COMMUNITIES OF COMPLICITY

DISLOCATIONS

General Editors: August Carbonella, *Memorial University of Newfoundland,* Don Kalb, *Central European University and Utrecht University,* Linda Green, *University of Arizona*

The immense dislocations and suffering caused by neoliberal globalization, the retreat of the welfare state in the last decades of the twentieth century, and the heightened military imperialism at the turn of the twenty-first century have raised urgent questions about the temporal and spatial dimensions of power. Through stimulating critical perspectives and new and cross-disciplinary frameworks that reflect recent innovations in the social and human sciences, this series provides a forum for politically engaged, ethnographically informed and theoretically incisive responses.

Volume 1
Where Have All the Homeless Gone? The Making and Unmaking of a Crisis
Anthony Marcus

Volume 2
Blood and Oranges: Immigrant Labor and European Markets in Rural Greece
Christopher M. Lawrence

Volume 3
Struggles for Home: Violence, Hope and the Movement of People
Edited by Stef Jansen and Staffan Löfving

Volume 4
Slipping Away: Banana Politics and Fair Trade in the Eastern Caribbean
Mark Moberg

Volume 5
Made in Sheffield: An Ethnography of Industrial Work and Politics
Massimiliano Mollona

Volume 6
Biopolitics, Militarism and Development: Eritrea in the Twenty-First Century
Edited by David O'Kane and Tricia Redeker Hepner

Volume 7
When Women Held the Dragon's Tongue and Other Essays in Historical Anthropology
Hermann Rebel

Volume 8
Class, Contention and a World in Motion
Edited by Winnie Lem and Pauline Gardiner Barber

Volume 9
Crude Domination: An Anthropology of Oil
Edited by Andrea Berhrends, Stephen P. Reyna and Günther Schlee

Volume 10
Communities of Complicity: Everyday Ethics in Rural China
Hans Steinmüller

Volume 11
Elusive Promises: Planning in the Contemporary World
Edited by Simone Abram and Gisa Weszkalnys

Volume 12
Intellectuals and (Counter-)Politics: Essays in Historical Realism
Gavin Smith

Volume 13
Blood and Fire: Toward a Global Anthropology of Labor
Edited by Sharryn Kasmir and August Carbonella

Volume 14
The Neoliberal Landscape and the Rise of Islamist Capital in Turkey
Edited by Neşecan Balkan, Erol Balkan and Ahmet Öncü

Volume 15
Yearnings in the Meantime: 'Normal Lives' and the State in a Sarajevo Apartment Complex
Stef Jansen

COMMUNITIES OF COMPLICITY

Everyday Ethics in Rural China

Hans Steinmüller

berghahn
NEW YORK · OXFORD
www.berghahnbooks.com

First published in 2013 by
Berghahn Books
www.berghahnbooks.com

© 2013, 2015 Hans Steinmüller
First paperback edition published in 2015

Library of Congress Cataloging-in-Publication Data

Steinmüller, Hans.
  Communities of complicity : everyday ethics in rural China / Hans Steinmüller.
    p. cm. -- (Dislocations ; v. 10)
  Includes bibliographical references.
  ISBN 978-0-85745-890-2 (hardback : alk. paper) -- ISBN 978-1-78238-914-9
(paperback : alk. paper) – ISBN 978-0-85745-891-9 (ebook)
  1. Rural life--China--Zhongba (Enshi Shi, Hubei Sheng) 2. Social ethics--China--
Zhongba (Enshi Shi, Hubei Sheng) 3. Zhongba (Enshi Shi, Hubei Sheng, China)--
Social life and customs. I. Title.
  HN740.Z46S74 2013
  303.3'720951--dc23

                                                                    2012032936

British Library Cataloguing in Publication Data

A catalogue record for this book is available from the British Library

Printed on acid-free paper

Front cover image by Hans Steinmüller.

ISBN 978-0-85745-890-2 hardback
ISBN 978-1-78238-914-9 paperback
ISBN 978-0-85745-891-9 ebook

Le quotidien, c'est l'humble et le solide, ce qui va de soi, ce dont les parties et fragments s'enchainent dans un emploi du temps. Et ceci sans qu'on (l'intéressé) ait à examiner les articulations de ces parties. C'est donc de qui ne porte pas de date. C'est l'insignifiant (apparemment) ; il occupe et préoccupe et pourtant il n'a pas besoin d'être dit, éthique sous-jacente à l'emploi tu temps, esthétique du décor de ce temps employé. Ce qui rejoint la modernité. Par ce mot il faut entendre ce qui porte le signe du neuf et de la nouveauté : la brillance, le paradoxal, marque par la technicité ou la mondanité. C'est l'audacieux (apparemment), l'éphémère, l'aventure qui se proclame et se fait acclamer. C'est l'art et l'esthétisme, mal discernables dans les spectacles que donne le monde dit moderne et dans le spectacle de soi qu'il se donne à lui-même. Or chacun, le quotidien et le moderne, marque et masque l'autre, le légitime et le compense.

Henri Lefebvre, *La Vie Quotidienne dans le Monde Moderne*

Contents

List of Illustrations   viii

Acknowledgements   x

Notes on the Text   xiii

Introduction   1

Chapter 1   A Remote Place from Three Angles   36

Chapter 2   Gabled Roofs and Concrete Ceilings   67

Chapter 3   Work Through the Food Basket   98

Chapter 4   Channelling Along a Centring Path   130

Chapter 5   The Embarrassment of *Li*   154

Chapter 6   Gambling and the Moving Boundaries of Social Heat   176

Chapter 7   Face Projects in Rural Construction   198

Conclusion   Everyday Ethics, Cultural Intimacy, and Irony   223

Appendix A   Newspaper Report   234

Appendix B   Expenses for the Construction of a House   237

Appendix C   List of Money-Gifts and Tasks   239

Appendix D   Subsidies Given to Three Households   241

Glossary   243

Bibliography   257

Index   271

List of Illustrations

Photographs

All the photographs were taken by the author, except A.1 and A.2, taken by *Enshi Evening News*.

1.1	The Valley of Bashan	46
1.2	The Memorial Arch	53
2.1	The 'houses of hanging legs' (*diaojiao lou*) were the most common architectural style of farm houses until recently	70
2.2	A 'Western house' (*yanglou*) or 'small comfortable house' (*xiaokang lou*)	71
2.3	The structure of the columns and the roof is built first, and only later walls are inserted	77
3.1	The stubborn old man	99
3.2	The periodical market of Bashan	104
3.3	Bashan Slope	106
3.4	Picking tea	112
4.1	A traditional house altar with the scroll 'heaven, earth, emperor, ancestors, and teachers'	143
4.2	The meal for the 'high relatives' (*gao qin*)	143
5.1	Guiding a child to kow-tow in front of grandmother's coffin	155
5.2	Preparing the offer of a pig and a goat (E. *zhu yang ji*) for the funeral of the mother-in-law	159
6.1	Just for fun (*hao wan'r*)	183
6.2	The *shaofo* game	188
7.1	The model household	207
8.1	A friendship across ages	231
A.1	Shi Han does research to understand the situation of peasant families	236
A.2	Carrying a bamboo basket, he participates in farm work	236

Maps

1.1   Enshi, Hubei, neighbouring provinces, and major cities   37
1.2   Hubei Province   38
1.3   Zhongba, Bashan, and the surrounding villages   52

Tables

2.1   Comparison of wooden and brick houses   91
3.1   Production of staple crops and cash crops in Bashan   105
       township
4.1   List of tasks at a family celebration   140

Figures

2.1   Basic floor plan and central axis of a house   73
2.2   The central axis and the ridgepole at the house   85
       inauguration
4.1   Seating order at a formal banquet   144

Acknowledgements

My greatest debt is to the people of Bashan who welcomed me into their homes and made it possible for me to call Bashan my 'second home' (*di er guxiang*). I sincerely hope that if anyone from Bashan ever reads this, he or she will feel that I have done justice to the complexity of everyday ethics there. I should also like to thank all those competent men and women in the prefecture, city, township and village governments, who in their position as representatives of state and party received and hosted me.

To respect their privacy, I use pseudonyms for all names of persons and of places below the prefectural level. I have called the village where I have spent most of my time 'Zhongba', which is literally 'central platform' or 'central flatland' in English – central as it is for its inhabitants in several senses that will become apparent. The township to which Zhongba belongs I call 'Bashan', that is the 'Ba mountain', 'Ba' being an ancient place name of this region.

My PhD studies and research were funded by an ESRC 1+3 Quota Studentship, a research bursary of the Universities' China Committee in London, and the Raymond and Rosemarie Firth Award of the Department of Anthropology at the LSE; for all this support I am very grateful.

In Beijing, I owe a great deal to Zhang Xiaojun for arranging my fellowship at the Department for Sociology at Tsinghua University. Under his guidance, I was able to make my first careful steps in Chinese academia, and teach my first course at university level. I have benefitted immensely from the discussions with him and his students. Wang Liru, Jason Li, and Duan Qiuli worked hard with me to improve my Chinese. Cai Ayi and Zhang Zhongyang, Chen Naihua, Hu Guanyu, Meng Wei, and Sa La supported me in different ways in Beijing. To all of them I am very grateful, but most of all to Guo Yan and all the members of the Guo family in Beijing and London.

Around China, many people hosted me generously in their native places: Long Tao and his parents in Changsha, Wu Liang and his parents in Dongyuan, and Xu Chenlin in Shanghai. Twenty years after I had first met him, Lü Yuansheng received me in Qiandaohu to complete another exchange between Bavaria and Zhejiang. In Madian, Zhong Rumei, Xiang

Yuanjing, Xiang Jun and his grandparents adopted me like a son into their family. Their generosity cannot be reciprocated with words alone.

At various universities, I was received as a guest: by Xu Gang, Wang Yue, Huang Xing, and Li Yuanxing in Hefei; by Ma Wei, Ha Zhengli, and He Xuefeng in Wuhan; by Luo Yiyun and Chen Tao in Jingmen; and by Zhou Shugang, Chen Zhihua, Qiu Shibin, and Xu Chuanjing in Enshi. I am grateful to all of them.

In Enshi, my first thanks go to Gong Zhixiang, who became my first friend there, for his encouragement, his support and his humour. Bevan Dau, John Mortimer, and Lila Rodriguez always left their door open for me, and gave me the space to relax and to change my perspectives. Peng Ji, Sheng Li, Yang Qi, and Zhang Xizhou showed me how to have fun (*wan*) in Enshi. Ran Zhenfu, Chen Lixin, Rao Xinyu, Liu Baoshi, Huang Juan, Wang Guowei, Guo Jiabin, and Bevan Tian hosted me with infinite generosity. Most of the very few things I know about Enshi's history I have learned from He Xiaogui. Cai Wen at the library of the Hubei Institute for Nationalities and Xiang Changming at the library of Enshi prefecture opened their doors for me, and let me read as much as I wanted in their libraries.

In Paris, I am grateful for the friendship of all those people who shared my Chinese experiences, but in particular Alejandro Abbud Torres Torija, Laurent Beduneau-Wang, Markus Berger, Pablo Blitstein, Guillaume Dutornier, Georges Favraud, Maelys de la Rupelle, and Lu Wei.

Back in London, several draft chapters were presented at the writing-up seminar at the Department of Anthropology, LSE. I have greatly benefitted from the comments and suggestions made there. I feel deeply grateful to all the members of our thesis writing seminar, which was a cohort of extraordinary personalities.

I am indebted to those who read parts of this book at various stages, and offered comments, criticism, and corrections: Eona Bell, Pablo Blitstein, Judith Bovensiepen, Vicky Boydell, Ankur Datta, Sarah Grosso, David Gierten, Solange Guo Chatelard, Carrie Heitmeyer, James Johnston, Li Ren-Yuan, Andrew Sanchez, and Lenz Steinmüller.

I have learned a lot from my discussions with David Gibeault and Tan Tongxue, and I owe them much for their hospitality and their friendship. Chang Xiangqun, Zheng Shanshan, and Zhang Hui also taught me many things, and they offered practical advice during fieldwork when it was most needed. Meryl Xue, Zhou Lei, Zhang Hui, Chen Chen, and Xu Chengpu helped me substantially with translations into Chinese and back, for which I am very grateful. Before and after fieldwork I participated in the workshops of Richard Sennett's Culture Project at LSE, and I have benefitted a lot from the interdisciplinary exchange there. Torsten Schröder and Jürgen Kufner gave much appreciated advice on how to draw maps. Heartfelt thanks also to all the friends who offered me a place to crash during my trips to London.

Parts of this book have been published in different form in journals. Chapter 6 is a revised version of 'The Moving Boundaries of Social Heat. Gambling in Rural China', *Journal of the Royal Anthropological Institute* 17:2 (2011), 263–280. Various sections of the two following articles have been used in different chapters of the book: 'How Popular Confucianism Became Embarrassing: On the Spatial and Moral Centre of the House in Rural China', *Focaal: Journal of Global and Historical Anthropology* 58 (2010), 81–96 and 'Communities of Complicity: Notes on State Formation and Local Sociality in Rural China', *American Ethnologist* 37:3 (2010), 539–549. I gratefully acknowledge permission to reprint revised versions of these articles and I appreciate the criticisms and suggestions made by the anonymous reviewers of these journals.

Charles Stafford and Stephan Feuchtwang provided gentle and perceptive supervision throughout the research and writing up of my doctoral dissertation. They never failed to answer emails in time, to read through my most esoteric drafts, and to encourage me to continue with this project. I am deeply indebted to them for their guidance, their support, and their example.

Solange Guo Chatelard has been my *compañera* almost since I began to discover the Chinese world. She has shared many weeks in Zhongba with me, and with her sensitivity and her compassion created new bonds with old and young. It is impossible to think of all these years without her loving presence.

My family unfailingly supported me when I was travelling *in der Weltgeschichte umananda*. Whether from a distance or at home, my parents and my siblings have always provided the deepest source of sustenance and continuity.

NOTES ON THE TEXT

Transliteration

All translations from languages other than English are mine, unless otherwise indicated. Throughout the text, Chinese words are written italicized in the standard pinyin form. The glossary provides the pinyin and the character equivalents for Chinese words used in the book. Words in the Enshi dialect that differ markedly in pronunciation and meaning from standard Mandarin Chinese I have marked with an 'E'. All other Chinese words in italics are part of the vocabulary of standard Mandarin, and only marked with a 'P' (for *putonghua*, i.e. standard Mandarin Chinese) if it was necessary to distinguish them from the Enshi dialect (e.g. 'street' is 'E. *gai*' and 'P. *jie*'). The names of persons and places are also given in pinyin form, except for names where different forms of romanization are more commonly used (such as Chiang Kai-shek instead of Jiang Jieshi).

Kinship Abbreviations

I have used the following customary kinship abbreviations:

F	=	father	M	=	mother
S	=	son	D	=	daughter
B	=	brother	Z	=	sister
H	=	husband	W	=	wife

Further kinship relations are indicated by combinations thereof, e.g. MZB = Mother's Sister's Brother.

Units and Measurements

Chinese *Renminbi* are given throughout in the unit of Yuan. The exchange rate in 2006 and 2007 was approximately 1 Yuan to £0.07 (€0.11). Weights are given in Chinese *jin*, with 1 *jin* equivalent to 0.5 kg. Areas are given in Chinese *mu*. According to the official measurement, one *mu* is equivalent to 666.66m^2 or 0.0667 hectare. As no cadastre exists which lists plots of agricultural land, the areas of agricultural plots are mostly local estimates.

INTRODUCTION

Shouts cut through the morning mist: 'One, two, ... three!', 'Slower!', 'Come on!'. Eight men lift the ridgepole onto its socket on top of the roof. At this moment the yelling of the helpers is shot through and then drowned out by the noise of countless firecrackers. Display fireworks are ignited and hiss into the fresh morning sky. The helpers on the concrete roof of Yang Minghu's house, all the relatives and neighbours in the front yard, everyone stands still in the smoke and noise. Slowly the smoke clears, and the wooden roof truss appears on top of the second floor.

This is a January morning in 2007, and we are at the inauguration of the Yang family's new house. The helpers have just finished hoisting the ridgepole (*shang liang*): this is the culmination of the house inauguration ritual, the house inauguration being itself the culmination of a long construction process, and all in turn the result of several years of hard work and saving.

Yang Minghu is a farmer in the village of Zhongba. The income from the 5 *mu* of tea plantations that he and his wife cultivate would not have been quite enough to maintain a family of four, pay for the schooling of his children, and still build this new house. During the year, it is mostly his wife who picks tea leaves on the slopes and sells them to the tea traders in the evenings. Yang Minghu himself works outside the farm on odd jobs, most of which is 'bitter labour' (*ku li*), i.e. unskilled manual work on construction sites.

When he got married in 1996, Yang Minghu had built a new house with brick walls and a concrete roof. At the time, the family did not have enough money to build a second floor, and most of the walls of his house were left unplastered. In 2006 he had finally gathered enough money together to build a good second floor, and hired a distant relative of his wife, a carpenter and builder, to do the construction work. Master Lan came together with one helper, and worked for about two months at Yang's house. In consultation with Master Lan, Yang Minghu decided to have a gabled wooden structure on top of the second floor ceiling, covering the rear half of the roof, whilst the other half was left as a terrace. This was rather uncommon: these days, most people leave their houses with a plain, concrete roof; and so the traditional ritual of 'hoisting the ridgepole' (*shang liang*) is replaced by another, more simple one, called 'pouring the concrete' (*dao ban*). However, Yang Minghu, who is a gifted craftsman himself, chose a mixed version with a small gabled wooden structure; and so the construction concluded with the traditional ritual of hoisting the ridgepole.

The main ritual expert for such a house inauguration is the carpenter. Master Lan had brought his own Master, the eighty-five-year-old Master Nie, the evening before the inauguration. In the middle of the night, they called on the 'patron saint' of carpenters, Lu Ban, and asked for his goodwill and protection. The two carpenters performed incantations and stylized recitations (*fengchenghua*) throughout the night, while Yang Minghu, his fourteen-year-old son Yang Jun, and eight helpers, ran into the forest to fell the tree that would become the ridgepole. The tree was carried back to the house before dawn, amid the noise of the firecrackers that Yang Jun was setting off. At dawn, the carpenters quickly shaped the tree into a squared beam. They performed another long set of recitations, and fixed a red cloth to the middle of the ridgepole as a sign of prosperity and good luck. The morning light was just brightening, when the helpers lifted the ridgepole on top of the roof.

'Modern' houses of bricks and concrete do not have a ridgepole, and no carpenters are hired. This was the only time in about fifteen house inaugurations, during the eighteen months I spent in this village, that I saw the carpenters worship Lu Ban, and do their recitations. Maybe aggravated by my presence, there was a certain awkwardness about the ritual and the recitations. At several points the younger carpenter Bai did not want to perform them, and Master Nie had to encourage him.

The new house provides the family with a huge living space. Some of the rooms will be used as storage rooms and some left empty for quite a while. Several older neighbours told me that this was just how the times were now: everyone is building spacious houses. In the past people would not have thought it necessary to build such a large house if someone 'just had one son'.

Construction activity has been booming in the last couple of years in Zhongba village: in this village group of about fifty households alone, thirty houses were built in the last ten years. A new house of bricks and concrete – instead of the wooden houses of former times – is the first major investment a family will make. A good part of this investment comes from money earned outside, labouring in major cities like Guangzhou, Shanghai, and Beijing. The building of these new houses is both an expression of the continuation of the family line, and of the vast social change taking place in local communities.

Once the ridgepole was up, everyone went downstairs, for an abundant breakfast. In fact, the notion of 'breakfast' does not exist at such celebrations; it was a huge meal, exactly the same as those that would be served for lunch and dinner (including the liquor for the men). After breakfast the two carpenters and the helpers got ready again to put the straight planks (E. *chuange*) on the roof. When they were more or less done with that, everyone went outside to bring the tiles up to the roof. All the people present, including the guests, formed a long line, and each handed the tiles to the next person to him or her, up to the second floor.

Some young guests did not want to help to carry the tiles: Tian Zhong, for instance, who had come back from Shanghai just two days before. Yang Jun's cousin Yang Hui, however, was helping; she had just come back from Shenzhen. Both in their twenties, they are labouring in factories in Shanghai and Shenzhen, and came home for the Spring Festival period.

I passed the tiles to Yang Yuanbing who was standing next to me. Yuanbing had become one of my best friends in the village. After having spent fifteen years in the cities he got married two years ago, and has stayed at home ever since. At this inauguration, he was the 'main coordinator' (E. *zhi ke*) of all the helpers, and the day before he had suggested to his uncle Yang Minghu that I should help at the house inauguration as well.

When he and Yang Minghu asked me, I happily accepted. It is the custom in this region to write a list of all the helpers and paste it on the wall of the house for everyone to see. The fact that my name would appear on this list (*shang ming*) attested, I thought, to the fact that after eight months I had finally been accepted in at least one way as a regular neighbour in the village, and furthermore that I had a significant relationship (*guanxi*) with Yang Minghu and the Yang family.

One of the aunts in the family was charged with the task of 'receiving the guests' (*ying bing*), i.e. offering a cigarette to each guest as they arrived. After some consultation, it was decided that it would be appropriate to have me take over this task together with the elderly aunt: I would realize later that getting me to offer cigarettes to the guests would show everyone that I was a friend of the family. And it was also an easier and lighter task than the hard work of those who were cooking or shifting the tables.

We were still carrying the tiles up to the roof when the first guests started to arrive, and Yang Yuanbing called me downstairs. He asked me to stay near the main door and hand over cigarettes to the people arriving. Many people knew me, smiled and joked when they realized that I was 'helping out' (*bang mang*). It is not that difficult to hand over cigarettes, of course, but it gave me an enormous feeling of security and even pride to fulfil this little task. The house inauguration at Yang Minghu's family was a turning point during my fieldwork. To be allowed to see the rituals of the carpenters, and to be asked by the Yang family to help out at their celebrations, were unprecedented signs of acceptance into the local community. It contrasted greatly with the many frustrations and misunderstandings I had had before: with officials who did not trust the innocent purpose of my research, and with villagers who treated me politely, but as a stranger; the loneliness I felt when it seemed to me that I could not share or express anything of real significance with those around me; the moments of embarrassment when it became obvious that I had been naïve and disrespectful.

Such a moment of exuberance, of the 'noise and heat' (E. *naore*) of firecrackers and banquets, contrasts with the routine of everyday life, a routine that had often seemed rather monotonous to me in the weeks and months before. What also gave this house inauguration its heightened significance was that the values and purposes of so many everyday actions were rendered visible for a moment. The drudgery and the striving of Yang Minghu and his family, the ongoing exchanges and negotiations between relatives and neighbours, even the cautious accommodation of an outsider like me, all this seemed resolved for a moment, and somehow meaningful and dignified in its ritual expression.

Yet in reality the question of the meaning and value of any social action cannot find an unequivocal answer, and commentary and negotiation will inevitably continue on questions such as which kind of house to build (of bricks or of wood?), how to perform a ritual (to worship Lu Ban or not?), how to stage such a family celebration (which food should be served, and who should be invited?), how to behave vis-à-vis the members of your family, your relatives, and your neighbours (to help, like Yang Hui, or not to help, like Tian Zhong), and what about outsiders like me? Answers to these questions have to be found continuously, and they depend as much on the experienced constraints of a changing empirical context, as on the values, ideas, and models of the actors themselves. They necessarily refer to wider moral frameworks which more often than not are fragmented, contradicting, and uncertain. They are articulated in ordinary action and discourse, and this articulation of moral frameworks is what I call everyday ethics.伦理

Based on eighteen months of participant observation in the village of Zhongba and the market town of Bashan, in the Enshi region of Western Hubei Province, this book explores such everyday ethics as they are experienced in this specific locality in rural China. To this end, I describe and analyse family, work, rituals, and local politics.

Everyday Ethics in Rural China

Several ethnographies of Chinese rural communities in the last decade
have focused on the transformations in values and moralities in the Reform era (e.g. Croll 1994; Yan 1996, 2003; Liu 2000; Ku 2004; Oxfeld 2010).
What they all highlight is how basic moral orientations are becoming ever
more difficult to ascertain for many people. The loosening of political control, the growing impact of markets in most spheres of society, consumerism and rising levels of inequality, in short, all the rapid changes in
Chinese society in recent years are subverting moral frameworks which
are believed to have been more stable before.

Such an environment of moral uncertainty presents certain challenges
to the observer. Yan Yunxiang, for instance, concludes his ethnography of
family relations in a village in Northeast China with a bleak assessment of
the ascent of immoral individuality (2003: 206ff; 2005). He describes in detail how the conjugal family has become the most important basic social
unit at the cost of extended families and kinship networks, and he relates
this change to the rise of romantic love (instead of arranged marriages),
and the increased significance of notions of private space. In his final assessment this growing individualism in family relations is not matched
by a public sphere that could check and balance it. In particular amongst
the village youth, he sees a development of individuality towards an
'unbalanced egotism' and the rise of the 'uncivil individual'. Their individualism is confined to the sphere of private life and only emphasizes
individual rights, without equal respect for other individuals and a com-
mitment to civic duty (2003: 206). Fundamentally responsible for this
situation is the 'socialist engineering' of the state, which made an independent 'public sphere' impossible (2003: 235; 2005: 651ff). His prediction
for the future is gloomy: 'Given that the socialist state remains hostile to
independent societal forces and autonomous actions in the public sphere,
the disjunction between the public and the private is likely to continue, as
is the imbalance between civil duties and self-interest in the growth of the
individual' (2005: 651).

It should be noted that Yan's conclusion is a moral statement itself. Behind his disquiet at the selfish individualism, and the gap between public
and private, stands an ideal in which these fissures could be overcome: an
individualism 'rightly understood', which brings together private interest
and public duty.

In his ethnography of rural Shaanxi in the 1990s, Liu Xin has recorded a
similar moral confusion (2000). Yet his theoretical take on it is quite different to that of Yan Yunxiang. Liu does not only point out the displacement
of former moral frameworks, but eventually emphasizes the complete

arbitrariness of moralities and values in contemporary rural China. In his view, there is a lack of any mode of a moral economy, and what remains are 'arbitrary combinations of cultural forms' that have lost their intrinsic meanings. He writes: 'There was no consistent "moral" order to guide and determine social action or cultural meaning; instead, the *"order* of things" rather than "things" already in an order became the subject of debate. Thus arguments about rules of the game have become the game itself, as the players constantly challenged and contested *how* this game should be played' (Liu 2000: 182).

Yan's decrial of moral decline and Liu's affirmation of moral arbitrariness serve as a starting point to further explore moral and ethical questions in contemporary rural China. To this end, let me first address the ways in which anthropology in general could engage with moralities and ethics.

Consistency and Irony

Ethics and moralities have rarely been explicit objects of enquiry for anthropologists. Whereas many anthropologists have dealt with issues that might be loosely categorized as ethical or moral problems (such as religious values, law and custom, honour and shame, for instance), they have rarely addressed them directly as such. This might be partly due to the tendency in sociology and anthropology to reify society or culture as a moral whole. Frequently 'morality' or 'ethics' have been collapsed into 'whatever other terms we have been enthusiastically using to explain collectively sanctioned rules, beliefs, and opinions: sometimes "culture", sometimes "ideology", sometimes "discourse"' (Laidlaw 2002: 312). James Laidlaw tracks this tendency back to the 'collective metaphysics of Durkheimian sociology which reduced the obedience to moral law to a question of social integration' (Laidlaw 2002; similarly Wolfram 1982 and Robbins 2004).

Recently, several anthropologists have proposed moralities and ethics as a field of study for anthropology (Howell 1997; Lambek 2000, 2010; Faubion 2001; Laidlaw 2002; Robbins 2004; Zigon 2007, 2008; Heintz 2009).[1] These outlines attempt new ways of going beyond the impasses of domination versus resistance, and structure versus agency; indeed, it is precisely the 'totalizing vision of societies' (Laidlaw 2002: 322) on the one side, and the ascription of resistance and agency on the other, that is questioned (cf. Lambek 2004b, 2008a). Foregrounding moralities and ethics instead privileges ongoing judgement, negotiation, and ambiguities in lived social realities.

What is common to these contributions is the attempt to study local moralities and ethics in particular practices and through the details of everyday life. Michael Lambek, for instance, writes that 'the ordinary is intrinsically ethical and ethics intrinsically ordinary' (2010: 3). His proposal to study 'ordinary ethics' provides an anthropological alternative to the prioritizing of conscious, verbal reflection and the downplaying of the moral element of ordinary action. Lambek understands ethics as 'intrinsic to the human condition, to the ordinary, to action, to the presence of criteria' and hence for him 'a sharp distinction between ethics and morality as, respectively, freedom and convention, doesn't work' (Lambek 2008b: 30). Laidlaw, on the contrary, is closer to such a distinction between ethics and morality, in which ethics properly is the reflective 'exercise of freedom'.[2] Zigon, similarly, draws a clear distinction between ethics and morality (2007, 2008:17ff, 192ff). He first distinguishes two kinds of morality:

> Morality, on the one hand, is a kind of habitus or an unreflective and unreflexive disposition of everyday social life. This embodied morality is not thought out beforehand, nor is it noticed when it is performed. It is simply done. It is one's everyday embodied way of being in the world.

> Morality can also be considered at the discursive level. That is to say, we can speak of morality as those of an organized religion or state structures, of what is considered, by the speaker of this discourse, as right, good, appropriate, and expected. This discursive morality, then, is publicly articulated and influences the moral lives of those persons who have some kind of social relationship with these discourses, but they should not be considered as being representative or deterministic of any actually lived embodied morality. (2008: 17–18)[3]

Yet all these moralities are not yet properly 'ethical'. Zigon continues:

> Ethics, then, is a kind of reflective and reflexive stepping-away from the embodied moral habitus or moral discourse. It is brought about by a moral breakdown or problematization [Foucault 1984: 388]. This occurs when some event or person intrudes into the everyday life of persons and forces them to consciously reflect upon an appropriate ethical response. Ethics, then, is a conscious acknowledgement of a moral breakdown, or what we can also call an ethical dilemma, which necessitates a kind of working on the self so that one can return to the unreflective and unreflexive comfort of the embodied moral habitus or the unquestioned moral discourse. […] This theory forces the anthropologist to find moments of moral breakdown to study. When we speak of moral breakdowns we can no longer simply speak about the morality of a person or group of persons, instead anthropologists of moralities must focus upon the problematization of morality. For it is at the intersection of morality and ethics, at this breakdown, that it becomes possible to see how morality plays a role in the everyday lives of the people we study. (Zigon 2008: 18)

To recapitulate: Zigon proposes two kinds of morality ('embodied' and 'discursive'). Ethics is the second-level reflection of morality, which becomes necessary in situations of 'moral breakdown'. This distinction is a good starting point,[4] yet I want to make two points of caution here: first, ordinary everydayness is granted no reflexivity. Everyday morality here is an unquestioned and unconscious 'disposition'. Conscious reflection only takes place in the 'ethical moment' of the 'moral breakdown'. Second, there is a tendency to describe those situations as 'moral breakdown' where people explicitly talk about moral dilemmas. Whilst I accept the basic distinction between moralities and ethics, I will argue throughout this book that much of everyday life in rural China already possesses the reflexivity that is characteristic of what Zigon calls the 'ethical moment' of the 'moral breakdown'.

In their outlines of an anthropology of ethics or morality Lambek, Laidlaw, and Zigon have also called for a renewed engagement with moral philosophy. Indeed there are several contemporary moral philosophers who have studied moralities against the background of concrete social arrangements, such as Alasdair MacIntyre (1981, 1988, 1990) and Charles Taylor (1985, 1989, 1997). For my purposes, I will start with Taylor here.

In *Sources of the Self* (1989) Charles Taylor has drafted the contours of the Western self in intellectual history. Although extremely interesting and inspiring in itself, it is not so much the content of this Western identity, but the methodological tools he proposes that interest me here. Taylor starts off his argument phenomenologically, positing that human action always includes 'strong evaluations'.[5] Different to 'weak evaluations,' which only refer to the practical problems in the realization of wishes or desires, 'strong evaluations' aim at the value of wishes, desires, or choices themselves. As such, they 'involve discriminations of right or wrong, better or worse, higher or lower, which are not rendered valid by our own desires, inclinations, or choices, but rather stand independent of these and offer standards by which they can be judged' (Taylor 1989: 4). Weak evaluations are contingent, whereas strong evaluations are categorical. Strong evaluations are 'gut feelings' about questions like dignity, meaningfulness, fulfilment, 'the good life', and they involve claims about nature and the status of humans. Inasmuch as they are experienced as independent of the arbitrariness of our desires, they are also experienced as being in need of an 'articulation by a moral ontology', and this is what Taylor calls 'inescapable moral frameworks'.

Any question about identity ('who am I?' or 'who are we?') needs such a surrounding moral framework for a meaningful answer. 'To know who I am is a species of knowing where I stand' (ibid.: 27), that is, to have an identity is to have an orientation within a moral space mapped by strong evaluations and qualitative distinctions. It is precisely because identity incorporates strong evaluations and qualitative distinctions that it in turn can play 'the role of orienting us, of providing the frame within which things have meaning for us' (ibid.: 30). According to this linked understanding of identity and morality, 'the portrait of an agent free from all frameworks rather spells for us a person in the grip of an appalling identity crisis' (ibid.: 31). The full definition of someone's identity usually involves not only his stand on moral and spiritual matters but also some reference to a defining community. But modern conceptions of individualism picture the human person as potentially finding her own bearings outside the webs of interlocution which have originally formed her. Against these popular understandings of modern individualism, and against the rationalist groundings of Kantian ethics, Taylor bases his moralities in a phenomenology of moral action. In this way, Taylor also opens a way of conceptualizing different moralities which do not centre on a notion of separated individuals (ibid.: 2.2). With this approach, he comes fairly close to several recent attempts in anthropology at describing forms of 'agency' or 'self-realization' in contexts that are explicitly anti-liberal (e.g. Hirschkind 2001; Mahmood 2005).

Let me highlight two points from Taylor's propositions: firstly, meaningful action contains 'strong evaluations' which build up 'moral frameworks'. These can be explored phenomenologically. For my case, I will attempt to neither presuppose a particular Chinese self nor a universal normative ethics. Instead I shall explore how such moral frameworks emerge in action. What I will call 'everyday ethics' refers to discourses and actions that include 'strong evaluations' in Taylor's terms. Secondly, there is a drive towards a consistent articulation of 'strong evaluations' into 'moral frameworks'. Taylor's work represents one of the few recent attempts in moral philosophy to provide a justification of values, morals, and identity. Much of his writing can be seen as an intellectual effort to propose ways in which consistency (between the contingent and the categorical, and between different moral frameworks) could be achieved.

From a more postmodern perspective, Richard Rorty recommends serenity towards our urge for consistency regarding identities and morals. In *Contingency, Irony, and Solidarity* (1989), he starts from an overview of philosophical thinking about language, identity, and community. Rorty documents how Western thinkers have seen all three as increasingly contingent – as products of time and chance, which lack a justification outside of themselves, such as divinity, fact, truth, or reason. Theology and metaphysics had been trying to find these angle points; later historicism had replaced these questions with historical and social circumstances. According to Rorty, historicists have either emphasized self-creation and autonomy (e.g. Nietzsche, Kierkegaard, Heidegger) or tried to argue for solidarity and a more just society (e.g. Marx, Mill, Dewey, Habermas). The problem remained of how to bring self-creation and justice, the private and the public, together. Rorty's book 'tries to show how things look if we drop the demand for a theory which unifies the public and private, and are content to treat the demands of self-creation and of human solidarity as equally valid, yet forever incommensurable' (1989: xv). He proposes instead to be a 'liberal ironist'. Whereas 'the metaphysician' tried to find social hope in theory, and private perfection in literature, 'the liberal ironist' reverses this relationship:

> Within a liberal metaphysical culture the disciplines which were charged with penetrating behind the many private appearances to the one general common reality – theology, science, philosophy – were the ones which were expected to bind human beings together, and thus to help eliminate cruelty. Within an ironist culture, by contrast, it is the disciplines which specialize in thick description of the private and idiosyncratic which are assigned this job. In particular novels and ethnographies which sensitize one to the pain of those who do not speak our language must do the job which demonstrations of a common human nature were supposed to do. Solidarity has to be constructed out of little pieces, rather than found already waiting, in the form of an ur-language which all of us recognize when we hear it. (1989: 94)

Whereas the metaphysician had tried to base solidarity on a definition of 'humanity' or 'human essence', Rorty suggests that it should be based on 'the ability to see more and more traditional differences (of tribe, religion, race, customs, and the like) as unimportant when compared with similarities with respect to pain and humiliation – the ability to think of people wildly different from ourselves as included in the range of "us"' (1989: 192). These similarities are not recognizable in abstract definitions, but can be gleaned from concrete descriptions. Rorty emphasizes the ethical potential of literature and ethnography: these 'thick descriptions' might enable us to share, re-live and understand something of people we previously thought of as 'others'.

It is the work of the 'liberal ironist' to destabilize and dismantle what Rorty calls 'final vocabularies'. These were the vocabularies with which the 'metaphysician' had tried to give an absolute interpretive closure to the problems of identity and morals. The 'ironist' however offers re-descriptions of such claims to final vocabularies, which prove them contingent. Rorty is aware that such ironies can be hurtful to others – many people prefer to be taken at their word. He has described the problem precisely:

Ironism [...] results from awareness of the power of redescription. But most people do not want to be redescribed. They want to be taken on their own terms – taken seriously just as they are and just as they talk. The ironist tells them that the language they speak is up for grabs by her and her kind. There is something potentially very cruel about that claim. For the best way to cause people long-lasting pain is to humiliate them by making the things that seemed most important to them look futile, obsolete, and powerless. Consider what happens when a child's precious possessions – the little things around which he weaves fantasies that make him a little different from all other children – are redescribed as 'trash,' and thrown away. Or consider what happens when these possessions are made to look ridiculous alongside the possessions of another, richer child. Something like that presumably happens to a primitive culture when it is conquered by a more advanced one. The same sort of thing sometimes happens to nonintellectuals in the presence of intellectuals. [...] The redescribing ironist, by threatening one's final vocabulary, and thus one's ability to make sense of oneself in one's own terms rather than hers, suggests that one's self and one's world are futile, obsolete, powerless. Redescription often humiliates. (Rorty 1989: 89–90, also quoted in Lambek 2004a: 4)

For an anthropologist who is to take the position of an ironist, this is particularly relevant in two ways: in relation to other intellectuals, including other anthropologists, and vis-à-vis the people one is writing about. The advice against the possibilities for humiliation in ironic re-description does however not mean that they are merely playful, frivolous, and decadent. By the twists of ironic re-description, one might reach deeper layers of shared knowledge that are based not on abstract definitions, but on shared experience.

Neither is ironic re-description reserved to intellectuals: ordinary people also continuously engage in their own descriptions of themselves and others. Obviously, their re-descriptions take other forms than the novels and ethnographies the liberal ironist consumes. If much of everyday speech and action aims at a consistency of selves and moralities, often enough the articulations of everyday speech and the implicit intentions in everyday action are not brought into consistent balance. Everyday talk and everyday action are often *uneigentlich*, they are not 'literal' in the sense that they have a single interpretation, a single possible re-description.

Such an interpretation of irony implies that it is not 'merely' rhetorical. This proposition has been put forward in a number of essays written by anthropologists, in particular in the edited volumes *Irony in Action* (Fernandez and Huber 2001) and *Irony and Illness* (Lambek and Antze 2004). Michael Lambek emphasizes that there are two kinds of irony: 'irony of commission and irony of recognition' (Lambek 2004a: 2). Or in other words: rhetorical irony ('intentional and "made"'), and situational irony ('interpreted and "found"'). This 'rough distinction' should serve to 'off-set the assumption [...] that irony is properly to be consigned to the rhetorical, as an intentional mode of presentation' (ibid.). Lambek points out further that anthropologists, and social scientists in general, often take both people's talk and the situations they are in quite literally. The actions and intentions that those anthropologists write about are represented as decisive, sure, and dramatic. Ordinary people are not granted what seems to be the privilege of intellectuals: a doubtful and relativist perspective (ibid.: 5).

In everyday life people encounter categorical moral propositions, and some they treat with awe, whilst they are ironic about others. The way these questions are dealt with depends much on the contingent circumstances of the everyday. What I call 'everyday ethics' are exactly these various forms of moral engagement in everyday practice.

We can pause here and look back at the decrials of the 'loss of morality' in China now. If it is not that ordinary people are becoming schizophrenic, they will still have some 'strong' value judgements in Taylor's sense. Hence they do have some kind of moralities – just different ones (different from the past, and probably different from those of the observer). Yan Yunxiang's condemnation of the selfishness of the young, and the decrial of the gap between 'the public' and 'the private' is something that Taylor would acknowledge as part of the experience of modernity. Highly sensitive to the unsettling and fragmenting moral experience of modernity, Taylor's work is an attempt at delineating common moral frameworks in 'the West', behind which stands the aim of a consistent moral self, and a unification of the moralities of the private and the public. And just as Yan Yunxiang's work itself has an implicit moral intent, it surely is a similar one: it aims at a consistent moral self and a reconciliation of 'private' and 'public'. Contrary to that, Rorty argues that we should give up on this question (and the implicit recourse to what he calls 'final vocabularies'), and accept contingency. In its emphasis on never-ending contingency (every situation could be framed in various moral frameworks, and the frameworks themselves are continuously put in question), the conclusion of Liu Xin's ethnography is rather similar to Rorty's philosophical position. But Rorty goes further: he affirms contingency, and suggests self-creation through re-description and solidarity based on a shared sensitivity to pain. Following Liu and Rorty, I will focus on the *décalage* between different moral frameworks and contingent situations, not with the aim of a final closure, a solution to the gap between self and society, private and public, contingent and categorical, but as an exploration of all the different ways in which these opposites meet each other: in confrontation, irony, and (mis-)representation. It is exactly the momentary articulation of moral frameworks in the everyday, at the conjunction of the categorical and the contingent, which is the main theme of this book.

The Everyday

I have referred above to a basic distinction between the moral and the ethical, quoting from Jarret Zigon (2007, 2008): morality is understood as an everyday habitus or discourse, and ethics as the second-level reflection of morality. According to this distinction, ethics really takes place only in the moment of the 'moral breakdown', when people are forced to reflect on what they generally take for granted. This definition relies on the opposition between the 'unreflective' moral habitus or unquestioned moral discourse versus the 'reflective' stepping-away of ethics (Zigon 2008: 18). Whilst I accept the distinction drawn between morality and ethics, I remain sceptical about assigning the everyday as an entirely 'unreflective state' to the former.

Zigon quotes Heidegger's concept of *being-in-the-world* to illustrate further the 'unreflective moral dispositions of everyday life' (Zigon 2007: 135). *Being-in-the-world* (*In-der-Welt-sein*) and the related concept *being-there/here* (*Dasein*) were Heidegger's substitutes for subject, object, consciousness and world in his magnum opus *Being and Time* (*Sein und Zeit*, Heidegger 2006 [1927]). *Being-in-the-world* is the most generic and existential mode of being that is essentially open to the world and relational. As such, it is open to the possibilities of differentiation, all of which begin in moments of 'breakdown'. The possibilities that 'the They' (*das Man*) follow is basically what creates the 'everyday' (*Alltag*). The 'everyday' of 'the They', however, is the epitome of inauthenticity (*Uneigentlichkeit*) for Heidegger, and he makes very clear that this kind of everydayness is negative. The real aim is to take 'authentic' (*eigentliche*) decisions. Zigon uses Heidegger's notion of a 'breakdown' to differentiate between morality and ethics, yet he does not address what for Heidegger was a central question: the distinction between authentic and inauthentic decisions.

If Heidegger was thoroughly uninterested in contemporary society and history, his work – most importantly *Being and Time* – should also be seen in the context of his time. In 1926, when he started writing *Being and Time*, everyday life in the big cities of Europe posed with ever greater urgency precisely this problem of authenticity versus inauthenticity, and related to that the problem of how to order experience in time.[6]

Around the same time, many other intellectuals were absorbed with similar problems. Several major novels written in Europe in the 1920s, in particular Joyce's *Ulysses* (1968 [1922]), Proust's *À la recherche du temps perdu* (*In Search of Lost Time*; 2002 [1913-1927]) and Musil's *Der Mann ohne*

Eigenschaften (*The Man without Qualities*; 1994 [1930-1942]), all share an obsession with an everyday life where every detail has become problematic. Written retrospectively, they all express the anxieties of life in the European metropolis before World War I, a time when the aristocracy and the old order still had a strong standing, but at the same time rapid urbanization, industrial production, and mass consumption were changing every detail of ordinary life. The interruptions and rapid change made an ordering of everyday experience, and a periodization of past, present, and future, increasingly difficult. What these three modernist masterpieces share is the attempt of their authors/narrators by listing all the details of everyday life and reflecting on them to recover memory and ultimately a way of making sense of the present – whilst they are irrevocably projected into the present throughout.

Like these authors, many others began to consider everyday life in the cities as a problem in itself: it was in everyday life where the rapid social changes of 'modernity' were felt most acutely, both the continuous arousal of the senses and the endless boredom brought about by capitalist rationalization. Georg Simmel, Walter Benjamin, Siegfried Krakauer and others were describing the 'minimal unity of the present', in which it became ever more difficult to order one's experience into sequences of memory and anticipation. In the words of historian Harry Harootunian:

> the condition of possibility of an experience of the present – the now – depended on the synthesizing capacity of consciousness. The modern, it was believed, was manifest when the unity formed by this synthesis was constantly dislocated, when consciousness was bombarded with givens that challenged its capacity to assimilate and classify in continuity and sequentiality. At that point, the world – the ever-present now – declared war on consciousness; traumatized it with shock, sensation, and spectacle; and introduced interruption, so that it could no longer dominate its objects and was forced to retreat into the sanctuary of pure memory and a pure past. This is the world that Georg Simmel described in his study of mental and metropolitan life and that Benjamin later divided into 'voluntary and involuntary memory.' This minimal unity of the present, however precarious, was increasingly seen by thinkers as the actual and unavoidable experience of everydayness that everywhere in the industrializing world – colonized and noncolonized – was identified as distinctively modern. (Harootunian 2000b: 4)

In this way, the problem of the everyday has been often seen as a distinctive feature of modernity.[7] Futurists, Dadaists, and Surrealists celebrated the dynamic, the unpredictability and the changes of this new fragmented everyday. Others were sceptical and frightened at the constant bombardment of the senses, the fragmentation of experience, and the loss of time-frames it brought. The valorization of the everyday as danger or possibility was then also a moral and a political problem. Heidegger's denigration of ordinary everyday life and his initial involvement in Nazi politics may not be coincidental.[8] The temporality of the everyday that for Heidegger was vulgar and inauthentic has been qualified by Walter Benjamin and others as progressive (Harootunian 2000b: 100). It was a similar problematization of everyday life to which Marxist intellectuals responded by proposing new forms of social critique and political action.[9] First in Russia, and then in many other socialist nation-states, the party-state was put in charge of limiting the disruptive forces of everyday life, and reducing the everyday into a determinate future and past. Since the Russian Revolution in 1917, consecutive socialist regimes have tried to actively 'politicize' every aspect of everyday life – an aim that was first formulated for the new Soviet regime by Trotsky in his *Problems of Everyday Life* (1973 [1924]). In this and later writings, Trotsky insists on the revolutionary transformation of the everyday, including popular custom, culture, and the family. Yet his 'permanent revolution' had to give way to bureaucratization and state-building. Trotsky's ousting after the death of Lenin, and the ascendance of Stalin, is the first instance where the conflicts between 'revolutionaries' and 'bureaucrats' became apparent, and it prefigures the lasting tension between 'reds' and 'experts' in China (cf. Schurmann 1968). While in the Soviet Union under Stalin a highly centralized party and state administration was built, in China the alternating tendencies of 'red' activism and bureaucratic consolidation resulted in a comparatively less omnipotent central state, due in particular to the temporary victories of reds over experts during the Great Leap Forward and the Cultural Revolution (cf. Shirk 1992). Whereas Mao favoured mobilization and Stalin ideological surveillance, both Stalin's and Mao's regime had one central objective: to control and regulate the everyday.

But in those mainly agrarian nations, the new everyday was experienced in very different ways when compared to urban Europe. If urban centres such as St Petersburg,[10] Shanghai,[11] or Guangzhou also experienced enormous social and cultural changes that led to similar problematizations of everyday life, what distinguished them from Britain, France, and Germany was that the experience of modernity itself here always included a twisted and inflected positioning vis-à-vis European modernity itself. To some extent, Chinese socialism can be seen as such counter-reaction against European modernity and capitalism. The seductive and corrupting attractions of capitalism had to be fought every day and everywhere. This new politicized everyday was introduced to the countryside after the establishment of the People's Republic of China in 1949.

The (Post-)Socialist Everyday

Communist mass politics relied to a huge extent on propaganda work. Perhaps the most important victory of the Communist Revolution in China was the change of discourse, of world-views, and time scales that it achieved (e.g. Liu 2002). Whilst many terms of Western modernity (including those linked to society, state, philosophy, literature, science etc.) had been introduced mainly via Japan since the beginning of the twentieth century, and whilst some of these had already reached the countryside during the republican era,[12] the biggest influx of modernist vocabularies amongst ordinary people in the countryside really began during the 1950s under the Maoist government.

From very early on, the communist party focused its propaganda effort on non-literary visual and oral media, which were accessible to illiterate peasants. Media such as cartoons, revolutionary songs, peasant dances, and public announcements were adopted from the Soviet Red Army, whereas others were taken up from Chinese popular culture: posters, woodblock prints, folk songs, and popular opera. Theatre in particular was a preferred way to get messages across (Peterson 1994: 100; Holm 1991; Ward 1985).

Most villages got their own village administration buildings in the first years of the People's Republic. In these offices of the 'production brigade' (*shengchan dui*), political assemblies were held regularly, in which all adult villagers had to participate. Every village now had an assembly room, and many of these were furnished with equipment such as radios and loudspeakers to announce their sessions. In the mountains of Enshi, not every peasant household was effectively in reach of a loudspeaker, but wherever possible, loudspeakers were installed at the production brigade offices. In the 1960s most villages had at least one loudspeaker installed at their village office, which was invariably used for propaganda purposes.[13]

Another important new means of communication were the local cinemas built in most townships. Film projectionists were charged with showing films in the cinema hall in the township, and intermittently in the villages. The plots of these films were invariably revolutionary stories: depicting the suffering in the 'old society' caused by landlords, KMT officials, and capitalists, the catharsis of the revolution, and the building of the 'new society'.

But probably the most important form of propaganda and communication were the mass meetings that were held regularly now in production brigades. It was in these sessions and the following campaigns that most ordinary peasants became familiar with the new discourses. One particular form was the genre of story-telling practiced since the land reform, called 'talking bitterness' or 'pouring grievance' (*su ku*). This meant the recounting of the suffering in the 'old society', of the hardships endured at the hands of nationalist armies, in particular forced conscriptions, and of the exploitation by landlords and capitalists. In these practices, the most obvious effect was a devaluation of the past, characterized by oppression and exploitation, and the contrast of that past with the present and future. A particular way of telling narratives and relating to oneself was established as the 'social and political norm in life' (Liu 2002: 371).[14]

Closely connected with all this propaganda effort was the development and spread of a simplified national language based on Beijing dialect (Harrison 2001: 234–237), and the promotion of literacy in the countryside. The 'campaigns to eliminate illiteracy' (*saomang yundong*) are generally taken for granted as one area where the Maoist government was particularly successful. Yet this claim has not remained unquestioned.[15] Teaching peasants how to read and write did not constitute a priority for the Maoist army during the Yan'an period and the first years of the People's Republic when political mobilization in the forms described above seemed much more urgent. The first real push towards mass education campaigns came with the collectivization campaign starting in 1955; literacy was seen as necessary for peasants as work team members (to count work points, for instance), and in particular for peasant officials.

The kind of 'peasant education' (*nongmin jiaoyu*) that was promoted from the mid-1950s cannot be separated from these necessities of state-building and rationalization in a planned economy. The corresponding 'state literacy ideology' defined popular literacy in terms of functional necessities in the planned economy and in relation to the state; in particular, literacy amongst peasants was defined as 'knowledge of 1500 characters, plus an ability to comprehend popular books and newspapers, write simple notes and keep account books, and perform simple calculations using the abacus' (Peterson 1994: 114). The curricula taught were explicitly designed for this purpose, and so the 'three tier literacy primer' according to which character sets were taught to students included a) characters related to the 'reading and recording of work points, labour assignments, accounts and receipts, the names of collective institutions (such as team, brigade, supply and marketing cooperative, unified purchase agreement, etc.), as well as the names of local crops, farm implements, local leaders'; b) 'county level administrative and political institutions, names of places and persons'; and c) 'vocabulary relating to the structure of the state, official ideology, and major state personalities' (ibid.: 115).

Several political scientists have argued that the Maoist revolution, which has often been interpreted as a 'penetration' of local society and an extension of state power, really had the unintended consequence of a strengthening of the 'cellularized' structure of rural society, that is, a kind of turning inwards of local communities (Shue 1988). At the same time as the state bureaucracy was growing to unprecedented levels, local communities became ever more entrenched in the 'honeycomb' structures of local allegiance and acquaintance. Connections to the outside world were limited and determined by the state and the ideologies of peasant literacy, with their focus on local economic competence and the administration and ideologies of the nation-state, befitted and reinforced this 'process of encystment' (Peterson 1994: 115).

During the consecutive campaigns of the Maoist era, people were mobilized in class struggle sessions and village walls were covered with 'big character posters' (*dazibao*). After the land reform, in which many poor farmers had been given land, the same plots were 'taken away' again in the collectivization campaign of 1955. The 'Great Leap Forward' with the grotesque 'concerted effort to melt steel and iron' (*dalian gangtie*), ended in the biggest famine in Chinese history. Those who lived through it still remember the year 1959, when they ate tree bark and several villagers in Bashan died of hunger. Then came some years of relaxation, in which responsibilities were given back to the household and to the work team, and independent agricultural production was encouraged. Before long, the next campaign would initiate the Cultural Revolution: 'destroy the four olds and build the four news' (*po sijiu, li sixin*), referring to the 'four olds' of old thinking, old culture, old habits and old customs. In 1966, students of the primary and middle school smashed and destroyed all the signs of 'feudalism' and 'superstition' that they could get hold of: statues of saints and Buddhas, earth god shrines, old books, tombstones.

Whilst the socialist everyday of Cultural Revolution era China has become a repressed memory, capitalist modernity and a global consumer culture are now omnipresent in urban life in China. As the literary critic Tang Xiaobing puts it succinctly, 'To all appearances, everyday urban life as normalcy now seems successfully instituted; for good reason, this is celebrated as a genuine cultural revolution in late twentieth-century China' (Tang 2000: 277).

Interpreting popular culture, literature, and cinema, Tang argues that whilst revolutionary socialism aimed at overcoming everyday life through heroism and utopia, in contemporary urban life, the everyday (that is heterogeneous, entertaining, consumption-oriented) has now become hegemonic (Tang 2000: 273–294).[16] In this urban life, the rural 'flashes back' sometimes, both as a 'rustic simplicity and authenticity' that has now acquired a different attraction (ibid.: 284), but also as the unsettling co-presence of migrant workers and rural poverty (cf. Guang 2003).

Yet has 'the everyday' not always been the core of any ethnography in modern anthropology? Has the method of participant observation, including the recording of all the 'imponderabilia of everyday life', not been that which has defined social anthropology since Malinowski? It might be more than a coincidence that Malinowski established the method of participant observation with the publication of *Argonauts of the Western Pacific* (1922) and subsequent work in the same decade that Joyce, Proust, and Musil published their major novels, and when Benjamin started working on the *Passagenwerk*. The anthropologists themselves were living similar metropolitan lives to those of these writers, including all the plethora of individual choices between different goods, lifestyles and attitudes, all intrinsically connected with mass production. Obviously, most anthropologists were not writing about everyday life in the metropolis, but about some faraway places. Surely much of the appeal, and enchantment, of these ethnographies came from the distance and remoteness of their objects (Ardener 1989: 211). The remoteness of the place of fieldwork was not least characterized by the relative absence of modern everyday life.

As I will argue in the chapters of this book, the modern everyday is now very much present in the villages of Bashan. First of all, there is a variety of consumer goods and means of communication, including TVs, mobile phones, and internet.[17] There is a boom in house construction using new materials (most importantly concrete). The areas of production and consumption are thoroughly integrated into market economies. Levels of literacy have continuously risen and more and more people communicate with ease in standard Mandarin. On top of all this, people are very aware of the 'outsiders' view' on their local practice, including the state condemnation of backwards rituals and the modernization discourses of 'civilization' and 'population quality' (*renkou suzhi*). In the following chapters I will try to show how people confront the moral challenges of this new everyday life.

Having explained some of the meanings that I wish to convey by using the terms 'ethics' and 'everyday', in the following two sections I will sketch out briefly two related theoretical fields to be explored in this book, that is, Chinese moral frameworks and cultural intimacy.

Chinese Moral Frameworks

The hierarchical relations of the family and the state have provided 'inescapable' moral frameworks for most people in rural China, in the past and today. Popular Confucianism emphasized the hierarchy and appropriate behaviour in the relations of father-son, husband-wife, and emperor-official. Whereas Confucian doctrine emphasized appropriate behaviour in particularistic relations, first of all those of the family, the legalist schools put the state first and emphasized universal rules and *raison d'état*. If either sometimes had more influence on the imperial state, it can be said that Chinese governance was characterized by the continuous tension between the 'relational ethics' of Confucianism and the 'universalistic' ethics of legalism (Yang 1988: 415ff). This tension continues, but in modern China, 'universalistic ethics become dominant while relational ethics go under-ground and constitute an oppositional force in the form of the gift economy', writes Mayfair Yang (1988: 422). I will discuss in more detail further below what exactly is meant by Confucian relational ethics going 'under-ground' (see also Steinmüller 2010).

In any case, such relational ethics dealing with the moral frameworks of the family are still extremely important to people in Bashan. In the first two chapters I will describe how the moral frameworks of the family are linked to different spaces, both material and conceptual. Such 'moral spaces' are built up by what is taken as central and what as peripheral. There are several different relationships between a centre and its periphery: the imperial court and the faraway mountains, the modern city and the backward countryside, the brick house on the market street and the wooden house on the hill, or the house of a family and the world outside the house. In these relationships the centre stands for uprightness and regularity, whereas the periphery is innocent and irregular. Recognizing a centre also implies recognizing a moral space: as the apex of one hierarchy, the centre has the power of defining propriety.

People in Zhongba and Bashan understand their own place as remote in relation to the central government and to the modern cities of China. But centres are not only there as distant references; they also exist here, in the local and domestic. If people refer to faraway centres, they also engage in place-making practices in which they create their own centres. Stephan Feuchtwang describes 'territorial place-making' in China in the three practices of centring, linking, and gathering. He proposes these three 'gestures' as a Chinese 'art of location' which contrasts with European practices that emphasize display and representation (2004: 178ff; 2005). Centring means establishing a place by giving coordinates and points of reference which mark a centre. An example for such a centre would be the main axis of a house around which a territorial place is given by the 'square' of the cardinal directions.[18] Around such a centre, references (which can be points in the landscape, resources, or people) are linked and gathered.

Centring implies a categorical moral element: vis-à-vis a centre (be it self-made or referential) one has to act in particular ways. At the same time, various centralized moral spaces can be overlapping and sometimes put in opposition to each other, and so the categorical demands need to be adjusted to the contingency of the everyday. The adjustment towards propriety takes place in everyday talk and action, and it is verbalized in

Chinese expressions such as *guanxi* (relationship), and *li* (propriety and ritual).[19]

These local moral discourses are part of a cultural vocabulary that appears in various different contexts. Adam Chau's monograph on local religion in Northern Shaanxi contains several inspiring theoretical propositions in this regard (Chau 2006). He describes how the same 'cultural logics' and 'social mechanisms' motivate and organize action in everyday life and in popular religion:

> The building of temples, the staffing and management of temple personnel, and the staging of temple festivals rely on volunteerism (based on an understanding of mutual aid and reciprocity), division of labor, a combination of paternalism and folk democracy, and a system of informal networking and contracting (e.g., the hiring of specialists). These are the same mechanisms, social skills, and cultural know-how used in building a family house, managing the household, staging life-courses events such as weddings and funerals, finding a spouse for one's child, and rural marketing. Similarly, the same cultural values or desires that are realized in folk social life are replicated and enacted in popular religion (e.g., the significance of hosting and the pursuit of red-hot sociality). (Chau 2006: 143–145)

Inasmuch as such 'values or desires' imply moral evaluations, they can also be called 'moral frameworks'. Yet to say that the same values (or moralities) are realized in all these different social spheres is true only on one level: at the level of everyday language. The same expressions are used to describe relationships and networks (*guanxi*), appropriate exchange (*lishang wanglai*), rules (*guiju*), propriety and etiquette (*li*), hosting (*qing ke*) and 'red-hot' exuberance (E. *naore*, P. *renao* or *honghuo*). But what to make of the extremely contradictory evaluations of such values in different situations? Social relationships can be affectionate but also instrumental, ritual and rules can be appropriate and decent, but also ossified and oppressive, and social heat can be festive and lively, but also corrupt and decadent. It seems simplistic to claim that it is just the same essentialized cultural values and desires that are evaluated in different ways. What rather happens here is that elements of a moral framework are metaphorically and metonymically represented; and they are never exactly reproduced one-to-one in the next instance.

But these moral frameworks are not 'merely' local. As the Chinese countryside has been thoroughly integrated into a nation-state and a wider political economy, there are other political and economic circuits which over-determine them, whilst they are at the same time re-created by everyday moral interaction. If such a negotiation is always 'political' in one way or the other, it also assumes an outrightly political form in the relationship between local practices and the state.

Local State Formation: Involution and Intimacy

The relationship between local sociality and the state reproduces a tension that is parallel to the categorical and the contingent elements characteristic of everyday ethics: the tension between the official and the vernacular representation of society. 'Official' representations are first of all those discourses in standard Mandarin that are enunciated in schools, government offices, and in the state-oriented media. Opposite to this are 'vernacular' discourses in local dialect that take place in face-to-face communities. But the opposition between official and vernacular is not only a linguistic one: images, architecture, and everyday action can be also become official or vernacular representations. These two never quite meet, and throughout this book I will focus in particular on their interplay and on those instances where they contradict each other.

The differences between official and vernacular, centre and locality, public and private, are crucially important in any social space, and as such not unique to contemporary rural China. What you hear in the news, what you are taught in school, and what is said in government announcements is generally quite different, and sometimes diametrically opposed, to what people say and do at home. In several chapters I will give detailed examples of the differing official and vernacular representations of such things as popular ritual, gambling, and corruption.

These ambiguities appear particularly salient when people are confronted with an outsider who wants to enquire precisely about such things. Covertness, embarrassment, cynicism, and irony are communicative strategies that make it possible to acknowledge both sides of the contradiction, to avoid confrontation, and to maintain communication. These are ways of doing 'face-work', as described by Erving Goffman (1955, 1959): actions that help to avoid inconsistencies between someone's face, as the positively attributed representation of a social person, and what someone actually does. Doing ethnographical work implies learning how to do face-work, i.e. learning the conventional ways of concealing and revealing such inconsistencies. In my fieldwork, this meant for instance learning how to talk about such things as geomancy, family celebrations, or corruption. Countless awkward situations produced by my foolish questions and clumsy behaviour assisted this learning process.

Yet the communicative strategies employed to deal with the ambiguities in the outside representations of local sociality point towards something beyond the awkwardness of doing ethnography: something that I want to describe in terms of Michael Herzfeld's concept of 'cultural intimacy'. Herzfeld defines 'cultural intimacy' as 'the recognition of those aspects of a cultural identity that are considered a source of external embarrassment but that nevertheless provide insiders with their assurance of common sociality' (2005: 3).

There is a 'coded tension' between official representations, generally linked to nation and state, and vernacular forms in face-to-face communities; this tension expresses itself in embarrassment, cynicism, or irony. Such are the reactions when 'cultural intimacy' is exposed; and they can both confirm the official representation, and satirize it. As these expressions are shared and common, they bind people together in intimate spaces of self-knowledge.

The distinction between official and vernacular does not coincide with social or political inequality: the powerful also have a sense of cultural intimacy. Ethnographic and anecdotal accounts show how shared metaphors of the state and the people are used by both officials and ordinary citizens strategically. Both use 'practical essentialisms' of themselves and of the state, in a kind of action that Herzfeld calls 'social poetics'.

In his discussion Herzfeld draws heavily on the study of rhetoric and semiotics, and one might wonder whether the 'social poetics' based on 'cultural intimacy' are not 'merely' symbolic. At least one reviewer of Herzfeld's book submits this predictable criticism: that it focuses on the cultural and symbolic representation of state and nation, but 'is that enough? Are there no "objective-correlatives"? If there are, how on earth do we find them? Where nation and state coincide, the answer may be, "in the objective power of the state"' (Cohen 1998: 8). In other words, the gap between official representations and local sociality that is characteristic of cultural intimacy might be a consequence of processes of state formation that increased the 'objective power of the state'.

Power is rather difficult to measure 'objectively'. In political science, this has been attempted by focusing on the efficiency of state power and assessing 'good' and 'bad' governance. In the case of the modern Chinese state, the problems of state power and government efficiency have been phrased by various observers in terms of 'state involution' (Duara 1987; Siu 1989a, 1989b; Wang Shaoguang 1989; Lu Xiaobo 2000; Murphy 2007). These approaches deal with different periods of state-making in modern Chinese history, and reach slightly different conclusions. But they all share a basic line of argument: that the lasting efforts towards the formation of a modern state from the republican era onwards did not result in an efficient, formal bureaucracy, and a transparent state machine, but re-produced and reinforced 'traditional modes of operation' and 'patrimonialism'. Whilst on the outside a shiny façade of formal rationality is constructed, inside a personalistic cancer is growing. In all of these accounts the state or society are seen to be somewhere they should not be. To argue in this vein necessitates a vantage point from which one actually knows where each should be; and this vantage point is usually a Eurocentric concept of the nation-state.

Most of these approaches are inspired by Clifford Geertz's description of 'agricultural involution' in Indonesia (Geertz 1963). The concept of 'involution' has been also widely used in the economic history of China (Elvin 1972; Huang 1990). In her outline of an alternative history of the 'rice economies' of East Asia, the historian Francesca Bray calls for approaches that go beyond the 'language of failure' implicit in concepts such as 'involution' or 'growth without development'. Both notions imply either an attribution of essential otherness, or a negative account of Chinese history, measured in terms of what was not achieved when compared with European history (Bray 1994: xiv). I take this point of caution that concepts of 'involution' when applied to the state might lead to the analytical pitfalls of eurocentrism and orientalism.

In fact, the condemnation of 'traditionalist' and 'personalistic' ties is not only characteristic of these state involution approaches but it is also the most common public representation of official corruption in the People's Republic. In chapter 7, I will argue that the ways in which this involutionary cancer is officially denigrated and locally recognized are just as productive of shared commonality, as are similar practices related to community rituals, gambling, and what is called 'superstition' (*mixin*). Those who share a sense of the same intimacies, and express their shared intimacies in indirect ways, form what might be aptly called a community of complicity.[20]

These communities of complicity cut across the boundaries of state and society. The involution approaches all emphasize the fact that state and society are deeply entangled. I want to go one step further and deal with the state at its most intimate, a state that is 'a constitutive force at the heart of the social world' in Erik Mueggler's words (2001: 5). Instead of correlating these senses of intimacy to the 'objective power of the state', I will try to relate them to a history of state formation in everyday lives.[21]

Fieldwork Conditions

I arrived in Enshi prefecture for the first time in November 2005. By then I had been travelling for two months through the provinces of Anhui, Jiangxi, Hubei, and Hunan. Some initial contacts I had made in London and Beijing had proven disappointing, and so I spent a lot of time looking for a suitable place to do fieldwork. I relied on Chinese friends and academics from local universities, who introduced me to different villages, in which they had done research, or where they had grown up themselves. Because the purpose of 'participant observation' is largely incomprehensible to many farmers and officials alike, it was essential to have someone to introduce me. Being presented as the friend of someone local (who was a student or teacher in some city, for instance) made things much easier. Additionally, the letters of acceptance I carried from Tsinghua University in Beijing were helpful for local officials (much more so than any document from a foreign university). 这不是很好.

In Wuhan, the capital of Hubei province, I met with researchers at the Centre for Rural Governance of the Central China University for Science and Technology. Professor He Xuefeng and his colleagues offered to introduce me to potential field-sites, and a student there, Luo Yiyun, accompanied me to several villages near Jingmen city. From there, I went into the mountains of Enshi prefecture, and, with the help of some researchers at the Hubei Institute for Nationalities, visited several villages in Enshi, amongst them some in Bashan township. After that I continued travelling on my own for another month, over Chongqing to Guizhou, Hunan, and finally back to Beijing. Over Christmas I took the decision to return to Jingmen and start my fieldwork in one of the villages Luo had first shown me.

Luo Yiyun went there again with me in January and helped me to present my plan to the village officials. I thought it would be sufficient to negotiate my stay with the village administration, and in fact the village mayor arranged for me to live in her house. After one month in the village, I also met with representatives of the next higher government level, the township. But no one from the higher government levels knew about my presence in the village: one day a teacher in a neighbouring village called the police to ask what the foreigner was doing there, 'a foreigner that goes around everywhere and asks questions all the time'. The policemen were not sure what to answer, and forwarded the question to higher government offices. The problem continued several steps up the bureaucratic ladder to the 'foreign affairs office' of the city government. No one had ever heard of such a case there, and so the officials became seriously suspicious about the research and intentions of this foreigner. I had not contacted these higher government levels before and had started my research without a formal permit from them. Finally the chairman of this office decided that to be on the safe side it would be best not to allow me to stay and continue my research, so as to avoid any further trouble. My case was then thoroughly investigated, I was interviewed for several days in the local police station, my laptop was confiscated, and I was barred from continuing my research in Jingmen. The documents and credentials I produced, from the LSE, the German Embassy, and Tsinghua University in Beijing, were seen as irrelevant; instead a research permit from the National Bureau of Statistics of the People's Republic of China was demanded – something which is almost impossible to obtain.

My biggest mistake was that I had not contacted the government offices at the city and prefecture level at the beginning of my stay, if only to greet them briefly and let them know that I was there, a gesture conveyed in the expression *da zhaohu* in Chinese, meaning both to say hello and to notify. As an outsider and a visitor I was also a potential intruder and troublemaker, and I was by default in the position of the supplicant vis-à-vis the local government officials. According to local convention, the minimum requirement would have been to at least present myself and pay my respects. Once a first contact is made, then progress can be made. Yet in my case the officials were informed of a *fait accompli*, and as a result they decided to avoid potential trouble with someone who had arguably shown that he did not know how to behave himself.

I had 'lost' three months because of this incident, and then had to start anew at another field site. This second place was Enshi. Here I contacted the prefecture-level government and its 'foreign affairs' office first and then gradually got to meet officials from different consecutive levels of government (prefecture, county, township, and village). This time I spent much more time in meetings and banquets where people exchange words and treats, and get to know each other. I had underestimated the importance of such personal contact, and in particular of eating together. My relationship with local officials still remained rather tense, but no one ever questioned again that I was allowed to do my research.

Officials of the 'foreign affairs' office of the prefecture and city government then took me again to Bashan township, and after some negotiations with the township officials, it was decided that I could settle down in Zhongba village. Zhongba was the first village in the region where most paddy fields were changed into tea plantations, in the 1990s; it is now a specialized 'tea village' with about ninety-eight per cent of its arable land planted with tea. It had been a showcase of local development already in the 1970s, when it was a 'red flag brigade' (*hongqi dadui*), and in more recent years it was given the titles of 'model village' (*shifan cun*) and 'civilized village' (*wenming cun*). Whilst the former villages Houmei and Bailong'gou now also belong to the administrative village of Zhongba, the attention of the government is broadly focused on the part that was formerly Zhongba village. Visitors are often taken around one circuit of the '8'-shaped round road of Zhongba. The relative prosperity of Zhongba was surely one of the reasons why the officials suggested that I should do my fieldwork in this place.

It was arranged that I should live in a side room of the village administration building. This building consists of several parts, each one with a different function. The former village administration building is a traditional wooden peasant house, which was transformed into a tea factory in the 1980s. Next to it is the new 'office building' housing the village administration, and the office of the village doctor. These offices had been the former primary school of the village, until 2002 when the school was closed. Now the classrooms upstairs are unused, whereas the rooms downstairs are the village offices. My room was directly above the surgery of Dr Hu, the village doctor. During the day, the village officials were often in their offices, but they rarely stayed overnight in one of the rooms upstairs. Li Shifu always arrived first and left last: a woman in her forties, she has been responsible for several years for the maintenance of the building, and she cooks for the village officials.

Although I had wanted to live in the household of a peasant family, I accepted the cadres' arrangement to stay in the village office at first. When I brought up this issue again after a month or so, I encountered little comprehension. The answer was usually that for my own 'security' (*anquan*) and comfort it would be more convenient to stay in the village administration building. After a while I gave up on the plan to move in with a family, and stayed in the village administration throughout my fieldwork.

During my first week in Zhongba, a local official accompanied me on foot to households in the neighbourhood; but soon I was left on my own. For most of the time, I was able to move rather freely in the villages of Bashan. But the government officials still had their eye on me. It was clear that many of the officials in neighbouring villages were reporting my movements to the township government. For instance, one day in the village administration of a neighbouring village, I overheard a conversation between a village official and a township official, who assumed that I would not understand the local dialect: they were talking about the calls that officials had made to the township government reporting that I had been to this village and which families I had visited. Yet this surveillance was mostly presented as being motivated by concern for my comfort; and overall, I enjoyed a lot of freedom in my research.

The relationship with the local officials would remain tense throughout most of my time in Bashan. In particular, my relationship with the party secretary of Zhongba, Fang Bo, was rather complicated. Sent down from the township government, he had assumed his office the same week that I arrived in Zhongba. He was twenty-eight years old then, just two years my senior. For most of the time, Fang Bo remained suspicious towards me: he could not see how my presence could be of any advantage to him. Instead he was worried about me causing trouble for which he would be held accountable. As a result he tried either to limit his contact with me, or he gave me suggestions and exhortations on what I should and should not do during my stay. The person in the village administration who was always unreservedly friendly with me was Li Shifu, the cook, who never failed to call me over for a meal.

I also sat for many hours on the low chairs in Dr Hu's office, which was always crowded with patients. In this way, Dr Hu was the nodal point of many networks of relationships, and many people also came to him with problems beyond the limits of his medicine: he was frequently called on to mediate in delicate matters and to settle disputes. But I spent most of my time with the family of Song Haomin, the farmer who was leasing the village's tea factory, and with the neighbours Tian Shanwei, Yang Yuanbing, Liu Laosan, Xie Kaisong, Wang Wei, and many others in Zhongba and Bashan.

During fieldwork, I spent much time exploring Zhongba and the valleys and hills of the neighbouring villages by foot. I would get up early, and walk along the roads of Zhongba village, and then over into the neighbouring villages of Bailong'gou and Houmei; later on I extended my walks into many other surrounding villages. By the end of my fieldwork I had visited all the seventeen villages of Bashan township at least once. This was not only because I liked hiking, or because I thought that 'I would see more walking' – as I often said to locals who asked me why I would not pay for a motorbike to drive me. One of the main reasons was that I did not know what else to do; after the first curiosity had faded, many neighbours had better things to do than to chat with me all day. Roaming the roads and paths of Bashan seemed a good way of exploring the countryside. Often someone would call me over, and invite me to sit down. In such situations I often tried to do some semi-structured interviews, but only sporadically recorded them. It took me a long time to understand what people expected of me when they invited me to sit down and have a meal. At the beginning I often accepted quickly, not understanding the most basic etiquette, which necessitated at least a semblance of polite refusal – after all, with a shared meal a relationship of reciprocity is established.

Soon I was also invited to weddings, funerals, and other occasions of 'eating wine' (E. *qi jiu*), that is, the family and community celebrations which I will discuss in chapters 4 and 5. Sometimes I also joined people in their work: I participated in the tea picking which is done throughout the summer months, helped on construction sites, and worked for several weeks in the tea factory owned by Song Haomin.

My problematic relationship with the local officials, and the image that many ordinary people had of me, changed substantially after I appeared several times in the local newspapers and on TV. First, a friend at the Hubei Institute of Nationalities in Enshi had the idea of writing a story about me for the local newspaper, and the idea was enthusiastically taken up at the propaganda department of Enshi city. A one-page report appeared in the *Enshi Evening News* about my presence and research in Bashan, and a ten-minute film clip was broadcast on Enshi TV, the local TV station. Many people in Enshi and Bashan saw the report, and afterwards strangers called me by my Chinese name on the roads of Bashan and Enshi. But many peasant families do not have cable TV (which is necessary to watch the local TV station), nor do they read newspapers, and so to them it made little difference. The reactions of the neighbours in the village were divided; some told me that it was an 'honour for the village', whereas others said to me in person that it was a farce, and made up. In the documentary I appeared to be lauding the local government and the development of the village and the township in the highest terms.[22] During the interview I was sitting next to the party secretary of Zhongba, Fang Bo, and one deputy head of the township government: I could hardly have criticized governmental policies in their presence. This was but one occasion in which I felt embarrassed about my own inability to reconcile different relationships of trust and indebtedness.

I had to learn many things in order to be able to share everyday life in Bashan, most importantly the local language. I had taken Mandarin classes on and off throughout my university studies, but when I arrived in China for the first time in summer 2005, I could scarcely strike up a conversation. So I took some more language courses in Beijing for about four months, which gave me a better basis, but was still barely enough. When I then went on a long trip through several provinces in search for a field site, I came to realize that most people in the countryside were not even speaking the standard Mandarin (*putonghua*) that I had learned, but local dialects instead. The local dialect of the Enshi region is close to the Sichuan dialects of northern Mandarin Chinese, and most native speakers can communicate with speakers of standard Mandarin. But a good many local idiomatic phrases are not readily understandable even to native speakers of standard Mandarin. It took me quite a long time to be able to communicate in the local dialect, and even at the end of my fieldwork I had not resolved the language problem to my entire satisfaction. But after one year more or less, I was able to have ordinary conversations in dialect, although I certainly missed many nuances.

My language skills also limited my access to local people. For a very long time, I had more contact with those who could speak standard

Mandarin. A related problem was my very limited access to women (who generally spoke less standard Mandarin than men). It would not have been acceptable for me to spend long periods talking even with married women, unless I was on very familiar terms with their families. The problem became obvious to me when my partner visited me in the field: she had much easier access to women than I had. After some time, I became good friends with several families, and had also long conversations with the women in these houses. Even though I do not explicitly problematize the issue of gender in this book, I have attempted to integrate women's perspectives on the changing ethical landscape of Zhongba and Bashan.

During my fieldwork I frequently wondered how the particularity of Zhongba and my fieldwork situation might have influenced my research. As a 'model village' Zhongba is certainly far more prosperous than most villages in the region. To a certain extent I could relativize what I saw in Zhongba with visits to other villages of Bashan, and by comparing the situation in Bashan with my experience in other regions of China. And even though the conditions of Zhongba are very peculiar to that village, they have also provided an interesting case study, in particular in terms of the 'face' that the new government policies toward the countryside are producing – a topic I deal with in chapter 7.

Another particularity of Bashan and Enshi is not dealt with in detail in this book: its status as a 'minority district'. Even though Enshi district became a 'Tujia and Miao Minority Autonomous District' in 1983, and Bashan township a 'Dong minority autonomous township' in 2003, there are no cultural and linguistic boundaries, and no self-ascribed identity, besides the one printed on ID cards, to distinguish those that are 'Dong', 'Tujia', 'Miao' or majority Han Chinese in the region. It is beyond the scope of this book to deal with the intricacies of 'minority identity' and the history of 'minority relations' in the region explicitly, but I will touch on the subject at several points.

Chapter Outline

Many anthropological monographs give the 'setting of the ethnography' after the introduction. The field site is located in historical time and geographical space. Both are empty frames into which a community is put, and the 'setting chapter' distracts attention from the question of how place and time are made.[23] I want to problematize the ways in which a local place is subjected from the outside; in rural China this cannot be done without reflecting the perspective of the central state. Accordingly, in the first chapter I present the place of my ethnography from three angles:

local historical sources about the region; contemporary media and government discourses; and local practices linked to the family. Whilst in the first two the region appears as rural, remote and peripheral, the last angle deals with how locals place themselves in a spatial and temporal centre. In all three angles, there are similar ambiguities between a locality and its outside representation, and between local sociality and the state.

The second chapter deals with the changes in the siting and construction of the houses in Zhongba, further elaborating on the connection between place-making practices and everyday ethics. Recently many people have built new houses of bricks and concrete, instead of the traditional wooden structures. By and large, the new houses are located along asphalt roads, and they are built by hired labour and with pre-fabricated construction materials – changes which all correspond to a different local political economy characterized by the growth of wage labour. Yet the social mechanisms and values realized in the construction processes are fairly similar for both wooden and brick houses.

The third chapter is about the different forms of work that people engage in, against the background of a rapidly changing political economy. I outline the general changes in the political economy of the township, and show the mechanisms of marketization with the example of the introduction of tea as a cash crop. Work in tea production is valorized and measured against labour in the cities on the one side, and work in agriculture on the other side. A survey of different occupations provides the background for an understanding of the meanings of work in the countryside today. The moral frameworks of family and work form the basis of the next two chapters, which deal with community celebrations.

The celebrations of life-cycle events, such as weddings and funerals, house inaugurations and birthdays, are occasions of major expenditures and important social gatherings. In such rituals, one central element is the propriety of social action, which is reciprocal within hierarchical frames. In the fourth chapter, I attempt to analyse this propriety in the changing meaning of its Chinese term, *li*. The 'centring' action of *li* is then described in the context of family celebrations in Bashan, and in particular in the case of one wedding.

The fifth chapter delineates several ambiguities around ritual practices. Many elements of ritual or *li* have become embarrassing since they had been and continue to be denounced in public. At the same time there has been a revival of many 'traditional' practices since the loosening of political control in the 1980s. Through the examples of funerary rites, the commercialization of family celebrations – one funeral in particular – and my own participation at ritual celebrations, I sketch both official and vernacular perspectives. These phenomena are characteristically embarrassing for the Maoist and modernist state, yet they are essential for local sociality. In this way they are productive of 'cultural intimacy' (Herzfeld 2005), which is also the overarching theme of the last two chapters.

In the sixth chapter, the moving boundaries of accepted sociality are explored in the context of gambling. I elaborate on the meaning of local notions of the opposition of capability versus luck/fate, and situate them in the changing political economy of rural China. What comes out implicitly both in life-cycle rituals, and in gambling, is the ironic stance of local sociality vis-à-vis the state. The local state and its 'face' is the topic of the following chapter.

Taking the example of the local implementation of the developmental policies for rural areas, the seventh chapter deals with the local state, and the relationships between villagers and officials. I describe local discourses about good and bad officials, what villagers expect from local government, and what they expect from each other. Through the Chinese notion of 'face' (*mianzi*), I deal with the boundaries between 'insiders' and 'outsiders' with regard to local government, and in relationship to the household.

In the concluding chapter I try to bring together the theoretical elements that have emerged in the previous chapters, and re-group them around the core theoretical notions of this book, which are everyday ethics, communities of complicity, and irony.

Notes

1. Jarret Zigon (2008) provides a summary of previous anthropological engagements with 'morality' and outlines an anthropological perspective for future research.
2. Laidlaw proposes a narrow definition of 'morality' following Nietzsche and Williams, reserving the term 'for ethical systems where self-denying values inform lawlike obligations' (Laidlaw 2002: 317). 'Ethics', on the other hand, he equates with 'the exercise of freedom' and he concludes his outline of an 'anthropology of ethics' writing that '[w]herever and in so far as people's conduct is shaped by attempts to make of themselves a certain kind of person, because it is as such a person that, on reflection, they think they ought to live, to that extent their conduct is ethical and free' (Laidlaw 2002: 327).
3. In the conclusion of the same book Zigon considers morality in three spheres: '(1) the institutional; (2) that of public discourse; and (3) embodied dispositions' (2008: 162). It is not spelt out clearly, but presumably (1) and (2) are subsections of the 'discursive level' of morality.
4. And it follows the European tradition of using the Latin word for the concrete and the Greek one for the abstract. Arthur Kleinmann (1998) and Niklas Luhmann (1991) use similar definitions: Kleinmann distinguishes 'moral process' (as experience and engagement) from 'ethical discourse' (which is abstract, principle-based, reflective and intellectualist). The sociologist Niklas Luhmann understands by morality 'a special form of communication which carries with it indications of approval or disapproval' and by ethics 'the description of morality' (1991: 84–85). Luhmann adds

that at least since the eighteenth century, ethics has become a 'theoretical reflection of morality,' whereas before it had been a 'description of a normative-rational special sphere of nature' (ibid.).

5. The distinction between weak and strong evaluations is first made in Taylor 1976, but elaborated in the first chapters of Taylor's main work, *Sources of the Self* (1989), from which I paraphrase here. I have also used the summary of Taylor's work in Joas 2000 [1997]: 124–144.

6. The literary scholar Hans Ulrich Gumbrecht has written a 500-page 'essay on historical simultaneity' entitled *1926. Living at the Edge of Time.* The book is a collage of events and writings that all took place in 1926, from the vantage points of Berlin, Buenos Aires, and New York, but ranging widely into many other 'everyday worlds'. It concludes with a longer essay on three 'Being-in-the-Worlds of 1926' including that of Martin Heidegger. In this essay Gumbrecht tries to show 'that some of the principal philosophical concerns in [*Being and Time*], some decisive elements in the structure of its argument, and perhaps Heidegger's entire contribution to Western philosophy can be read as originating in a reaction to the emotional, intellectual, and political environment of 1926' (Gumbrecht 1997: 442). Using a more sociological method, Pierre Bourdieu has similarly analysed the social and historical conditioning of Heidegger's thinking (Bourdieu 1991 [1988]).

7. Gardiner (2000) and Highmore (2002) give summaries of theories of the everyday in Western modernity from Simmel to De Certeau. Harootunian (2000b) describes the condition of the everyday both in Europe and Japan, and compares the writings of Tosaka Jun, Kon Wajiro, and Kobayashi Hideo in Japan to those of Siegfried Krakauer, Walter Benjamin, and others in Europe. If the 'mystery of the everyday' as part of an experience of accelerated modernization was similar both in Europe and Japan, the kind of responses were rather different; and based on this difference Harootunian aims at a critique of the uniqueness of European modernity, an assumption that is prevalent in cultural studies and history.

8. As rector of Freiburg University, member of the Nazi party, and public intellectual, Heidegger actively endorsed Hitler and National Socialism. Aside from his personal involvement, the connections of his philosophy to Nazism have been subject to extended debates. The debate was revived in France in 1987 with the publication of Victor Faria's *Heidegger et le Nazisme.* Many eminent thinkers have contributed to this debate, including Derrida (1987) and Bourdieu (1991 [1988]).

9. The philosopher John Roberts has reviewed these debates starting with the Russian Revolution and culminating in the work of Henri Lefebvre (Roberts 2006). Mapping out these debates, Roberts is seeking to re-establish the concept of the everyday as a 'basis for a critique of culture' and defend the 'continuing possibilities of cultural theory as a revolutionary critique of the social totality' (2006: 3–5). His criticism is addressed mainly to the trends in contemporary cultural studies (in the wake of Michel de Certeau's work) to romanticize creative consumption and cultural resistance.

10. For modernist art, architecture, and literature in St Petersburg in the second half of the nineteenth century, a 'modernism of underdevelopment' that led to the Russian Revolution, see Berman (1983: 173–286).

11. See, for instance, Lu 1999 and the contributions to Zhang 1999.

12. Chen Zhongshi, for instance, describes in his novel *White Deer Ground* how teachers and students introduced new words like 'democracy' (*minzhu*) and 'masses of the people' (*renmin qunzhong*) during the republican era (Chen 2008 [1993]). The conflicts and misunderstandings around these new words were presumably similar in Bashan, where Communist activists at the primary school also carried out

propaganda work during the Japanese invasion. For the original translation of Western terms into Japanese and from there into Chinese, see Masini 1993 and Liu 1995.

13. The spread of such 'non-literate' media was pervasive: 'by 1975, for example, 93 per cent of rural production teams in China and 70 per cent of rural households were linked to some form of wired broadcasting, in addition to which there were more than 106 million loudspeakers in rural areas, one for every seven persons' (Peterson 1994: 99, footnote 16, quoting Burns 1987).

14. Reviewing a text by Fang Huirong which deals with memories of the land reform in the countryside, Liu Xin concludes that 'the effectiveness of the Communist power-practice lies in its success in creating a new temporal horizon that allowed the present to always stand out as a glory against background of a painful past' (Liu 2002: 386).

15. Vilma Seeberg, for instance, concludes that contrary to official declarations, there was actually very little improvement in both school age and adult-level literacy between 1949 and 1979, with literacy levels remaining constant at around 32% (Seeberg 1990: 268, 278).

16. Several other authors have attempted to capture and theorize contemporary everyday life in China in similar ways; see, for example, the essays in Dong and Goldstein 2006. Inspired by Walter Benjamin's explorations of consumer goods, architecture, and street life in Paris, Michael Dutton has tried to bring the experience of everyday life in urban China together in a montage of pictures, texts, and quotations. Similar in spirit and style to Benjamin's *Passagenwerk* (1982), Dutton's *Streetlife China* (1998) is a motley collection of observations, quotations, and reflections. But Dutton runs the risk of granting too much of the 'agency' of resistance to the acts of consumption in everyday life, and too much autonomy to the realm of the everyday (Harootunian 2000a).

17. The arrival of all these consumer goods and the changes in house construction are similarly reported in most recent ethnographies of rural China (e.g. Yan 1996; Ruf 1998; Han 2001; Ku 2004).

18. The Chinese character for 'square' (*fang*) also means 'place' (*di-fang*). The spatial concept of 'four quarters' (*si fang*) around a centre has been the most important structuring principle of Chinese cosmologies from the Shang dynasty onwards (cf. Wang 2000: 20ff; Wheatley 1971).

19. These notions, and related ones such as *ganqing* (feeling), *renqing* (human feeling), *zeren* (responsibility), have been used in various ethnographies to theorize Chinese moralities. See Yang (1994), Kipnis (1997), and Ku (2004), for instance.

20. My outline of communities of complicity, which are based on indirect expression and action (such as embarrassment, cynicism and irony), is similar in some ways to the rhetorical approach of Frederick Bailey (e.g. 1969, 1991). But there are some differences in the direction of our arguments: while Bailey tends to focus on power games (and perhaps sometimes reduces social reality to such games; for example, see how he presents the relationship between ethnographer and informant, 1991: 68ff.), I am more directly concerned with the constitution of community. Whereas Bailey focuses on strategizing and deceit, I focus on indirection and irony. Hence if he shows the 'prevalence of deceit' (1991), my aim would be to show the 'prevalence of indirection and irony'.

21. This resonates with several other attempts in anthropology to study 'everyday forms of state formation' (e.g. Joseph and Nugent 1994; Fuller and Benei 2001; Krohn-Hansen and Nustad 2005). Instead of pre-assuming a monolithic state, the state itself is understood here as an ongoing ideological project which is never completed (cf.

Abrams 1988; Mitchell 1991). Accordingly, the boundaries between state and society are blurred (Gupta 1995), and the quotidian boundary-making between state and society has become the main focus of analysis.

22. I include a translation of the article that appeared in the *Enshi Evening News* in Appendix A. The content of the newspaper report and the TV documentary were almost identical.

23. Corsín Jiménez (2003) argues that space is a dimension of social relationships themselves. He contrasts his approach of 'space as a capacity' with the common theoretical understanding of space as 'territory' that is inhabited, classified, or signified, which he traces back to Durkheim. My inspiration for avoiding a 'setting chapter' is Erik Mueggler's ethnography, *The Age of Wild Ghosts*, in which he tries to invert this 'common trope of ethnography' (2001: 10).

Chapter 1

A REMOTE PLACE FROM THREE ANGLES

In the 43rd year of the reign of the Kangxi emperor (1704 CE), the poet and playwright Gu Cai embarks on a long journey into the mountains west of Yichang. He carries letters of invitation from his friend Kong Shangren, to visit Xiang Shunnian, the head of the chieftainship Rongmei. These chieftainships (*tusi*) do not have a Mandarin administration like the rest of the Empire, their populations speak languages partly incomprehensible to Chinese-speakers from the plains, and their rulers often cannot read and write Chinese. But the rulers of Rongmei and the other chieftainships in the region have been vassals to the emperor for centuries, and they have strong ties with officials and literati in the plains. Xiang Shunnian in particular is known to be a cultivated man who encourages and sponsors poetry, theatre and music at his court in Rongmei.

With the adversities of the weather, the mountain paths through endless woods, and the dangers of bandits and beasts of prey, it takes almost a month to reach Rongmei after leaving Yichang, the last town in the plains. Gu Cai carries with him the most recent play written by his friend Kong Shangren, entitled *The Peach Blossom Fan* (*Taohua Shan*, 1993 [1702]).[1] After Gu Cai's arrival in Rongmei, Xiang Shunnian has the play rehearsed and staged at his court in Rongmei. Together they spend a pleasant three months at the court in Rongmei, with many evenings of conversation, music, and poetry.

After his return, Gu Cai wrote down in verses what he had experienced in the mountains. Entitled *Travel Notes from Rongmei* (*Rongmei Jiyou*, 1991 [1704]), he left behind his lyrical elaborations for posterity. The *Travel Notes* are a poetic compliment to this area and his host Xiang Shunnian. Exchanging complimentary compositions and poems was one of the distinguishing marks of the empire's scholar-officials, and Gu Cai's *Travel Notes* bear witness that the chief (*tusi*) Xiang Shunnian was accepted by the literati as a peer. The book is full of poems about the landscape and the people of Rongmei. Setting the stage for the entire book, the first page contains a long comparison of the Rongmei chieftainship with 'the peach blossom land' (*taohuayuan*) of a well-known Chinese legend: a beautiful land that is far away in the mountains, where people remained honest and simple, and untouched by the oppression and chaos of the valleys.[2]

But Gu Cai also writes in his *Notes* about the more prosaic and miserable aspects of life in the Wuling mountains, the inaccessibility, the adversities of nature, the constant danger of bandits, and the poverty and misery of the peasants. In the history of the region there has been certainly much disorder, both political and social, as in many other regions of central China. But compared to the plains along the Long River in Hubei and also to the Sichuan plateau, the mountains of Enshi prefecture in Southwestern Hubei have had much less contact with the outside world. This is an outpost of the mountain regions of western Hunan, of Guizhou and Yunnan, where many people with languages and customs completely different to the Han Chinese were living. Compared with them, this area was much closer to the empire. Yet it is still 'remote' enough to be compared to the 'peach blossom land' of the legend. Even today people sometimes use the expression to describe the mountains of Enshi.[3]

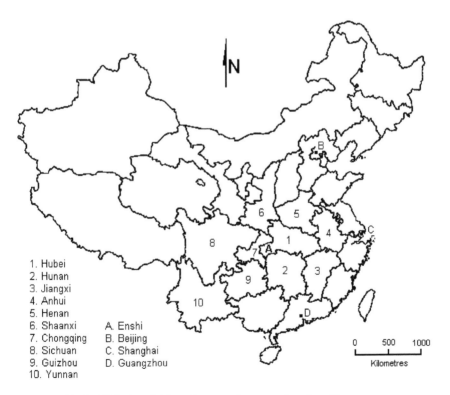

1. Hubei
2. Hunan
3. Jiangxi
4. Anhui
5. Henan
6. Shaanxi   A. Enshi
7. Chongqing   B. Beijing
8. Sichuan   C. Shanghai
9. Guizhou   D. Guangzhou
10. Yunnan

Map 1.1 Enshi, Hubei, neighbouring provinces, and major cities

The reminiscences of Gu Cai set the stage for the topics to be explored in this chapter: the image of a remote region as an idyllic and romantic place, sometimes utopian in its beauty, and disconnected from the demands and oppression of a civilizational centre; sometimes wild and dangerous, a jungle where 'natives' live maintaining martial traditions, and possibly rather unrestricted sexual conventions; and sometimes just images of backwardness and ignorance.

In what follows I will trace three discursive frameworks around different centres and what is remote to them, and by doing so, situate the place of my ethnography historically and spatially. The first two frameworks are the hegemonic discourses in which this remote mountain region is described in late imperial China, and now. Both of these are relatively far away and removed from the experiences of ordinary local people. The third one is the framework of families and lineages, and here people are actively living in a time and dwelling in a place that is not envisaged in the hegemonic discourses. In local tourism, lineage practice, and geomancy, such local practice enters partly convergent and partly conflictive relationships with hegemonic discourses.

The Enshi region of Southwestern Hubei Province lies in the Wuling Mountains, which stretch over north-western Hubei province, the southeastern corner of Sichuan province (Chongqing), and along the border of Guizhou and Hunan provinces. On a map of the People's Republic of China, it looks as if this region is right in the middle of the country (see map 1.1 and 1.2). In fact nowadays this area is thoroughly integrated into the

Map 1.2 Hubei Province

political system of mainland China, and cultural and social differences between its inhabitants and the Han Chinese of Sichuan or Hubei are not obvious. Yet this is now a 'Tujia and Miao Autonomous Prefecture' (*tujiazu miaozu zizhi zhou*), i.e. a minority district receiving a particular treatment within the political hierarchy. As a relatively inaccessible mountain region, this area shares many characteristics with the other borderlands of the Chinese empire in the south. Throughout the Ming and Qing dynasties, the populations of these borderlands lived in constant exchange with the Chinese empire: sometimes in vassalage, sometimes in revolt, but altogether relatively independent. Many of these regions were eventually populated with Han settlers in the eighteenth century, when the Qing Empire reached its widest expansion.

When Gu Cai visited Rongmei, the area was predominantly governed by local chiefdoms (*tusi*), which were related in a particular vassal system to the Chinese empire. The Rongmei chiefdom was then one of the most prosperous and Gu Cai's reminiscences show how learned and highly cultured the people at the court of its chief Xiang Shunnian were. The only place that was then governed directly by the Mandarins of the empire was the town of Shinanfu, which later became the capital with the same name as the prefecture: Enshi.

This vassal system of governance ended in the 12th year of the reign of emperor Yongzheng (i.e. 1735 CE), with a reform that 'did away with the vassal chiefdoms and instead installed officials sent by the imperial court' (*gai tu gui liu*).[4] At the same time Chinese merchants and officials had started to promote and distribute two New World crops that had come mainly from the Portuguese and Spanish trading in the seaports of southern China: potato and corn. Originating from the highlands of South America, these crops proved to be particularly apt to the highlands of southern China, and played a major factor in the migration and 'colonization' of many new areas in south-western China.

During this same period, almost a million people left the plains of Jiangxi and Huguang[5] in two huge waves of migration and went to Sichuan and Guizhou.[6] Many immigrants followed the Yangzi upstream; some of them stopped at the ports of Yichang and Badong, and entered the mountains of what is now Enshi prefecture. A second group of immigrants was escaping from army conscription and floods in western Hunan and northern Guizhou and came to take advantage of the new possibilities of the vast land in the Wuling mountains that had hitherto been jungle. These population movements were partly promoted and guided by mandarin officials; the message spread amongst the settlers that they could take as much land as they could till up in the mountains, with only 'the horizon in front of their eyes as a frontier' (*yi muguang wei xian*). That, at least, is what is still transmitted in family histories and legends. The majority of families that are now living in Enshi prefecture can trace their ancestry back to one of these waves of immigration. In Bashan township, for example, there was a large group of immigrants from Jiangxi that had a common temple and a Jiangxi assembly (*jiangxi laoxianghui*) at the market town. This group probably took part in the first wave of migration. The second wave of migration also affected Bashan: many families still retell family legends and genealogies in which the origin of their families is traced back to places in Hunan and Guizhou (the most frequent places of origin of the families in Bashan are Baoding and Anhua, two small towns at the border of Hunan and Guizhou provinces). These legends and genealogies will be part of my third angle, described below. But first let us look at how the mandarins of the time described this mountain region.

Angle 1: Local Gazetteers

Whereas relatively few written sources about this region exist from earlier times, at the beginning of the eighteenth century the number of such sources increased rapidly. The majority of these are reports written by visitors and local gazetteers produced by the scholar-administrators of the region.

In imperial China, the mandarin administrators had to compile at regular intervals local gazetteers (*difang zhi*) of every county in the empire, including a basic census, customs, geographical conditions, flora and fauna, transport, local history, virtuous elders and widows, maps of the capital city and its official buildings, imperial posts, legends etc. Different in scope and content, such local gazetteers sometimes included veritable ethnographies. In the following I will cite some of the local gazetteers of Enshi County and the neighbouring regions compiled during the Qing dynasty (1644–1911 CE).

In most of these texts several features of the native 'highlanders' are continuously emphasized. One of the most commonly used words to characterize such mountain dwellers and their habits in these gazetteers is *chunpu*, which can be translated as 'simple' or 'unsophisticated'. Generally it is used as a positive attribute, implying that someone is 'honest' and 'upright'. Yet good nature and honesty could easily turn into naivety, and even unruliness and savageness. Indeed the martial characteristics and the unorthodox religious and sexual conventions of these people are frequently emphasized:

> All the relevant local gazetteers compiled before 1949 say that the highlanders were given to believe in gods and spirits, often different from those worshiped

by townsmen. They also say that these highlanders were extremely frugal, straightforward, physically strong (both sexes), arrogant, and quarrelsome. The compilers, urban scholars themselves, took a disapproving view of these strange, unruly attitudes and behaviour, particularly the highlanders' sexual libertinism and their litigiousness. People of this breed were prone to protest and revolt. Their history in the nineteenth and twentieth centuries is indeed frequently punctuated by insurrections. (Ch'en 1992: 31)

In fact, such a description is by no means exceptional, or peculiar to peripheral regions. There are numerous similar texts about Han Chinese in many regions of China, showing the unease of the Mandarins at the superstitious beliefs, heterodox cults,[7] sexual licence,[8] and litigiousness[9] of ordinary people. The content of the local gazetteers must be considered against their social background: their authors were scholar-officials within the hierarchies of the imperial bureaucracy. Thus the gazetteers were primarily intended for registering information that was necessary and useful for the administration, including geography, censuses, and the economic and political situation. Therefore, the gazetteers frequently read like handbooks for the mandarin administrators. But the central concern of the scholar-administrators was not just the facts about the regions, but how the morals and governance within the empire might be influenced. Unlike other forms of governance, the administration of imperial China was based much more on moral example than on factual control and command chains – and hence moral commentary and judgement was most important when dealing with peripheral people.[10]

At the same time, the authors were often writing about the districts where they themselves had some responsibility, and so they would sometimes try to embellish the situation. The most important benchmark of 'civilization' in imperial China was the level of Confucian learning. Hence one often finds phrases which emphasize the extent to which the local population was dedicated to learning, and how many excellent scholars came from this region, despite the extremely low probability of this in poor mountain areas. The following passage is an example of such achievements against all odds:

Enshi is located in the middle of thousands of mountains, and it cannot be reached on boat or carriage. The people there are very honest and sincere, and the customs simple and upright. The practice of learning and studying is wide-spread and well-established, and the people are not afraid of the effort and costs it implies. The gentry and the officials understand that good reputation and moral principles are the highest values and they judge each other by it. There are few thieves, and simple-minded bandits are afraid of the law. There is a lot of production in agriculture and handcrafts, which is sold for just market prices. [...] Even though agriculture and living conditions are hard, people live happily to old age here. (Enshi County 1982 [1868]: 285)

Obviously, such a eulogy is full of set phrases, politeness, and circumlocution. In a sense, the mandarin officials could hardly write in any other way, because if they had pointed out all the difficulties of the region under their own administration, including poverty, immorality, and ignorance, surely higher officials would feel compelled to take measures.

Yet at some point it became necessary to indicate the negative side and the potential dangers of the mountain populations. Rather than being presented as factual statements about contemporary problems, such issues were more often cast in a historical narrative, hinting that such barbarity and savageness had since become civilized.

The local gazetteer of Enshi compiled in 1868, for example, contains an interesting piece about the 'three transformations of local customs in Enshi' (*en yi fengsu san bian shuo*; Enshi County 1982 [1868]: 291–292). It describes how during the Yuan, Ming, and Qing dynasties, the local population oscillated three times from relatively 'simple' and 'honest' (*pu*) customs towards 'sophistication' (*hua*) and then fell into immorality and decay. But in the long term and across these cyclical developments, there was a change 'from simplicity to sophistication' (*you pu er hua*).[11]

The last of these three transformations took place in the eighteenth century after the abolition of the vassal system; the main factor driving this transformation was the huge influx of settlers mentioned above. The new settlers brought with them agricultural skills, trade, and knowledge, yet they must have met with a lot of mistrust at the same time. And whilst the natives seemed 'honest and upright' at first, they must have surely appeared 'naïve and ignorant' at other times. Over several generations people in the region continued to distinguish between 'natives' and 'incomers':

> The people of this place can be divided into 'native families' (*benhu*) and 'incomer families' (*kehu*): the first have been living here as natives for several dynasties, whereas the latter came as merchants and migrants after the reforms of the Qianlong period. Generally speaking, one can say that the natives are of honest and upright character, whereas the incomers are sophisticated and urbane. (Enshi County 1982 [1868]: 287)

Over centuries of migrations and cultural exchange, incomers have become 'natives' when compared to new incomers. In late imperial China, the syncretic cultural expressions that developed in local society were taken as the particular customs of a mountain people, which was nevertheless 'Chinese' in the sense of being part of the empire. Yet in the 1950s, when communist officials and ethnographers initiated a huge national project of 'minority classification', the local customs were so significantly different to those of other Han Chinese that it seemed justified to classify the people of this region as a singular 'minority'. The name that was chosen for this minority was another expression for the 'native families' (*tujia*, or earlier *benhu*). The most striking difference between their folk customs and those of the majority of Han Chinese was that their conventions of patriarchy and lineage were seen as much less orthodox: in particular mortuary practices, ancestor worship, and the inheritance of property were quite peculiar, and could be interpreted as conveying less patriarchal authority overall.[12] Nevertheless, at the time most locals thought of themselves as 'Han Chinese' (*hanzu ren*) or at least 'Chinese' (*huaren*) precisely on the basis of patrilineal ancestry. This is the typical Chinese way of lineage and kinship identity; I will describe in more detail below how it is still very important in local society. But first let me explore some more theoretical associations about civilizational projects and faraway places in China and elsewhere.

Civilization and Remoteness

The ways in which local society and culture are described in the gazetteers should be understood against the background of the 'civilizational project' (Harrell 1995) of the Qing empire at the time. This could also be called a 'colonial project', as a state civilization was pacifying and populating a formerly infertile mountain region.[13] In fact, the extension of the Chinese empire towards the south and west was a very long historical process.[14]

Many aspects of the interaction between the empire and the nomadic people of these borderlands are strikingly similar to the relationship between valley civilizations and hillside nomadic people in South-east Asian history. Generally, state civilizations formed on the basis of paddy rice cultivation in the valleys, whereas nomadic people lived as slash-and-burn cultivators, and also as hunters and gatherers in the mountains. Writing about the Buid hunter-gatherers in the Philippines, Gibson argues for instance that the egalitarian qualities of Buid social life, and their avoidance of dependency and hierarchy, emerged in the interaction with their aggressive Christian neighbours (Gibson 1986). The latter tried constantly to engage the Buid in long-term relationships of debt and political patronage, and thus integrate them into the political and economic hierarchies of the lowlands.

James Scott has summarized this kind of interaction as the interplay between 'centrifugal' and 'centripetal' forces in South-east Asia (Scott 2001, 2009): empires and states tried to subdue as many people as possible, to extract taxes and conscribe soldiers. But time and again the pressure on the population reached a threshold, in particular when natural disasters and war hit the densely populated valleys. Then people often migrated to the higher mountain areas, where there was considerably less state control, tax and tribute, and less pressure of orthodoxy. According to Scott's argument, this is primarily due to the choice of one particular mode of agriculture (paddy rice cultivation versus slash-and-burn, hunting and gathering) and lifestyle (including heterodox religious beliefs). Yet it is also a 'political choice' in relation to the civilizational centre of an empire: 'people voted with their feet'. The histories of the highlanders were documented most of the time by officials of the state bureaucracies, and thus from the perspective of the state. Moving the focus from the state-governed valleys to the 'freedom' of the mountains, Scott speculates 'how a history of South-East Asia would look like that would be not dynastic and state-centred?' (Scott 2001: 103).

It is not my ambition to write a history of the Wuling Mountains from the perspective of the peasants there. I merely want to point out how a similar structuring of the relationships between a remote area and a civilizational centre can be found both in the local gazetteers in the Qing dynasty, and the presentation of the region in China now; and how these images play an important role in local representations. One point that Scott makes appears crucial: that it is necessary to see hillside people and ethnicity always in relationship to a centre – speaking of remoteness, of highlands, and of ethnicity would not make sense without reference to a centre (something that is 'close', some 'valleys', or some 'majority').

Such a consideration of 'the remote' resonates with several other theoretical outlines. In social anthropology, the obvious reference for 'valley' and 'hill people' would be Edmund Leach's paper on *The Frontiers of 'Burma'* (1960). One could just as well consider literature in colonial history, subaltern studies, or other studies of marginalization and oppression. I want to make another digression here with a short text by Edwin Ardener. In a paper on 'remote areas', he provides some theoretical considerations on what being remote in relation to some centre might imply (Ardener 1989 [1987]). Geographical remoteness is one feature (areas are 'remote' because of difficulty in physical access, i.e. mountains or deserts, for instance); but more importantly, 'remoteness' is defined 'within a *topological* space whose features are expressed in a cultural vocabulary' (ibid.: 214). Using examples from his field sites in the Cameroons and in the Hebrides (both rather remote places), Ardener elaborates a semantic field, the cultural vocabularies, of such 'remote areas'. One important element of this semantic field is the 'event-richness' or 'event-density' of the remote. In dominant central areas, many things happen with regularity: there is order and hierarchy. In remote areas, however, many happenings have an 'event-quality', in the sense that they are singularities taking place at a particular time and in a particular place. Living in relative solitude and in the relative absence of the automatisms of the centre (those introduced by governmental administration and markets, for example), people do not regularly share the same time and space.

This is especially true when these events are placed in relation with the centre: the roads and the people that connect the remote to the outside are particularly significant, far more so than any road in a metropolis.[15] What intensifies the significance of the connections to the centre is the always implicit fear of intrusions from the centre; remote areas are always open to the outside, and protected only by their remoteness. People acquire significance in a similar way, as innovators, tinkerers, entrepreneurs, and above all as strangers. Remoteness means that one does not share the same time or space, or the same centres of familiarity. At the same time the remote always remains open and vulnerable to intrusions from the centre. This condition necessitates a disturbed and rich adjustment of realities, for both the inhabitants of remote areas and for hegemonic incomers. This kind of spiritual struggle produces what Ardener calls 'event-density'.

Ardener's piece can also be taken as a comment on the politics of identity and ethnicity: the question of 'who we really are' imposes itself in particular in the 'remote area'. Or to put it in another way: 'the feature of a "remote area" [...] is that those so defined are intermittently conscious of the defining processes of others that might absorb them' (Ardener 1989: 223). Indeed, the question of the 'identity' or 'ethnicity' of a majority such as Han Chinese or WASP US Americans barely seems to make sense, and it is surely less frequently asked then the question of the 'ethnicity' of China's 'minority nationalities' (*shaoshu minzu*) or indigenous people in the US.

Situated in a metropolitan culture themselves, and writing about 'others' who are more often than not 'remote', anthropologists also partake in the construction of relationships between centres and what is remote to them. The anthropologist who leaves 'civilization' and lands in a canoe on the beach of a remote island is epitomized in the scenery that Malinowski describes at the beginning of the *Argonauts of the Western Pacific*.[16] It seems that 'distance lends enhancement, if not enchantment, to the anthropological vision' (Ardener 1989: 211) – and this might be one particular reason for the difficulty of 'doing anthropology at home' and 'studying up'. Yet to record what the world looks like from a faraway place might be just as respectable a contribution – a contribution that can help an understanding of how power works between centres and what is remote to them.

Angle 2: Development Discourse and Tourism

Bashan township is about 20 kilometres from Enshi, the capital of the prefecture with the same name. Driving on the bus from the city of Enshi towards Bashan, one passes ragged hills, paddy fields, and tea plantations. Most of the road follows the Bashan River upstream. This road, and one national road which crosses the area of Bashan township in the east, are the two major traffic arteries of Bashan. Built in the 1930s, the national road was one of the first 'public roads' (*gonglu*) in the prefecture. Both roads followed old traffic routes for the trade in opium, tea, and herbal plants during the Qing dynasty (cf. Ch'en 1992: 95).

On the public bus it takes a little less than one hour to travel from Enshi to Bashan. There are houses along almost all of the road, the majority of them of concrete and bricks, built very recently. After an hour the bus enters the valley of Bashan. The plain area there forms a triangle, with two little streams flowing into it at the two southern corners, coming together, and then leaving it as the 'Bashan River' at the northern corner of the valley. The road then passes the new landmarks of the 'Dong Minority Township' (*dongzu xiang*) that Bashan has recently become: the 'Dong Pagoda' (*dongzu ting*) with its nine echelons of projected roofs and the 'Bridge of Wind and Rain' (*fengyu qiao*), covered with a large ornamented wooden

Photograph 1.1 The Valley of Bashan

canopy. Both of these intricate wooden structures were commissioned by the township government in 2004, shortly after Bashan was granted the status of a 'minority township'. From the 1980s, different levels of the administrative hierarchy were given 'self-governing' (*zizhi*) status if a certain ratio of the local population was registered as a recognized minority. Enshi Prefecture was renamed a 'Tujia and Miao Autonomous Prefecture' (*tujiazu miaozu zizhi zhou*) in 1983. In the last administrative re-structuring in 2003, the former townships of Bashan and Tanjiazhai were brought together into one new 'ethnic township' (*minzu xiang*), on the basis of about one third of the population being classified as Dong minority.

Soon after the first houses, one arrives at the 'bus station' of Bashan, which is really just a street crossing. The landmark here is the huge five-storey *Seven Yields* supermarket that opened in 2007. Most days of the year, this crossing buzzes with motorbikes, three-wheelers, cars, trucks, and people walking. The two streets that formed the old market of Bashan are high up on the slopes in the south-western corner of the valley. Curled between the main road and a small stream that comes out of a rock here, is the 'Upper Street' (E. *shang gai*) or 'Old Street' (E. *lao gai*). In the 1970s a huge concrete reservoir was built here to collect water, ensuring the drinking water supply of the township. About 150 metres down from the Upper Street is the 'Lower Street' (E. *xia gai*), which consists of three smaller roads. In between the two parts, on a flat hill, are the buildings of the township government (*xiang zhengfu*), until the 1990s called the 'district government' (*qugongsuo*). Behind the government buildings a hill overlooks the whole valley plain. The fortified watch tower that had been on the summit in the Maoist era was torn down in 1984, and in 2005 a 3-metre high red teapot was built on it, symbolizing the glory of the 'tea township' that Bashan is.

Until the 1980s, the northern border of the market town was the Bashan River, which makes a sharp curve to the west at the end of the Lower Street. The only buildings on the northern side of the river had been the huge halls of the old tea factory, in which all the tea of the township was processed. In 1987, the tea factory was closed, its buildings torn down, and soon after this flat area was quickly covered with new-built houses. Since then the settlement has grown extensively, and already covers half of the plain area in the valley. Since 2006 there has been a development plan to build houses in a new quarter that would cover almost all of the river plain within the next few years; when I left Bashan in 2007, the roads for the new development plan covering the rest of the valley had already been built.

Whilst this new part of the town is thriving, the older part of Bashan has hardly changed. The Upper Street in particular has been in decline since the 1980s. Several houses are empty and dilapidated, and local residents often pointed out that nowadays even the families in the countryside are better off than the poor people in the Upper Street. A man in his forties, who lives with his family on the Upper Street, said to me: 'Look at this place, it is all decaying. In Zhongba they at least have tea, and got wealthy with it. No one cares about us here.'

The decrepit houses on the Upper Street aside, for most people from the villages, the market town is an important economic and political centre: it is the nearest market place, both for the peasant market on every second day, the tea marketing in the region, and now for the retailers and two major supermarkets. Politically, it is the next level above the village administration. Goods, officials, and ordinary people all pass through the market town on their way to and from the villages.

Surrounding the valley of Bashan, villages stretch out on the hills and slopes. There are no visible settlement agglomerations that would form what is called a 'natural village' (*ziran cun*) in Chinese; most farmhouses are spread over the mountains, with several houses occasionally making up a hamlet. Many of the newer houses are built along the gravel and asphalt roads, whereas the older houses are scattered on the slopes. Most of the area close to the market town is now planted with tea, and only very few paddy fields remain. On the steeper and unfertile slopes corn and vegetables are planted. The woods in the area are slowly recovering now after the Maoist era, when almost all trees were lumbered.

The geographically advantaged areas, like the smooth slopes of Zhongba to the south-east of the market town, the valleys of Pangqiao to the south and Daliangxi to the north, are full of tea plantations, and densely settled. Other villages, more remote from the market town, often have more subsistence crops like corn and rice. This is so in particular in the part of Bashan that was formerly the old township of Tanjiazhai. Here there is very little tea, and cash crops like vegetable, fruits, and sometimes tobacco deliver markedly less income.

Both in Bashan and in the surrounding villages, I was often told that this place was 'backward' and 'remote'. When I asked people what they thought of the place they were living in, and what they thought about their future in this place, some typical answers were:

'This place is too remote and backward. There is no way of going forward here.'

'This is an unlucky (*beishi*)[17] place.'

'I would like to become a proper person (*zuo ren*), and find possibilities to develop. But I tell you it is really difficult in this place.'

'We are so poor here.'

At the same time locals were willing to admit that at least their conditions were better than in other mountain villages, far away from asphalt roads and other transport connections. In this way, one could draw a continuum from a remote mountain village like Zhongba, to the market town of Bashan, to the capital of Enshi prefecture, to the towns in the plains of Hubei, to the coastal cities (like Shanghai or Guangzhou) and the capital of China, Beijing – and perhaps from there to London and New York. The first and most obvious difference between the places along this continuum is the level of economic development and perceived wealth. Mostly corresponding to economic wealth, people and places are graded according to levels of 'civilization' (*wenming*) and 'population quality' (*suzhi*).

The concepts of 'civilization' and 'population quality' have become central in discourses about governance and culture in the last two decades. They certainly correspond to some extent to a political economy in a state of massive change. Some have argued that these keywords have taken over the function that 'class' had in Maoist discourse (e.g. Anagnost 2004). Similar to 'class' in Maoist discourse, 'population quality' is something that describes the whole being of a person, not just certain aspects of it. The same is true of both 'civilization' and 'population quality': a person is judged to have a certain amount of it altogether, and not in one or other aspect of his or her behaviour.[18]

It seems like a contradiction in terms to say that a peasant (*nongmin*) would have high 'civilization' or 'population quality'. However, a peasant who is educated, or skilful in doing business, or has experience in dealing with people from outside the village, or is a competent village-level official, can be said to have 'high population quality'; yet this would not be said in reference to the person being a peasant.

In the China of the reform era, the 'peasant' is the object par excellence of the discourses and policies of 'raising population quality' (*tigao renkou suzhi*). 'Population quality' can refer to all characteristics of a person, such as education, manners, health, and strength; and peasants are represented not only as 'ignorant' and 'uneducated', but also as overworked, sunburned, and soiled (*tu*). In most government doctrines and developmental programmes related to the countryside, the phrase 'to raise the population quality of the peasants' (*tigao nongmin suzhi*) is taken together with improving educational levels, infrastructure, and housing.

With 'the peasant' as the main object of this discourse, and the level of economic development as a corresponding variable, the countryside in general, and a remote mountain region in particular, must appear as a place of poverty with low levels of 'civilization' and 'population quality'.

Yet the bucolic and idyllic side, which in earlier times fascinated poets like Gu Cai, is still present nowadays. In recent years, similar portrayals of pastoral beauty are connected with minority politics and tourism. The first minority classification of the 1950s soon lost momentum when in the Maoist era everything was tuned to politics of class struggle. Only since the beginning of the 'reform and opening' policies have ethnic politics become important to the ordinary population again. In 1978 ethnic classification was revived as a national policy: local government had to provide information about ethnic identity in the national census, and at the same time the national government announced particular funds and subsidies for minority districts. During the 1980s, many new 'minority districts' were classified; they were granted special autonomy rights, and received special treatment from the national government. In fact, the prefecture of Enshi became one of the youngest 'autonomous minority prefectures' (*shaoshu minzu zizhi zhou*) of the People's Republic of China when it was declared in 1983.

The basis of the classification was not very specific: difference in 'language, customs, economy, and psychology' (Brown 2004: 158). But even this was rather difficult in a region like Enshi, where it turned out that Han Chinese, Miao, Tujia, and Dong were living next to each other, and were not even conscious of being anything other than 'Chinese'. Thus government officials finally classified the minority status of individuals according to surname: names that had long been mentioned in the accounts of local chiefdoms as 'native families', such as Xiang, Tian, and Peng, were classified as 'Tujia'. Family names like Yang, Wu, and Yao, that evoked similar family legends as the Dong people of Guizhou, were classified as Dong. Until the present day, there has been much blurring and manipulation of the categories and identities of 'minorities' in the area (cf. Brown 2002). There are various benefits of officially recognized minority status: it provides justification for some affirmative policies (e.g. in the university entrance exam requirements for local students), and most importantly, it serves as a justification for national and provincial subsidies given to disadvantaged regions. Additionally, the minority status of the local population adds to the 'local speciality' (*difang tese*) of a place, which can become a marketable asset. 'Local speciality' and 'ethnic difference' (*minzu tese*) provide an edge in the promotion of local industry; and so in Bashan they are advertised in the promotion of the local tea and tourist industry.

In Bashan township, there are now two tourist sites being built by the local government. At the same time, the cultural office and a task force working group of the township government are working hard to 'dig out' (*wajue*) and revive 'minority culture' (*minzu wenhua*). In summer 2008, the vice chairman of the township proudly told me that they had organized a trip to a Dong village in the neighbouring province of Guizhou, from where they brought a lot of songs, dances, and cloths of the Dong minority. A group of singers and dancers was trained to perform for the visitors at the new tourist spot, and in autumn 2008 the first performances of 'Dong' and 'Tujia' culture were given at the new tourist park.

Let me quote from a leaflet entitled 'Charming Bashan', which was prepared by the township government of Bashan, and which is fairly typical of how the township is described for tourism. Similar texts appear on the websites of the township, and are distributed to outsiders visiting Bashan:

> The customs and morals of Bashan are pure and honest (*chunpu*) since time immemorial. The people of the Dong land are friendly and hospitable. This is an ancient and mystic land. The sons and daughters of the Dong land have lived here generation after generation, they have passed down their culture, and have created their unique customs and folkways, an altogether resplendent traditional culture. [...] Wander around the organic tea plantations, watch the girls picking tea, listen to one of the love songs of the tea mountains, and you will feel as if you were in paradise! [...] The society and the enterprises of the Dong Minority Township of Bashan are flourishing and developing [...]. Communication networks and motorways are connecting it to the regions outside the mountains [...]. The education facilities of the entire township are advanced, and have yielded excellent results. [...] Since the beginning of the new millennium, the entire township has entered a new heyday in the construction of a civilized new countryside [...]. The basic facilities in the countryside have been improved a lot, the civilizational level and overall quality of the peasants has risen a lot; observers will take delight in seeing that every village is becoming wealthy, and every household civilized.

In texts like these, there is an emphasis on the 'achievements against all odds' comparable to the one we found above in the local gazetteers: this mountain region is relatively inaccessible and infertile; yet even so there are all the basic facilities of a modern society, there are hospitals, schools, and telecommunication networks, and there is economic development.

But what is more, the event-density of the remote becomes a marketable asset in tourism. What in modernist discourse would seem only poor and underdeveloped (not least because of being remote) acquires a new quality of itself: what happens there is singular, meaningful, and authentic. The tourist can feel the simplicity and beauty of such a life when he 'wanders around the organic tea plantations' and 'watches the girls picking tea'.

Neither the longer history of the region in relation to the Chinese empire, nor the emerging discourses of 'minority culture' are obvious in everyday life in the countryside. Most people ignore what is written in gazetteers or in tourist pamphlets. In the following I will discuss the way in which locals see their place and their history.

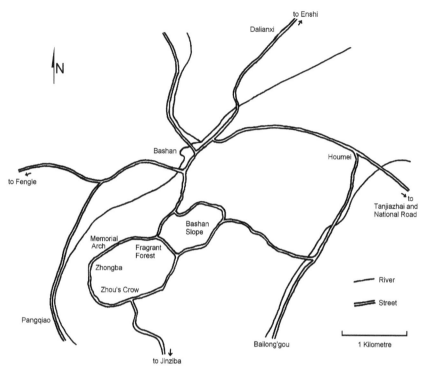

Map 1.3 Zhongba, Bashan, and the surrounding villages

Angle 3: Family Places and Histories

About one kilometre along a smoothly ascending asphalt road towards the south-east of the market town, one reaches the village administration building of Zhongba. Here, at a place that is locally known as 'Fragrant Forest', the two circuits of the 'figure-of-eight'-shaped asphalt ring road meet (see map 1.3). Zhongba proper is a hamlet on the hills towards the south, overlooking the deep valley of the Bashan stream flowing from Pangqiao into the valley of Bashan. Not too far from this hamlet, there is a stone memorial arch (*paifang*) erected during the Qing dynasty, honouring a virtuous widow of the Ruan family.[19] People often refer to this locality simply as 'Memorial Arch'. Following the asphalt road higher up, one reaches the village group 'Zhou's Crow', so named after the Zhou family which lived here in the past. The legend goes that the Zhou family had a feud with a neighbouring family. When the neighbours came one night to destroy the tombs of the Zhou family, the call of a crow woke the family up, and they were able to chase away the neighbours. At Zhou's

Crow, the round road takes a huge curve and comes back to the centre of the 'eight' that it forms. The northern cycle of the 'eight' road encompasses the flattest and most fertile fields of 'Bashan slope' directly above the market town. These commonly used place names are now also categorized administratively as 'village groups' (*cunmin xiaozu*) of Zhongba. Together they formed the old village of Zhongba, or the 'Red Star Brigade' (*hongxing dadui*) as it was called during the Maoist era. Many older people still refer to it by this name, whereas the new administrative village of Zhongba created in 2003, to which two neighbouring villages, Bailong'gou and Houmei, also belong, has mainly remained an administrative unit.

Photograph 1.2 The Memorial Arch

Landmarks, toponyms, and administrative units are all ways in which people attach themselves to places. Beyond that, how do the villagers of Zhongba see the place they live in and its history? As mentioned above, the first answers are frequently standard sentences of a standard discourse about 'civilization' and 'population quality'. Yet behind these obvious answers given to an outsider coming from a modern and developed centre, there are much more complex ways in which people are situated and situate themselves in a local space and a local history. Of course, all individuals have personal memories attached to places which are meaningful and significant to them. Here I am not dealing directly with the memories of any particular person, but rather with some frameworks of memories, or discourses. In the remaining part of this chapter I explore two such frameworks that are significant in everyday life in local society: the histories and places of families, and those of geomancy (*fengshui*).

Family Histories

Memories and places linked to the lineage and the family are especially significant to local people. This can be obvious in place names such as 'Liu Family Village' (a neighbouring village in Bashan) and 'Zhou's Crow' (even though the Zhou family has long left Zhongba), or in the Memorial Arch that belongs to the Ruan family. Almost every long-established family has its own legends about where they came from and how and when they migrated to this region. More often than not these legends are connected to customs which are particular to one family or lineage. The members of the Ruan family clan of Bashan, for instance, were very poor when they came to the Enshi region, escaping from floods in Guizhou. They were so poor that they carried walking sticks, the distinguishing mark of beggars at that time. That is why the men of the Ruan family use long walking sticks in their worship of the ancestors during the Spring Festival. The stick is covered with red paper, and put next to the house altar in the main room of each household.

There are countless stories about the rules of a lineage (*jiagui*) such as this one about the men of the Ruan family using these sticks during the rituals of the Spring Festival. Rules fix such things as the time of the 'family reunion meal' (*tuannianfan*) during the Spring Festival, food taboos, and particular kinship addresses.[20]

The history of families is always framed in the language of a lineage-family (*jiazu*), and it is almost always told and transmitted by men. Women have an ambiguous role, because in a patrilineal and patrilocal kinship system, a woman goes from her natal family to that of her husband, and so is in between two family lines. Women maintain links with both families, and hence do not stand unequivocally for one patriliny. Related to that, the 'family tradition' (*jiachuan*), the legends that are told about the origin of the family and its prominent members, are told predominantly to boys. If the names of family members are written down in a family genealogy (*jiapu*), women often do not appear, or appear just with the surname of their father. When I asked elder women for their surname, they often answered with the surname of their husband.

If a written genealogy (*jiapu* or *zupu*) exists, then sometimes these stories are written down as well. But in this region, written genealogies are very rare. The few that existed were destroyed under Maoism, and since the 1980s they have only been rewritten in exceptional cases. Another marker of genealogical position has, however, existed throughout: the genealogical name of each man.

Traditional Chinese names consist of three characters. The first one is the surname of the family (*xingshi*), the second one is the generational name shared by all males of one generation (*beifen*), and the third one is the individual given name (*mingzi*).[21] The generational names are taken from a series that is a poem of mostly 12, 24, or 36 characters. In the past these poems were written down in the genealogies of a patriliny. As an obvious sign of the continuation of the male line, generational names were given to boys; girls – who would leave the patriliny anyway – do not generally have a generational name. Even though genealogies were burned and ancestor worship, together with most practices linked to the patriliny, forbidden during the Maoist era, almost every large family in Bashan continued the practice of the generational names until very recently. Almost every elder man from an old-established family knows the poem of the generational names of their family by heart.

When a son is born, the family name and the generational name are already given. The grandfather would then look at the combination of the surname and the generational name, together with the 'eight characters' (*ba zi*) of the year, month, day, and hour of the birth. As given in Chinese peasant almanacs, every year, month, day, and hour has two Chinese characters attached to it. The 'eight characters' of the birth hour result from the combination of two characters for the year, two for the month, two for the day, and two for the hour. Together these eight characters are the basic information about a person, necessary for any divination and geomancy concerning that person. Diviners and geomancers then put the 'eight characters' into complex relationships with sets of cosmological elements, like the two cosmic forces yin and yang, the five elements (*wu xing*, which are fire, water, wood, earth, and metal), the sixty-four hexagrams of the Book of Changes (*yijing*), and a whole plethora of other symbols.[22] These elements themselves stand in relationship to each other and influence each other. Certain combinations of symbols bode well, whereas others prefigure bad luck.

Any Chinese character can contain such cosmological symbols. The basic character of the element can be directly present: the character symbol for 'column' (柱 *zhu*), for example, contains the wood radical (木 *mu*). Besides that there is space for all kinds of associative thought: rain (雨 *yü*) will be related to a water element, as will thunder (雷 *lei*) because it contains a 'rain' radical.

The ideal of Chinese divination is that the person (as represented in the 'eight characters') is in harmony with the moving forces of the cosmos; and so the challenge when finding a name is that the combination of relationships represented in the 'eight characters' of a person are put into harmony with the name of the person. This is generally the task of the grandfather of the baby, who is most concerned about the continuation of the male line of his family. Sometimes the grandfather calls on a diviner to help him with this task.[23] In 2007 most families in Bashan continued this practice of name-giving following the birth of a son.

However, young parents, in particular those who do not live with the grandparents of their children, often chose the easier customs that are common in the cities now. They omit the generational name, and so the child's name is composed of only two characters: the surname and the given name.[24] Alternatively, people may freely choose a two-character given name without paying attention to the customary generational name. But even then, most men still remember their own generational name, even though it is not written down anywhere and they have never been called by this name.

The practices mentioned so far relate to the time and history of a family and a lineage. These practices were once markers of Chinese identity as a whole. They have been passed on in the 'little tradition' of the countryside, whereas in the 'great tradition' of China, they are no longer central. Whereas at the time of Gu Cai, the people in the mountains were different by virtue of not having lineage practices as strong and strict as other Chinese in the plains, now they are different by virtue of having a richer tradition of lineage practice when compared with other Chinese.[25] In the cities the lineage has lost much of its compelling force as a social unit, and generational names are increasingly rare to find.

It is a historical irony that part of the cultural and social practices surrounding the lineage should nowadays have become operational to the classification and representation of this region as a 'minority district'. The original minority classification of the Dong, Tujia, and Miao in this area was largely based on surnames, i.e. membership of a certain family or lineage (see Brown 2002; Wu 2003). At the same time, the self-identification of locals remained far more closely attached to their lineage identity than to the new designation as a minority, which they had written in their identity cards.

The Space of Fengshui

The 'eight characters' of a person's birth hour have a particular influence upon that person's life cycle as a whole. In the practice of geomancy, they are also crucially linked to the spatial positioning of houses and tombs. *Fengshui* is the traditional Chinese practice of geomancy: a popular cosmology that connects astrological signs and cosmological elements with the shape of the lived landscape.[26] Interpreting the particular *fengshui* of a place is done to take advantage of its positive 'energy', and to adjust to it. Most lay people hire an expert geomancer (*fengshui xiansheng* or *yinyang xiansheng*) for this work. Whilst the practice has long been suppressed by Chinese governments as 'feudal superstition' (*fengjian mixin*), it has remained immensely popular, especially in the countryside. In Bashan as of 2007, it was compulsory for anyone building a house or a grave to consult a geomancer, who would help to situate the house or grave according to the *fengshui* of the place.

It should be stressed that the *fengshui* of a house, grave, or any other place, is dependent on the people that live in that house, are buried in that grave, or dwell in that place. In *fengshui* beliefs, the person, the built environment, and the landscape are all placed in relation to each other, and no ontological separation is made between people, architecture and landscape.

Let me give an example with the following story of a farmer from Zhongba village. Tian Shanwei's house is just next to the village administration building in Zhongba, and so he was my neighbour when I was living there. He is the youngest brother of three. Being his seniors, the first two brothers 'divided the family property' (*fenjia*) first. That is, they received their part of the family property, built their own houses next to the parents' house, married and established families. As the youngest brother, Tian Shanwei stayed in the house with his parents, even after he got married. This is quite common in the region: the youngest stays with the parents, and will inherit the house after their death.[27] However, Tian Shanwei was very hard-working and ambitious, and wanted to build his own new house. He chose a place right next to the primary school and village administration building of Zhongba. Usually calculating the *fengshui* of a place is indispensable before choosing the place and situating the foundations of a house. But in this case, he chose a place on the downward slope side of the road, which arguably did not have very good *fengshui*.[28] Nonetheless he accepted this disadvantage, given that this was the only place available next to the school, an important consideration as Tian Shanwei and his wife planned to open a small shop to sell groceries and foodstuff to the students. The house was finished in 1990, and until recently the family was doing relatively well. In 2003 Tian Shanwei started feeling ill more and more often; he was sleepy all day, and later he could not move at all. Even the easiest movements consumed all his strength, and for the last four years he has barely been able to do any work. The many doctors he visited could not help him at all, and finally doctors in the prefecture hospital in Enshi diagnosed him with a 'chronic osteomalacia'. As a result he had to spend a good part of his meagre income on hospital bills, operations, and medicine.

In 2007, things went from bad to worse, and his sixty-five-year-old father was diagnosed with cancer of the throat. He survived the cancer, but after several operations he now breathes through an artificial hole in his throat. During one operation his vocal cords were damaged and he subsequently lost his voice. Because both men in the family are now barely able to work, Tian Shanwei had to borrow a lot of money from the local bank, and more still from relatives and friends. He became more and more convinced that this house was bringing him only bad luck, and that he had to move somewhere else with his family.

To the immense surprise of most people in the village, in autumn 2007 he started to build a huge new house right next to his old one. Before building the house, he carefully consulted several fengshui experts and selected a place according to their recommendations. He plans to sell the old house to an outsider, 'because it is easier to deal with outsiders' he says. In fact, people from other villages are eager to move to this relatively prosperous village, which is close to the market town, but it is probably also implied that an outsider would know less about the bad luck haunting the family in the old house.

Whilst fengshui is closely linked to the fate (*mingyun*) of a family and a household, it is sometimes extended further and linked to a lineage, a hamlet, or even an entire township.[29] An old and respected man in the market town of Bashan, Wen Yunfu, explained to me the *fengshui* of the entire township:

> Bashan has four 'exterior spots' (*waijing*) and four 'interior spots' (*neijing*). The four exterior spots are: Grass River Bend in the East, Fragrant Flower Forest in the South, Red Rock Temple in the West, Cock Forest in the North; the four interior spots are: Red Rock in the East, the 'blue snake catching the turtle' in the South, the Chicken Branch root in the West, and the Two Lions Gate in the North.

For every one of these spots, Wen could tell several stories about Bashan's local history. These eight spots mark a square in the four cardinal directions

East, South, West, and North. I could not ascertain all the meanings that the particular markers carry, but Wen Yunfu assured me that the inner and outer spots together were features of excellent *fengshui* for the township.

Fengshui as a popular practice is always open to manipulation as well. In fact one of the main aims in Chinese geomancy and divination is to influence and manipulate in some measure the cosmological forces at work. In this way, the knowledge of *fengshui* can be instrumentalized by the powerful to impinge upon the aspirations of others.

The following is a story that is often told about the *fengshui* of one of the side valleys of the Bashan triangle plain. In between the 'Chicken Branch Root' and the 'Two Lions Gate', a small valley opens into the north-western side of the triangle plain of Bashan. Over the centuries, the stream has formed a deep meandering valley in between rugged hills and rocks. At the point where one enters the valley, coming from the plain, one passes a high rock on the left side. People say that long ago, this rock was much higher and that it provided the valley behind it with very good *fengshui*. In particular, the Gong family who was living there was said to prosper because of the good *fengshui* of the valley: talent and ability (*rencai*) abounded in the valley, sons of the Gong family became high officials, and the Gong family as a whole was very prosperous. At the time of the Qianlong emperor the prosperity and success of the family aroused the envy of a mandarin in the capital of the prefecture, Shinan (now Enshi). Hence he had his henchmen demolish this rock, and dig a hole (*quekou*) into the summit of this hill. Thereafter, no member of the Gong family was ever successful in the imperial exams again, and the family declined.

This legend goes well with a true story that is commented upon in similar ways. As mentioned, the valley in this same place follows the meandering line of the stream. In the past, after strong rainfall the stream often flooded the fields along the valley. During one campaign of the 1960s[30] the cadres of two production brigades had the idea of opening several tunnels into the rock formations, so that the stream would flow in a straight line, and the fields would remain dry. With the help of dynamite detonations, five long tunnels were opened through the rocks, and since then the river has left its old river bed, and flows through the new cave tunnels. At the time, locals opposed the opening of the tunnels, arguing that it was not worth the effort. But the most serious disadvantage was that the *fengshui* of the valley would be destroyed.[31] However, during the Maoist era this could not be said openly in public, and even now it is embarrassing for some people to talk in public about something like *fengshui*. Yet many old people in the valley are convinced that their bad luck comes from the bad *fengshui* of the valley.

Such stories highlight the complicated relationship between local ideas of *fengshui* and the state. In fact during the empire local government was often suspicious about such practices that were later called 'feudal superstition' (cf. also Feuchtwang 2002 [1974]: 8ff). Yet the imperial state rarely went as far as to directly intervene in local practices; instead a gentle guidance by 'correction' and 'exemplar' was generally favoured (cf. Hamilton 1989). It was only from the beginning of the twentieth century that practices such as *fengshui* were broadly devalued amongst educated elites, whilst they remained common with ordinary people. During the Maoist era, local 'superstition' was fervently denounced and systematically attacked.

On the other hand, at various points throughout imperial history, *fengshui* was consecrated as a legitimate practice. Cases are reported of geomancers who were employed by emperors and promoted to civil service ranks (Feuchtwang 2002 [1974]: 230). Classics of *fengshui* were included in the imperial encyclopaedias of the Qing dynasty.[32] The plans of capital cities, and the official architecture from the imperial palaces down to the *yamen* and temples in the townships, followed similar principles. Often it is difficult to decide what was the venerable 'imperial cosmology' and what was the popular practice of *fengshui*, in particular so because many of the references in both are the same, for instance the symbols of the *Ritual of Zhou* (*zhou li*), of the *Book of Changes* (*yi jing*), and of Five Elements (*wu xing*) theory.[33]

As is exemplified in the legend about the malicious mandarin who destroyed the *fengshui* of the Gong family hamlet, people commonly assumed that the powerful and wealthy also tried to manipulate *fengshui*. And they must have done so rather successfully – 'if not, how could they have become powerful and wealthy in the first place?' This kind of circular argument sometimes assumed seemingly ironic or even grotesque proportions: older peasants would repeatedly tell me that the power and success of Mao Zedong and other leaders was actually based on their intimate knowledge and versatile manipulation of *fengshui*. One famous story tells how during the civil war between Nationalists and Communists, Chiang Kai-shek, the leader of the nationalist Party, tried to find the tomb of Mao Zedong's father, dig out the remains, and destroy the tomb. In this way he would destroy the *fengshui* of the Mao family, and Mao Zedong would be subjected to misfortune. But when the neighbours of the Mao family heard about the plan, they took off the name badges of the tombs in the village, and so the soldiers who Chiang Kai-shek had sent could not find the tomb. In anger they wildly destroyed several tombs in the village – a most outrageous and horrible act, as devastating the tomb of a family is the same as destroying the integrity and prosperity of the whole family line. The *fengshui* surrounding the tombs of the Mao family, however, was preserved and further provided for excellent fortune, whereas the infamy of digging out the graves of innocent families led to misfortune and the eventual defeat of Chiang and the nationalists.[34]

The irony here is that it was precisely in the name of Mao that the practice of *fengshui* was persecuted in the past. In recent years, *fengshui* has become a respected object of study for architects, historians, and even designers in mainland China. Even though there is still widespread suspicion against it as a 'superstitious' practice, there are also many books and experts who try to prove that *fengshui* is really 'scientific' (*kexue*) and thus does not contradict in any way the promulgated world-view of party and state, of which scientism is a major part.[35]

Yet in the countryside, references to *fengshui* and related practices like astrology and divination are never made in public. They will be spoken about only in private, and almost always with a somewhat ironic undertone. In the Maoist era, exposing the *fengshui* practices of others would have amounted to serious imputation and denunciation, and many people still relate to it in secretive, partly embarrassed, ways.

To relativize these practices of place- and history-making further, it should be mentioned that nowadays many young people adopt quite an indifferent attitude towards the legends and rules of the lineage, and also the practices of *fengshui*. With the economic growth of the last decades, watching TV and gambling have become the most prevalent leisure activities, and very rarely are the legends about family origins told to the younger generation. In particular the young people who have been working in China's major cities often find such story-telling a 'backward' (*luohou*) custom for old 'peasants' (*nongmin*) – a custom that is 'countrified and coarse' (*tuli tuqi*) – and in this way apply the same continuum of the hegemonic discourse of 'civilization' (*wenming*) and 'population quality' (*suzhi*).

Because people are aware that *fengshui* beliefs have been called 'superstitious' and 'backward', conversations about *fengshui* are beleaguered by a sense of wariness and stealth. Tian Shanwei – the farmer who was concerned about his ill fortune – and Wen Yunfu – the knowledgeable elder – revealed their stories about *fengshui* to me only after we had known each other for a long time. By this time we shared some kind of 'insider knowledge': that, actually, many people would condemn such stories as peasant backwardness. And yet at the same time, we also knew that these stories and beliefs were of crucial importance in local sociality. Such an intimate knowledge, then, is what makes a community of complicity.

* * *

The village of Zhongba, and the entire Enshi region, is still relatively 'remote' in present-day China. The most obvious attempts to connect it to the outside world, to link its economy to the wider national and global economy, and to somehow reduce its remoteness, can be seen in the huge efforts by the national government to improve its transport infrastructure. During the time that I spent in Enshi from 2005 to 2007, the first motorway and railway were being constructed from Yichang to Chongqing via Enshi, which will connect the Enshi region to the national transport networks. Many people assured me that the next time I came to Enshi, it would be a much more 'convenient' (*fangbian*) journey. These new traffic lines will facilitate transport in the region but even though they may bring the region closer to the outside world, it will in all likelihood remain 're-mote' in some sense.

In local practices, such as the re-telling of family histories, name-giving, and geomancy, people make certain places meaningful. Beyond that, they also convey a sense of time that is very different from the one suggested in hegemonic discourses. The time and space of these local practices is that of families, lineages, and local communities.

However, family histories and geomancy are quite different in how they are related to outsiders: whilst the histories and places of a family and a lineage are of decisive importance for the narratives of 'minority culture' and tourism, *fengshui* is a much more intimate form in which people are connected to their own time and place. In the beliefs and stories of *fengshui* there are sometimes dramatic representations of the intrusion of outsiders into such a local space (as in the stories about officials destroying the *fengshui* of a place). Local officials appropriate and re-invent lineage and family histories, yet they frown upon the practices and beliefs of *fengshui*.

Whilst in hegemonic discourses this area is designated as 'remote' and 'backward', locals have their own spatial and temporal frameworks, in which they are in one way or another at the centre of the world. Or as Ardener puts it: '"remoteness" is a specification, and a perception from elsewhere, from an outside standpoint; but from inside the people have their own perceptions – if you like, a counter-specification of the dominant, or defining space, working in the opposite direction' (1989: 221).

In this chapter I have tried to show such 'counter-specifications' in the spaces of families and of *fengshui*. There are others as well. In the following chapters we will see similar ambivalences in community celebrations and rituals, in gambling, and in local politics. In a sense, most of this book is about the ways in which local people create their own spatial and temporal framework with their own centres; that is, how they build their own 'local moral worlds' (Kleinmann 1998). Yet such local worlds never exist in isolation and this book is also about the complicated relationships between these local spaces and wider national and global frameworks. We have seen that local places and histories are not 'just' and 'simply' local; local places are made as a combination of outside specifications and inside counter-specifications. Likewise, everyday ethics are not simply the actions and discourses of a local moral world, but rather the actions and discourses which reflectively engage the local moral world with outside frameworks, both moral and spatial.

Notes

1. Set during the fall of the Ming Dynasty (1368–1644 CE), this historical drama became very famous soon after its first publication. Richard Strassberg describes the social and historical background of the book in his literary biography of Kong Shangren (Strassberg 1983).
2. This story was first written down by Tao Yuanming in his *Records of the Land of Peach Blossoms*. It goes as follows: a fisherman follows a river upstream in the Wuling Mountains of Hunan (which neighbours current-day Enshi). He enters a cave where the stream originates, walks into it, and finds the 'Peach Blossom Land' on the other side of the cave. The people there have long since left the plains, escaping chaos and war during the Qin dynasty. Entirely ignorant about the outside world, they live happily in their idyllic surroundings. The fisherman eventually goes back to where he came from, promising the people that he would not tell anyone in the outside world about their existence. Yet once back there, he goes to his prefect (*taishou*) and tells him. The government official sends out troops to find the 'land of peach blossom', but from then on no one has ever found it again. This story is so widely known that the expression 'a Land of Peach Blossoms outside this world' (*shiwai taoyuan*) has become a set phrase (*chengyu*) in modern Chinese.
3. When Fei Xiaotong visited the Wuling mountains in 1991, he could not resist the comparison either: 'The scenery of this mountain region equals the descriptions of Tao Yuanming in his *Records of the Land of Peach Blossoms*. It is really all curious peaks and narrow gorges, beautiful rocks and gentle forests' (Fei 1999 [1991]: 239).
4. *Gai tu gui liu* is an abbreviation for *gai tusi gui liuguan*, literally 'to change from the vassal chiefs to the imperial officials'.
5. The former province of Huguang comprised what are now the provinces of Hubei and Hunan.
6. These large population movements were called 'Huguang fills Sichuan' (*huguang tian sichuan*), meaning 'populating Sichuan from Hubei, Hunan, and Guangdong' (cf. Xiao 2005).
7. There are countless cases of Mandarins condemning the erroneous beliefs (*xie*) and licentious cults (*yinsi*) of local populations (see for instance Stein 1979, Wang Jian 2003, and the contributions to Shahar and Weller 1996).
8. E.g. Sommer 2000.
9. The Confucian classical tradition emphasized social harmony, and so people were encouraged to repress 'selfish' desires and avoid unnecessary lawsuits. Contrary to these exhortations, however, courts were often sought after and litigation masters (*songshi* or *songgun*) helped ordinary people to file law suits (see Macauley 1998).

10. Cf. Hamilton 1989 for a brief general description of governance in imperial China. The moral exemplar continues to be a key element of governance and social control in modern China, a society that Borge Bakken has described as *The Exemplary Society* (Bakken 2000).

11. It is remarkable that *hua*, the word here translated as 'sophistication', also means 'civilized' and 'Chinese'.

12. Melissa Brown argues that these differences were the main reason for the classification as 'Tujia' minority (Brown 2004: chapter 5).

13. Several historians have called the Qing expansion a 'colonial' one, such as Laura Hostetler, who describes the development of the ancillary sciences of ethnography and cartography in the *Qing Colonial Enterprise* (Hostetler 2001).

14. For general overviews of this history, see Wiens 1954 and Perdue 2005.

15. 'Remote areas are obsessed with communications: the one road; the one ferry; the tarring of the road; the improvement of the boat. [...] The world always beckons – the Johnsonian road to England, or the coast, or wherever it is, is an attraction to the young, for it leads from your very door to everywhere. It is quite different in this respect from a city street. The road to Cathay does not flow from no. 7 Bloomsbury Mansions' (Ardener 1989: 219). To paraphrase the last sentence: the road from Bashan to the city of Enshi leads to every place in the entire world, whereas Kingsway in front of the LSE does not actually lead anywhere.

16. 'Imagine yourself suddenly set down surrounded by all your gear, alone on a tropical beach close to a native village, while the launch or dinghy which has brought you sails away out of sight' (Malinowski 1922: 4).

17. *beishi* literally means 'against the prosperous time', and thus 'behind the times' or 'unlucky'. In the local dialect it is also used as a swearword: calling someone a '*beishi*' person means that he/she is a good-for-nothing.

18. Some anthropologists have suggested analysing these discourses as a form of neoliberalism (e.g. Yan Hairong 2003; Anagnost 2004). Yet such an analysis is problematic, first because of the holism and meta-narrative it purports, and second because of the difficulty of applying Western concepts (like liberalism) to Chinese society. A discourse such as the one about 'population quality' might be less useful for controlling people and maintaining a motivated modern proletariat, but more so for hierarchically classifying a population (see along these lines Kipnis 2006 and 2007).

19. In various dynasties of imperial China, it was a common practice to erect such memorial arches for widows who refused to remarry or committed suicide after the death of their husband. Such arches were approved by the emperor directly, who conferred the honorific title onto a widow and her family. The memorial arches stand as material traces of the imperial politics of elevating moral exemplars of virtuous behaviour (see Elvin 1984 and Mann 1987 for general discussions of female virtue and the imperial state, including such memorial arches). According to local legend and the inscriptions on the memorial arch, the widow of the Ruan family did not remarry after she had lost her husband at a young age, and dedicated the rest of her life to bringing up her children and grandchildren. See photograph 1.2.

20. In his doctoral dissertation, the 'native' anthropologist Wu Xu has shown how certain food habits are linked to family and lineage identities in Enshi. On the basis of an extremely rich ethnography, he goes further to argue that the central category along which people see their own identity is their lineage and its history, rules, and customs – and not at all the official 'minority' categories (Wu 2003).

21. For example in Mao Zedong, Mao is the surname, Ze the generational name, and Dong the given name.

22. The building blocks of this exceedingly complex popular cosmology are the same as those of *fengshui*, i.e. Chinese geomancy. They are summarized comprehensively in Feuchtwang 2002 [1974].

23. If a serious discrepancy appears between cosmological elements in the 'eight characters' of a child, there are further options allowing one to strike a balance: one possibility is to 'call an adoptive father or an adoptive mother' (*bai gandie/ganma*). This adoptive parent can then exert the necessary influence that the child lacks. For example, the parents of a child were of the opinion that the elements 'earth' and 'water' were lacking in the 'eight characters' of the son, and therefore felt that the company and protection of a mason would do him good. They asked Liu Laosan, a mason living next to the village office, to become the 'adoptive father' (*gandie*) of the child, and the boy went on to spend many days of his school vacations at the house of this 'adoptive father'. Similarly, the lack of the element 'wood' can be compensated by having a carpenter as an adoptive father. It might also be that imbalance comes from the influence of parents, uncles and aunts on the child. In particular, the 'eight characters' of the father and the brothers of the father have a strong influence on the child. If they do not combine well with those of the child, an option is that the child 'changes the kinship address' (*gai kou*) of the relatives in question. That is, the child will call his father 'uncle' and his uncle 'father' for instance. All of these practices were still relatively common in 2007.

24. My Chinese name is built in this form: Shi Han, where Shi is the surname and Han is the given name.

25. This is true when compared with the family and lineage practices of urban people, but the observation cannot be generalized: the situation is a very different one in the south-eastern provinces of Fujian, Guangdong and Jiangxi, where local lineages, ancestor worship and popular religion had been much stronger for several centuries.

26. For a general introduction to *fengshui*, see Feuchtwang 2002 [1974]; for an overview of the history of *fengshui* and contemporary practices, see Bruun 2003 and 2008.

27. Often the youngest son is the favourite of the parents, and he takes care of them when they are old. In this case he often demands support or reimbursement from his brothers. Negotiations and quarrels between siblings about caring for the old are very common.

28. One basic rule of *fengshui* is that a grave and a house should have a slope on the back, and a free view on the front side.

29. Apparently in Taiwan people 'did not speak of the *dili* [=*fengshui*] of whole towns; but numerous mainland sources show this was a possibility' (Ahern 1979: 165 footnote); see also Feuchtwang 2002 [1974]: 257–259.

30. People in Bashan remembered this as part of the national campaign 'Learn from Dazhai in agriculture' (*nongye xue dazhai*). In 1963, Mao Zedong had issued this slogan for all rural communes in the People's Republic to emulate the achievements of the Dazhai commune in Shanxi province, in particular in land reclamation through hard manual work. On this campaign and agrarian radicalism during the 1960s and 1970s, see Zweig (1989).

31. According to *fengshui* beliefs, a stream is a dragon (*long*), and in general a meandering stream is more auspicious than one which flows in a straight line.

32. Inclusion in the imperial encyclopaedias implied public recognition and validation – in the course of the edition of these huge encyclopaedias, many books comprising heterodoxies and heresies were banned and destroyed as well. The 1726 edition of the Imperial Encyclopaedia, the *Complete Collection of Illustrations and Writings from the Earliest to Current Times* (*gujin tushu jicheng*), contains eighteen separate

works on geomancy (Feuchtwang 2002 [1974]: 9). In his book on Chinese geomancy, Feuchtwang lists several manuals from this compilation, including one entitled *Liu Ji's agreeable geomantic Aphorisms* (*liu ji kanyu manxing*) and the *Three-pole Geomancy of Immortals* (*sanji xianren dili*) (ibid.: 307). Like these two, the other titles in the imperial encyclopaedia refer to geomancy by the names *dili* or *kanyu*, rather than *fengshui*. Whilst *fengshui* was the more popular colloquial term, geomancy was generally referred to as *dili* and *kanyu* in classical Chinese (cf. Fan 1992: 37).

33.   Arthur F. Wright has described the 'cosmology of the Chinese city' as an 'imperial cosmology' that was systematized early on (in the Western Han dynasty, 206 BCE – 8 CE) and changed only slightly over the next two thousand years. 'The system of ideas known as *feng-shui*', he writes, 'represents the only accretion to the cosmology of the city from the fall of Wang Mang [23 CE] to the end of the imperial order [1911 CE]' (Wright 1977: 54). Wright traces elements of both the 'imperial cosmology' and *fengshui* in the design of Chinese capital cities, and implicitly acknowledges that at least in some cases it is difficult to distinguish between them, as, for example, when he writes: 'The hill's location north of the palace complex and its contours [...] strongly suggest the influence [...] of *feng-shui* theories, but I have found no textual evidence for this' (71). But Wright does not problematize the distinction between the imperial cosmology and *fengshui* itself. It seems quite likely that in many instances the reference to *fengshui* was understood as invoking an alternative cosmology and an alternative (im-)moral order. Hence if elements of 'imperial cosmology' and of *fengshui* were blurred, certainly it was more common to legitimize something as part of the 'imperial cosmology' in public and outside representation, whereas *fengshui* was referred to in more private and intimate surroundings.

34.   This story, told to me by several people in Bashan, is reported together with many other tales and legends about past emperors in *The Recorded History of Grave Robbery* (Ni 2008). It is also widely discussed online (e.g. http://blog.sina.com.cn/s/blog_4851fade01008cng.html [accessed on 18 October 2011] and http://www.cacc.org.cn/news/show.asp?articleid=7432 [accessed on 18 October 2011]).

35.   The official view on *fengshui* is divided and ambiguous. On the one side, it is generally marked as a misguided 'feudal superstition' when it appears in the state-oriented media. For example, a list of the contents that internet censors are encouraged to 'trim or delete' includes the following item: '[programmes and websites which] publicize fortune telling, *fengshui*, divination, ghost healing, and other feudal and superstitious activities' (State Administration of Radio, Film, and Television 2009: 2.6). At the same time, courses on *fengshui* are taught at several universities. In 2009, a course entitled 'Construction and Fengshui' at the University of Science and Technology in Wuhan caused much debate. Various people accused the university of 'teaching superstition', whilst others emphasized the scientific character of *fengshui*. The university finally decided to close down the course. See *Xin Jing Bao* (*New Beijing Newspaper*), 19 March 2009, 'fengshui shi che tou che wei de mixin, hai shi kexue?' (Is Fengshui out-and-out Superstition or Science?).

Chapter 2

GABLED ROOFS AND CONCRETE CEILINGS

The first road in Zhongba on which vehicles could drive was built at the end of the 1960s, but this road was paved with asphalt only in the 1990s. Until then, people used to carry all their goods and agricultural products on their backs. The main criterion for the location of a house then was its distance to the market town. When people came to this area as migrants in the eighteenth and nineteenth centuries, they often settled as extended families in hamlets together. The geographical conditions in the mountain regions did not favour bigger settlements, and so there are no single-surname villages such as exist in many other regions of China.

The compound or 'courtyard' (*yuanzi*) of an extended family was a crucial basic unit of conviviality. Even though in theory there could be various surnames in one compound, in fact most frequently all the households in one compound belonged to one single surname. Other surnames may have been included by forms of 'lower' marriage, such as matrilocal marriage or adoption. It was unheard of for a young man to marry a woman from the same compound. Within these courtyards there lived only people of 'one's own family' (*zijia ren*), and everyone was known only by kinship address. It was also the basic living space in which children grew up; inside the compound one was amongst one's own family, and did not have to pay too much attention to one's appearance. Inside the compound the 'skin of one's face is thick' (*mianpi hou*), meaning that one does not have to care much about questions of 'face', image, shame, and dignity: these problems became important only once one left his immediate surroundings of the hamlet and met outsiders.[1]

Now there still exist several such compounds in Zhongba and in other surrounding villages. One of them is the hamlet of the Yang family, opposite the village administration building where I was living. Just as in most other hamlets I have seen, the boundaries between the hamlet and neighbouring houses of other surnames are now very loose: some members of the Yang family have built houses nearby outside the hamlet, and not all brothers and uncles get along well. Some even have better relationships with neighbours of other surnames than with their own lineage members. Nevertheless, it was in this hamlet that I still heard people referring to their entire lineage as 'their own family' (E. *geren jia*), and obviously all members addressed each other only by kinship terms. But such a hamlet is now rather the exception than the norm. Other settlement patterns have become increasingly common. During the land reform of 1950 and 1951, every individual and household was classified as a member of a different class. Wealthier farmers had to cede their land and houses, and families of 'poor' and 'middle' peasants came to live in the houses of 'rich peasants' and 'landlords'. In Fragrant Forest the huge house of the Ruan family, for instance, was given to two poorer families. Several families of the surname Tian came from Bashan Slope and were given land previously belonging to the Ruan family too, and built their houses there. Additionally, there were a number of poor farmers from other villages who were re-settled into this village, which was relatively wealthy and close to the township of Bashan. These re-settlements did not group houses together in compounds, but in single houses of one family instead.

Now people follow entirely different criteria regarding the location of their houses. The broader roads on which vehicles can drive, and in particular the asphalt roads built since the 1990s, had a decisive impact on settlement patterns: houses are now predominantly built next to the asphalt road. Those planning a new house often leave the immediate hamlet, and build their new house as close as possible to the next road.

The houses that are built now are also very different to the older ones: the most important construction material is no longer wood, but cement, bricks, and sand. The differences in house construction correspond to wider politico-economic and social transformations.[2] In this chapter I will draw some of these connections, by exploring how settlement patterns and house construction have changed in Bashan. After an overview of architectural types and of the local discourse on 'hot' and 'cold' locations, I describe the construction and inauguration of two houses. The first case study gives a detailed account of the inauguration of Yang Minghu's new house, the same one with which I started the introduction to this book. The second case study deals with the house of his neighbour Tian Dejun, an example of the new houses of bricks and concrete. Based on these two examples, I compare wooden houses and brick houses, and delineate continuities and discontinuities in the practices of house-building in the villages of Bashan.

The Centres of Houses and Valleys

Three Types of House

It is difficult to ascertain what the forms of architecture and construction in the Enshi region were before the huge immigration of Han settlers into this area. It is likely that the houses of ordinary people were simple wooden structures, often with walls of bamboo and tree bark.[3] At least since the administrative reform under the reign of the Yongzheng emperor in 1735, and the consecutive arrivals of masses of immigrants from other regions, the art of carpentry and construction, and the situating of houses according to geomantic knowledge, developed in fairly similar ways in this area when compared with other neighbouring Han Chinese regions. Carpentry was an art for initiates, transmitted from master to apprentice, and included much more than the mere skills of working with timber. A master carpenter would know about the meaning and significance of each part of the wooden structure, in particular the length and width of beams and columns;[4] he would be knowledgeable about the numerous rituals accompanying the construction and inauguration of a new house, most importantly those of 'hoisting the ridgepole' (*shang liang*) and of 'opening the door of wealth' (*kai caimen*). This knowledge is said to come from the 'patron saint' of the carpenters and builders, Lu Ban. Old carpenters are often very knowledgeable about related magical arts, including those used to open wells, to cure illness, and create curses and anti-curses. All this knowledge and the magical verses used are collected in the 'books of Lu Ban' (*lu ban shu*), of which most carpenters have a hand-written version, copied from their masters.[5]

Until the 1970s there were three basic architectural types for houses in this region. First are wooden houses that are called the 'houses of hanging legs' (*diaojiao lou*). This is a wooden structure based on pillars, with planks built in between them. The name refers to the most outward pillars of the projecting roof, which stand alone whereas the other pillars are integrated into the walls. The freestanding pillars hang like 'legs' from the roof (see photograph 2.1). Sometimes the walls between the wooden columns are filled up with bricks and chalk. The side rooms have a ceiling and above it a second-floor attic; the main room is covered only by the over-arching gabled roof. Generally in these wooden houses people live on the ground floor; the attics are used for storage or are left empty.

The second architectural type is a house with load-bearing walls of stamped mud and/or adobe, which is called an 'earth house' (*tu fangzi*). This technique of building is the most common one in the plains area of the Long River in central China, and it is more widespread in the valleys of this region which are more readily accessible.[6] In Bashan, which is very mountainous, like most of the prefecture, it was not very practical to build such houses. Hence until now, such houses could only be found in villages closer to the city of Enshi, which do not have too many mountain slopes. In the villages around the market town of Bashan, including Zhongba, there are extremely few of these houses.

The third type is the four-side courtyard, built also of wooden structures. Surrounded by walls, such a house can include several forecourts, leading up to a major courtyard that is often paved with flagstones. Walls and courts create a deeper level of interiority, which protect and emphasize the central room of the house. This form was reserved for wealthy families in the township and city.[7] As has been documented in many other regions of China, '[t]he several successive courts and receiving rooms gave the greater ceremony needed by a wealthy family or by government and allowed a hierarchy of privacy not seen in the more egalitarian farm house.'[8]

Yet nowadays none of these three traditional structures is built anymore. Most houses built since the 1990s are 'Western houses' (*yang fangzi, yanglou*) or 'small comfortable houses' (*xiaokang lou*),[9] that is, multi-storey structures built of baked bricks, with concrete floors strengthened with bar steel, ceilings of concrete slabs, and pre-fabricated doors and windows. Ideally, the walls will be plastered, or sometimes covered with tiles (see photograph 2.2).

Photograph 2.1 The 'houses of hanging legs' (*diaojiao lou*) were the most common architectural style of farm houses until recently

Photograph 2.2 A 'Western house' (*yanglou*) or 'small comfortable house' (*xiaokang lou*)

The Centre of the House

A basic structure is common to most houses of ordinary people in the countryside, no matter whether the houses are wooden or concrete, one- or multi-storeyed, humble or luxurious: in the middle of the house, there is one big central room, the main room of the house (E. *taowu, tangwu,* P. *zhengwu, zhongtang*). One enters the house through a two-wing door into the main room, which is always on the eaves side, and never on the ridge side of the house. Single-wing doors lead from the main room into the side rooms. Standing in the middle of the house and looking towards the main door, the left room is the 'higher room,' which is generally the room where the parents sleep; children sleep in rooms on the right side, or in rooms further away from the main room.

The main room is also frequently used to store things like corncobs (hung on poles), tea leaves, machines, and motorbikes. The side rooms are used as sleeping rooms and for storage. The kitchen is almost always at the corner of the house; at its centre is a hearth with two built-in cauldrons. These are fired with wood in an oven directly under the cauldrons; older houses do not have a chimney, and so their walls and ceilings are black from the grime and smoke of the fire. Now most houses have brick-laid chimneys, and in recent years the use of methane-gas cookers has been promoted by the township government.

On the back wall of the main room, facing the door, is the 'ancestral shrine' (*shenkan*, or E. *jia xian*), built of wooden shelves. At its centre, there is a vertical carved tablet, or a paper scroll, with the Chinese characters for 'heaven, earth, emperor, ancestors, and teachers' (*tian di jun qin shi wei*). On both sides of, and parallel to, this vertical line, which marks the centre (of the house, and of society), the positions of different gods or goddesses (usually including Guanyin, the goddess of mercy, and Zaowang, the stove god) are also marked vertically. In smaller characters, the name of the main branch (*tang*) of the surname of the household is written. On the wooden shelf beneath it, there may be incense burners, candles, ancestral tablets, pictures of deceased ancestors, and statues of deities. Often there is a square wooden table beneath the shrine, which is also used to put offerings and worshipping utensils on.[10]

During the Maoist era, these shrines were destroyed as signs of 'feudal superstition'; in most houses a poster of Mao Zedong or other heroes of the Communist Revolution replaced them in the same place. This could include the 'four leaders' (Mao Zedong, Zhu De, Zhou Enlai and Liu Shaoqi) or the 'ten great generals' of the Communist Revolution.[11] Sometimes there are now also pictures of a modern city (with skyscrapers and cars), a waterfall or any other 'romantic' tourist spot, or huge scrolls with the Chinese characters for 'double happiness' (*shuang xi*), 'happiness' (*fu*), or 'long life' (*shou*). But in most of the houses, these pictures are on the side walls or side doors, and the heroes of the Communist Revolution – mostly Mao himself – are in the position formerly reserved for the ancestral shrines. Only few families have repaired ancestral shrines with inscriptions, but the majority of houses have a simple wooden board beneath the Mao poster, on which candles, incense, and other utensils for worship are stored.

The central axis of the main room is the line from the ancestral shrine towards the main doors (see figure 2.1). This axis is generally adjusted to the rules of *fengshui* by a geomancer who is hired before the construction of a new house. Determined by the geomancer's compass (*luopan*), the central axis also presents a moral compass in various senses that will become apparent. It is of crucial importance in family celebrations, with which I will deal in chapters 4 and 5. Just as the geomancer links and gathers the flows of energy (*qi*) in the landscape and seeks to maximize their effect on the place of dwelling, the head of a household invites and hosts relatives, neighbours, and friends at ritual occasions. Complementary to the narratives of families and *fengshui* presented in the last chapter, here we have a practice of centring, linking, and gathering in the material space of the house.

Cold Hills and Hot Valleys

In the villages close to the market town everyone who has the necessary money to build a new house will build one of bricks and concrete; almost no one builds traditional wooden houses anymore. People living in older wooden houses often explained to me almost apologetically why they still live in these old houses: a reason might be, for example, that they have only one daughter, and invested all their money in her education. If there is a young son in the family that could marry soon, however, his father, or he himself, will do whatever it takes to build a new house, of bricks and concrete. Without such a house it is often rather difficult for him to find a bride willing to move with him into his house. The wooden houses are seen as 'backward' (*luohou*) and 'behind the trend' (*gan bu shang xingshi*). Almost no one thought of these houses as 'authentic' and 'idyllic' in the way that many outsiders (including Chinese visitors and myself) would see them at first. I often asked people whether they could not find any beauty in the old houses. Only very few elder people sometimes mentioned that the older houses were in fact quite practical and comfortable. The wooden walls and the gabled roof provide very economic heat management that seems particularly well adapted to the climate of this semi-tropical mountain region: the tiles on the gable

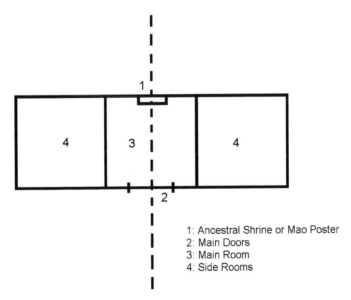

1: Ancestral Shrine or Mao Poster
2: Main Doors
3: Main Room
4: Side Rooms

Figure 2.1 Basic floor plan and central axis of a house

roof block out the heat in the summer, and air can drift in under the high ceiling of the gable. During the winter the wooden walls provide sufficient shelter against the cold. Contrary to this, the masses of bricks and concrete of the 'modern' houses store heat in the summer and cold in the winter. Yet these advantages seem obvious only to some older people; an old man, for instance, would say that he has been living all his life in his old house and does not want to move into a new one, in the sense of 'one should not move the roots of an old tree'.

But the most prevalent association evoked by the wooden houses is that of backwardness. In the popular imagination, a wooden house is far away from the public road, up the mountains, where one walks on mountain paths, where it is muddy when it rains. Such a place cannot be reached by motorbike or truck. And in most situations reality corresponds to this image. It is rather difficult to build a house of bricks if the place cannot be reached with trucks to transport sand, cement, bricks and all the other construction material. Thus the new houses even more compellingly have to be next to the public road.

Houses that are high up in the mountains and far away from roads are said to be 'lonely' and 'cold' in the vernacular. Contrasted to this is the 'liveliness' and 'hotness' (*renao*) of the street and the market. This is related to the cultural ideal of having a household that is 'lively and hot' (*renao*), of which the most obvious sign would be to have many children crowded under one roof.[12] The liveliness, noise, and heat implied in the word '*renao*' (E. *naore*) similarly is the ideal characteristic of a festival, a banquet, a market, or a business.[13] The older wooden houses on the slopes are more difficult to reach, the journey to the market is more expensive, and children have to walk a long way to school. Women of marriageable age much prefer a husband who has a house close to the street and the market, and it has become increasingly difficult for young men from places high up in the mountains to find spouses. Let me give an example from one of the more remote villages of the township.

One day in the summer of 2007 at the house of a neighbour in Zhongba, I got to know Dr Cao and his brother Cao Wenxiu, who come originally from one of the most remote villages of the township. Dr Cao now works in the hospital of a neighbouring township, while his brother is still a farmer in the village. Their village is about 25 km from the market town, and it takes almost an hour on the motorbike to get there. When I got to know Dr Cao and his brother, they soon started to tell me in a very emotional way about how poor their village was. In these faraway places 'traffic connections are not convenient' (*jiaotong bu fangbian*); children have to walk for several hours to get to school or stay with relatives in other villages that have a school; there is no business whatsoever, and people are very poor.

Most young people leave this place, and those men who remain cannot find wives. Dr Cao had seen a report about me on Enshi TV, and explained to the people present that I came from a foreign country, was a research fellow at Tsinghua University in Beijing, and was responsible only to the higher government offices of the city and the prefecture. And so he invited me several times to visit their village, and 'write a report' (*xie baogao*) and 'report to higher government levels' (*xiang shangji huibao*). I went up to their village a couple of days later, and spent some days with Cao. The Cao family was extremely hospitable to me, and introduced me to several neighbours. Even though they had exaggerated a little bit, it is certainly true that their place is relatively poor and remote. It is really rather difficult for young men here to find a wife, as local girls marry out, and most women from outside are not willing to move up to this place. There is quite a high ratio of bachelors in their thirties and forties, many of whom will probably stay single. There are only two brick houses out of fifty houses in the entire village group.

Compared to this village, Zhongba is a relatively advantageous place: it has a fairly good asphalt road, and is also rather close to the market town of Bashan. During the one and a half years of my fieldwork there, at least forty new houses were built in Zhongba. In the village group of Fragrant Forest alone there were about ten new houses, and so I had plenty of opportunities to observe the construction process. Without exception, all of these houses were built of bricks, and almost all of them were built next to the asphalt round road of Zhongba. Most of these families had previously lived in houses higher up on the slopes, and built their new houses on fields they owned next to the asphalt road. It is comparatively easy for young men to find wives here; there are also a number of families with a single daughter who found sons-in-law that moved into the household of the bride (*shangmen nüxu*). Such uxorilocal marriages contradict the ideal of the patrilocal lineage, and the husbands who assent to them generally come from poorer families. Tian Laosan, a woman in Fragrant Forest, was a widow for only a short time after her first husband died: it was quite easy for her to find a new husband, something that would have been much more difficult had she had been living in a remote and poor place.

Conversely families from more disadvantaged places try to increase the chances of their sons on the 'marriage market' by building new houses. A new house is frequently one of the most important parts of the preparation for a marriage (cf. Murphy 2002, chapter 4). Hence the people who hesitate most in building new houses are those without a male heir. The carpenter Yang Mingmao and his wife, for instance, did not have children, and so they adopted a girl from a neighbouring family that already had two children and would have violated the laws of family planning with a third child. In 2008, Master Yang was still living in an old wooden house, and he told me that they would spend their savings on the education of their thirteen-year-old daughter. For the future he hopes for a good son-in-law; he explained to me that there is no reason now to build a new house, as his daughter might marry elsewhere.

The local discourse of 'social heat', in which the streets and the market town are 'hot' whereas the mountains are 'cold', provides another example of a place-making practice of centring, linking, and gathering. Here, the liveliness of the streets constitutes a centre, in relation to which the 'coldness' of the mountains marks remoteness.

Building Wooden and Concrete Houses

Building a new house is an extremely important step in the life of a family. In the following I deal with the process of the construction in greater detail, and compare the construction processes of wooden and brick houses.

In principle, farmers who want to build new houses have to apply for permission from the village council first. The construction of a new house means effectively that farmland (for which farmers only have right of use) is transformed into plots for houses. During the boom in house construction in Zhongba that I witnessed, this permission was granted in most cases. Only in cases where there was a severe conflict of interests or where buildings reached exceptional size did the village officials hesitate. In such cases, all available networks must be mobilized for permission to be obtained.

Generally, houses are built without a fixed architectural plan, and many installations are improvised, and added once the owner has saved enough money to spend on the next item in the new house. Often brick houses remain unplastered (both inside and outside) for a long time, until the owner has saved enough money for the plaster.[14]

Until the 1970s, not much pre-fabricated construction material was bought, besides the roof tiles. The wood might have been partly bought and partly felled from the family's ground (or at the time the production brigade's); it was all chopped and worked into columns, beams, and planks at the construction site itself.[15] Almost all the workers were neighbours and relatives, who would mutually help out in such cases. The only man who had to be hired was a master carpenter.

After a foundation had been set (often only with stones), the first step of building a wooden house was to erect all the carrying columns, and then the structure of columns and joists supporting the building. The plank walls would be inserted later: once the structure was complete, one could make the roof, so that the building would at least have some shelter against the elements (see photograph 2.3).

During the time of my fieldwork, I did not have the opportunity to observe the construction of an entire wooden house. But some families have chosen a hybrid form, between the concrete and wooden structures; on top of the brick structure, they build a gabled roof. No matter whether the walls are wooden or of bricks, a gabled roof can afford some of the advantages that the old wooden houses had. Whereas a roof of concrete slabs will store heat in the summer and cold in the winter, the gabled roofs provide for fresh air in the summer and warmth in the winter.

Besides that, in particular in areas that are further away from the public roads, it is quite difficult to transport cement and sand, and often easier and more convenient to transport lumber and roof tiles, which are needed for the gabled roof. And for some people, the ritual related to hoisting the ridgepole might have some attraction and meaning in itself. 'Hoisting the ridgepole' (*shang liang*) is traditionally the most important event when building a new house. The community celebration of a house inauguration is called 'the wine of hoisting the ridgepole' (*shang liang jiu*). I have participated in two such events, and will describe below one of those, in which I was called upon as a helper. The following is another description of the event with which I began the introduction of this book: the house inauguration at Yang Minghu's family in November 2007.

Photograph 2.3 The structure of the columns and the roof is built first, and only later walls are inserted

Wooden Houses: Hoisting the Ridgepole

Yang Minghu and his family built their house just outside the Yang family hamlet opposite the village administration building where I was living. The members of the Yang family were among the first people I got to know after my arrival in Zhongba. In fact on the very first day that I moved into the side room of the village administration building, I was taken to the house of his cousin (*tangxiong*) Yang Mingxu, and later also met Yang Minghu himself. He made quite an impression on me: sun-burned, slim and short, with a grey goatee beard, in worn-out peasant clothes, he was talking very confidently and volubly. Without much paying attention to the fact that I could not really follow his Enshi dialect, he talked in what seemed a very friendly and humorous manner. After he had left, the young village official who was accompanying me said that this man was known as a 'boaster king' (*chui niu wang*).

Over time, I got to know him very well, together with all the members of his family; they were one of the families I became closest to. This was not least due to their exceptional children. Yang Hua and Yang Jun often came over to my room to call me to play with them or to come over to their house. The eleven-year-old Yang Hua is very outspoken and courageous for her age; she is quite naughty sometimes, and not doing well in school. Her older brother Yang Jun often came over to the square in front of the village administration building; since the new basketball court had been finished there in the autumn, he frequently played there with his friends.

As someone who had been working all his life in the countryside and on construction sites, a very capable craftsman, yet relatively poor, Yang Minghu built his house in a rather peculiar way: instead of buying the usual red baked bricks, he rented a stone grinder from an acquaintance, bought cement and sand, and started producing his own cinderblocks. They are arguably quite a bit cheaper,[16] yet they need a lot of work, and most people would say that they did not look as good as red bricks.[17] Over the summer of 2006, I often saw Yang Minghu, working alone or with a helper, carrying stones from behind his house to the stone grinder, and then mixing the ground pebbles with sand and cement. In autumn he had made enough bricks for a second floor, and called over a distant relative of his brother as a builder. Master Lan had the skills of both a carpenter and a mason; but he is always introduced, by himself and by others, as a carpenter.[18] He came to stay, together with a helper, for about two months at Yang Minghu's house, working on the construction site every day. Yang Minghu also helped, and sometimes he paid another one or two helpers; but the main work was done by Master Lan: the construction of the walls and the gabled wooden structure on top of it. By mid-January, most of the work was finished; yet the ridgepole, to be placed at the centre of the gable, and the tiles were still left.

They were left for the ritual event of 'hoisting the ridgepole' (*shang liang*), which finally took place on 19 and 20 January 2007, just three weeks before the Chinese New Year.[19] I had been at Yang Minghu's house often during the construction period, and knew of the scheduling of the ritual, when I heard the first firecrackers at dawn on 19 January from their house: the cooks and helpers were arriving. At midday, Yang Hua ran over to the village administration building to invite me to come to their house.

The relatives and neighbours were preparing everything for the celebration that evening and the next day. Yang Minghu's nephew Yang Yuanbing was the main coordinator (E. *guanke*, or *zhike*, or *zongguan*) of the helpers at the event. Together with Yang Minghu he arranged the various tasks for different people. Yang Minghu's 'network of relationships' (*guanxiwang*) is not very wide, and so it was not an easy task to find enough helpers. In fact they were still lacking several people in the afternoon, and Yang Yuanbing suggested I could help out as well. Yang Minghu effusively thanked me when I accepted, and repeated several times 'thank you so much, thanks, thanks'.

One particular task for this celebration is the felling and transportation of the tree that will become the ridgepole. This is done before dawn when 'no dogs bark and no cocks crow' (*mei you gou fei mei you ji jiao*), and the carpenters would then 'give sacrifice to Lu Ban' (*ji lu ban*). The host calls eight middle-aged men, who should each have at least one son already, and have good relationships with the host, to help with this task. Of these eight men, four are neighbours, and four are affinal relatives. The four neighbours that were helping at Yang Minghu's house were Tian Benping, Tian Benjun, Hu Xungao and Uncle Yang. Yang Minghu had helped out at their houses several times during the last year: this work is done as mutual labour exchange. In addition to these four men, there were four others who were all male relatives of Yang Minghu's wife. These eight men had already arrived, and prepared the ladders and poles with which to lift up the ridgepole the next morning.

Because the man that would write the red 'book of presents' (*liben*) had not arrived yet, Yang Yuanbing himself was writing the list of helpers.[20] Yuanbing's hand was shaking and trembling a lot when he was writing, perhaps because he was smoking so much, but probably also because he was quite nervous, and the brush was too big, so that the characters did not look nice. It was one of the first times that he had done this job. The list includes the host, Yang Minghu, the 'branch name' of the Yao family, the formal four-character expression for the celebration of a house inauguration, 'the building has been finished' (*huagou luocheng*), and the date at the end of the list.

When he was done, he put it on the wall, just with some sticky tape. Some moments later I and another man realized that Yuanbing had forgotten to include the name of the man who would be writing the 'book of presents'. This is obviously an unacceptable omission, and so Yang Minghu and Tian Benping (one of the respectable older neighbours) discussed for some time what to do. I wondered why they did not just immediately write a new list (apart from the omission, two smaller mistakes had been struck out, and it was not beautifully written in the first place). Their discussion was about the 'rules' (*guiju*) of writing the list, and whether it was acceptable 'according to the rules' (*an guiju*) to take the list down and write a new one. They talked about this for a while, and then decided that writing a new one would not be a problem. Yang Yuanbing wrote it again, and twice again, until he finally wrote it without a mistake. It still did not look perfect, but at least was without mistakes. This was the first indication to me of the overall emphasis on the smoothness and correctness of everything that happens during such a celebration.

In the afternoon the relatives started to arrive. The relatives that came now, on the day before the main celebration, were most importantly the affines of Yang Minghu. Besides his own sisters with their husbands, who came from various places, the biggest group was the agnatic relatives of his wife, who came all together in a bus from Fengle, about 30 km from Bashan. They brought many presents for the celebration: liquor, firecrackers, a huge tablet with the character of 'double-happiness' (*shuang xi*) on it, and money-gifts, which they all gave together. Master Lan, the carpenter-builder who had led the construction process, was also amongst the group of affines, and also contributed to the presents. He had brought his own carpenter master, the eighty-five-year-old Master Nie, who would help him to perform the rituals and incantations that night.

All the helpers were fulfilling their tasks, and my own task was to give cigarettes to everyone who arrived. At the beginning I went forwards too much, towards the incoming guests. Yang Yuanbing told me later that it would be sufficient for me to just wait at the door for the guests, and offer one cigarette to everyone once they arrived at the door. It was he who had suggested that I could help out here, and so he guided and corrected me as well.

After an abundant dinner, most people stayed in the house, chatting and gambling. I left at 9 P.M. and walked back to the village administration building. There I hurried to write some notes down, and get some hours of sleep. People had been advised that on the following day the celebrations would start around two hours before dawn, i.e. 3.30 A.M. I woke up just in time to walk back up to the house with Tian Benjun, one of the helpers.

When we arrived there were two circles of men sitting around basins with glowing charcoal, warming their feet. Most of them had not slept all night, and one group of older men were playing cards. Soon Yang Minghu, Yang Yuanbing, and the two carpenters Lan and Nie got ready to go upstairs to remember Lu Ban.

In the middle of the room upstairs, with the roof still open, they brought a bowl filled with maize corns, in which they stuck three candles. The room upstairs had a scroll outside with the following script on it: 'Behind the luxurious house new trees form a forest, in front of the beautiful residence the mountains look like a painting' (*huashi hou xin shu cheng lin, yu zhai qian bian shan ru hua*) on the two sides, and 'the future is bright and beautiful' (*qiancheng si jin*) on top. In the room, there was a huge scroll at the top of the wall, on which was written 'The Ziwei star is shining high above' (*ziwei gaozhao*).[21] Then below this script, on the back wall of the room, a table was placed with a bowl of maize corns and candles, paper money (already with round holes in it, that made it into paper coins), incense, several other bowls with liquor, and some little 'red envelopes' (*hongbao*) with scripts on them. They also brought a large cockerel, bound by the legs.

No one said a word and I wondered if the people were uncomfortable that I was there. Whilst Yang Yuanbing and Yang Minghu were just standing in the back and watching, the two carpenters got ready to worship Lu Ban. The old master Nie took the rooster, held it with one hand, and scratched the rooster's comb with his finger nails, until blood was dripping down. Then he pressed some drops of blood into one of the bowls on the table, and wrote some signs onto the paper money with the blood by moving the head of the chicken (actually very little blood came out of the comb). When Master Nie was finished with that, he put the cock down on the right side of the table, took the paper money and separated it into notes. Yang Minghu and Yang Yuanbing went outside to the platform there. I wondered whether other carpenters would now perhaps recite some 'flattery speech' (*fengchenghua*), as people had told me earlier: rhymes wishing prosperity and wealth to the family.[22] But nothing was said. Did my presence have any influence on them?

Master Nie took the paper money, burnt some on the table, and then lit three smaller packs on the floor in front of the table. Then he took more paper money, and burnt it at four points outside the door on the platform, the four points forming a big square in front of the door. It seemed that they had now finished; they took most of the material on the table, and prepared to go. When the old master was leaving the room by the side door to go down the ladder, the younger master pulled him back, and they discussed something of which I only understood the word 'rules' (*guiju*), supposedly about the proper ways of performing this ritual, and maybe whether it was necessary to do some more recitations.

Then the two carpenters went down, with me following them; Yang Minghu and Yang Yuanbing stayed upstairs and cleared away the things. The two masters took the rooster, and went away into the dark towards the neighbours' houses. I did not dare to follow them. I stood for a while, hesitating, in front of the house, and finally went in. After a while everyone came back into the room and sat down. Then two tables were prepared for the helpers to eat, just as festive as the evening before, with all the food here. But it was the women who had prepared it, as the two cooks had not arrived yet.

After the meal the eight men – the four neighbours, and four men from Fengle – prepared to go. With them were Yang Minghu and his son Yang Jun, me, and the two carpenters. Yang Jun was carrying a bamboo basket with axes and ropes to fell the tree, candles and firecrackers. It was now around 4.30 A.M., and still completely dark. Several men carried electric torches so they could see in the darkness. We walked down the public road, passing the village, and down to a slope about one kilometre from Yang Minghu's house. With the help of Master Lan, Yang Minghu had already determined beforehand the tree that would become the ridgepole.

When we arrived at the tree on a steep slope, Yang Minghu quickly climbed up the tree to a height of about 3 metres, and tied a liana around it, so that others could pull it to fall in the right direction. At the same time the two masters put three candles on the ground immediately next to the tree on the side of the slope and lit them. The two carpenters got ready, and Master Lan did some more recitations before they hit the axes into the trunk. The two masters then swung their axes into the trunk, and did not rest until they had felled the tree, which they did very quickly and smoothly. When the tree was down, it was cut with a saw to the appropriate length of the ridge beam (about 6 metres), also without stopping, and rather quickly. Whilst the carpenters were sawing, Yang Minghu stood next to his son Yang Jun, and constantly whispered into his ear.

The other men had been waiting around. Now they put a red cloth on the trunk of the tree, quickly took the tree, and carried it away. Even though the tree was not very big, it was not easy for such a small number of men to carry it on such a steep slope and down to the road, but they did it very fast.

I was walking behind with Yang Jun; he set off firecrackers, beginning when we were still on the slope. When the men carrying the tree had arrived at the road, he started to set off more and more firecrackers, and I helped him by carrying the sack, and giving him a lighter and cigarettes.

I also took a turn beneath the tree further up the road. When I was carrying it, I realized how heavy it was, perhaps heavier for me as, being taller than anyone else, I was taking on more of the weight. Yang Minghu was telling his son to stay behind the tree, and how to burn the firecrackers: that he should spare some, and burn more once they got to the village, and then at the house. When we arrived at the public road opposite the Yao family hamlet, people at the house also set off some firecrackers there to 'receive the beam tree' (*jie liangshu*); at the house Yang Jun then burned those firecrackers which remained.

They placed the tree in front of the house, on two benches, and then everyone just watched for a while. The men had a short rest, but then quickly prepared ropes around the tree; some went upstairs with the ropes, and then all together pulled the tree up onto the platform. The tree was pulled up in front of the house, which is also a 'rule'. I was helping on top of the platform, pulling on the ropes. When the ridgepole had almost reached the ceiling, Yang Minghu crawled over to lift it onto the roof: a firm grip and a hand movement, and the ridgepole tumbled over the edge of the concrete slab. Up on the platform the tree was put onto two wooden blocks to hold it and then everyone went down; now it was for the two carpenters to do their work. They worked the tree with their axes, and within half an hour they had chopped it into a square plank.

Whilst the carpenters were working, dawn was slowly breaking, and when they were done, it was daylight. Most people had got up now, and some were watching the carpenters at their work. When the carpenters had finished chopping, Master Nie measured and marked the exact middle of the ridgepole. Then he prepared the red cloth that was to be fixed there. The red cloth has to be of a certain size and certain things have to be put in it: a peasant almanac, ink, a brush, several coins, and some nails.

When Master Nie had cut the red cloth, he wrote 'long as heaven and old as the earth, old as the earth and long as heaven' (*tian chang di jiu, di jiu tian chang*), meaning 'everlasting' or 'as enduring as the universe' (which is 'heaven and earth', *tiandi*), across the top side of the ridgepole, which would be covered with the red cloth. In the middle of the two lines of this script, he wrote a huge character that was made up of various different characters, going out into circles and crosses. When he had finished that, he took the two brushes he had used, two black boxes of ink, two peasant almanacs (*nongli*), some nails, and then covered them with the red cloth. The young carpenter Lan took four coins, and used them to fix the red cloth onto the ridgepole, hitting them into the wood like nails. This red cloth will remain on the underside at the centre of the ridgepole – in many old houses they can still be seen.[23]

After this the old carpenter started his recital again, wishing fortune and prosperity for the family. Then the two carpenters moved to either side of the ridgepole, to the places where the ridgepole would rest on the wall, and Yang Minghu and his son Yang Jun stood on either side with them. The old Master again made some recitations, and then both carpenters started chopping with their axes a little into the ridgepole, taking off two small shavings of wood. They exchanged the wood-shavings with father and son, for two little 'red envelopes' (*hongbao*) of money.

Now the old carpenter Nie started his recitations again. It seemed the younger Master Lan did not want to say anything, but then one of the older men told him that he had to say something as well. He said a sentence or two, when they were chopping into the ridgepole before giving the wood pieces to Yang Jun, but nothing more. Whilst everyone else was getting ready to put the ridgepole up onto the wall, I heard him saying a couple more sentences in a loud voice. During the whole procedure I was standing outside the room, on the platform.

The four men who were helping were on the roof holding the ends of the two ropes that were fixed on each side of the ridgepole. The day before, Master Lan had prepared two little planks that would go under the ridgepole on the wall, holding it. On top of these, at the point where the ridgepole would sit, they put the little pieces of wood that the carpenters had given to Yang Minghu and Yang Jun, and some laces in various colours.[24] The men then pulled up the ridgepole, and at that moment, two huge boxes of display fireworks and several bands of firecrackers were lit outside on the platform. Everything went smoothly, and when the ridgepole was placed up on the wall, the firecrackers were just burned out.

The house inauguration established a centred space that is schematized in figure 2.2. The table on which the carpenters worshipped Lu Ban is an improvised altar (1), and is in the same position where later the ancestral shrine will be (in Yang Minghu's house, the ancestral shrine was already there on the ground floor, as they had just added a second floor). Above it, the central scrolls are stuck to the wall (here, the 'ziwei'-scroll, and 'the future is bright' scroll). On each floor, two side scrolls complemented the central scrolls (4). At the supporting points of the ridgepole (3), the carpenters chopped off the shavings, and swapped them for red envelopes with father and son. At the very centre of the ridgepole (2), Master Nie painted 'heaven and earth' on the wood, and then fixed a red cloth to it, containing brushes, almanac, and nails.

What we have here is a centred domestic space, which is established through the reciprocal action of the family represented by father and son, and the two carpenters. This is a local practice of centring, but it includes various references to higher-level centres. The carpenters worshipped Lu Ban, their patron saint; the Ziwei star represents the authorization and protection of the ruler (be it the emperor or Mao Zedong); the incantations

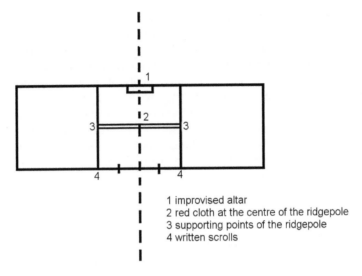

1 improvised altar
2 red cloth at the centre of the ridgepole
3 supporting points of the ridgepole
4 written scrolls

Figure 2.2 The central axis and the ridgepole at the house inauguration

of the carpenters and the objects in the red cloth are tokens of success within and allegiance to a wider political and cosmological order, as they represent good wishes for material prosperity, familial harmony, and scholarly success.

After breakfast people were again resting, chatting, and gambling. Then the two carpenters and some other helpers got ready to put the straight planks (E. *chuange*) on the roof. When they had finished doing that, everyone went outside to bring the tiles up to the roof. All the people present, including the guests, formed a line and each person handed the tiles to the next, up to the second floor.[25]

Working in line with the older people and the neighbours, I thought that this must have been similar to the spirit of the communal work in previous times. During the Maoist era, most agricultural work was done in the collectives of the work teams. But communal work has a long history stretching beyond state socialism: local farmers often engaged in informal labour exchange, in particular when a neighbour or relative had work that could not be done alone (e.g. during the harvest, when slaughtering a pig, and at the construction of a new house). Until recently, a great part of the construction of a house was done by neighbours and relatives 'helping out' (*bang mang*); i.e. they were given meals and sometimes accommodation, but not paid. In the last few years, however, it has become more common to hire waged labour instead.

The most important participants in this ritual were the two carpenters, Yang Minghu, and his son Yang Jun. The carpenters' performance is crucial for the future prosperity of the family. Because of that, it is important that they are properly paid (the red envelopes) and hosted (with good food). In rural China, stories abound about carpenters who were not hosted well or had misunderstandings with their hosts and then cursed the new building.[26] They will wall in objects, or leave them in the crevices of the wooden structure. Hence it is crucial that the cycle of reciprocity with the carpenters is always balanced out: they have to be hosted with the best food, and they have to be presented with red envelopes, visibly, and several times during the inauguration.

Houses are generally built by fathers for their sons, or together with their sons. They are often built directly with a view to the son's wedding – a new house in the modern style increases the chances of finding a bride immensely. Ideally, the son should be like a 'ridgepole': saying that someone is 'made like a ridgepole' (*dongliang zhi cai*) implies that this person is a pillar of society, and a valuable member of the community.

And so Yang Jun was the centre of attention during the inauguration; he had to stand next to his father when the carpenters made their last recitation before the ridgepole was lifted up. He was the one who gave the carpenters a ceremonial little 'red envelope' in exchange for their work. His father complained about him at some points, and ordered him around; but then he came over again and again to whisper something into his ear. When they pulled up the tree onto the roof, Yang Jun wanted to go onto the roof with the other men, but his father said to him that he should stay in front of the door on the platform, and watch the carpenters do their work.

He had to show that he understood the 'way of being filial' (*xiaodao*). This contrasts with the arguments that they had sometimes in the family, and the problem of Yang Jun not being such a good student. The night before the inauguration Yang Jun wanted to gamble with the men, but they told him off, saying that he was only fourteen years old and still a 'student' (E. *xuesheng wa'r*). As it turned out, later that year he would drop out of school, and leave the countryside to labour in a factory in Shenzhen, far away from his family.

Brick Houses: Pouring the Concrete

On the other side of the road, a little bit further up the hill from the hamlet of the Yang family, there are several houses belonging to the Tian family, which do not form a single hamlet. These include the new house of Tian

Dejun, one of the many new houses of bricks and concrete built during my time in Zhongba.

I also became familiar with the Tian family relatively early into my fieldwork. Again, a major factor was my contact with the children, in this case, Tian Dejun's son Tian Dong, who is the same age as Yang Jun. Often when I passed by their house, Tian Dong called me over to 'play' (*wan*), which with him would often mean reading books together, practising some English, or watching TV (where he would explain to me the classical Chinese expressions used in historical TV series).

Tian Dejun has one older brother, Tian Delin, who is a relatively successful businessman. Tian Delin was in the army in the early 1980s, and when he came back home he was able to rely on several close friends that had served with him. This was decisive for his success in the construction business: he started off as a small contractor, and soon got several bigger contracts, including those to build public roads in Bashan and Zhongba. Now he is relatively well off and lives in the city of Enshi.

Working in his brother's construction company, and in several odd jobs in the city of Enshi, Tian Dejun had made almost enough money to build a new house in 2006. He planned to build a completely new house in the 'modern' style. In the summer of 2007 he started with the preparation; he called an excavator to prepare the ground and started buying the construction materials. These included sand, cement, plaster, bricks, steel bars, window- and door-frames. The bricks most commonly used in the region are fired sand-lime bricks; sometimes cinderblocks, cast of sand, pebbles and concrete, are also used. The steel bars are needed for reinforced concrete; the doors, and the windows are other major items that have to be bought in advance.[27]

The hired excavator did all the raw work, moving the earth on the slope to create a level surface for the house, and digging out trenches for the foundation. On the following days several neighbours helped out with the earthmoving works, and to build the foundation sockets. In the construction of the new houses, this is generally the only thing which is done in mutual informal labour exchange. Obviously it is expected that Tian Dejun will also help the neighbours that worked at his house, when they need his help.[28]

From early on, one of the most important helpers in the construction process was Xiang Jixiang, the brother of Tian Dejun's wife. Xiang Jixiang is well known locally, not least because of his appearance: with his long black curly hair and beard he looks rather daring.[29] Together with his wife, and his brother-in-law, he has spent several years in the city of Tianjin in northern China. When he came back, he opened a karaoke bar in the city of Enshi, and later another one in the neighbouring county of Jianshi.

Often karaoke bars also offer some kind of escort services or are linked to massage parlours. It is well known that the owners and managers of bars need to establish good relationships with officials, the police, and with some 'grey' or 'black' elements in society in order to be successful, to get the necessary permits, and to be protected against both police raids and abusive customers.[30]

Xiang Jixiang left this business some years ago and moved back to Zhongba. He bought a truck, and delivers construction material and stones for other people. But he benefits hugely from the kind of 'symbolic capital' that he has amassed in Tianjin and Enshi: he is widely respected, and partly feared. His reputation as someone who is very loyal to his close friends and who has influential connections is an excellent basis to do business locally.[31]

During the summer and autumn, I spent many days at the house of Tian Dejun, often with Tian Dong, but sometimes also helping with the construction work. Xiang Jixiang was doing most of the transportation of the lumber needed for the formwork of the concrete. He came over with his truck on several occasions to transport trees from the house to the sawyer in the market town and back. I went with him and Tian Dejun twice, helping them to load the poles and planks from the truck.

I was invited by Tian Dejun to come over on 4 August 2006, when they would be celebrating the 'pouring of the concrete' (*daoban*). I went over to their house in the early afternoon, set off some firecrackers that I had bought as presents, then entered the house. At the banquet table I sat with the older neighbours, and next to Tian Delin, the businessman brother of Tian Dejun. Tian Delin was hosting me together with the old men; and he offered many toasts of liquor to all the men on the table. I did not see the host Tian Dejun much that evening, and when I did see him he looked very serious and somehow nervous. His arm was bandaged: he had broken it some days before, when he fell down from the scaffolding at his construction site.

After dinner, most of the men went to the side rooms of the house to play Mahjong, and I was dragged along to sit down and play. We played until late that night, and only in the evening did I realize that they would be 'pouring the concrete' of the roof at midnight.

Tian Dejun had hired a contractor, who arrived with ten workers at 11 P.M. They prepared their machines, and started to pour the concrete on the second floor at midnight. The group of ten workers mixed the concrete with a machine and then carried it up to the roof. I wondered why the pouring was set at midnight; Tian Dejun told me first that it was because the group of workers had another job during the day. But later his son and another uncle told me that it was really because the geomancer they consulted had told them that they should do it at exactly this hour.

The accident when Tian Dejun had broken his arm was extremely significant. Tian Dong told me that the geomancer (*fengshui xiansheng*) and a Daoist priest (*daoshi*) had performed several incantations and rituals (*fa shi*) in their house, of which Tian Dong did not understand much. He just remembered that the Daoist priest was spraying around the blood of a rooster's comb. Tian Dong understood that this was meant to protect the new house against evil influences and ghosts. He added that 'the people here believe quite a lot of superstitions'.

The next morning, Tian Dong came over to my room, and invited me to come and have breakfast at their house again. This was the main day of the celebrations, when all the ordinary guests would come. Most of them arrived in the afternoon. The people with the red 'book of presents' were busy writing down all the money that had been given. The largest sums came from Xiang Jixiang and his other sister, who lives in Tianjin and did not come in person. They gave 1000 yuan each, as well as some dozens of *jin* of baijiu. Apparently all the liquor that they had for the celebration was given by the relatives, but the liquor was the only present given in kind; the rest was in the form of money-gifts.

Obviously, most of the symbolism of the wooden structure that was once so crucial for the building of houses is of no significance for concrete houses. This is most visible in the roof, which is not a gabled wooden structure, but most frequently a flat concrete roof. The concrete is poured into a wooden form; and sometimes pre-fabricated concrete slabs are used. There is no need for a carpenter master, and there is no main ridge beam, and so the ritual described above cannot be performed. Without the performances of the carpenters 'hoisting the ridgepole', this kind of house inauguration seems much less 'ritualistic'; what remains is the common banquet for the guests, who offer their money-presents.

Comparison of Wooden and Concrete Houses

Let us sum up the differences between the older wooden houses of the 'hanging legs' (*diaojiao lou*) and the new brick houses that are called 'Western houses' (*yang fangzi, yanglou*) or 'small comfortable houses' (*xiaokang lou*). To produce two opposing ideal types, one could say that wooden houses are built in hamlets, whilst brick houses are built along asphalt roads. The owner of a wooden house is a farmer who lives off the land and maybe some unskilled manual labour, whereas the owner of the new houses has considerable income from outside agriculture, either from labouring in the city, or from doing business. Such additional income is needed because most of the labour and construction material used for the construction of the new houses has to be bought with money, and in the majority of circumstances agricultural incomes are not sufficient to afford them. In the construction process, voluntary labour exchange between neighbours and relatives plays a much more central role in the building of wooden houses. Generally the only paid worker is the carpenter/builder, who also commands specialist ritual knowledge. For the construction of brick houses, however, most of the workers are hired labourers, and the most important foreman is the mason, who does not need all the specialized ritual knowledge of the carpenter. The construction material for the wooden houses is predominantly local natural raw materials, like lumber and stones, whereas for the brick houses a great deal of pre-fabricated and mass produced materials (cement, sand, chalk, bricks, bar steel, electric installations, tubes) are needed.[32] It would be exaggerating, however, to say that wooden houses are not connected to the electricity network and hence have no electrical installations: in Bashan as of 2007, I have not seen one house that is not connected to electricity, even in the most remote mountains.

To conclude the construction process in wooden houses, a major ritual is held which all turns around 'hoisting the ridgepole' (*shang liang*). Modern brick houses do not have a gabled roof nor ridgepoles, and so the ritual is called 'pouring concrete' (*dao ban*). Whereas the first one looks very much like a ritual, with incantations, chicken's blood, taboos, and rules, the second one looks more like a stripped-down and commercialized version of the former: what is visible on the outside is the labour of the hired workers, and a banquet where each guest brings a money-present. The two types of houses represent respectively tradition and the countryside, versus modernity and the city. This representation is most obvious when spelled out to an outside visitor (like a government guest, a tourist, or an anthropologist): wooden houses are the idyllic dwellings of a mountain people, conserved for ages. Brick houses are the visible signs of progress and development in the built environment. In table 2.1 all these binary oppositions are listed against each other.

Needless to say, reality is never exactly in tune with a binary schema like this one. In both my examples here, we saw that elements of both sides were mixed together. Yang Minghu's house is not completely built of lumber, yet it has a gabled roof with a ridgepole, and so he arranged the more traditional ritual for the house inauguration. Whilst there was more voluntary labour exchange than at Tian Dejun's house, Yang Minghu still paid several labourers in cash, and bought a lot of the construction materials. The smoothness of the building process and the appropriateness

Table 2.1 Comparison of wooden and brick houses

	Wooden house	Brick house
Settlement pattern	Hamlets of lineages	Individual households along asphalt streets
The owner and host	Farmer, who works part-time in manual labour locally	Farmer, who works either in the city, or does business locally
Leading worker	Carpenter	Mason
Construction labour	Relatives/neighbours volunteering during entire construction process; only the carpenter master is paid	Neighbours only helping out to lay the fundament; rest wage labour
Construction materials	From the family's grounds: stones and wood; minor parts bought	Almost everything bought on the market; pre-fabricated materials (bricks, cement, sand, slabs, electricity installations, tubes etc.)
Concluding house inauguration	'hoisting the ridgepole' (*shang liang*), diverse ritual activity, and banquet	'pouring the concrete roof' (*dao ban*); not much ritual activity visible; commercialized banquet
Government-promoted view presented to the outsider	Idyllic houses of minority people	Progress and development visible in the built environment
Prevalent imagery	Countryside, tradition	City, modernity

to *fengshui* beliefs was equally important, albeit in different ways, at both construction sites. Altogether, there are several features that are fairly similar at Yang Minghu's and Tian Dejun's house construction:

1. everything has to happen smoothly
2. the basic floor plan and the role of *fengshui*
3. the importance of the son
4. the role of the affines
5. informal labour exchange

First of all, the whole process of the construction, and in particular the last steps leading up to the final celebration of 'hoisting the ridgepole' or the 'pouring of the concrete ceiling', should happen smoothly. An unexpected or ill-fated event has to be managed with extreme circumspection, so as not to become a bad omen: the lifting of the ridgepole and the ritual action at the house of Yang Minghu or the accident of Tian Dejun are examples of this.

Secondly, the floor plan of both old and new houses is centred around one main room, which is entered from the outside through the main double-wing doors; side rooms are entered from this main room. The siting and location of a house, and in particular the direction of the main room, is done according to an interpretation of the *fengshui* of the place.[33] For this task a geomancer is hired; he will advise equally on the judicious time for 'hoisting the ridgepole' as on the time for 'pouring the concrete'. As far as I can judge, this was still common practice in 2007. However, it is tricky to estimate how much people follow *fengshui*; the subject still seems sensitive as a kind of 'superstition', and hence most people talk about it only in private and to others they trust. Sometimes older men told me that nowadays people no longer pay much attention to the *fengshui* of their houses. Mostly they referred to cases where people wanted to have their new house built next to the public road at all costs, and so some houses are built facing the road, with their back looking down the slope. This is against the basic *fengshui* principle, that the back of a house should be always 'shielded' by an upward slope. And it is also rather impractical, as the ground floor needs to be supported by stilts. Whereas it was generally confirmed that most people were attentive in some way or other to *fengshui*, these houses with their backs towards the down-slope seem to confirm that there are at least some people who do not pay that much attention to it. Thirdly, houses are built for a son and hence for the future of the male line. Accordingly, the participation and role of the son during the celebration is crucial. Yang Jun and Tian Dong were perhaps the most important figures of these two events, yet they experienced fairly different celebrations.[34]

Fourthly, the affines of the family played a very important role during the house construction and in the celebration. Tian Dejun's brother-in-law Xiang Jixiang, and Yang Minghu's brother-in-law Master Lan both contributed in very important ways to the construction process. Xiang Jixiang drove his truck several times, and used his broad network of acquaintances to help Tian Dejun. Master Lan was the main carpenter and builder at Yang Minghu's building site, and even though he had to be paid for that, he had to give presents at the celebration as well. Both represent two rather different kinds of skills and function: Xiang Jixiang has a truck and a network of relationships crucial for transporting construction materials and getting things done; Master Lan has the skills of a builder, and the traditional knowledge of a carpenter necessary to hoist the ridgepole in the proper way.

And finally, in both cases the informal labour exchange with neighbours and relatives was important, yet again in very different ways. Whilst at Tian Dejun's house, people helped out only with the groundwork, at Yang Minghu's house even the guests at the banquet on the last day all helped to put up the tiles. Whilst Yang Minghu is a craftsman who himself worked a great deal on the construction site, Tian Dejun paid for most of the labour done on his construction site.

The social mechanisms and values that are commonly realized during the process of a house construction all revolve around the basic social institution of the family and the household. The house represents the family to the outside world, and it is the most immediate materialization of the expectations and aspirations linked to the family. Building a house implies a centring movement on various levels: in space (the location of the house, the *fengshui* of the floor plan, and the ritual action at the house construction) and in time (the continuation of the family line). These spatial and temporal reference points open up a centred space, which metaphorically equates to a moral space. The house and its construction also represent then a centring of moral choices and a centre of moral judgement.

The moral framework that is represented here is that of the family, its continuation, and its reciprocal exchanges with relatives and outsiders. If everything during the construction processes happens smoothly, this centred framework is also meant to further the prosperity of the family. For all this, the proper way of dealing with neighbours and relatives is essential: one needs social capabilities in order to reciprocate in labour and ritual exchange. To have a family, to work for its continuation, to live in a house that is centred, and to deal properly with relatives and neighbours; all these are categorical moral demands. At the same time, these categorical demands have to be continuously adjusted to contingent realities.

In this chapter, I have also mentioned the awkwardness which such moral requirements sometimes present, in particular those of 'traditional' ritual. Remember the reluctance of the younger carpenter to recite the ritual incantations at the Yang household, and the secretiveness surrounding the *fengshui* beliefs and the Daoist rituals at the Tian household. People only told me about these stealthily and in private, after the event. And fourteen-year-old Tian Dong explicitly stated how such things are labelled in official discourse: they are 'superstitions' ('the people here believe quite a lot of superstitions'). Hence, if there are various continuities in the construction of wooden and brick houses, the representation of moral frameworks in house construction is now also fractured by the awareness of outsider commentary on these frameworks. These expressions of awkwardness and indirection point towards a community of those who are 'in the know'. The complicity they share is based on shared experience in local sociality on the one hand and on an intimate knowledge of the condemnation of some elements of it (e.g. ritual) on the other. Before I further discuss the formation of such communities of complicity, the next chapter will deal with their basis in everyday work and consumption.

Notes

1. French anthropologist David Gibeault writes about Wujiagou in Northwestern Hubei, which has apparently conserved much more of this kind of social space: 'The Chinese like to formulate their reactions towards a social environment in terms of the "skin" (*pi*) of the "face" (*mian*). At home, in the hamlet, the skin is "thick" (*hou*): one can joke, you cannot be outraged, and everything can be said. Outside, the skin is "thin" (*bao*): one is on one's guard, mindful, and dignity becomes timidity. This is true for every instance of displacement from village to village; between the hamlets of Wujiagou, however, the relations are so close, and the exchanges so frequent, that only the adults are sensitive to their mutual strangeness. The reason for this exception is simple: marriage is approaching, and all young men who notice a young woman visiting, all the young women who spot a young man walking by, – are all possible spouses. The occasion demands a sense of shame' (Gibeault forthcoming: 4–5).

2. For a magisterial outline of the 'fabric of power' embodied in the social space of the house in late imperial China, see Bray 1997, chapters 1–3.

3. Cf. Gu Cai 1991 [1704]: 11; Xu 2006: 67; Peng 2000. Xu and Peng also mention the active promotion of 'orthodox' customs by the state officials from the eighteenth century in this respect: e.g. the 'fire beds' (*huo chuang*), in which males and females of various generations slept together, were strictly forbidden (Peng 2000: 7ff). Separate rooms for couples and children fixed the clear separation of inside (*nei*) and outside (*wai*) in the living space, corresponding also to female and male spaces.

4. There are numerous rules about the length of different parts of the house, and of pieces of furniture (e.g. Xu 2006: 67; Peng 2000: 8). Many include the number 8 (*ba*), which is similar in pronunciation to the Chinese character '*fa*', indicating prosperity. These carpentry rules were probably introduced in this region by carpenters that came with the migration waves of the eighteenth century (Peng 2000: 8).

5. Whilst cheap copies of such books are available on street book stalls in Bashan and in Enshi, people would often insist that these are counterfeit versions. The real 'books of Lu Ban' would be worth a fortune, but they are never sold in public. Klaas Ruitenbeek has translated and commented the *Classic of Lu Ban* (*lu ban jing*), one of the most commonly used version of these books (1986, 1993). Wolfram Eberhard has translated several folk tales and one *Illustrated Book of Lu Ban* (*huitu luban jing*) published in the early twentieth century in Zhejiang (1970), and Ronald Knapp has given numerous detailed descriptions of popular Chinese architecture, including references to carpentry (1986, 1989, 1999).

6. These two different ways of building houses, the wooden houses (*diao jiao lou*) on the one side, and the house built of stones and mud, with wood only used for the planks

of the roof (*tu fangzi*) on the other, distinguished families that were or had become 'natives' (*tujia*) to the mountains, and those that were outsiders (*kejia*) from the plains.

7. An example in Bashan was the courtyard of Wu Yongxing. Wu Yongxing had been the biggest and most influential merchant of Bashan in the last years of the Qing dynasty. The headquarter of his company, with his own private courtyard, on the Lower Street was for a long time the biggest and richest house in Bashan: a huge complex with three forecourts, carved wooden windows, carved painted entablature, guest chambers and a main reception hall. During land reform in 1950 Wu Yongxing's house became the primary school of Bashan. The beautiful wooden structure with several internal courtyards was torn down and replaced by a multi-storey building of concrete slabs in the 1980s. In 2003, the primary school moved out to another building, and since then the school building has been occupied by Bashan's nursery school.

8. Dillingham and Dillingham 1971, as quoted in Ahern 1979: 159. On the same page Ahern cites several cases from Taiwan, Guangdong, and Shandong that all confirm 'the creation of multiple interior barriers in front of the main hall' as a 'mark of high status or wealth'.

9. 'small and comfortable' (*xiaokang*) is one slogan referring to the level of wealth that ideally should be attained by every Chinese family; it is one of the main catchphrases in Deng Xiaoping's teachings. For the ideological underpinning of this slogan of being 'relatively comfortable' in an 'egalitarian society', see Lu Hanlong 2000.

10. The scroll with 'heaven, earth, emperor, ancestors, and teachers' is common in many parts of central China. Yu Yingshi traces its origins back to the thirteenth century CE (Yu 2004). For the history and features of ancestral shrines in the Wuling Mountains, see Tian 2007.

11. i.e. Zhu De, Peng Dehuai, Lin Biao, Liu Bocheng, He Long, Chen Yi, Luo Rongheng, Xu Xiangqian, Nie Rongzhen, and Ye Jianying.

12. Since family planning has been enforced in the 1980s, most families have only one or two children.

13. I will deal in more detail with such notions of 'social heat' or 'red-hot sociality' in chapter 6; see also Chau 2006, chapter 8.

14. This basic approach of slow gradual addition and improvization has also been described by Francis Hsu in his ethnography of West Town, Yunnan province, in the 1940s: 'West Town houses are in various stages of completion at any given period of time, and work is always in process' (Hsu 1948: 39).

15. Specialized sawyers using mechanical saws to produce planks only appeared in the 1980s. Now many people have their planks sawn with these machines, but the columns and beams are generally still axed by hand. In the course of my fieldwork, I had plenty of opportunity to see carpenters do this work: I often admired the dexterity with which they would chop a tree into a square beam, with only a small axe and a linemarker (*modou*): a string that is dipped in ink, strained from one head of the tree to the other, pulled up a little bit at the middle, and then flicked against the trunk. In this way the ink marks a straight line, which the carpenters use as a guide to get the edges of the beam straight.

16. Red-burned sand lime bricks cost between 0.25 and 0.28 Yuan per brick in 2007 in Bashan. Without calculating his own labour, Yang Minghu said that by producing his own cinderblocks, he would spend less than half the amount on brickwork.

17. Because many people construct their houses over long periods, adding another section when they have sufficient money, the walls often remain unplastered for years, and so the bricks and their colours are visible.

18. Sometimes he was also called the 'ink control master' (E. *zhang moshi*), a nickname based on the ink line marker (*modou*) that the carpenters use.

19. The timing is significant: it was possible to carry out the construction work dur-
    ing the winter, which is the 'idle period' (*nongxian*) of the peasant calendar, when
    not much is to be done on the slopes and on the tea plantations. Yet a house should
    not be without a roof during the Spring Festival period, when everything should
    be provided for people to relax and to celebrate family reunions. The 'hoisting of
    the ridgepole' ritual is common in many regions of China, but there exist only very
    few descriptions in Western languages. Ruitenbeek reviews briefly several Chinese
    descriptions (1993: 68–71) and Knapp summarizes the rituals accompanying house
    construction (1999: 40–51).
20. Usually the man that writes the 'book of presents' also writes the list of helpers and
    all the paper scrolls that are stuck on the door-frames of the house at such an event.
21. Ziwei is the name of a star which is said to be the star of the emperor. The first ele-
    ment of the name is the colour 'purple' (*zi*), which is a colour associated with the
    emperor. Yang Yuanbing explained this inscription to me in the following way: 'the
    Ziwei is a majestic star on the sky; you can also say that a big leader, like Mao Ze-
    dong, is a Ziwei.' Others emphasized that the inscription will prevent bad people
    and ghosts from coming close to this house.
22. Examples are: 'carve the head of the beam to 1.8 inch/ and the sons and grandsons
    will all prosper' (*liangkou kaiqi yi cun ba, erzi ersun dou fada*); or 'four seasons of wealth
    and vast sources of wealth/ all the ways to wealth shall be easy and smooth' (*siji facai
    caiyuan guang, tiaotiao cailu dou tongchang*). There are countless verses like that, all
    wishing prosperity, and sons who succeed in education, health and happiness. Many
    also accompany the movements and actions of the carpenter. So, for instance, when
    he wraps a red cloth around the beam three times, he will say 'wrap it on the right
    and turn it three times/ give birth to a dear son/ wrap it on the left and turn it three
    times/ become an excellent scholar [literally 'the first in the imperial exams']/ give
    birth to a son who exceeds in the examinations/ and the host's family will prosper
    year after year' (*you chan san zhuan sheng guizi, zuo chan san zhuan dian zhuangyuan.
    sheng guizi, dian zhuangyuan, zhujia fada wanwan nian*).
23. The beam is never covered with a framework nor with paint, so the wood can breathe.
    It was explained to me that if the wood is well selected (i.e. not distorted or grow-
    ing askew), it will not shrink or twist much when the sap is drying. I had wondered
    whether a completely fresh tree would not cause problems if it was placed directly
    into the built structure.
24. The colours possibly represent the five colours of the five elements (*wu xing*). This
    element is not mentioned in the *Illustrated Book of Lu Ban* (*huitu luban jing*), partly
    translated by Eberhard (1970), but most other objects that Nie and Lan used in the
    ritual (including brushes, ink, coins, and nails) are the same as in this Lu Ban Book.
25. Yang Minghu had bought 5000 tiles, for a roof area of 75 m² (that makes 15 m² for 1000
    tiles). The tiles cost 160 Yuan for 1000 tiles or 800 Yuan for 5000 tiles.
26. Eberhard has collected numerous folk stories dealing with wily craftsmen (see 1966
    and 1970), and Huang Shu-min recounts one more recent case (1998: 37–38).
27. In Appendix B I include a cost calculation of the most basic expenses for construc-
    tion material and wages to build an average two-storey house comparable to that of
    Tian Dejun. The basic masonry with concrete floors and ceilings, windows and doors
    alone amounted to about 80,000 Yuan, which does not include any plaster, painting,
    or internal installations of water and electricity.
28. A good relationship (*guanxi*) and reciprocity are always emphasized in such mutual
    labour exchange. For example, Old Ma was an outsider in the community, and had
    good relationships with only a few people. When he started constructing his new

house in the summer of 2007, no one helped him dig the foundations, and the old man did most of the work alone with his son. When I asked some men in the Yang family why no one was helping Old Ma, they said the answer was obvious: he has never helped anyone here, so they would not help him either.

29. There are very few men with long hair in Bashan. In the past it was a custom to show one's mourning (in particular for a deceased mother) by not cutting one's hair for several months, and I knew of at least one case where a son followed this custom. Jixiang let his hair grow for other reasons. One neighbour said explicitly that he has his hair like that 'to scare others' so that they would show respect when dealing with him.

30. A bar-owner proudly explained this to me as follows: 'I have relationships both in the "red way" (*hongdao*) and in the "black way" (*heidao*)' – the 'red' refers to the colour of the communist party, and the 'black' to the 'black society' (*hei shehui*) of hoodlums and gangsters.

31. His household was also amongst those that benefitted the most in the development programmes of the government. With substantial financial help from the government, his new house has been constructed in the 'minority style' (*minzu tese*), and visitors that are shown around the model village of Zhongba are often taken to his house. A factor here again is his daring appearance, with his beard and shoulder-long curly hair. Occasionally he likes to dress up in colourful 'minority-cloths', appearing as a kind of Dong noble savage to the visitors. The first time I visited Bashan, I was taken around Zhongba and also to his house by local officials. Xiang Jixiang was just building his new house then, and came over from the construction site when we arrived at his house. His appearance left a vivid impression on me then.

32. Cf. the list of construction materials and wages needed for an average two-storey house in the 'modern' style in Appendix B.

33. This is different to Taiwanese cases in the 1970s as reported by Emily Ahern, where no attention was paid to *fengshui* (or *dili*, as her informants called it in Taiwan) in the construction of new houses. She was told that 'it's a bother to build *dacu* [old traditional houses] because you have to be so careful about the *dili*. With *yanglou* [new urban houses] you do not have to build according to the *dili*; *yanglou* are built according to the road' (Ahern 1979: 164). Weller confirms this, based on fieldwork in a Taiwanese township in the late 1970s: 'Although modern houses are generally built without the help of a geomancer, his help is still considered necessary for houses built in the traditional style. In either case, people often ask geomancers to determine the proper placement of the domestic altar' (Weller 1987: 147). In Bashan in 2007, most new-built houses did not have an elaborated house altar. But most of the new houses either had a poster (often of Mao Zedong) and/or a wooden shelf to mark the position of the house altar, and for most new-built houses the central axis had been adjusted by a geomancer.

34. Tian Dong and Yang Jun are quite different characters too. As mentioned above, Tian Dong was more interested in studying English, Chinese, and watching TV with me, whereas Yang Jun favoured playing basketball, and sometimes asked me for cigarettes as well. When I left Zhongba in 2007, Tian Dong was just preparing to enter higher middle school (*gaozhong*), and Yang Jun had left school to go and work in a factory in Guangzhou.

Chapter 3

WORK THROUGH THE FOOD BASKET

Most of the slopes and paddy fields of Zhongba are now covered with tea shrubs, planted in uniform rows. Interrupted only by some small groves, the dark green of the tea leaves is the dominant colour of the landscape throughout the year. In Fragrant Forest, two stripes of paddy fields stick out: straw cobbles in autumn and winter, irrigation water covering the fields in spring, bright green rice plants in early summer that dry into a withered yellow before harvest, all provide a stark contrast to the tea shrubs surrounding them. Just outside the Yao family hamlet, these two fields are the only rice paddies left in Fragrant Forest. They are owned by two cousins: Yang Mingde and Yang Mingxi. Both men are in their late fifties and work in the fields year in year out, come rain or shine. Many others are not used to this kind of work rhythm anymore; when it rains they often stay in their house. The young in particular refuse to do the kind of work in the fields that is seen as the embodiment of being a peasant: ploughing with a water buffalo or standing barefoot in the mud planting rice.

The cousins jointly own the last water buffalo left in Fragrant Forest, and in spring they sometimes take the buffalo to other villages higher up the mountains to plough for other farmers there. All their neighbours in Fragrant Forest have long since sold their buffalos, which are not needed in the tea plantations. Aside from their small rice paddy fields, Yang Mingxi and Yang Mingde also plant corn, potatoes, and vegetables. With all these crops, it is necessary to know about the annual agricultural cycles. They use the Chinese lunar and solar calendars to be certain about the dates for sowing and harvesting, and they have countless sayings and rhymes that attempt to predict changes in the weather. For the tea plantations, this knowledge is not of such crucial importance, even though at least the first tea picking is always done between two specific dates of the peasant solar calendar.[1] Such things do not matter a great deal to those that work in the cities.[2]

Yang Mingde has two daughters, both of them married in Enshi city. As neither of them is planning to move to their father's house, Yang Mingde does not see any need to build a new house, and continues to live in his old wooden house in the family hamlet. So does Yang Mingxi, who lives just next door. When his brother Yang Minghu moved out and built his own house (see previous chapter), Yang Mingxi stayed in the old house where they had grown up. His two sons have been working in Guangzhou for many years now. Both are unmarried, and they have not come home for the Spring Festival for two years now.

Without being explicit about it, Yang Mingxi and Yang Mingde are stubbornly holding on to the ways of yore that revolve around working the land. When asked why they are continuing in this vein, they say that they have done so all their lives, and that the rice they plant themselves is better than the rice that you buy in the market. Here again, the two cousins stand out: the neighbours who have given up on paddy rice production now buy all their daily rice in the market in Bashan.

In fact, the two cousins do not buy much at all on the rare days when they go to Bashan or to the city of Enshi. Normally young people would buy some snack next to the road, have 'breakfast'[3] or even sit down for a meal at a stall. 'He never buys anything in the city', Yang Mingde's wife Yao Wei told me, and while she meant to convey respect for his frugality, she also pointed out that some people might find such behaviour exaggerated and stingy nowadays. Yang Mingde's first wife died young, and Yao Wei married him only four years ago. She had been living in Shanghai for about ten years with her first husband, until she divorced him. Yao Wei is very much used to city ways, and had some problems in getting used to the life in the village, although this was made easier by the fact that her

Photograph 3.1 The stubborn old man

family is from the Upper Street, the poorest street of Bashan, whereas Yang Mingde is from Zhongba, which is the wealthiest village in the township.

With their refusal to buy foodstuff and snacks in Bashan, Yang Mingde and Yang Mingxi confirm their 'peasant values' of thrift, frugality, and a suspicion of fancy new consumer goods. Both through their own agricultural produce and the goods they consume, they participate in commodity markets to a much lesser degree than their own children and than most of their neighbours. They also plant some tea, which they sell on the market, as everyone does. But the majority of their agricultural production is for their own consumption. In fact, most of the food they consume is from their own products, with some minor exceptions such as liquor, salt, and soy sauce. Meat is provided by the pigs they feed, slaughtered before the Spring Festival, and cured with smoke to conserve it. They have several small vegetable plots and they grow their own tobacco.

Yet these two stubborn old men are very much an exception. Even though the majority of the population of Zhongba, as in the other villages of Bashan, is registered as 'agricultural population', it is in fact only a minority who earns all their income from agriculture. Most people engage in a variety of different occupations, which are all linked to commodity markets to various extents. There has been a huge increase in the varying alternatives and options for work, occupations, and livelihood strategies. This diversification is complementary to and a consequence of the commodification of labour.

Besides many other things, commodification also means that work becomes measurable in terms of a common denominator (mostly money – but according to one's theoretical stance also other more abstract forms of value). Thus measurable, work becomes negotiable. I will stress below the heightened moment of choice between different occupations and different forms of work. While this element of choice goes some way towards explaining changing attitudes towards work, it also appears that the penetration of production and consumption by the commodity form, enabling the comparison of (formerly) incomparable forms of human labour, gradually de-valorizes certain forms of work. This is the case in particular with agricultural work.

The commodification of the productive sphere goes hand in hand with the commodification of the realm of consumption. Both in everyday labour and in everyday consumption, people have to face a multitude of choices, which also have moral implications. Here the old values of hard physical work and thrift, to which the Yang cousins still adhere, are a foil for the moral references of the majority of young people. To them, such values of old seem backward, and they aspire to different kinds of work and consumption. In local business, labour migration, and in conspicuous consumption, they refer to a different set of centres and moral frameworks. In this chapter I deal with work and consumption and their moral implications. To provide some background, the next section gives a short outline of the political economy of Bashan, and in particular the growth of tea production and marketing.

The Local Political Economy and the Rise of the Tea Industry

Like most of rural China, the highlands of Western Hubei, Western Hunan and Eastern Sichuan were characterized by small-scale peasant farming close to subsistence levels for much of their modern history. This 'modern' history can be said to have started with the huge influx of immigrants in the seventeenth and eighteenth centuries. Before that slash-and-burn cultivation, together with hunting and gathering, were still pre-eminent. The settlement of this mountain region was facilitated by the introduction of intensive farming, and in particular by maize and potato, which were suitable to the climatic and geographic conditions in the mountains (Wu 2003: 51ff). Compared to the plains regions of China, commercialization and urban development arrived only fairly late to this area, by the end of the Qing dynasty, almost at the beginning of the twentieth century. But even then, agricultural commercialization – in this area driven mainly by the trade in opium and tong oil – failed to effect major social transformations.[4] Peasants produced mainly for their own subsistence, and there was almost no trade in staple crops, given the transport difficulties in the mountains (Ch'en 1992: 44, 51). Inter-regional trade was limited to an exchange of cash crops (tong oil, opium, tea, medicinal plants, timber) with minor consumption goods (e.g. cotton yarn, cloth, paraffin, kerosene, salt, sugar, and tobacco) (ibid.: 89). But all marketing systems in the region were 'traditional' in the sense that they were mainly based on small-scale production, and independent small buyers (ibid.: 96).

In the late Qing dynasty and the Republican Era, farmers were integrated into the local economy mainly via periodical peasant markets. The periodical market of Bashan took place on days 1, 4, and 7 of every ten-day period (*xun*) in the lunar calendar. G.W. Skinner has developed a fine-grained theory for the social importance and distribution of these markets (1964, 1965a, 1965b). According to Skinner's theory, the general unit of a hierarchy of central places in rural China was the 'standard market town'. Given that most rural households visited only one periodical market on a regular basis, the 'standard marketing area' comprised all villages that were dependent on one market town. The distribution of the traditional peasant markets, according to Skinner's prediction, takes the shape of hexagons which include around eighteen villages. Even though the area of Bashan and the neighbouring townships is very mountainous, cut through by deep valleys and unfertile hills, the spatial distribution of the traditional markets in this area seems to correspond relatively well to Skinner's theory, according to my observations.[5]

After the Communist Revolution, and the founding of the People's Republic in 1949, land was collectivized under several campaigns that were fairly similar in this area to the rest of central China. By the end of the 1950s almost all farming was done in collectives of production brigades and work teams, according to set quotas and procurement prices. Commerce and trade were strictly limited and controlled by governmental agencies. According to the different waves of political radicalization and liberalization, individual economic activity (including sideline and subsistence production) was curtailed or partly encouraged, and the policies towards periodical markets changed correspondingly, from complete prohibition to considerable leeway.[6] In the 1950s the markets continued on a reduced scale; and after the 'Great Leap Forward' in 1958 they were completely forbidden for several years. Several old people remember still the sadness of several years without markets, of 'cold days' every day (cf. Skinner 1965b: 372). The idea was that people 'would have more time to labour' instead of wasting their time hanging around at the markets. Whilst markets resumed in the 1960s, there was still considerable control over them, and they were stopped again during the Cultural Revolution. The limitation of independent marketing activity, together with the strict regulations on people's mobility, created a very important connection linking farmers to the wider social networks outside their villages (cf. Selden 1993).

Impeded by the transport difficulties in the mountains, the basic conditions of small-scale agriculture close to subsistence levels continued far into the Maoist era. The first major road from Enshi City to the township seat of Bashan was built in the 1950s, and the first roads to the villages in the township only from the 1970s. But until the 1990s people carried all their crops and goods in baskets on their back. It is safe to assume that much of the agricultural production in Enshi prefecture by the end of the Maoist era was still subsistence farming.[7]

After several local attempts to introduce more managerial capacities to single work teams, loosening of quota restrictions, and allowing sideline activities at the end of the 1970s, the collectivist system of agriculture was abandoned at the beginning of the 1980s. By 1983 most production brigades had out-contracted their land to individual households, in the so-called 'Household Responsibility System' (*jiating lianchan chengbao zerenzhi*). In this system, which continues to the present day, peasant households receive their land based on an average per head of adult members in the form of a contract of use rights to the land for fifteen or twenty-four years. The average amount of land is very small in most of central China; in Bashan township it is about 0.7 *mu* plain land and 1 *mu* slopes per capita, which results in 2.8 *mu* for a family of four.

However, grain production continued to be controlled by government procurement agencies until 1990. The grain depot and buying station of the township in Bashan was finally closed in 1991. Sideline activities were condoned from the 1980s, and have gradually been encouraged by the government since then. Among the most common were growing vegetables and picking herbal plants for the local periodical market, minor handcrafts, and temporary construction as builders, carpenters and unskilled workers. At the same time rural industries were established, at the beginning mainly by village and township administrations, in the 'Township and Village Enterprises' (TVEs). In Bashan this was mainly the local tea industry; in the 1980s several tea factories were built by the local government, to be managed by the village administrations. Later all of these were leased or sold out to private bosses. I will describe in more detail below the process of the introduction of monocultural tea plantations, tea production and tea marketing in Bashan.

At the end of the 1970s, there was a loosening of the regulations regarding independent marketing activities. In Bashan the periodical peasant market appeared for a time with three market days during every ten-day period (*xun*). In the 1980s[8] the market days soon changed to the days 1, 3, 5, 7, and 9 of the lunar calendar, and this scheme continues to the present day. The market still plays a very important role in the life of the people in the villages around Bashan. Many people go down to Bashan on market days, not only to exchange goods, but also to talk and meet with people from the market town and from other villages (see photograph 3.2).

But it seems that the modernization of the local transport network and the establishment of modern retailers will bring an end to the periodical peasant markets in the near future. 'The very logic of market periodicity assumes inefficient transport and weak demand density' (Skinner 1985: 412), and hence improved transport and permanent facilities in the market places will bring an end to periodical markets. Many households in Bashan now have motorbikes, and asphalt roads are reaching most villages. In recent years, numerous new shops and retailers have been established on the streets of Bashan, and in January 2007, the first major supermarket opened its doors.[9]

Since the mid-1990s, the huge growth of capitalist enterprises in China's major cities, together with the relaxation of governmental control on population movement, have led to a huge internal labour migration from the countryside to the cities, and from central China to the coastal provinces.

Photograph 3.2 The periodical market of Bashan

According to official data, about fifteen per cent of the population registered in Enshi Prefecture in 2006 were 'floating population', that is, they were not at that time living in the prefecture.[10] The number of people who are not registered and accounted for in official statistics is presumably considerably higher. According to my observations in Zhongba, almost every man below the age of forty has worked at least temporarily in a major city, such as Shanghai, Beijing or Guangzhou.

At the same time, small-scale and staple crop farming has steadily declined in importance as a source of income. It is now impossible for many farmers to maintain a socially acceptable living based on an agricultural income alone. Responding to these changes, the central government has recently shifted the general direction of rural policy from taxation towards subsidization. This was also due to the fact that during the 1980s and 1990s, the general agricultural tax and the countless fees collected from the farmers had led to many conflicts, and in some other regions to collective protests (cf. Lu 1997; Perry 1999).[11] In 2001, the national government decided to lift the tax burden; the general agricultural tax was cut in several phases and then completely abandoned. This meant an acknowledgement by the national government that henceforth small-scale agriculture would no longer play a prominent role in the national tax budget nor in the gross national income. Since 2005, the central government has implemented policies directed towards the countryside under the heading of 'The Construction of a Socialist New Countryside' (*shehuizhuyi xin*

新农村永受

nongcun jianshe). At the same time the public and academic discourse has moved from the 'peasant burden' (*nongmin fudan*) to the comprehensive 'three problems of the countryside' (*san nong wenti*), that is, the problems of the peasantry, of agriculture, and of the countryside in general.[12]

农民   农业   农村

The Introduction of Tea Monocultures in Bashan

Since the 1990s, there has been a growing trend towards cash cropping and commercial farming in rural China, which is actively encouraged by local governments (see Zhang and Donaldson 2008). In Bashan, the production of staple crops (including wheat, potato, rice, corn, soybean) has decreased massively in the last decade, whilst the production of cash crops, such as tea, fruits and vegetables, has increased in the same proportions (see Table 3.1).[13] The most important of these cash crops in Bashan has been tea: in the last fifteen years, Bashan township has seen a complete transition towards commercial and monocultural tea production. This is still small-scale farming based on household units, but the production and marketing is now completely commercialized. This transition corresponds to one explicit aim of local governments in Enshi, namely to promote 'specialized townships', i.e. entire townships specialized into one crop: one tobacco township, one melon township, one tea township, etc.

Table 3.1 Production of staple crops and cash crops in Bashan township

	1996	2006
Staple crops harvested in summer (wheat and potato) in tons	4203	3227
Staple crops harvested in autumn (rice, corn, soybean) in tons	21317	9477
Of that: Rice production in tons	10850	3319
Area of staple crops harvested in hectares	6940	4690
Tea leaves production in tons	720	2795
Area of tea leaves planted in hectares	1377	4543
Fruit production in tons	225	2899
Area of fruit production in hectares	- no data -	317
Vegetable production in tons	8205	21450
Area of vegetable production in hectares	590	1700

Source: Bashan Township 2006

However, the conversion to monocultural tea has not been very easy for many farmers. The township government, and one official in particular, played decisive roles in promoting the tea monocultures. Yao Kejin was a young official, who did not have much education, but did have a great deal of charisma. His family is from Bashan Slope, the part of Zhongba that is closest to the market town. These slopes are relatively flat and have the most fertile land of the whole of Bashan (see photograph 3.3). Almost half of the houses here belong to two big surnames, Yang and Yao.

When he became the head of the township government in the 1990s, Yao Kejin strongly advocated tea production and the change to tea monoculture, starting at home, in the hamlets of his own family on Bashan Slope. At first, the farmers there were extremely hesitant, and many refused to dry out their paddy fields and fill them with tea plants when government officials tried to convince them to do so. Many people remember Yao Kejin scolding his own uncles and aunts for not wanting to plant tea. The farmers were afraid that they would not have enough to eat if they did not plant rice. There was a common saying at the time:

chaye shang shuitian	If the tea leaves enter the paddy fields
hui dao wu jiu nian!	We will return to 1959!

(1959 was the year of the famine after the Great Leap Forward, when people ate tree bark and grass, and many died of hunger.) Facing strong opposition from the local farmers, Yao Kejin insisted, using very rough methods. Besides insulting people who were his own relatives and who were higher up in the generational hierarchy, he also used such drastic methods as cutting the irrigation channels to the paddy fields of several

Photograph 3.3 Bashan Slope

families and thus forcing them to plant tea shrubs in the dried-up fields. *Rude*
After several years of 'thought work' (*sixiang gongzuo*) with the farmers,
backed up by extension services providing know-how and advice, the
establishment of government-owned tea stations producing tea saplings,
and support for the first tea processing factories, slowly most farmers in
Zhongba and the surrounding villages switched to tea production. Yao
Kejin died in 1997 from cancer; he was only in his forties. His tomb is at
Bashan Slope, and is very well kept. The people's fear and awe for him
became reverence and gratitude after his death. Now most people say that
he was a very rude man, but that his ideas were right, and that he brought
wealth to Bashan.

In several villages close to the market town tea is now by far the most
important crop. There are very few places where older peasants still plant
staple crops. Potato, sweet potato and corn are not important anymore
for the incomes of the peasants, and many farmers who still plant a small
amount of these crops just feed them to their pigs. Rice has almost completely disappeared, and now the farmers here buy their rice in the market at Bashan.

In the history of tea production in Bashan, local government played
a crucial role. Government involvement has scaled down considerably
when compared to the days of Yao Kejin, but local officials still offer extension services, attempt to enforce standards for quality and hygiene
in the tea factories, and guide tea farming, processing, and marketing
towards 'standardization' (*guifanhua*). A number of 'model households'
(*shifan hu*) are chosen by the township government. Ideally, these households would have information on tea production, marketing, and quality
measurement, and would provide a model for neighbours in their village
groups. But in reality, it is often only the tin 'model-household' plates next
to the doors of these households that distinguish them from others. Similarly the extension services of the township government that are meant to
give support and advice to both tea farmers and small tea factories do still
exist, but have lost much of their importance in recent years. Every now
and then there are workshops on tea production; but overall government
officials do not have much influence over the tea growing itself anymore.
The situation is different with the tea processing in the tea factories: the
factories have to be registered at government offices, they have to pay taxes and they have to fulfil regulations on standards and hygiene. In particular, the biggest tea factories in Bashan have close links with officials in
the township government, for various reasons: whilst hygiene and quality standards in the local tea production are still only loosely enforced,
it is particularly at the bigger factories that government officials attempt
to promote 'standardization'. Frequently the township government also

offers low-interest loans and subsidies for these purposes. Additionally, the bigger factories have to pay high taxes.

Whilst government is still involved in tea production and processing, the marketing of tea leaves takes place without any government interference or control. I will describe in more detail below the market that takes place every evening on the streets of Bashan. In different ways, the tea farmers, the bosses of the tea factories, and their workers are all participating in commodity markets. The same is true of the other forms of work in which people engage, including migrant labour and countless odd jobs.

The Choice of Work

Tea Labour

Within the premises of the village administration of Zhongba, there is a tea factory owned by the village council. The tea factory shares the same history as many other 'Township and Village Enterprises' all over China: in the 1980s it was first a village enterprise, owned and managed by the village council. Since the 1990s most of these enterprises have either been sold or leased to private businessmen (which were often the same government officials who were managing them before). This tea factory has been leased out to various private bosses who were producing tea there, and for more than three years now, Song Haomin, a peasant from Zhou's Crow, has been renting the tea factory from the village administration.

Just like me, and even for somewhat similar reasons (including issues of rent and payments), Song Haomin and his family also had a rather tense relationship with the village administration and the village secretary in particular. That was probably what brought us together, besides the wonderful hospitality and warmth of the entire family. Often when I came home in the evenings, when the village administration had closed, and all the cadres and the cook had left, Song Haomin's wife invited me to eat with them, and I spent long hours chatting, playing games, watching them working and sometimes also working myself in the tea factory. I learned during this time that all the favours they offered me, in particular eating together with them, should be reciprocated by little presents on my part. The fact that I was helping them in the tea factory must have astonished many onlookers and the family members themselves at the beginning, but over time it was casually accepted.

From the very beginning I was taken aback by the working hours in this tea factory. It was common to work all night and the whole of the following day without a long break, until one load of tea was completely processed. That sometimes meant continuous work for up to thirty hours.

After such a shift, one usually cannot sleep well, and dozes for a little bit until the next shift starts, often just sitting in a chair, or lying on the tea leaves. The rhythm of work is only interrupted by days of rain, when no tea can be picked; or sometimes by an important family celebration, like a wedding or a funeral that one has to attend.

Only in autumn, when no more tea is picked, do the tea factories close. From November to mid-March, during the idle months of the peasant calendars (*nongxian*), many tea workers and tea farmers will do other odd jobs, and the tea entrepreneurs will engage in maintenance work and arrangements for the next tea season. During these months, much time is spent with the family, or visiting relatives and friends.

In the local tea factories, there are generally two different forms of payments for the workers, one according to a monthly salary, the other one according to the amount of tea a group of workers processes, that is, payment per piece (*an jian*). The first, called *diangong*, is payment according to labour time or time-wage; the second, *baogong*, is payment according to the result of labour or piece-wage. Like many other bosses of small tea factories, Song Haomin paid all his workers on a piece-wage.

Marx has elaborated the transition from time-wage to piece-wage as a form of raising the intensity of labour and making superintendence of the labour force partly unnecessary; instead it facilitates the subletting or out-contracting of labour. Hence according to Marx, 'piece-wage is the form of wages most in harmony with the capitalist mode of production' (Marx 1962: 580). In his rich ethnography of the workers who constructed Brasilia, Gustavo Lins Ribeiro draws on Marx's basic formulation to describe the inventory of different forms of super-exploitation in project work paid according to time (*tarea*) or final product (*empreitada*) (Ribeiro 2006: 147ff). In Ribeiro's presentation, piece-work, together with incentives like bonuses for overtime and a legal uncertainty over labour relations, all serve to replace outside forms of labour control and surveillance with self-control by the workers, via what Ribeiro calls a 'fetishism of the salary' (ibid.: 159ff).

It is apparent not only to Marx and Ribeiro, but to the tea workers of Bashan as well, that piece-wage means essentially material rewards, whereas time-wage implies a more complex relationship, and frequently a closer link between the boss and his employees.

I had several conversations about the difference between *diangong* and *baogong* witih Tian Benjun, a peasant in Zhonga who has been working in tea factories for fifteen years. It is often the case that the quality of the tea produced by the *diangong* is better, because the worker does not have so much pressure to produce quickly to earn money. On the contrary with the *baogong* the salary of the worker is higher, and the production is quicker. When asked what the ideas or motivations of the boss might be, Tian Benjun answered that they would probably be the same as those of every other boss in the world: 'Obviously the bosses want to spend as little money as possible on salaries, and have the best quality possible. In that the bosses are the same everywhere.'

I asked Tian Benjun why Song Haomin was now only paying his workers per amount of tea processed (*baogong*) and not per month (*diangong*), and he said that it might be because it is more difficult to pay a *diangong*; it demands more long-term organization. Song Haomin lost quite a lot of money in 2005 with the workers he was hiring per month as *diangong*, probably because of their lack of skill, and his naïve trust of them. Paying workers per piece frees him of such considerations; the workers themselves are responsible for producing good tea. Another worker told me that the *diangong* are generally more suitable for smaller tea factories. Most of the big factories are only hiring *baogong*. With the *diangong* the boss has to be there most of the time and take care of the work; but Song Haomin, for example, wants to go out and buy and sell tea and so cannot be there all the time. In this case it is more convenient for him to have *baogong*.

A boss usually has a closer personal relationship with a *diangong* than a *baogong*. Someone working as a *diangong* has often started very young as an apprentice (*tudi*) learning with his master (*shifu*), and if he stays on as a *diangong*, he becomes almost a family member. The relationship to a master is indeed similar to a kinship relationship; as well as the transfer of skills, protection, mutual support, obedience and emotional attachment are expected. Often the relationship between master and apprentice lasts for their lifetimes, and it is not uncommon for a middle-aged man to go during the Spring Festival period to his master to give him the same gifts he would give to his wife's family. Such master–apprentice relationships are very common in the traditional crafts, in particular masonry and carpentry.[14] Skilled tea workers are also called master (*shifu*) and sometimes have apprentices. If there is a master–apprentice relationship between the boss and a young worker, then the young man will be never paid by piecework, but always to the days and months of work. For some young men it was a matter of pride to talk about the good relationship they have with their master, and the secure income they have as *diangong*. 'I am even paid when it rains', a twenty-year-old told me confidently.

That contrasts a great deal with the *baogong* work, which is often seen just as doing 'bitter labour' (*xia kuli*). It is quite clear to many people involved in local tea production that nowadays piece-wages are increasingly favoured over time-wages; and that this is mirroring a more general transformation. I heard on several occasions the comment that '*baogong* fits more to how people work nowadays'. My neighbour Yang Yuanbing explained to me that this is the case because piece-work is correlated to a whole different outlook, a way of thinking. 'Nowadays it's always more about "economic thinking"' (*jingji sixiang*), and this kind of 'economic thinking' has become more and more pervasive, he said.

In recent years, tea labour has also lost the attraction it had in the 1990s. Many men in their thirties and forties have worked earlier in the tea factories, but no longer want to do it. First, the salaries are almost the same as they were fifteen years ago,[15] when there was much less tea production, and a high demand for skilled workers in tea processing. That means that the salaries earned in tea production are, relatively, much lower now. Then there were only very few people that could make good tea, and they were relatively well paid. Making tea is something that needs some skills; and nowadays there are many people making tea in Bashan. As there were fewer skilled tea workers in the past, it paid much better then.

Tea Markets: Farmers and Traders

The tea season starts in spring, around March. During the first months, people are mostly picking tea-buds (*yacha*), which are the raw material for the most expensive teas. Later on, more and more big leaves (*da yezi*) are picked; these are much cheaper, and used for teas of lesser quality, including black tea for export.[16] During the months of the tea harvest (from March until August), the tea farmers sell tea-buds and leaves to intermediate traders, or directly to the small tea factories, of which Bashan township has more than a hundred. If it has been raining a lot, no tea is picked, because tea leaves that are soaked with water are impossible to work with in the tea factories. During the peak of tea production, almost every evening at dusk the roads of the surrounding villages and the market place of Bashan are busy with farmers carrying their tea leaves on their backs and tea merchants on their three-wheeler motorbikes.

Aside from the tea factories of Song Haomin and Hu Yanglong, the house of Yang Mingxu is a main gathering place for the tea trade in the summer evenings in Fragrant Forest. The boss of a tea factory in Bashan has an arrangement with Yang Mingxu to use his front court every evening to collect tea, and for a small commission, Yang Mingxu helps him to buy tea from the local farmers. During the summer months, the tea pickers arrive every evening at Yang Mingxu's house, carrying bamboo baskets and huge sacks of tea. An average tea worker can pick between 50 and 100 *jin* per day. Often it is the tea pickers themselves who carry these huge loads to Yang Mingxu's house in the evening. Yang Mingxu weighs the tea leaves on portable scales, and then checks the quality of the tea by plunging deep into the tea sacks with his hands, grabbing handfuls of

Photograph 3.4 Picking tea

leaves. He probes the quality not only visually, but also by touching it and smelling it. He then offers a price accordingly, which is mostly accepted by the tea pickers. In fact the tea pickers have usually enquired beforehand about the tea prices that are being offered. In the evening the talk about the tea price is the principal topic of conversation; and instead of 'Where are you going?', people greet each other by asking 'How much are green leaves in Bashan?' and 'How much did you sell tea-buds with this and this trader?' The answer shouted out by a neighbour who has just sold his tea is mostly quite imprecise, like '6 Mao, 7 Mao, 8 Mao, all different prices are there'. In fact many people, in particular the tea traders, use their mobile phones to call relatives and business partners who they trust to find out about the tea prices.

It happens quite often that someone arrives at the gathering point around one tea trader, learns about the tea prices from others standing about, finds them unreasonably low and goes off to the next trader. The network of tea collecting points corresponds to the general road and transport network of Bashan: in the most remote mountains there are only very few traders collecting tea, and the central gathering point is the township of Bashan. Soon after the introduction of the tea monocultures in Bashan, tea factories and tea traders entered into open market competition every evening during the tea season, and the government has never entered into this area of tea marketing, between the primary producers and the first processors. In consequence, there is a thriving tea market, which is most visible on the streets of the township of Bashan every night in summer: all along the roads, at the doors of several shops and tea factories, there are tea traders with their weighing machines, and around them crowds of tea farmers selling their leaves. The streets are crammed full with the three-wheeled motorbikes of the small tea traders and with people, many carrying tea sacks on their backs.

The large numbers of people coming to this 'night market' (*yeshi*) soon attracted small merchants who sell foodstuff and other petty goods on the side of the road. Now all the major shops in Bashan also open until late. Both in the small market stalls and the bigger shops, business thrives in the evenings, as many tea farmers have just picked up their daily wages and so have disposable income in their pockets. It is common for people to treat themselves to expensive vegetables, meats and other foodstuffs once in a while after earning a good day's pay. Moreover, parents sometimes want to buy special gifts like foods and sweets for their children or loved ones. During the tea season the night market of Bashan is even more buzzing and 'hot' (E. *naore*) than the periodical peasant market of Bashan, which is held in the morning.

The tea price depends on the quality of the tea, which in turn depends on the weather conditions (it is generally lower when it is raining). The market mechanism of supply and demand is quite complex, and is driven mainly by the intermediate traders. In those villages that are not in walking distance of the Bashan market, most of the tea is bought by these traders, who come on motorbikes to the houses of the peasants, or to street crossings. The tea price that is given to the peasants is generally lower depending on to the distance from the markets and tea factories, and is mainly driven by the contacts and activities of these traders. In some villages that have good tea leaves, sometimes the traders drive up the price to even higher levels than on the market in Bashan, whereas other villages that have only little and poor tea leaves are generally disadvantaged because few traders frequent these places.

These traders are called *yan'erke* in the local dialect: like 'swallows' (*yanzi*), they 'fly back and forth' between different places.[17] In standard Chinese, they are called *erdao fanzi*. Literally meaning 'someone who trades between two ways/realms', this last expression is quite interesting in itself. According to one dictionary it means 'private businessman or trader who makes exorbitant profits by buying cheap and selling expensive'. Another Chinese dictionary is more specific: 'profiteer that takes advantage of the differences between prices set by governmental agencies and black market prices' – which clearly relates it to the two 'ways' (*dao*) of governmental regulation versus the market economy. In Maoist discourse this was a favoured description of tradesmen and capitalists. Sometimes older people still use the word in the derogatory sense it had earlier, to criticize these traders who take a good part of the profit from the tea farmers on the one side, and the small tea factories on the other side.

Usually the *yan'erke* work for one or several tea factories, and agree to buy and sell the tea for certain prices, allowing for a minor profit for themselves. The biggest tea bosses of Bashan have many *yan'erke* working directly for them; and the biggest tea bosses generally know best the different prices for raw tea leaves in different villages, whilst the smaller ones, who have fewer contacts, are often in danger of losing out on price margins, as they know less about all the price developments in other villages. The *yan'erke* themselves might try to increase their profit, and some of them drive huge distances, sometimes up to 30 km into the neighbouring counties, in order to capitalize on minor price differences.

Some of the *yan'erke* are young men who have spent several years in the cities, and have returned temporarily to the countryside. Song Fei, for instance, the son of Song Haomin, worked as a *yan'erke* for some time. He and his friend Du Jie had spent several years in Wuhan and in Shanghai, but after they had returned for the Spring Festival in 2007, they did not want to go back to the city again, and instead tried several jobs at home. And so they worked for several weeks as *yan'erke* in Bashan, using Song Haomin's three-wheeler. Song Fei and Du Jie constantly compared the trade of a *yan'erke* with their other principal option: going back to the cities as migrant labourers.

Migrant Labour

A huge majority of young people are migrating to the major cities of China. Even in the villages of Bashan where tea plantations and the tea industry offer a source of income, the majority of the young leave the countryside. Almost all men and women in their twenties have at least been to the cities for a period of time. It has also become increasingly common to leave babies and children with their grandparents, and so many women also spend long periods working outside the village (cf. Ye et al. 2005).

When asked what they would like to become later, most students in middle school (*chuzhong*, grade 7–9, 13–15 years old), and the majority of the male students in the local primary school would tell me that they would like to become a 'boss' (*laoban*) and 'do business' (*zuo shengyi*). The majority of these boys will migrate to the cities, following their dream of becoming rich. Similarly, young people who temporarily came back to the countryside for the Spring Festival or for other reasons would frequently ask me which types of business I would recommend to make money.

Most of the adult population in Bashan have attended primary school and some have also attended a few years of middle school. Even though the general level of education has improved recently, it is still fairly common to leave school after the first degree of middle school (*chuzhong*) at grade 9. Teenagers who leave school at this age are often still too young to leave their families, and will stay at home for some time. When asked what they are doing, they generally say 'find things to do' or just 'play' (*wan*) – given that it is not very honourable, neither for them nor their parents, to leave school at this early age. Sooner or later, most of them will leave the countryside to find work in the cities.

Yang Minghu's son Yang Jun (who played such an important role in the house inauguration: see introduction and chapter 2) was one of the most self-confident teenagers I met in the village. He would often come over to the village administration building to play basketball, or invite me to come over to his house. To the chagrin of his parents, his marks in school were always fairly low, and he insisted on leaving school after grade 9 of middle school, in 2007. He was eager to leave the village, and found a relative of his mother who was recruiting a group of about eighty teenagers from Bashan and Fengle to go to Guangzhou and work there in a factory. His parents showed me the papers that the intermediary had distributed to the families of these teenagers, describing the work conditions and providing contact details in Guangzhou. They would work for about ten hours a day in the factory, first for a basic salary of 450 Yuan a month; as soon as they had acquired some skills, there would be the possibility of better payment, and of overtime hours.

There are four main reasons for rural migrants to return to the countryside: unemployment, illness or injury, pregnancy, and family obligations (Murphy 2002, chapter 7). Whilst these are more immediate reasons to return to the countryside, in the long term the majority of migrants will return to the countryside at some point, most often to build new houses and marry (cf. Murphy 2002, chapter 4). In between, people have to face the choice of working in the cities or staying in Bashan. Many did not find themselves at ease in the cities, given the discrimination and exploitative labour conditions they often had to face there.

In autumn 2006 a group of older men in their forties and fifties from the village went to Beijing to work. An intermediary had promised them good jobs on construction sites, with a minimum salary of 50 Yuan per day. But once they arrived in Beijing, they found out that it was actually not that easy; the boss said that he would not need them immediately, so they should look for jobs in the interim. Once back in the village, one of them told me that as they were not able to speak much standard Chinese (*putonghua*), 'people in Beijing just took us as country bumpkins (*xiangbalao*)'. They spent several days together entertaining themselves, or 'playing' (*wan*) according to the Chinese expression. One day they walked from the hall that they had found as accommodation in the suburbs to Tiananmen Square in the centre of Beijing, a march of several hours. After having visited Tiananmen, they got back on a bus to Enshi. One of them summed up their experience as follows: 'Having fun in such a little vacation in Beijing cost us about 1000 Yuan each'.

Song Fei and Du Jie, the two young men who did some work in the tea trade in Bashan, also spent several years in the cities. But last year they decided to stay for one year in Bashan; life in Shanghai and Guangzhou had been hard enough for them, and they said they could not find good jobs this year. At the same time they share with most of their contemporaries a disdain for agricultural work; if they dressed like the older generation and worked on the slopes, or as workers on construction sites, or even as labourers in the tea factories, their peers would show contempt, and such work would certainly be a big drawback for the image they would like to convey towards potential girlfriends. Young people in their twenties who engage in agricultural work are rather an exception. The majority of younger people who come back from the cities and spend a longer period in the countryside just do odd jobs, like driving passengers around on motorbikes as a motor-taxi.

Odd Jobs

Providing a motorbike passenger service has become a very common casual job for young men in Bashan. Most days would see a huge crowd of young men on their motorbikes and three-wheelers at the main crossroads of Bashan, waiting for passengers. Taking passengers from the market town to the villages, a man can make between 30 and 50 Yuan a day in Bashan. But most of the young men working in this occupation would readily admit that this was not a long-term occupation, and that they are considering other jobs or going to the cities again.[18]

Since local construction is booming, work in construction is another outlet where many men can find temporary jobs. In the cities, construction work is one of the most common occupations for migrants from the countryside; many therefore have experience in this field, and some have even become 'masters' (*shifu*). But for the majority it is just another odd job, and they only do basic manual labour on construction sites. Such work – carrying shoulder-poles, for instance – is the essential meaning of '*xia kuli*', i.e. of being a coolie – one of the few Chinese loanwords in the English language.

One man from the Yang family hamlet, Yang Mingxiang, has found another odd job to make ends meet: he buys scrap and junk from farm houses and resells it in the market town. On the slopes of the old village of Zhongba, I know of at least five other farmers whose main profession is the same. All of them have a three-wheeler motorbike, on which they transport plastic, bottles, and any kind of junk and scrap. On a good day they can make a rough profit of about 30 to 50 Yuan. Most of them resell their junk to two intermediary dealers in the township. One of them, Tao Qiang, is the brother-in-law of Yang Mingxiang from Zhongba, and most of the junk dealers in the village sell to him. Tao Qiang has made a small fortune in this business, and has recently bought a house in the market town, which is considered to be a clear sign of his social advancement. This stands in stark contrast to the bad reputation that junk dealers have in general; at the same time it is a characteristic of the reform era that some people got rich doing jobs that were generally considered inferior.[19] But locally a successful junk dealer like Tao Qiang would not be seen as having less social prestige than any cadre or white-collar employee.

The Value of Work

We have seen so far a plethora of different occupations and odd jobs, which are all integrated into local and national commodity markets. Related to this, the ways in which work is valued have changed. Until recently, hard work, particularly farm labour, was highly valued. Many older people still hold strongly to such values, and retell stories about people who got rich because they were hard-working. Expressions like 'keep house with hard work and thrift' (*qin jian chi jia*) or 'strive through hardships and earn a living with toil' (*qin pa ku zheng*) are frequently written on the scrolls at the door-frames of houses, and are commonly used to instruct children. Most families had their own vocabulary of such sayings, including rhymes and stories, emphasizing that a proud member of the family and lineage would be honest, hard-working and reliable, and thus conferring moral responsibility towards the ancestors and the family on the younger generation.

But nowadays agricultural work is generally only done by the older generation. Many young people, especially those who have some higher education or those who have lived in the city for extended periods, often have a low opinion of agricultural work: it is a 'damned peasant work' (*si nonghuo*) that will never get you anywhere. On the other side, old people would sometimes complain about the moral decline of the young; for example, an old farmer told me: 'In the past people had scrolls like "keep house with hard work and thrift" (*qin jian chi jia*) on their door-frames.

When I see the young people now, it makes me think they should write "eating, drinking, and revelries" (*chi he wan le*) instead.'

Whilst such crude condemnations are still rather rare, most people agree that nowadays what counts more than hard physical work is someone's 'brains' (*tounao*) and 'intelligence' (*congming*). Obviously, 'brains' are not good in themselves: they can be put to various uses. Tea bosses need them, as do *yan'erke*. Such 'intelligence' can easily become morally ambivalent, for instance, when good relations are severed by piece-work, or when *yan'erke* become selfish profiteers.

To be successful in business, one also needs a wide network of social relationships. This is particularly the case for the local 'bosses' (*laoban*), which so many of the young aspire to become. A boss generally has a strong network of relatives and friends, including reliable connections in the government hierarchies, and often also amongst local hooligans or gangsters. While such relationships are often modelled on kinship relations – in particular brotherhood – they can also stand in obvious contradiction to the obligations towards the family, such as the moral duties of a filial son, for instance.

Migrant labour, many of the odd jobs mentioned above, and the activities of the bosses take place outside and away from the moral framework of the family. It is here, when people are seen to be abandoning the moral framework of the family, that the moral ambiguity of commodified work and consumption is felt most acutely. Let me give an extreme example with one of the local gangsters of Bashan.

Kang II

Several men in Bashan are known and feared as 'gangsters' (*liumang*)[20] and 'hooligans' (*hunhun*). The most famous representative of this 'grey society' (Tan 2007) is Kang 'the second' (*Kang lao'er*). Kang II is an ex-convict who has served several prison sentences since the early 1980s for various crimes including assaults, robbery, and battery. After spending a total of fifteen years in different prisons and labour camps all over Hubei province, Kang was eventually released in 2002. Instead of moving to another town or province, Kang moved back to Bashan where his family lived and resumed an ordinary life there. Having spent most of his adult life 'floating' (*liulang*) and in prison, the first thing Kang did following his release was to find a wife and settle down in order to build a family. Relatives introduced him to his current partner, and in the same year he built a house on the market street. For the purchase of the plot, for the necessary government permits, and for construction material, he allegedly used former contacts, and took advantage of the awe and fear that most people feel towards him. According to local gossip, neither the township government nor the local police dare to interfere with him. Many people in their forties or above remember the stories of Kang II and the feats of him and his gang. But most of the time nowadays Kang goes around the town unnoticed. One contemporary of Kang's claimed that in the 1980s when they were only in their early twenties they knew no better, but that then Kang II and his cohort matured and became ordinary citizens: 'There was no clear line back then to distinguish what was right from what was wrong, we did not have a sense of the law (*mei you falü de gainian*). Now he's just a man like everyone else, he has a family and works hard to earn his living.'

Kang has gone some way towards proving that he can lead the life of an ordinary and conventional person. He lives with his wife and two children in their house on the market street, helps his wife to sell snacks, and engages in occasional jobs in the construction business. His network of relatives, friends, and acquaintances is very wide, of which the number and amounts of gifts for family celebrations such as weddings, funerals, and birthdays are the most obvious sign in local society. In these ways, he receives recognition in the local face-to-face community, including from many people that would have avoided him in former times.

Whilst many people condemned his past, others also emphasized that because of his experiences as a gang member, he was a particularly 'loyal' person (*jiang yiqi*). In particular amongst young men, who had lived in cities for some time, there was also a certain element of admiration when he was mentioned. They would make comments like the following: 'In the past Old Kang was a tremendous and tough guy (*xiong*).[21] But nowadays no one is afraid of him anymore. Actually I have a friend in Enshi who is much tougher and more powerful than he is.'

Expressions such as 'loyalty' (*yiqi*) and 'toughness' (*xiong*) remind one of the attributes of life along the 'rivers and lakes' (*jianghu*). This expression is used to refer to a life outside the community, 'floating' (*liulang*) from one place to the other, and relying only on friends and brothers. Novels of 'rivers and lakes' are a traditional genre of Chinese literature, dealing with knights errant and their ethics of brotherhood. In contemporary Chinese, *jianghu* is also often used to refer to the 'black society' (*heishehui*) of gangs and mafia-like organizations.[22]

Old Kang has left the *jianghu*, and has settled down. Yet the way in which people talk about him, and in which he still demands respect, is clearly influenced by his past. In the way that he presented himself to me, and in the stories others told me about him, he always seemed to fall between the contradictory characterization of a criminal and an upright member of the community.

In the past, Kang obviously lived in contradiction to what is expected from everyone in terms of family and work. Even though he has settled down now, his appearance still reminds people of the *jianghu*. Kang exemplifies the ambiguities between the family and other moral frameworks outside. The young men who leave Bashan and spend long periods of time 'floating' in the cities often confront similar moral dilemmas, and their morality of brotherhood and loyalty sometimes runs into contradiction with family moralities. But most of them will return to Bashan and marry, just as Kang did.

Relating to all these different forms of work, and the accompanying values and moral frameworks, people have to choose between a number of possible options. This is the case not only in the realm of production, but also the realm of consumption. Commodification in both areas is closely tied. As much as one's work and consumption are individual choices, they will be also continuously judged by others, and generally they are related to a family, and not to an individual alone.

The Choice of Consumption

A person's work and consumption are strong markers of their social identity and standing. In local discourse, they are both frequently related to a person's success or failure in providing for their family. General criteria used for judging 'happiness' are the family-related objectives of wealth, sons, and long life.[23]

In an article on Chinese notions of happiness and self-fulfilment, Wang Mingming (1998) demonstrates how people in villages in Southern Fujian saw happiness in exactly these terms. He further elaborates on how people rationalize achievement and failure based on two elements: someone's capability (*nengli*), on the one side, and someone's 'fate' (*ming*), on the other. The most basic meaning of *ming* is someone's life, but it also means their fate (see also Harrell 1987). Wang delineates the opposition of 'capability' (*nengli*) and 'fate' (*ming*) as a local 'social ontology' (*shehui bentilun*), and compares it to the opposition of 'structure' and 'agency' in the social sciences. 'Capability' and 'fate' are also very important notions in Bashan. When asked about their life stories, and in particular the reasons for the successes or failures in their lives, many people would end either by stressing their capabilities (*nengli* or *benshi*), or by bluntly relating them to their good 'fate' (*ming*). Every time I insisted on this point, trying to force people to choose only one of these factors, they would admit that in fact both elements play a role, and the relationship between them can never be finally determined. When dealing with one's own success or failure, 'fate' is often a post facto rationalization; relating someone else's success or failure to either capability or fate generally implies a moral judgement. What is also crucially important here is how someone is presenting her or his capability and fate to others. Let me illustrate this with the following story.

Tian Jiafu is a farmer in a relatively remote village of Bashan township. He had been away from home for about ten years, labouring in Hangzhou and Shanghai, and came back to his home village only last year. On one evening I spent in his house, he told me about his wedding, the various ways he had tried to earn money, and how he had built his house the previous year. He had been very poor when he was young, and had tried to make some money with a small shop he opened in the village. But because his father and his brother liked to drink liquor in his absence, they gave too much to people that could not pay, and lost lots of money with this shop. Later Tian Jiafu tried to make money by trading in herbal medicine. He had heard from a friend that very high prices were paid for a certain medicinal plant in Long Shan, a city in neighbouring Hunan province. But when he went there, he realized that they were actually paying only half the price for which he had bought the plants in Enshi. With that business he lost another 10,000 Yuan, and came back to Enshi with debts.

At the time he had proposed marriage to a girl in a neighbouring township. Her father was a teacher in the local middle school, and head of a much respected family. Tian Jiafu would have had no chance with his proposal if he had told her his real situation (that he had huge amounts of debt), and so he remained silent on this issue. In fact, he 'tricked' (*pian*) her, he admitted himself. She only found out about his heavy debts after the wedding. However, she stayed with him, and has been a very loyal and extremely hard-working wife ever since.

After three years working in Hangzhou and Shanghai, he called on her to come with him to the city as well. They came home together last year, to build a new house in their home village. Actually, Tian Jiafu did not want to build a new house; he thought that their old house was still fine, and he would have preferred to invest the 30,000 Yuan that they had then to start some minor business in the region. But he said that a new house had been his wife's foremost wish for years. In the end they built the new house, and not with (cheap) concrete bricks, but with red clay bricks, which would look nicer and show everyone that they had now achieved quite a comfortable living standard. His wife wanted so much to show everyone in the village that they had overcome poverty now.

Whether someone's good fate is visible to the public depends not least on whether it is shown in public. Both Tian Jiafu and his wife had had a very hard life so far, and they had never had many opportunities to show that they had achieved something. By building their beautiful new house, their moderate wealth is made clearly visible to the public of the village community.

This story was told to me by Tian Jiafu himself, and I think it is safe to assume that his wife would have told it in quite a different way. Perhaps he was not at all successful in dealing with money, and that just made it more reasonable for her to insist on building a house, a stable investment that he would not be able to squander away. In any case, it was not possible for me to go deeper into the demands, needs and desires of either of them, and in particular of his wife. Nevertheless, this story illustrates, I think, a central opposition: namely the one between re-investing and display, between striving and showing off, in the spending of money. When assessing someone's capability (*nengli*) and someone's fate (*ming*), people will look both at their hard work and also at the proper ways of displaying, of spending. The problem of whether to show prosperity to others (so that it would be recognized and become meaningful) or whether to save money, re-invest, or just continue working, poses itself frequently.[24]

In the example cited above, Tian Jiafu says that he would have preferred to re-invest his money; but in the end he built the house out of compassion for his wife, because she had been living such a hard and miserable life by his side ever since their wedding. The house was primarily an investment in their outside appearance, in the face (*mianzi*) of their family.[25]

The outside appearance of a family, and with it the display of a good *ming*, does not stop at the façade of a new house (cf. the previous chapter), but also includes a whole range of installations, furniture, and other items to be found inside the houses. In many households one can find tiled hearths, kitchen surfaces, and toilets, heavily varnished furniture, TV sets, hi-fi systems, mobile phones, and some have washing machines, fridges, and computers. These are all the material expressions of a *xiaokang* ('small and comfortable') society, according to the official slogan of Deng Xiaoping. Whilst such items provide for the private pleasure of domestic consumption, they are also necessary tokens of an individual and a family's standing in the local community, as seen in the example of Tian Jiafu.

It is generally expected that people spend money (for instance on food and clothing) appropriate to their social standing and give presents appropriate to their social relationships. One of the strongest criticisms is to call someone 'miserly' (*xiaoqi*) and 'stingy' (E. *seba*, P. *linse*). Gossip about neighbours who do not spend much on their clothes, and in particular on the food they eat, is very common. While in the Maoist past this was praised as simplicity and frugality (*pusu*), in recent times such people are called 'old-fashioned' and 'backward' (*luohou*); they are accused of stubbornly sticking to their old habits, the customs of the old generation. These are precisely the kind of comments that some of the younger generation made about the Yang cousins, who refused to buy food in the market of Bashan. In these ways, individuals and families are judged locally according to their food, clothes, exchanges and so on. The changes in everyday consumption also represent the huge social, cultural, and political changes of the last decades. 'To see the [political] situation through the bamboo food basket' (*cai lanzi li kan xingshi*) is a popular saying in Chinese; taking it as a motto, Lu Hanchao has analysed social and cultural change in urban China in the twentieth century, focusing on such basic realms of everyday life as water, light, food, and clothing (Lu 2006). In Bashan too people often described past and present events in terms of such everyday life concerns as subsistence.

In the course of numerous conversations with me, local people illustrated past events with examples of the way they dressed and what they ate before the Communist Revolution and in the Maoist era. They would remember times when everyone wore straw shoes (E. *cao hai*) or went barefoot throughout the year, and when farmers owned only one pair of trousers. Until the 1970s, corn and potatoes were the basic staple crops, and people could not eat their fill of rice, let alone meat, which was a rare commodity. Daily meals were 'small vegetables with a bit of staple' (*xiao cai ban bian liang*), i.e. potatoes or corn mixed with a bit of rice, and accompanied by some vegetables.

This offers a stark contrast with today's food: rice is now the basic staple, and corn and potatoes are mainly fed to the pigs. When people eat corn or potatoes now, they say that this is just 'to have fun' (*haowan*), as an interesting variation in the cuisine. To some extent these foodstuffs have now become expressive of local identity, when people offer them to guests in their households, or in restaurants in Enshi city that advertise 'country-style menus', such as 'corn rice' (E. *baogu fan*) and 'potato rice' (E. *yangyu fan*) (see Wu 2003: 99–129).

Most food now, and all the other consumer items mentioned, is bought with money from the markets of Bashan and Enshi. This kind of consumption corresponds to the new forms of work described above: only very few old farmers, such as the Yang cousins, avoid both commoditized production and consumption. If such behaviour was lauded in the past, nowadays the earlier subsistence and revolutionary standards of hard work and frugality are continuously placed in opposition to the new standards of progress and modernity. People have to take decisions on an everyday basis according to which standards they want to build their houses, and buy furniture, food, and clothes, and how they want to show this consumption within the local community. In their choices of consumption, they refer to different and partly contradictory standards of approbation and moral frameworks.

Conclusion

People in Bashan engage in many different forms of work, and agricultural production has become only one amongst many others. Now different kinds of work are judged according to the monetary gain they bring about, and hard work has lost much of its pervasiveness as a value in itself. For the young it is clear that they will not be recognized and esteemed in society if they are just peasants, but that other things count more in contemporary China.

The different criteria of social approbation correspond to the background of the changing political economy of this township, and of rural China in general. I have painted in this chapter a picture of a myriad of odd jobs in which the men of Bashan engage. Both in the local tea industry, and in migrant labour, work is mainly carried out as wage labour. This stands in contrast to agriculture, where to a large extent people were still producing their own subsistence crops – and a minority of stubborn old people continues to do so. Tea and migrant labour, and all the other odd jobs, represent the increased immersion of local work and livelihoods in commodity markets; tea production and tea marketing provided an example of agricultural commercialization and local marketing activity. As we have seen with tea production, migrant labour, agricultural work and odd jobs, people now have a wider range of options when it comes to choosing the work they want to do. Increasingly, the criterion by which different types of work are measured against each other is the money that can be earned by them. This is particularly clear when agriculture is compared with tea and migrant labour. It is also clear when someone exercising a generally low-esteemed vocation, such as that of a junk dealer, becomes relatively rich, and enjoys social prestige on the basis of his wealth and social connections.

The commodification of labour goes hand in hand with commodity consumption. The extension of markets for agricultural goods and labour took place at the same time that markets for mass-produced consumer goods were growing rapidly. What is in the 'bamboo food basket' of everyday consumption, and what people think should be in it, has changed rapidly in the last decades. They face the changing times 'through the bamboo food basket' of everyday consumption, and the work that fills it – and what they face there is the leveller of commodification that means both a huge number of possible choices and a heightened awareness of social inequalities.

What the vast majority of the odd jobs described here have in common is that they are done for the sake of a household and a family, that is, the basic orientation of work towards the establishment and maintenance of family and household has not changed in the countryside. The household as the basic unit of production and consumption is not only reinforced by economic practice and cultural representation, but also legally and politically. In imperial China, tax collection and land rights were always related to household units, rather than individuals. That was made possible by censuses and the registration of households. Essentially, this is still the same now. At the beginning of the 1980s, land was distributed to households under the 'household responsibility system'. The agricultural tax was collected from households until its abolition in 2003. All of this was possible because of household registrations, which determined one 'household head' (*huzhu*) – almost always a man – and all other members of the household in relationship to him, i.e. wife, parents, children of the household head. Being the most important economic and legal unit, the household, as the home of one family, is also the most important unit when it comes to the family celebrations I deal with in the next chapters. The family as a unit of belonging and of social mobility is the most internalized moral frame of reference.

But the huge social transformations of the last decades have not left the family and household unchanged. The ways in which individuals contribute with their work to the maintenance of their family have led to a broad 're-drawing' of the boundaries of the household (cf. Entwisle and Henderson 2000). With the proliferation of different occupations, labour migration, and the growth of wage labour in general, incomes are now increasingly individuated before they are contributed to the household.

Related to this, there is now more space and time for work and consumption that is not related to the family: Yang Mingxi's sons, for instance, have not come back from Guangzhou for several years. 'They are providing for themselves out there, and I look after myself here', he says. But when they get married, they will come back, and probably build new houses in Zhongba. Until they return to the fold of the family, what they do to get by, and what they aspire to, falls mainly outside the frame of the family. For many young men, the absolute loyalties and personalistic ties of the *jianghu* become the most important moral references when 'floating' (*liulang*) outside.

Work and consumption are then in all these different ways characterized by a heightened moment of choice, and with it, an increased moral ambiguity. This moral ambiguity is also a central concern for the local and national state. Governments attempt to guide the behaviour of ordinary people both in the realm of production and consumption, and to teach citizens the appropriate relations between production and consumption, between accumulation and spending, on a short- and long-term basis. I will deal in subsequent chapters with such discourses in relation to family celebrations and gambling. Here as well there are various possible moral references that can be invoked: traditional 'peasant' values, Maoist morals of hard work and frugality, and the legitimization of the desires and pleasures of private consumption of today. In the following chapters I will further explore how people in Bashan negotiate these different moral frameworks between their own local sociality and the state.

Notes

1. That is, *lichun* ('beginning of spring') and *qingming* ('clear and bright festival').
2. Notwithstanding, most people in the countryside know the most important dates of the annual cycle (all Chinese holidays, beginning with the Spring Festival) and of personal events (birthday, weddings, funerals, etc.) according to the Chinese lunar calendar. The lunar calendar is also used to choose propitious dates and for divination.
3. Such as filled dumplings (*baozi*), filled pancakes (*xian'r bing*), fried flat cakes (*shaobing*), or oily sticks (*youtiao*), accompanied by soy milk or yogurt. None of these pastries were commonly found here in the past, as there are no cereals grown in the region, and so little wheat flour was available in the past. I have never seen farmers preparing this kind of pastry themselves at home, nor drinking soy milk or yogurt. However, they sometimes buy these things in the market, and especially for their children, which testifies to the importance of the younger generation in introducing new consumer habits (cf. Jing 2000).
4. Jerome Ch'en (1992) demonstrates how in the Wuling Mountains in the first decades of the twentieth century additional income from cash crops (mainly opium and tong oil, but also tea, pig bristles and medicinal herbs) did not lead to major social transformations, because of population increase, the exploitation of small peasants by landed elites, and the military (including communist, nationalist and bandit armies in the region). Philip Huang has made a similar argument on a more general level: in his two classical works on rural China (1985; 1990) he characterizes China's agricultural economy as a situation of 'involution': 'small-peasant production at subsistence levels persists, becoming ever more elaborated with commercialisation, intensified cropping, and household industry. As this pattern of change advances, peasant production, far from giving way to large-scale production, actually comes to obstruct the development of wage labor-based production by virtue of its ability to sustain labor input at returns that are below market wages. And far from giving way to labor-saving capitalized production, it actually obstructs development in that direction by pushing change in the direction of lower-cost labor intensification and involution' (1990: 13).
5. The periodical markets in the surrounding townships in 2007 are basically the same as those mentioned in the local gazetteer of 1868 (Enshi County 1982 [1868]: 134); and hence it can be inferred that the distribution of markets in this region presented a relatively stable system of market integration. Almost all of these markets re-appeared in the 1980s, and exist until the present day.
6. Cf. Skinner and Winckler 1969, and Skinner 1985, for an account of the continuous policy cycling during the Maoist era, always oscillating between mass mobilization, based on 'normative power (persuasion, exhortation, manipulation of symbolic rewards)', and economic recovery, based on 'remunerative power (material rewards, appeals to self-interest)' – according to Skinner at least eleven times back and forth (Skinner 1985: 395ff).

7. This is probably true for much of rural China: 'The power of this ideological vision [Chinese socialism] was so strong, and the collectivist reorganization so dramatic, that our attention has been diverted from the fundamental fact of the persistence of the peasant condition of subsistence farming' (Huang 1990: 17).

8. I could not find anyone in Bashan who remembers the exact year. According to the only official source about the periodical market I could find, 'the original market days in the township [of Bashan] were on the days 1, 4, and 7 of the lunar calendar. The number of people that frequent this market usually amounts to more than 10,000; and the streets from the gates of the municipal tea market to the district hospital are crowded with people pushing and squeezing. After the introduction of the household responsibility system [in 1981/82] the schedule was changed to odd days' (Enshi City Propaganda Department et al. 1994: 152).

9. But whereas Skinner predicted in 1985 that '[t]he historical role of periodic marketing in China's social and economic development is likely to end with the present century' (1985: 413), the periodical markets of Bashan and the surrounding market towns have continued until now.

10. This is the ratio of a total population of 3,879,007 and an 'out-floating population' (*liuchu renkou*) of 592,510 (Enshi Prefecture, Bureau of Statistics 2007: 105).

11. The *Report on the Chinese Peasantry*, published by the journalists Chen Guidi and Wu Chuntao in 2004, was a national bestseller, describing the plight of impoverished peasants in Northern Anhui and the gross injustices they had to endure from local officials.

12. The scholar-official Wen Tiejun is sometimes credited with having coined the expression 'three problems of the countryside' (e.g. 2000, 2001 [1999]). Aside from him, other influential public intellectuals participating in this debate are the sociologist and journalist Cao Jinqing (whose book *China Along the Yellow River*, 2000, has been widely read), and the official-turned-researcher Li Changping (who became famous with his book *Telling the Truth to the Prime Minister*, 2001). For an overview of these debates, see Day 2008.

13. This table is based on official statistics of the township government. As can be seen, the staple crop production of the entire township went from 4203 tons of summer staple crops (wheat and potato) and 21,317 tons of winter staple crops (rice, corn, soybean) on an area of 6940 hectares in 1996 to 3227 tons of summer staple crops (wheat and potato) and 9477 tons of winter staple crops (rice, corn, soybean) on an area of 4690 hectares all together in 2006. At the same time the area planted with cash crops (tea, fruits, vegetables) increased substantially, as did the volume of cash crops produced (from 720 tons to 2795 tons for tea leaves, from 225 tons to 2899 tons for fruits, and from 8250 tons to 21,450 for vegetables).

14. Basing his findings on his fieldwork in Chuxian, Anhui province, in the 1940s, Morton Fried remarks that '[t]owns are distinguished from villages also in the institution of apprenticeship […]. In the villages one learns by imitating and observing his parents, whether they are engaged in agriculture or in subsidiary handicrafts. In the town, young males are instructed in the techniques of some handicraft or commercial specialty, which entails a social relationship between master and apprentice that has no proper counterpart in the village' (Fried 1953: 24–25). I believe that Fried's judgement reveals a lack of knowledge about the traditional crafts in the countryside. Carpentry, for example, has had a long tradition of learning by apprenticeship, which was not limited to the cities.

15. Which was about 50 Yuan a shift for a *diangong*, and about 0.25 Yuan per *jin* of green-leave tea for a *baogong*. For the bud-tea (*yacha*), where both the raw material and the

processed tea are more expensive, and processing is more labour-intensive, the wages were between 1.5 and 2 Yuan per *jin*.

16. The tea trade with foreigners has a very long tradition in China. For more than a thousand years, Han Chinese traded tea for horses with Tibetans and Mongolians along the 'Tea Horse Road' (*cha ma dao*). Later, tea and silk become major export goods to be traded with Westerners in China's sea ports (cf. Wang 2006). Whilst all kinds of tea are exported now, black tea is produced almost exclusively for export. No one in Bashan drinks this tea, known as 'red tea' (*hong cha*) in Chinese, due to the colour of the tea water. Whereas green tea is roasted, black tea is dried in the sun and fermented. People often remarked that green tea is much better, and that the black tea is not only cheap, but also dirty, because it is left outside to dry – 'sometimes you even find cigarette butts in it', I was told. At the same time some people pointed out that black tea fitted neatly into the other culinary preferences, such as beef and lamb (instead of pork), of people like Mongolians and Russians, who live in 'cold climates' (*handai*).

17. Cf. Enshi Wanbao 2007c. This article describes the ordinary routine of the *yan'erke* in Enshi before the Communist Revolution; they carried their goods on their backs between the city and the periodical peasant markets in the surrounding townships.

18. Murphy also reports similar motorbike taxis in rural Jiangxi; as in Bashan, most young men there did not see this as a long-term occupation (Murphy 2002: 199–200).

19. The bestselling novel *Xiongdi* (*Brothers*) by Yu Hua, describing the life story of two brothers, offers a grotesque satire on the morals of the reform era, in which some people got rich overnight by dealing in rubbish. The two brothers Li Guangtou and Song Gang are almost the complete opposite in every respect: Li Guangtou is ugly, bad-tempered and sly, whereas Song Gang is handsome, upright and hard-working. The first gains incredible wealth as a junk dealer, and becomes an insatiable woman-iser. The second works all his life to earn a living for himself and his wife Lin Hong. Whilst he wastes his health in drudgery, his brother Li Guangtou seduces his wife Lin Hong. When he learns about the betrayal, Song Gang kills himself; in the end Lin Hong becomes the manager of a brothel, and Li Guangtou prepares to rent a space-craft and take his brother's ashes into outer space (Yu Hua 2005; 2006).

20. The word '*liumang*' can be translated as hooligan, thug, or rogue. The etymological origin of the word is 'floating people' who have no home and no stable profession. Criminals, beggars, ghosts, and foreigners might all fall into this category.

21. *xiong* means 'evil, ferocious, inhuman' in standard Chinese. In the Enshi dialect the word is also used as meaning 'capable, tough, and tremendous.' Another word often used in similar contexts in standard Chinese would be *lihai*. The character *li* origi-nally means sharp, fierce, and dangerous; it can also mean 'evil ghost', as in *ligui*. Both words are often used to 'compliment' some extraordinary achievement or at-tribute, and both connote a degree of moral ambiguity: that which is inhuman (such as ghosts and criminals) which can give rise to awe, but also fear.

22. The opposite of the *jianghu* would be the *miaotang*, i.e. the life of 'temple' and court, the realms of the official discourses of family and government. From the perspective of the *jianghu*, the *miaotang* is seen as full of compromise, cowardice, submission, and moral corruption, whereas in the *jianghu* absolute morals and absolute loyalty reign.

23. Obviously these aspirations have to be qualified: since family planning has been introduced, it is forbidden to have many sons. In addition, long life and wealth are not unambiguously positive.

24. As to the question of whether a young couple should spend money in building a beautiful house, or invest it in business, more frequently young wives opt for the

first, whereas young husbands opt for the latter, which is surely related to the weak position of young wives coming into a new household. An example from Chinese literature is He Xiulian and her husband Sun Shao'an in the novel *An Ordinary World* by Lu Yao (2002 [1989]: 266ff).

25. One could even compare the showing of a good *ming* to something like a Chinese version of doctrines of predestination (cf. Weber 1932 [1920]). Even if someone's *ming* was predetermined, one could never have absolutely certain knowledge about it. There are many attempts to reach that certainty, most clearly illustrated by the popularity of divination and *fengshui*. But on a more basic level, one could just work hard, and do something to show someone's good 'fate'. I hasten to add that there are many obvious differences between protestant ethics and Chinese ethics, above all the lack of a transcendent god and absolute judge, and related to that the idea of a 'calling' that could be shown in one's work.

— *Chapter 4* —

CHANNELLING ALONG A CENTRING PATH

Like many others of his age, Wang Wei stopped studying at the age of sixteen after he finished middle school. Two years later, a relative helped him to find work as a waiter in Shanghai, where he stayed for the next six years doing odd jobs. He started out cleaning and serving in a restaurant, worked as an electrician, later found a job in a massage parlour, and finally in the reception of a medium-sized hotel. Shortly after he returned to Zhongba for the Spring Festival in 2006 he met Song Yan, Song Haomin's daughter, and they became a couple (*tan pengyou*). Song Yan had also left school at sixteen, and whilst she is very bright, speaks perfect standard Chinese, and enjoys reading books,[1] she has never left Bashan. By helping her parents at home, she also made it possible for her younger brother and sister to attend school for some more years. But she does not begrudge the fact that she did not have the same chances, and just like her mother, Song Yan always has a smile and a good word for those around her, and seemed to me full of unshakable optimism.

When I arrived in Zhongba in May 2006, the two had just recently begun their relationship, and Wang Wei was working occasionally for Song Yan's father. As we were so close in age – Wang Wei is just one year younger than me – we spent a lot of time together. Several times during my fieldwork, my girlfriend came to visit me from Beijing, and then the four of us regularly went down to the township to eat at the street stalls. Often we joked with each other about which couple would get married first. In the winter of 2006, it became clear that it would be Wang Wei and Song Yan. The wedding was set for a date shortly after the Spring Festival in 2007, on the 18th day of the first lunar month, which was 7 March 2007.

After the tea season had ended, the workers had gone home, and only Song Yan and her parents stayed in the tea factory, doing maintenance work, and safeguarding the equipment. During the winter, hours were spent eating, drinking, and chatting, sitting on the low wooden chairs around the table in the small side room of the tea factory. Often the conversation would turn to the many family celebrations and banquets that one had to attend. And of course, the most important issue that winter was the preparation of the wedding of Song Yan and Wang Wei.

One of the first expressions that I learned in the dialect of the Enshi region is *qu qijiu* (P. *qu chijiu*), literally to 'to go and eat wine', but meaning to attend a celebratory banquet for an important event. It means to visit someone else's family celebration: a wedding, a funeral, a house-warming party, the birth of a child, a birthday (36, 60, 70, 80 years and every decade after that can be celebrated), or a celebration for a child who has passed the entry examinations to the university or the army. The most important life-cycle events of these are weddings and funerals, and they are called 'red and white events' (*hongbai xishi*), for the symbolic colours of happiness (red) and mourning (white). In the countryside, such celebrations are generally held at the house of the host family, whereas in the market town of Bashan or in the city of Enshi, people often invite the guests to a restaurant. 'To go and eat wine' implies that one would go to the celebration, give a money-gift, and participate in a lavish meal. The money-gift is called '*renqing*' locally, which means both the human feeling that the present is supposed to express, and the present itself. The family which is 'hosting the wine' (*zheng jiu*) has to prepare well in advance. Generally the day of a celebration is chosen with the help of a diviner who calculates the most propitious date and hour, according to the 'eight characters' (*ba zi*) of the year, month, day and hour of the birth of the main participants. Before the celebration, the host will invite neighbours and friends to 'help' (*bang mang*) in hosting the event. A list with the names of the people that are helping and their tasks is produced and hung next to the door of the house.

All these actions necessitate proper behaviour, etiquette and formality. The established practices and etiquette (*liyi* or *lijie*) at such occasions are particular forms of what is called *li* in Chinese, which can be translated as 'ritual'. Just as it is difficult to define ritual, *li* eludes an easy definition. Hence in the first part of this chapter, I want to briefly discuss *li* in relation to 'ritual', and give a theoretical outline of *li* as moral discourse and practice of 'centring'. Then I describe the basic elements of family celebrations in Bashan township; that is, what it means to 'hold a wine' (*zheng jiu*) and to attend a banquet, or 'eat wine' (*chi jiu*). The last part will feature the example of the wedding of Wang Wei and Song Yan, in which the theoretical outline of *li* can be exemplified. The next chapter will then place family celebrations in the historical context of the post-revolutionary Chinese countryside; it deals with the blending of vernacular and official perspectives in such rituals.

Li and Ritual

A stone's throw away from the village administration building and Song Haomin's tea factory, in the Yang family hamlet, I often had long conversations with Yang Yuanbing. A few days after the house inauguration of Yang Minghu, where he was the main coordinator, and I had helped out, I was sitting again with him, drinking tea and smoking cigarettes. Yuanbing could tell stories for hours, and this night he was recounting his experiences in the cities; he then delved into the history of the Yang family, and the customary rules of proper behaviour which had been so much more important in the past. He concluded on a pensive note, saying, 'this one character of ritual propriety (*li*) has been central in Chinese culture throughout its history.' I asked about *li* now, what did it mean to the people now? 'Obviously much has been lost', he answered, 'just like we don't have the office of the lineage elder (*zuzhang*) anymore here. But some things have also improved: now the younger generation can speak out if the older generation does something or says something that is wrong. And some people do still understand about the proper ways of *li*, some people who are educated and who have culture (*you wenhua*).'

The etymological root *li* means to perform a ritual or a sacrifice. Based on the proper ways of how to perform rituals, and by extension, how to behave properly, *li* is a central term of Confucian ethics. It appears prominently in the 'four classics'[2] which were used to teach reading and writing, and there are several other classics entirely devoted to the discussion of *li*: the *Rites of Zhou* (*zhouli*), the *Book of Etiquette and Ceremonials* (*yili*) and the *Book of Rites* (*liji*). There are many other highly influential texts emphasizing the importance of *li* for the maintenance of the social order, such as the *Book of Xunzi* (*xunzi*) and Zhu Xi's *Family Rituals* (*jiali*).[3] *Li* has been one central concept in the interaction between the emperor, the mandarin elite and ordinary people; and the rituals and moralities of *li* were at the core of Chinese forms of governance.

In contemporary Chinese *li* can mean many things. It is part of the expressions for 'politeness' (*limao*), 'etiquette' (*liyi*), 'ceremony' (*lijie*), 'custom' (*lisu*), 'worship' (*libai*), 'gift' (*liwu*), 'wedding' (*hunli*), and 'funeral' (*zangli*). In the very popular expression that 'courtesy demands reciprocity' (*lishang wanglai*), *li* also means propriety in reciprocal relationships.

It follows that *li* should be highly relevant to any account of Chinese ritual, of hierarchical relationships in China, and of popular practices such as banquets and gift-giving. But relatively few anthropologists of China have taken up the challenge of integrating the long history of *li* in Chinese philosophy and ethics. To give one example: Yan Yunxiang's monograph *The Flow of Gifts* (1996) is probably the most authoritative study of gift-giving in rural China in the reform era. Yet Yan does not relate practices of gift-giving and their historical change much to the written discourses on *li*. In a review essay, Wang Mingming recommends the ethnography for its detail and wealth of empirical data, and proceeds to criticize two main points: the first is that Yan Yunxiang is distorting the historical changes of gift-giving practices by contrasting Maoist and post-reform hierarchies with an idealized past. Secondly, Wang proposes to research further the long history of *li*, in particular its relationship with the tributary system of the empire (Wang Mingming 2003: 124).[4] Whilst Yan sometimes uses Chinese concepts of reciprocity, like *bao*, and of 'human ethics', like *renqing*, he does not go further and explore the more general and abstract concept of proper social behaviour which is *li*, and the vast Chinese literature on the topic.

Besides the academic compartmentalization that would assign the task of researching this literature to history and sinology, there are several other reasons why it is difficult to conceptualize *li* in anthropology. *Li* presents all the problems of an 'indigenous' notion, not mature enough to become a category within Western social science.[5] Being such a central concept in Chinese thought, it is extraordinarily difficult to translate, as it is linked to almost all other important concepts in classical Chinese thinking.[6] Most crucially, distinctions commonly made in Western philosophy and sociology, such as those between meaning and performance, between cosmology and practicality, and between bodily participation and reasoned reflection, are either completely absent or at least drawn in very different ways in Chinese theories of *li*.[7]

Such oppositions are at the core of many sociological theories of ritual. Comparing Confucian ritual theory and Clifford Geertz's notion of the theatre-state in Bali (Geertz 1980), James Laidlaw, for instance, argues that in the end it is precisely these opposites that characterize Geertz's outline, and which make it unfit to describe Chinese state ritual (Laidlaw 1999). While Geertz had set out to 'transcend the opposition between the form and substance of power – or the symbolic and the real – his image of the state as theatre actually reproduces that opposition' (Laidlaw 1999: 404). The persuasiveness of Geertz's metaphor of state ritual as theatre still depends on the distinction between on-stage representation and off-stage ordinariness. If rituals take place away from public view, without popular participation, or if their entire preparation and organization is ritualized as well, then it no longer makes sense to speak of ritual as theatre. Yet this is precisely what happens in state and court ritual in imperial China. Laidlaw further contrasts Confucian ritual theory with functionalist theories of ritual, dealing with Radcliffe-Brown's short invocations of Confucian ritual (Radcliffe-Brown 1952: 145–146, 157–160, ff.). Radcliffe-Brown's point was that ritual does not have the magical effects that participants might claim, but other psychological and social effects, which work towards the reproduction of the social order. In this sense ritual participants cannot step away and reflect upon their ritual. But this is precisely what happens with Confucian ritual theorists: unlike the sociologists who stand outside the social web and elucidate its mystifications, scholar-officials were primarily concerned with their own morality when writing about ritual. 'Scholar-officials who took up and elaborated theories such as Xunzi's were not commenting on the benign effects that certain illusory and superstitious notions had on other people. They were reflecting on activities central to their own way of life' (Laidlaw 1999: 414).

In this way, Confucian ritual theory always united committed participation in ritual and self-conscious rational reflection. Contrasting Chinese ritual theory with functionalist theory (personified in Radcliffe-Brown) and symbolic theory (personified in Geertz), Laidlaw concludes that Confucian ritual theory simply did not draw the differences that are at the heart of these sociological theories.

Writing on court ritual in imperial China, James Hevia (1995) and Angela Zito (1984, 1993, 1997) have put forward elaborate interpretations of how text production and negotiated performance are articulated in *li*. In *Cherishing Men from Afar*, Hevia gives a description and analysis of the British embassy under George Macartney, who arrived at the court of the Qianlong Emperor in 1793 (Hevia 1995). Hevia describes both Qing and British principles of organization as part of two 'imperial formations' and discourses of power, and contrasts this with earlier interpretations of the famous encounter, depicting it as cross-cultural misunderstanding or as one of the first contacts of the 'traditional' and 'closed system' of the Chinese empire with Western imperialism and modernity.

On the Chinese side, Hevia provides a sophisticated interpretation of Chinese ritual, or *li*. Similarly to Laidlaw, Hevia attempts to avoid the pitfalls of both symbolic and functional interpretations of ritual. According to Hevia, former scholarly treatments of Chinese imperial ritual were either symbolic (taking 'elements of the rite as either culture-specific or archetypal signs that communicate the meaning of the rite to the minds of the participants') or functional (taking 'ritual as an instrument by which social and political structures are made legitimate') (Hevia 1995: 17). In both, rituals refer 'to things outside themselves'; 'ritual action cultivates or inculcates shared beliefs (read culture) in order to produce group solidarity, while providing autocratic rulers an instrument for maintaining social control' (ibid.: 19). Quoting from Catherine Bell (1992) on general theories of ritual, and Angela Zito on Chinese *li* (1989), Hevia emphasizes that ritual activities themselves contain the production and negotiation of power

判断的

relations. These power relations are not unidirectional, and they are sub-ject to continuous practices of domination, resistance, and negotiation.

With respect to Qing imperial ritual, this is the all the more compelling if one takes note of the fact that '*li* is dispersed and diffused across various do-mains of practices and through various textual traditions. [...] In the reign of the Qianlong emperor, *li* was deeply embedded in the Qing imperium's world-ordering processes, in Confucian, Daoist, and Buddhist philosophy and practices, in household rules and management, and in the worship of ancestors, gods, and spirits, as well as in diplomacy' (Hevia 1995: 22).

Rites that are called *li* are generally concerned with a macrocosm–microcosm relationship; through metaphorical association, including part–whole relationships (synecdoche) and structural similarity (ho-mology), a relationship is established between the emperor performing a particular auspicious rite and, for example, a cosmic process.[8] Yet any metaphor can be turned into a metonymy, and so the metaphorical pre-sentation of hierarchical and cosmological order never reaches complete interpretational closure; it is continually re-worked, commented upon, ne-gotiated and manipulated.[9]

Both Hevia and Zito point out the central importance of the term 'cen-tring' (*zhong*) in the performance and discourse of *li*. Hevia describes the dealings of the Qing imperial formation with the Macartney embassy as a process of 'channelling along a centring path':

> Actions of all participants are continually reviewed for signs of excess and de-ficiency that would move the action toward extremes. We might say, therefore, that human actions are channelled between extremes, and that this channel-ling embodies the centering process. As it does so, channelling organizes hi-erarchical relationships that are considered to be the proper order of the world at the moment of ritual constitution. To put it another way, the centering pro-cess allows the differentiation and inclusion of the powers of others into the emperor's rulership as desirable superior/inferior relations. (Hevia 1995: 123)

Hevia calls this a 'patterning discourse' (1995: 122):

> The engagement between cosmic pattern and human classification continu-ally channels action away from extremes and toward a contingent spatial cen-ter that temporarily constitutes a cosmo-moral order made up of the Cosmos, earth, and humanity. This process is discernible in a variety of textual sources under the rubric 'centering,' *fengjian shi zhong*, negotiating a mean between overabundance and scarcity. (1995: 123)

Another expression often used in the memorials issued by the emperor and the mandarins is 'to square with proper circumspection' (*fangwei tuoshan*) (Hevia 1995: 153, 186); it also refers to the establishment of a hierarchical order, in which the four sides of a square are properly separated and bound together around the centre. In similar ways the levels of upper/lower (*shang/xia*) and inner/outer (*nei/wai*) are separated, and moral and cosmological attributes given to the respective positions (Zito 1993: 332).

The 'channelling' that Hevia writes about refers to the processes of preparation and negotiation that precede the main act (of imperial audience, in his case): this is then the only moment where a hierarchical order is completely spatialized. Before and afterwards there are long processes of negotiation, including strategies of domination and resistance. The same can be said about a Chinese banquet, or at least about the moment when an inferior toasts a superior in such a banquet (see Pharoah 2005, chapter 4, for instance). I will try to conceptualize some of the main elements of weddings and funerals below.

We could equally contrast functional and symbolic descriptions of family rituals with the theoretical perspective proposed by Hevia: a wedding, for instance, can be described in terms of the maintenance of the social order, and thus in particular the 'duties' attached to 'social roles' in a marriage, or the 'legal functions' of the marriage as a contract between two lineages (e.g. Freedman 1970, 1979 [1967]). Funerals have been described in relation to the cosmologies and symbolic structures signified in them (e.g. in a masterly way for food prestations and fertility, Thompson 1988). Yet both functionalist and symbolist descriptions always refer ritual action to something outside of it (reifications mostly, such as 'society' or 'cosmology'); related to this 'outside', *li* itself is secondary. Like Hevia, I want to describe *li* first of all in its own terms. Obviously what happens in rituals is related practically and metaphorically to social and cosmological processes. Yet the relationship is never unidirectional and unambiguous.

It is not only the general theoretical outlook, including the importance of 'centring' and the formulation of 'channelling along a centring path', that I take from Hevia and Zito. There is another element that both stress and which can be highly insightful for dealing with ritual activity in general and family celebrations in particular. This is the central role that the writing of texts played in *li*. Angela Zito points out in her work how *li* is both practical performance and an object of textual production par excellence (Zito 1984, 1993 and 1997).

She analyses the court rituals that were performed by the emperor as a 'text/performance'. Writing and editing were invariably necessary for the enacting of *li*. They not only provided guidance for ceremonial performance, but in 'ritual texts, the forms of the rites were iconically embodied and prefigured' (Zito 1993: 330). Appropriate writing produced texts that are called *wen*, which she translates as 'cosmic text-pattern' (ibid.: 331).

The emperor was not only the filial son of heaven, properly performing imperial rituals, but also the apex of the state apparatus of literati, and hence the perfect sage. As 'son of heaven' he embodies both perfect filial piety (*xiao*), and perfect textual production, i.e. *wen*, in the written edicts that he issues continuously and the editing projects that he leads. Below the emperor, the literati similarly legitimated their position and ruling by issuing moral texts. The 'ritualization' process of *li* necessitated both moral commentaries and their spatial embodiment in correct performance.

In moral prescriptions and Confucian learning, in architecture, and in the embodied performances of rituals, the ritualization process assumed analogous forms from the Grand Sacrifices of the emperor down to the family rituals at the village level. In this process the reproduction of texts by ritual specialists and 'peasant intellectuals' (such as Buddhist and Daoist priests, geomancers, diviners, and lineage elders) played a crucial role (see Hayes 1985). Zito suggests viewing this as a 'modelling of processes of modelling', which does not necessarily require a congruence of local symbolic detail (Zito 1993: 333). Several studies by anthropologists and historians have emphasized the eminent political nature of the local emulation of imperial ritual: for example Joseph McDermott writing on the community pact ritual of the Ming dynasty (1999) and David Faure on the popularization of lineage rituals (1999).

Yet what are we to make of the apparent contradiction that in the countryside most people attending the celebrations are not able to offer long and sophisticated interpretations of the meanings of rituals and the writings used in them? Regarding Chinese funerary rites, James Watson has famously argued that the beliefs of ordinary people and the meanings they attribute to rituals do not matter; he suggests that what matters is the correct performance only. He went on to argue that it is this correct performance, which he calls 'orthopraxy', that holds Chinese society together (Watson 1985, 1988). In the same edition on Chinese death ritual, historian Evelyn Rawski emphasizes, in opposition to Watson, the crucial role of texts and the attempts by the state to link orthodoxy and 'orthopraxy', and concludes that 'belief and performance are very hard to separate' (Rawski 1988: 22).

A historian like Rawski, Zito takes up Watson's insight that 'belief' and 'performance' are somehow separated; yet for her the question to be asked is not '*whether* or not belief and performance were linked but rather *how* they were linked, in what contexts and to what ends' (Zito 1993: 327). For Zito 'the nonseparation, the conflation, and the intimate interpenetration of body and mind, meaning and action, were precisely an effect of *li*. Any mode of analysis that automatically "ritualizes" *li* by separating these aspects from one another does it great disservice' (ibid.: 328).

The fact that many ordinary people are more focused on the right practice than the correct meaning is rather a characteristic of the dominating
function of literacy:

> Watson notices correctly that the elite tended not to concern themselves with
> the 'meanings' and 'beliefs' of their inferiors. We could go further and note a
> tendency in philosophical texts to repress the practical bodiliness of rituals. In
> this mutual masking of the whole (the body disappears in one place, meaning
> is evacuated in another) lies the area of negotiation between rulers and ruled
> that constituted the hegemony that encompassed them both. (Zito 1993: 332)

It might seem far-fetched to connect these texts on imperial court ritual
and their textual commentaries to the family celebrations in Bashan now.
Yet I believe it is possible to show that there are remarkable analogies.
Whilst it is beyond the scope of this book to go any deeper into the Chinese literature on *li*, I want to dwell on the social importance of textual
production for ritual action. In the family celebrations that I will describe
below, certain forms of writing are imperative: paper scrolls with appropriate inscriptions, a list of helpers, and a book in which visitors and the
presents and money they have given are listed.

Besides these texts that are produced for family celebrations and during rituals themselves, there are countless other texts and discourses commenting on and re-defining propriety in such celebrations (written and
printed ones, but also ritual speech, doctrinal statements, and everyday
conversation). The ability to comment upon *li* and to guide others towards
its perfection is invariably linked with a high level of 'culture' (*wenhua*)
and 'civilization' (*wenming*), i.e. it is equivalent to being literate.

If in the past the distinction between the performance of rituals by il-
literates and the textual commentaries on *li* by literati was a form of ideological domination, it seems to me that in contemporary China as in the
past, local ritual practice can only be understood if it is related to the ongoing textual and discursive commentary on it. In the next chapter I will
deal with contemporary commentaries on family celebrations in the countryside, which include discourses of modernity, progress and 'population
quality' (*suzhi*), elements of Maoist ethics, and romanticizing folklore. All
these also appear in everyday discussions about the propriety of family
celebrations and the prestige of the participants.

Amongst the commentaries being made about propriety in family celebrations, the issue which is most widely debated nowadays in Bashan
is the commercialization of these celebrations. On the one hand, the
proper use and spending of money (in particular for inviting guests and
when giving it as a gift) are inseparable from *li*; on the other, the recent
surge of money spent at such celebrations is criticized by many people.

Disproportionate gift giving and lavish family celebrations are also the object of governmental campaigns, but at the same time they are necessary to maintain social relationships, specifically for businesspeople and officials. In the next chapter, I will focus on such potential contradictions, and specifically the tension between the ways in which popular rituals are evaluated in official state discourse and in the local face-to-face community. In the rest of this chapter, I will present some of the basic elements of holding a family celebration, and then describe the process of 'channelling along a centring path' in one wedding.

The reason that I am dealing with all these different family celebrations together is that primarily in the Enshi region they all fall under the category of 'hosting wine' (E. *zheng jiu*) and 'eating wine' (E. *qijiu*). The category implies that a banquet is to be held, and a banquet necessarily includes wine: 'without wine there is no proper ceremony and rite' (*wu jiu bu zheng liyi*). All these family celebrations share other characteristics in the way that they are organized, which I will describe first.

Family Celebrations

Once the date for a celebration has been set with the help of a diviner, the host will inform relatives, neighbours, and friends of this date. It is common to send invitation cards, and if such a card is received, it is imperative to go; non-attendance would then be seen a grave sign of disrespect. In the countryside, only outsiders are explicitly invited, with an invitation card or just with a phone call; the immediate neighbours will learn about it quickly through the village gossip.

The host has to start preparing the celebration well in advance. Besides inviting the guests, he also has to ask neighbours and friends to come and help with different tasks during the celebrations. In the past invitations to help were written in calligraphy on red paper and sent to people; the invitations also served as proof that someone had gone to help out and thus could expect that the host would come and help at his house in the future. Nowadays the host just informally asks the helpers or gives them a phone call; yet when inviting helpers, many factors have to be taken into account. Helping at a family celebration necessitates a good relationship, and it is always reciprocal. Generally no one is paid for helping at such a celebration, but there are exceptions: the main cook, who is always a man (whilst his helpers are mostly female neighbours, and not paid); musicians and singers (mainly at funerals); and the ritual specialists (in particular the Daoist priests at funerals). But all the helpers receive one pack of cigarettes for every day they come to the house, and they have to be served with the same meals as the guests. At weddings, they receive a symbolic 'red envelope' with some money (often eight Yuan, eight being a lucky number) and a bag with a bar of soap, a towel, sunflower seeds, and sweets. In Table 4.1 I have reproduced a list of the basic tasks carried out at a family celebration:

Table 4.1 List of tasks at a family celebration

Chinese	Pinyin	Task
支客	zhike	Coordinator
迎宾	yingbin	Receiving guests
礼桌	lizhuo	Receiving money and presents, and listing them in the book of gifts (liben)
菜厨	caichu	Cooking dishes
饭厨	fanchu	Cooking rice
执盘	zhipan	Carrying dishes to the tables
调席	tiaoxi	Arranging the tables
奉烟	fengyan	Offering cigarettes to guests
奉酒	fengjiu	Offering liquor to guests
洗菜	xicai	Washing vegetables
安宿	ansu	Arranging places to sleep for overnight guests
生火	shenghuo	Responsibility for fireplaces and hearths
烧茶	shaocha	Preparing tea
支杂	zhiza	Shopping and other tasks

This is a basic list of indispensable tasks for any celebration. It can be extended for particular ritual necessities (e.g. Daoist priests at funerals, or carrying presents to and from the house of the bride at weddings) and according to the organization of the host and the main coordinator (sometimes tasks such as 'setting of firecrackers', *mingpao*, or even 'entertainment of guests', *yule*, are added). The distribution of tasks is clearly related to a person's position and status in the community: the main coordinator is always a respected senior man; the one receiving the guests is commonly someone who knows how to deal with people of all walks of life (a 'social person', *shehui shang de ren*); most of the helpers in the kitchen are women from neighbouring houses; carrying the dishes and arranging the tables is a task for younger male neighbours, often friends of the host; washing the dishes and doing the shopping are minor tasks for people that do not enjoy much respect. The lowest task is clearly taking care of the fireplaces (*shenghuo*). It is assumed invariably by an elder man, and often someone that is not held in very high regard.

As a rule, a list with these tasks and the people assuming them is written down on red paper and stuck on the wall next to the main door. Next to the tasks, the occasion of the celebration, the name of the host family, the branch name of the lineage (*tang*), and the date are written down. On all the door-frames of the house, but most importantly the main door-frame, written paper scrolls with inscriptions (*duilian*) are pasted. The writing of the list of tasks and of the paper scrolls is often done by the same man who writes the red books of presents (*liben*). According to his skills, he alludes more or less poetically to the occasion of the celebration; in the most elaborate versions poems are added to the list of tasks.

Another very important man is the cook. Unlike the other helpers, he has to be paid for his services.[10] Together with the host, he will buy the food for the banquets. Often the host orders the cook to prepare a certain kind of banquet of particular dishes, and then pays him[11] a general price according to the number of tables. Mostly the drinks (soda, beer, and Chinese liquor), and the cigarettes, are bought by the host himself.

All the helpers arrive the day before the main celebration to prepare the house for the celebration. Tables, chairs, and kitchen utensils are borrowed from neighbours, and brought to the host's house. In the evening the closest relatives, in particular the relatives of the wife and mother of the host, arrive. All the other guests arrive on the following day for lunch (or dinner at funerals). Guests are often counted by the number of tables. Nowadays round tables with ten chairs each are used; until the 1980s, square tables with eight chairs were common. The smallest number of guests I have seen were five tables, the biggest number fifty-eight tables: the number of guests is an obvious indication of the network of relationships (*guanxi*) of a person and a family.

Upon the arrival of a guest, he or she is greeted as a 'rare guest' (*xike*), offered a cigarette and a cup of tea, and shown a seat. Sitting around the fireplaces, people wait until a place at a table is free. Once all the people have finished eating, and leave their table, other people rush over to the seats. It is considered extremely impolite if the helpers start cleaning up the left-over dishes while someone is still eating.

Either before or after the meal, the guest will present a money-gift, which is listed in the book of presents; after the amount is listed, the men who keep account of the presents offer a pack of cigarettes[12] (and sometimes a pack of sunflower seeds and candies) in return to the guest. Until the 1980s people were more inclined to give presents in kind, but now it is only the closest relatives who add liquor, firecrackers, or foodstuff to their money-presents. People think very hard about the proper amounts of money to be given, and later the amounts of money given becomes a topic for endless conversation. There are occasions where certain presents in kind are necessary from certain relatives: at the birth of a baby the mother's parents give food and clothes for the baby; at a wedding close relatives of the family of the bride give blankets and other articles of daily use that will form part of the dowry; and at a funeral daughters and sons-in-law of the deceased are supposed to offer one pig and one goat (E. *zhu yang ji*).

The preparation of a family celebration therefore includes many actions that have to be well considered and calculated. For the host these questions are: whom to invite, which people to ask for help, how to distribute the tasks of the helpers, and what kind of dishes,[13] alcohol[14] and cigarettes[15] to offer the guests. For the guests the main question is what presents and how much money they should give. Both sides will aim at an appropriate social expression of their relative social standing, and of the relationships to each other, an expression which should sit at a mid-point between excess and deficiency.

Similar to the imperial ritual described by Hevia and Zito, this centring movement in a proper social expression also includes the reproduction of a hierarchical spatial and moral order. To recapitulate, in the commentaries on imperial ritual, one important aim was to 'reach a mean between overabundance and scarcity' (*fengjian shi zhong*) and to 'square with proper circumspection' (*fangwei tuoshan*) (Hevia 1995: 153, 186). In such expressions, 'centring' also refers to the spatialization of a hierarchical order, by fixing the four sides of a square, and levels of upper/lower (*shang/xia*) and inner/outer (*nei/wai*). In the family celebrations in Bashan, such a centring activity takes place in the main room of the host's house.

The most important ritual activities of a family celebration take place in this room, in particular at weddings and funerals. As mentioned in the chapter on house construction, every house has one main room, the central axis of which is adjusted to the rules of *fengshui*. At the back wall of the main room, facing the door, used to be the 'house altar' (E. *jia xian*), with the characters for 'heaven, earth, emperor, ancestors, and teachers' in the centre. Representing the order of the cosmos and the correct behaviour towards rulers, ancestors, and teachers, the central scroll was the materialization of the core principles of *li*.[16]

Nowadays the central scroll and the ancestral shrine are usually replaced by a poster of Chairman Mao. Even though only very few households have a proper 'house altar', most still have a simple wooden shelf beneath the Mao poster, on which worship utensils such as candles and incense sticks are stored. And even though only very few old people still regularly worship ancestors or deities at this place, the main room and the central axis from the wooden shelf towards the main doors is still of crucial importance in family celebrations (see photographs 4.1 and 4.2).

At most ritual occasions, guests are hosted in the main room. A great deal of attention is paid to the appropriate seating order at such occasions:

Photograph 4.1 A traditional house altar with the scroll 'heaven, earth, emperor, ancestors, and teachers'

Photograph 4.2 The meal for the 'high relatives' (*gao qin*)

the guest of the highest rank sits next to the ancestral shrine, the second-rank guest on his left, and then the others alternating on both sides down towards the least important guest, who is placed closest to the doors (see figure 4.1). In this way, the seating order mirrors the centring of the house itself, which I have described in chapter 2.

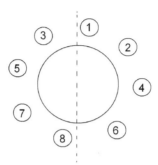

Figure 4.1 Seating order at a formal banquet

At all celebrations except funerals, the table at which two helpers receive money-gifts and write the list of presents is placed just below the place of the house altar (or the picture of Mao). At funerals, this room is made into a 'hall of filial piety' (*xiaotang*), and during the celebrations before the burial, the coffin is placed here exactly along the central axis. The house altar is covered with white cloths, and a square table is put in front of the coffin on the side of the main door. On this table, gifts and sacrifices are placed next to a picture of the deceased, to which the descendants kow-tow; this is where the hired musicians play, and the Daoist priests perform their chants and venerations. The most fundamental act of a wedding is the moment when the groom receives his bride at the door; both enter the main room and bow together in front of the house altar. This bowing, just like the kow-tows in front of the coffin at the funerals, is the main ritual event in a wedding; all the appropriate guidance of conduct before was preparing for this main act of 'centring'. At this moment the symbolic hierarchy in which bride and groom are placing themselves is completely spatialized. Then they go into their newly refurbished sleeping room, which is preferably the left side-room. Later, the relatives of the bride are hosted in the main room, properly seated as schematized in figure 4.1 above.

The Wedding

Aside from funerals, weddings are the most important ritual events in the life-cycle of people in Bashan. They present a wealth of ritual detail,

explicit rules and etiquette and have been described and analysed frequently (for instance in Freedman 1970, 1979 [1967], or Wu 2003: 244–246ff.,
for the region of Enshi). In most of the weddings that I saw in Bashan, I
participated only as a guest and observer. At two weddings of neighbours
in Zhongba I was invited as one of the helpers, and it was during these
celebrations that I learned the most about the ritual process in weddings.
One of them was the wedding of Wang Wei and Song Yan, which I will
describe here.

In autumn 2006, both Wang Wei and Song Yan were still denying that
they planned to marry; but soon after, I learned that their families had
agreed to call Tian Daliang, a distant maternal uncle (*jiujiu*, MFBS) of Wang
Wei, as a matchmaker. Even though most young couples get to know each
other on their own now, a matchmaker is still needed to mediate between
the two families and to help in the preparation of the wedding.

In the past, all the different stages leading up to a wedding were mediated by the matchmaker. Weddings were fundamentally a relationship
between two patrilineages, and a go-between was necessary in order to
avoid direct confrontations in the negotiations. After the first contact between the two families, and a period of getting to know each other (*ren-
shi*), the groom would come over to the house of the bride and have dinner
with her family. Later a date would be set for a betrothal party, which is
called 'inserting incense' (*cha xiang*) in Enshi. On this occasion the groom
and his family visit the house of the bride; he then has to worship her
ancestors, place incense sticks at her house altar, and kow-tow in front of
her ancestors. The groom also has to offer various presents to the family
of the bride, including clothes, red envelopes with money, incense and
paper-money, and food (in particular pork, and usually an entire pig). The
betrothal party establishes a contractual relationship between the two
families, and it is agreed that the couple will get married later. If one party
pulls out before the wedding for any reason, a return of the presents can
be demanded. After this agreement, the groom has to offer gifts (such as
food, liquor and money) to the parents of the bride on various holidays
and in particular during the Spring Festival. Throughout the marriage
process, the relatives of the bride are seen as ceremonially superior, and
it is emphasized that the groom's side (*nanfang*) has to obey and satisfy all
the demands of the bride's side (*nüfang*). A local saying expresses it in the
following way: 'Hold your head high when you marry off your daughter,
bow your head down when you receive a daughter-in-law' (*tai tou jia nü, di
tou jie xifu*). Based on her fieldwork in rural Taiwan, Emily Martin Ahern
has argued that wife-givers are accorded a ritually superior position to
wife-takers, basically because they have accumulated a debt which cannot

be repaid, and hence have to assume a heavy obligation towards those whose daughter they have taken (Ahern 1974).

Nowadays these rules have lost much of their ineluctability. The young couple will usually agree first between themselves, and the betrothal (still called 'inserting the incense') is in fact the occasion where they formally notify the parents that they will get married. Yet it is still compulsory for the groom to offer presents to the family of the bride, and the relatives of the bride have to be treated with the utmost respect. Wang Wei and Song Yan did not hold any formal betrothal party, but during autumn and winter 2006, Wang Wei helped Song Yan's father a great deal in their tea factory. He bought a new TV set for Song Yan's family and just before the Spring Festival, he gave the family a live pig. He also had to give red envelopes and money-presents to Song Yan's father, which amounted to several thousand Yuan. At the same time, he was refurbishing the kitchen and sleeping room that they would use in his house.

Even though Wang Wei sometimes emphasized to me the burden of the presents, and showed some unwillingness at helping out in Song Hao-min's tea factory (which he nevertheless did when they needed him), all together the exchanges between his and Song Yan's family seemed to proceed rather harmoniously. Yet piecemeal negotiations were undoubtedly taking place, pushed in particular by Wang Wei's mother (who is the head of her household, as Wang Wei's father married into the house as a 'son-in-law crossing the doors', *shangmen nüxu*, i.e. it was an uxorilocal marriage) and Song Haomin. Sometimes remarks and asides betrayed the positions and advances made. One occasion, in particular, was the wedding of a friend of Wang Wei's around the same time. Here the demands of the bride's side for the dowry were ridiculously high, driven not so much by her parents, but by the bride herself, who demanded all the luxury appliances of an urban household. If most members of the Wang and Song families agreed that her demands were exaggerated, and the ensuing conflict between the families deplorable, citing the case could serve different ends: pointing out what was excessive (as Wang Wei did explicitly several times), or emphasizing one's own humility (as Song Haomin conveyed implicitly, whilst never drawing an obvious comparison between his daughter and the other bride). What was clearly the goal of all the negotiations and comments was to reach a centre point between excess and deficiency, to the advantage and satisfaction of both sides.

With the help and mediation of Tian Daliang, both families agreed to set the date for the wedding on 8 March 2007. According to tradition, a propitious wedding date had to be chosen, which is to be adjusted to the 'eight characters' (*bazi*) of bride and groom. They quickly consulted the peasant almanac, but did not consider the 'eight characters' of bride and groom too seriously,[17] and instead chose a national holiday for the date of the wedding: 8 March is International Women's Day and a holiday in China. Such national holidays (in particular the national holiday of the People's Republic, 1 October) have become quite popular as dates for weddings.

As agreed before, I arrived on the morning of 7 March at the house of Wang Wei's family. Most helpers were there already busy preparing tables, food, and the paper scrolls. Whilst at the house of the groom this is the day of preparation, at the house of the bride this is the main day of celebration. In the morning, the groom goes together with the matchmaker and some of his close relatives or friends to the house of the bride, and brings presents. This is called 'to go li' (*guoli*). Being a close friend of Wang Wei, I went with him. The presents we were carrying included one huge canister of liquor, clothes for the parents of the bride, the dress which the bride would wear the next day, and red envelopes with money-presents for the helpers at the house of the bride. The liquor is used to host the guests and family of the bride, but a little bit of liquor has to remain and be brought back the same day.

At Song Yan's family home there were already many guests when we arrived. Wang Wei presented his gifts, and the red envelopes (containing 4 Yuan each) were distributed to the helpers. Another ten red envelopes were left for the girlfriends of Song Yan, who would accompany her that night. This is called 'ten sisters accompanying the bride' (*pei shi zimei*); sisters, cousins and girlfriends of the bride spend the night singing together with the bride. In recent times this custom has become less common, not least because so many young people are working in the cities, and accordingly it is difficult to find 'ten sisters' to sing together with the bride. If they are brought together, however, they will sing popular songs and karaoke, instead of the older songs of the region or the songs that describe the lives of women in marriage, that have been sung in earlier times.

The gifts that Wang Wei had presented were distributed by Song Shunze, who was the main coordinator of the helpers at Song Yan's house that day. Song Shunze then put incense sticks into radish slices and placed them on the table of the house altar, which is, in the case of Song Yan's family, just a table, with a poster of Mao Zedong above it, and not the traditional inscription. Then he poured three glasses of liquor under the table, and burned paper money, all to worship the ancestors of the house; this is called 'inviting the ancestors' (*qing zuxian*). We had a sumptuous dinner, and then went back to Wang Wei's house. There people continued sitting around, some gambling, until the evening.

In the evening all the helpers who were to go to the bride's house the following day to collect the dowry of the bride had already arrived; this is normally a group of young men, often friends of the groom. This group of helpers who 'go over to the [new] relatives' (*qu qin*) also has to be organized by the groom's family. In Wang Wei's case there were twelve helpers, on one truck, one three-wheeler motorbike for the group of helpers and the dowry, and one car to drive the bride back. I was part of this group of helpers, and each of us that evening received a red envelope containing 4 Yuan, a towel, a bar of soap, a pack of sunflower seeds and sweets, and a pack of cigarettes.

The following morning, I went down to Wang Wei's house at about 8 A.M., as his mother had told us the previous night to come at that hour. When I arrived most of the other helpers were already sitting around and waiting, while Wang Wei's parents, in particular his mother, organized the gifts that we had to bring with us. These included quite a lot of red envelopes for all the helpers at the house of the bride, cigarettes, and sunflower seeds. All the helpers and relatives who were there had a simple breakfast of sweet sticky rice (*mijiu*), and soon after that we got ready to go over to the bride's house.

By now the drivers of the car and the truck that were to go to the house of Song Haomin had arrived, and we set off. Besides the twelve men who would help carry the furniture and presents, Wang Wei's sister Wang Xin and their cousin Tian Dan went with us; they went to accompany Song Yan to the house of the groom. Wang Wei himself had to stay at his own house; according to the custom he had to wait for the bride.

When we arrived at the house of Song Haomin, we sat around for quite a while, and finally ate another meal. At the same time many guests were arriving. Song Yan was sitting in the back room, with the girls and younger relatives. Song Shunze, the main coordinator, repeated the same worship as the day before; he burned paper money, poured three glasses of liquor under the table, and put incense on the board beneath the Mao poster. Then he took another set of red envelopes that we had brought with us, and gave one to each of the thirty-three helpers at the house of Song Yan's father.

Song Yan's family had received a lot of presents, most of which were put in the main room: numerous bed sheets, covers and cushions (mostly from the closest relatives of their family), several bamboo baskets, thermos flasks, washing basins, wooden chairs and a fire basin. Normally these smaller things are given by the closest relatives of the bride, and besides that there would be a much richer dowry, given by the father of the bride. In this case, Wang Wei's and Song Yan's fathers had agreed on buying the dowry together and installing it directly in Wang Wei's house.[18] We then carried all these presents to the trucks; the last thing that was put on the truck was the basin for a fireplace, complete with charcoal and fire tongs.[19]

Song Yan had been waiting in the sleeping room, together with Wang Xin and Tian Dan, her mother, and some other cousins and aunts. When everyone was ready, Wang Xin and Tian Dan went out to wait at the threshold for her, and then her mother and an aunt accompanied her to the door. The aunt was holding an umbrella over her head, and Wang Xin and Tian Dan walked behind her; and so this little group of women around the bride walked her to the waiting car. On other occasions I have seen the bride cry, and sometimes her mother and aunts too, but today there were few tears.

When we arrived at the house of Wang Wei, our group of helpers took the presents off the truck, and stored them quickly in the house. This has to be done very quickly; only later will the things be ordered neatly and put up for display, mainly in the couple's bedroom. When we had put everything down, we went up to the house, the drivers parked the truck and the motorbikes at the house of a neighbour, and then everyone waited for Song Yan to leave the car. People had already prepared a lot of firecrackers in front of the house. Inside the main room, the table with the book of presents was put aside, and two red candles were placed on the house altar (red being the colour of weddings). On the floor, just before the house altar (a poster of Mao in this case), a red cloth was laid on which the couple would stand to bow.

Song Yan then got out of the car, accompanied by the bridesmaids Wang Xin and Tian Dan, and went up the road to the house. Amid the noise and smoke of firecrackers, Song Yan walked over to Wang Wei, who was waiting in front of the main room. There, he took her hand, and the two of them bowed together in front of the house altar (see photograph 4.1). They then walked into their bedroom at the side of the main room, and sat down together on the new bed. Sitting on the bed, Wang Wei's mother helped Song Yan to change her shoes to house shoes.

This is the central moment of any wedding: when the bride and groom bow together to the ancestors of the groom's family, and then go over to the bedroom and sit down on the bed for a while. All the guests stand in front of the main door, and next to the walls inside the house, and watch them attentively. The air is full of the smoke and noise of the firecrackers that are set off outside.

Being the central act of a wedding, the exact time at which the bride and the groom together cross the threshold of the main room is also decisively important; it is determined in advance by a diviner according to the 'eight characters' of bride and groom. It might happen that the bride arrives too early at the house of the groom. At one wedding I saw the bride and the groom wait for two hours outside the house, just until the exact hour that had been determined for them to enter the house and bow at the house altar.

The two thresholds and door-frames that have to be crossed are at the main door and the door to the bedroom. Both are adorned with appropriate paper scrolls (*duilian*): the main door with the announcement of the wedding; the door to the bedroom with a scroll that more or less directly alludes to what is supposed to happen inside this room.[20]

Soon we helpers had lunch, and in the afternoon, when many people had already eaten, two tables were put in the main room, for the most important meal of the day: the meal for the 'high relatives' (*gaoqin*). The closest relatives of the bride's family (brother and sister-in-law, and sometimes also the sister of the bride) are accompanied for a meal by the closest relatives of the groom's house (in this case mostly the uncles of Wang Wei, including the matchmaker Tian Daliang). On the 'higher' table (closer to the house altar) the groom eats with the men and on the 'lower' table (close to the door) the bride eats with the women. It is by no means always clear who exactly should sit down at these tables and who should not. This afternoon one maternal uncle (*jiujiu*, MZB) of Wang Wei was having an 'argument' with a paternal uncle (*shushu*, FB); that is, both sides insisted that the other one should sit down. In the end Wang Wei helped the maternal uncle to sit down; normally it would have been the paternal uncle who should sit down, but the relationship with the maternal side and the paternal side of relatives is somehow turned upside down in Wang Wei's family, because his parents had an uxorilocal marriage. In this case the maternal uncles are often taken to be like agnates of the family.

After the meals people sat around and played cards until the evening. Some late guests dropped in, but most of the crowd had left already. In a side room I was watching Wang Wei's mother and sister counting the money that they had received as presents. Altogether it already amounted to more than 10,000 Yuan, and there would still be some late guests coming in the evening and the next morning.

* * *

Even though much of the wedding preparation has lost the ritual imperative it might have had in former times, it is still crucial for all participants to adjust their behaviour to ritual propriety. Wang Wei and Song Yan may have met without the intermediation of a matchmaker, but the uncle Tian Daliang was still called on to help with the preparations and to mediate between the two families. Whilst no formal betrothal party was held, Wang Wei still had to pay his respect to his in-laws; he presented a pig for the New Year, helped out in their tea factory, and hosted them in his house at the wedding. Even though for both the wedding date and the hour of the crossing of the threshold, no one had calculated the astrological consonance of the 'eight characters' of Wang Wei and Song Yan, everyone still paid attention to a generally auspicious appearance.

In all these actions, propriety (*li*) was crucial: every movement was a 'channelling along a centring path', aiming at particular fixations of a centre and the hierarchical coordinates around it. The most important moment in which such a centre is spatialized is the moment when the young couple enters the main room of the groom's house, and bows in front of the house altar.

Undeniably the rituals that Hevia and Zito are writing about at imperial courts are quite different to the rituals that I am describing here. But there is a certain logic in *li* that is similar, and which is produced in analogy to former imperial rituals. Taking up Hevia and Zito's arguments, I have tried to describe this ritual process as 'channelling along a centring path'. The preparations both of the host family and the guests include a whole series of actions that have to be finely tuned in order to reach a middle way between excess and deficiency. All this 'channelling' culminated in the final act of 'centring', when the couple bowed together at the house altar of the groom's family. During the ritual process, all ritual elements and actions have to be adjusted to social propriety, and they are painstakingly negotiated and commented upon. Given the distance in time and space, it is all the more remarkable how 'centring' as a spatial and moral practice describes both imperial court ritual and contemporary family celebrations.

So far I have written about *li* as if it was an honoured principle of ritual governing moral action. But *li* has also become something which is deeply embarrassing, in particular from the perspective of the modern Chinese state. This embarrassment is the topic of the next chapter.

Notes

1. Song Yan asked me once if she could borrow the two volumes of the bestseller *Brothers* (*xiongdi*) by Yu Hua (2005 and 2006), which she had seen on my table. Three days later, she gave them back to me, and said it was an entertaining read. I could not believe that she had really read the 721 pages of the two volumes in just three days, and questioned her about the content. She had nuanced opinions on several characters in the novel, and offered extremely interesting comparisons to people we both knew in the village. *Brothers* had been the first long Chinese novel I had struggled through. Reading most days for about one hour, it took me three months to read the entire novel.
2. The 'four classics' (*si shu*) are *The Great Learning* (*daxue*), *The Doctrine of the Mean* (*zhongyong*), *The Confucian Analects* (*lunyu*), and *The Works of Mencius* (*mengzi*).
3. The latter was a central work of Neo-Confucianism used since the Song Dynasty. It has been translated and commented by Patricia Ebrey (1991).

4. Wang is reviewing the Chinese translation of Yan Yunxiang's book, which was published in 2000.
5. Instead of granting such 'indigenous' notions their theoretical potential, Western social sciences often takes its arsenal of theoretical tools for granted, according to David Graeber. He argues that much academic anthropology merely reproduces widely used concepts of Western philosophy and social science, instead of carrying out the intellectual task of re-working notions which are not inbred in elite traditions of Europe and North America. 'Where once anthropologists' key theoretical terms were words like mana, totem, or taboo, the new buzzwords are invariably derived from Latin or Greek, usually via French, occasionally German' (Graeber 2004: 98).
6. In what follows, I have greatly benefited from the literature review on *li*, both in Confucian writings and relevant anthropological theories of ritual, by Catherine Capdeville-Zeng (2008).
7. These dilemmas of Western 'representationalism' present considerable difficulties for the study of ritual. Dealing with 'the difficult relationship of modern ideology and the effort to understand "the social"', Daniel de Coppet points out how in French and English the word 'representation' lost its sense of an efficacious and creative activity in itself (which it had in medieval Christian funeral for example), and becomes a mere equivalence, a 'standing in' for something else, 'an image' separated from 'the real' (Coppet 1992). This historical 'slippage of meaning' might be related to the overwhelming tyranny of the 'ocular metaphor' in Western thinking, which Richard Rorty has described (1980). Surely the 'ocular metaphor' was not of such central importance in Chinese history; the sinologist Jean François Billeter for example contrasts the 'Western gaze' with the 'Chinese act' as central metaphors for knowledge (Billeter 1984).
8. Hevia (1995: 22), quoting from Hay (1983a and 1983b), is opposing metaphor ('a primary meaning extended to other contexts') to macrocosm–microcosm relationships, synecdoche and homology. This is a rather narrow understanding of metaphor, which can be also understood as an overarching category containing synecdoche and homology.
9. Stephan Feuchtwang proposes a very similar argument regarding the metaphorical relationship between Chinese popular religion and imperial organization (Feuchtwang 2001 [1992]).
10. Between 50 and 80 Yuan per day in Bashan in 2007.
11. Even though in most farmhouses it is the women who prepare food every day, the cook at a celebration is always a man.
12. Apparently it is only a local custom in Bashan to give an entire pack of cigarettes. In the northern part of the township (around the market town of Daliangxi) only one cigarette is given. In the past (and in some very remote villages in the mountains) dried raw tobacco (E. *yezi yan*) was given; normally only elder men smoke this tobacco, which to the young seems disgustingly countrified and coarse (*tu*).
13. There was a price range between about 50 and 200 Yuan per table of ten people, according to the number and kind of dishes.
14. The cheapest, locally brewed liquor cost about 1 Yuan per *jin*; the best one I saw in a celebration in Bashan cost about 15 Yuan per bottle, and was presented in wrapping on the tables.
15. The price range here was between 2 Yuan for a pack of 'Red Golden Dragon' (*hongjinlong*) and 8 Yuan for a pack of 'Seven Wolves' (*qi pi lang*). Sometimes people bring cartons of tobacco from other provinces, which most locals did not know; generally such a tobacco would look more expensive than it really was. Every helper has to be offered one pack of cigarettes for every day he or she is at the celebration, and

every guest one pack, so that about 300 packs of cigarettes are needed for an average celebration. Given that figure, the dilemma between saving on cigarettes versus the enhancement of prestige (by offering expensive cigarettes) is a very real one.

16. '*li* has three roots: heaven and earth are the root of life, the ancestors are the root of commonality, rulers and teachers are the root of order. If there were no heaven and earth, how could there be life? If there were no rulers and teachers, how could there be order? If only one of those three is missing, there is no peace and security for humankind. Hence, these are the three root principles of *li*.' Quoting these often-repeated lines from the book of Xunzi, the radical critic of Confucianism, Wu Yu, concludes: 'That is where the five-character tablet in our country comes from' (Wu 1985a [1917]: 110, cited also in Yu 2004).

17. Many people also consult the 'eight characters' of groom and bride to find out whether the union is feasible, i.e. whether the two sets of characters and signs combine and are 'in accordance with Heavenly intentions' (Freedman 1979 [1967]: 261ff). I know of at least one case in Bashan where the parents opposed a union because the 'eight characters' of bride and groom were interpreted as incompatible by several diviners.

18. The richest dowry that I have seen, transported on three trucks, included the following: a fridge, a washing machine, a TV set, a manicure table with a mirror, ten wooden chairs, an electric fan, blankets and bed covers (more than ten), one common round table, one Mahjong table, various thermos flasks, two big basins, and various small ones, for washing, several tea pots, a furniture set with four big closets, six chairs, two side closets, bamboo baskets, and a water spender.

19. People regarded it as particularly important that these tools for the fireplace were put on the truck last. This alludes to the fact that the couple will establish a new household with their own stove and fireplace.

20. At Song Yan and Wang Wei's wedding, it was the following scroll: 'The peach blossom opens half the night in the bridal chamber, the dear son is firm the entire night vigil in the nuptial room' (*dong nei taohua kai ban ye, fang zhong guizi jie wu geng*).

Chapter 5

The Embarrassment of Li

The written characters that we normally use in society are still [representative of] the bad habits of the imperial age. In the towns, most houses have scrolls such as 'obliged in gratitude to the northern palace' or 'the emperor's benevolence is without limit' on their doorframes. In the countryside, people habitually stick a red paper scroll on the walls of the main rooms, with the characters for 'heaven, earth, emperor, ancestors, and teachers' on it, and some who are particular about it even have a carved tablet with the same characters.

Such corrupt old thinking is rampant in China, and thus if we sincerely want to consolidate a republican polity, we have to expunge all the old thinking that is anti-republican in morals, literature, and elsewhere; and that as thoroughly as possible.

Chen Duxiu, *The Old Thinking and the Problems of the National Polity*, May 1917

Firecrackers were going off throughout the first night that I spent in Bashan, 15 November 2005. Every now and then, a new tirade of firecrackers reverberated, echoing through the entire valley. A huge funeral was going on in a house not too far from the hostel in the market town where I spent the night; the noise finally reached its peak at dawn, when the coffin was carried out of the market town to the place where it would be buried.

Later I became accustomed to the firecrackers and the 'funerary dirge' (*ai yue*) announcing funerals all over the valley of Bashan. Like the other family celebrations mentioned in the last chapter, funerals are prepared with utmost diligence, and are accompanied by lavish banquets. Besides weddings and house inaugurations, funerals are the single most important life-cycle events, and they entail a long and intricate ritual process. Over a period of several days, the descendants of the dead person prepare the funerary rites, and keep vigil around the coffin, which is placed in the main room of the house. On the last night before the burial, the guests come over for a banquet. The most important guests at this occasion are the daughters, granddaughters, and affines of the deceased: each affinal family comes with a band of musicians playing drums and *suona*.[1] The direct daughters and sons-in-law additionally offer a pig and a goat for the family of the deceased (E. *zhu yang ji*). All the descendants cover their heads with white cloths representing their mourning, and they perform countless kow-tows in front of the coffin (see photograph 5.1). During the last night, the closest relatives stay awake, whilst old men sing 'night songs' (E. *ye ge*) to mourn the dead and to entertain the living. At dawn, the coffin is taken out of the house and to the burial ground in a procession. The basic sequence of the ritual process at a funeral in Bashan follows the same standardized structure that has been described by James Watson as a defining feature of 'Chineseness' (1988), with some minor variations that are mostly due to the fact that Watson bases his description on fieldwork in south-eastern China (cf. Naquin 1988).[2]

Even though there are no customs of re-burial, as is common in the southern provinces (cf. Watson 1982), for at least three years after the funeral there is a major celebration every year on the 'Spring Sacrifice Festival' (E. *she* or *sheri*).[3] On this day the relatives of the deceased go to the 'new tomb' (*xin mu*) accompanied by a small music band, put streamers and umbrellas (E. *baogai*) on the tomb, and set off firecrackers. This procession is 'like a second funeral', yet on a much smaller scale. After three years, the 'new tomb' is transformed into an 'old tomb' (*lao mu*) at the Spring Sacrifice Festival, with another ceremony during which the tombstone is erected (*li mubei*) (see He 2008).

Photograph 5.1 Guiding a child to kow-tow in front of grandmother's coffin

The richness and pomp of funerary ritual in Bashan contrasted greatly with funerals in another region I had visited previously. Before I moved to Bashan in May 2006, I had already spent more than two months in a village in the district of Jingmen, in central Hubei province. During these two months, I did not see a single funeral. Just before I left this village in April 2006, I learned that two neighbours in the same village group in which I had lived had died whilst I was there. Nobody had informed me of anything special taking place, and there certainly had not been the endless firecrackers and the 'Yellow River Elegy' which would announce a funeral to anyone in the surrounding villages in Bashan. The funeral had taken place with only the closest relatives and neighbours attending. The public visibility of a funeral was reduced to a minimum level here. To have a funeral announced throughout the entire township by the noise of firecrackers, or to have a funeral procession on the public roads of villages and townships – as I had often seen them in Bashan – would have been unthinkable.

On a return visit to this village in September 2007, just before I left China, I talked with several older men about the funerary customs in their village. Only then did I learn that many of the customs I had thought of as specific to the Enshi region had also been common here: the basic funerary sequence was the same, and actually most peasants were still burying the dead in wooden coffins, which is against the official promotion of cremation. The dead had to be remembered every seventh day after the funeral, until the forty-ninth day (seven times seven); for three years a tomb was said to be a 'new tomb', and in the third year a ritual took place that finally transformed the dead into ancestors and the tomb into an 'old tomb'; this ritual was called 'completing three years of filial piety' (*san nian man xiao*), similar to what was done at the *sheri* in Enshi. But most importantly, the funerals themselves had been fairly similar in the past, including under Maoism. It was only from the 1980s that local government had started to crack down radically on funerary ritual. Ever since then bigger funerary celebrations had been forbidden, and cremation (*huozang*) enforced instead of the traditional earth burial (*tuzang*). Traditional funerals continued to take place, the old men told me, but with a very low profile, and they were not announced publicly.

Whilst it is impossible for me to assess all the reasons for this difference, it is clear that local government plays a crucial role in facilitating or precluding such ritual activities. Governmental campaigns to promote cremation and suppress extravagant rituals are much diminished in Bashan. One important factor which goes some way towards explaining the relative lenience of the local government is that Bashan is a minority township and Enshi a minority prefecture, where 'minority particularity' (*minzu tese*) and 'minority culture' (*minzu wenhua*) are promoted. The room for what is permitted and what has to be concealed from the public gaze is quite different here, but in both places it is conditioned in complex negotiations between local sociality and the local state. Not only are there larger regional differences (such as those between Enshi and Jingmen), but within the township of Bashan, and at every ritual occasion, the proper balance between dash and decorum is up for negotiation. Both the outer show, and what happens within more private spaces at such funerals, is of the utmost concern for ordinary people, and for the local state.

With regard to the everyday talk around ritual occasions, in particular funerals, in this chapter I highlight the tension between vernacular discourses in a local face-to-face community, and official discourses related to the state. I will do so first by quoting some comments that I heard about the revived practice of hiring Daoist priests for funerary rituals, and about other customs at funerals. Yet in Bashan the funerary rituals, including those of the Daoists, were tacitly tolerated by the local government.

What the local state is more obviously concerned about is the increasing 'commercialization' (*shangyehua*) of family celebrations, with which I deal in the second section. During recent years, the amounts of money-gifts exchanged have increased rapidly, and local government offices and media intermittently proclaim that this 'bad custom' (*exi*) should be limited. Embarrassingly, however, such 'commercialized' banquets are frequently staged by powerful officials, who are forced to do so to maintain their relationship networks. I will give an example of such a banquet with the funeral of the father of a high official in Bashan.

During my time in Bashan, I was not only an outside observer of these ambiguities in ritual propriety, but I also tried to participate in such rituals to some extent. By doing so, I put myself more than once into awkward situations. In the last section, I will describe my own problems of acting properly on ritual occasions.

As popular practices that are 'considered a source of external embarrassment but that nevertheless provide insiders with their assurance of common sociality' (Herzfeld 2005: 3), funerary rituals and 'commercialized' family celebrations are examples of 'cultural intimacy', according to Michael Herzfeld's definition. But they are so not only because of the elements of 'superstition' or 'commercialization' associated with them: the principle of *li* itself has become profoundly embarrassing over the course of the last century. Confucianism was attacked as 'the doctrine of *li*' (*li-jiao*) in the attempt to build a modern nation and modern citizens from the beginning of the twentieth century onwards (see Harrison 2001: 96ff.). Under Maoism, and in particular during the Cultural Revolution, government propaganda, party campaigns, and the education system all attempted systematically to destroy the traditional Confucian moral system, including its popular forms, such as family celebrations. Whilst political control has loosened a great deal since the 1980s, this past in which *li* itself has become embarrassing is still shaping how people relate to it now.

Superstition in Funerals

In recent years it has become increasingly common to invite a group of Daoist priests to funerals. They carry out elaborate rituals at makeshift altars and perform incantations reading from their books (*nian jing*). On the last night of the funerary rituals – which can last for up to seven nights – they perform the ritual of 'running around the coffin' (*rao guancai*), which is a stylized dance around the coffin. In an elaborate ritual, the daughters-in-law of the deceased have to follow them and spread paper flowers on the floor around the coffin (*rao guan sa hua*).

The most successful local group of Daoist priests comes from a neighbouring market town. There is a certain rivalry between different Daoist priests, but in general they have their own area and clientele where people hire them. In the valley of Bashan and the villages to the east, including Zhongba, Yao Ke'ai is hired most frequently. He is a retired primary school teacher, and makes a comfortable living from this profession. Even though locally he is called a 'Daoist priest' (*daoshi*), in reality he does not perform many of the Daoist rituals which the bigger groups have in their repertoire. Knowledgeable in *fengshui* and divination, at funerals he 'opens the way' (E. *kai lu*, P. *kai dao*) for the soul of the deceased.

Aside from the Daoist priests, there were always several old men performing 'night songs' (*yege*) or 'beating the night drums' (*da ye luogu*). In a group of at least four, they sit down around a square table, and sing to the accompaniment of small gongs and drums. Supplied by the host with tobacco leaves to smoke[4] and sugared ginger tea to clear their throats, they sing couplets and ballads for several hours. Their repertoire always includes stories of Confucius (*kong lao'er*, 'Kong the second' in the vernacular), classical legends (such as the *Romance of the Three Kingdoms*) or moralistic narratives (such as the *24 Examples of Filial Piety*). They will also include mourning songs for the deceased, and depending on the rhyming skills of the singers, they can bring in all kinds of local and personal detail.

Whereas the 'night songs' had always been part of the funerals, the activities of the Daoist priests were forbidden for many years. Only in recent years have they seen some revival. For the 'night songs' generally 30 or 40 Yuan is charged per man per night. The Daoist priests, however, charge more (around 50 Yuan per man per night), and often their group is also bigger. It is generally only families that are rather well-off who can afford to pay the Daoists.

One of the few funerals where I saw Daoist priests was in the Yang family hamlet in a neighbouring village. I went there with Liang Xianpei from Zhongba, and Master Liao, the foreman of the workers in Song Haomin's family. People were sitting in the side rooms, chatting and gambling, whilst the group of Daoists that Yao had hired was performing their incantations in the main room. I asked Master Liao whether he understood what the Daoists were singing and could explain it to me. He said – like most other people that I asked – that he did not understand a single word. He added that the 'night songs' are more fun, people would pay more attention to them because they were intended for their entertainment. But he concluded that Yang Mingmao, the son of the deceased, was quite well-off (as he could afford to pay for the Daoist priests).

Yang Mingmao works as a carpenter and is quite a sociable character. We had met each other several times at houses in Zhongba where he had been working, and he knew that I often visited the house of his brother-in-law Liang Xianpei. For the funeral, I had come over with Liang Xianpei and his family, who were most important guests that night, representing the in-laws of the family. Liang Xianpei came with a music band he had hired, and presented the 'offering of a pig and a goat' (E. *zhu yang ji*) which is expected from the daughters and sons-in-law of the deceased (see photograph 5.2).

Photograph 5.2 Preparing the offer of a pig and a goat (E. *zhu yang ji*) for the funeral of the mother-in-law

Several days after the funeral, I met Yang Mingmao on the street, and he invited me to come over to his house and have a meal. Eating and drinking with him, we came to speak about the funeral again. I asked him about the Daoist priests, and he confirmed that it had been quite expensive. He detailed the costs: 40 Yuan for each man per night, with eight men for five nights, made 1600 Yuan all together. Why had he hired them, I asked, as several people had told me that he had been the first one to do so in this village? He answered that he himself understood nothing about what the Daoists did. But it had been the last wish of his mother, and he had promised her that he would bring the Daoists over.

In everyday talk, the rituals of the Daoists, and anything else that could be called 'superstitious' ritual, was never spoken of outright. But while the memories of the Maoist condemnation of 'superstitious' tradition loomed large, local people found their own creative ways of reconciling public discourse and local practice. According to what people told me about the Maoist era in Bashan, the basic funerary rites had been the same – with the difference that there were many fewer money-gifts, no Daoist priests, and no band of drums (*luogu dui*). Whilst it was clear from early on that the more 'religious' elements of funerals (like the incantations of the Daoist priest) were forbidden, with several other elements it was not completely obvious what was allowed as proper commemoration of the death, and what was prohibited as 'feudal superstition' (*fengjian mixin*) and wastefulness (*puzhang langfei*). The 'night songs' of the old men were always retained – if now sometimes mixed up with Maoist language.[5] But the band of drums hired by the daughters and sons-in-law became a point of contention. It was forbidden during the Cultural Revolution, but often local cadres were not sure whether to enforce the prohibition or not.

At one funeral in the township, I overheard a conversation between Wen Yunfu and Lan Yanda, both respected old men who had previously worked as officials in the township, and were now retired. Lan Yanda defended the more conventional view that many aspects of the funerals are indeed wasteful and full of superstitions, and the government had some responsibility to set limits on such activities. Old Wen countered that all this is a proper 'commemoration' (*jinian*) of the dead, and expression of 'popular culture' (*minjian wenhua*). He said that by the end of the 1970s, he had already argued with other officials about that. His point was that 'after the death of "father Mao" (E. *mao laohan'r*) the entire nation was in mourning (*dai xiao*), and the funerary ceremonies were prepared with all pomp.' That clearly showed that proper remembrance and funerary rites were an issue of necessity and decency.

Later on, he recounted to me in private how he had played on the uncertainty as to what was permitted and what was forbidden in funerals.

Whereas the activities of the Daoist priests were clearly interpreted as 'superstition', it was not clear whether inviting bands of drums and *suona* was also a 'wasteful' and 'feudal' custom, or proper decency. As mentioned above, it is the task of the daughters and the sons-in-law to invite such bands for the funeral, which is seen as the most basic duty of a son-in-law to show respect for his wife's family. When the mother of Old Wen's wife died in 1974, most families did not invite music bands, as such a thing might draw attention to one's family. However, Old Wen felt that he had to do so; as an official in the township, he thought he would have some authority if anyone else criticized him. The funeral took place in Jinziba, a neighbouring township in the mountains, and he was not too familiar with the local officials there. But he decided to take the risk, and on the night of the funeral, he paid a group of musicians to walk over to Jinziba with him. At the funeral, everything went well, until the secretary of the village arrived. He had not seen a music band for several years, and thought that this was forbidden and should be reported to higher offices and prosecuted. The secretary started arguing with Old Wen at the funeral dinner, but it turned out that the secretary was un-educated (*mei you wenhua*) and naïve. Old Wen described how he impressed him by saying he was an official from Bashan township, and that he, Wen, had close and confidential connections with higher officials. In the end, the secretary apologized to Old Wen. 关系→一切的解决方法.

Wines for Nothing

The 24th day of the 12th month of the lunar calendar is a very important day in the annual cycle: traditionally it is called the 'little new year' (*xiao nian*). This day marks the beginning of the Spring Festival period, and in the past it was an important day of domestic worship in the houses. It is also a propitious day for weddings, and every year many young couples choose this day for their wedding. In 2006, I knew of at least five weddings taking place on this day in Bashan township and the surrounding villages. Many families had to visit several of them, being relatives, friends, neighbours or colleagues of the families.

I myself went to only one wedding on this day, the wedding of a neighbour in Zhongba whom I knew relatively well; at the banquet table after the bride had arrived, I was sitting next to Kang II and Xia 'the beard'.[6] Xia did business in the coal trade in Bashan, and is an old friend of Kang. They had already been to two other weddings on the same day, and the host had to beg them to stay at least for a meal. For people like them, it has become increasingly common to come only to 'have their money-present

送礼 →排个人情

registered' (*gua ge renqing*), i.e. to pay the expected money, and have it recorded in the red book of money-gifts that is written on these occasions.
Often people will only send their children to hand in the money-gift; and
it has also become very common to send the money with a neighbour
or someone else who is going to the event. At one of the biggest celebrations I have seen, the birthday of the mother-in-law of the current mayor
of Zhongba, one official of the township brought money-gifts from eight
other people who could not be present. All of the different names, with
the respective amounts of money, were duly listed in the book of presents.

After a lot of insistence on the part of the host, they finally stayed, and
ended up on the table at which I was sitting, together with the boss of a
tea factory, who regularly bought coal from Xia 'the beard'. Even though
they both already had red faces from the liquor they had drunk before,
they had to drink again, being all well-acquainted and related to each
other as business partners. At the table, they were toasting each other, and
I shared one-and-a-half glasses of liquor with them. Their conversation
turned to the different weddings of the day, mostly the money-gifts that
people had given. Xia had to go to two more weddings the same day and
Kang to three.

Since the 1990s, with the economic growth and the increased participation of local farmers in the money economy, the amount of money given as
gifts for family celebrations like weddings, funerals, birthdays and house
inaugurations has increased immensely. One of the most obvious signs of
this inflationary growth was during the period from 2006 to 2007, when
the minimal socially acceptable amount of a money-gift increased from
20 Yuan to 30 Yuan.

Like many other elderly people, Tian Benping often complained to me
about the 'commercialization' (*shangyehua*) of inviting guests for these
events. He explained to me in detail how businessmen and cadres, in
particular those that have huge networks of relationships (*guanxiwang*),
need to stage a party at least every four years; if they fail to do so, they
will lose too much money in the *renqing* that they give away every year.
The calculation is simple: if a businessman in Bashan spends between
4000 and 5000 Yuan a year on *renqing* money, he would need to take in
between 16,000 and 20,000 Yuan in one celebration every four years, ig-
noring monetary inflation (which has been considerable in the last years).
It is equally impossible for them to miss the celebrations of their friends,
relatives and business partners, because if they did so, they would incur
serious problems in those relationships. Tian Benping pointed out that he
himself would only invite guests for the most important celebrations, that
is, the weddings of his children, and funerals of his parents. All the other occasions, such as birthdays of parents, celebrations for children who

passed the entry examinations for university or were admitted into the army, he did not celebrate. It has become a deplorable new custom to stage banquets at such improper occasions, to celebrate such 'wines for nothing' (*wu shi jiu*), Tian Benping said.

It came as a surprise to me then that in August 2007 a lavish celebration for the sixtieth birthday of his wife took place at his house. I first thought that Tian Benping had contradicted himself, in his claims that he would not celebrate a birthday with a huge banquet. Tian Benping had been working in the government tea station that was producing tea saplings when tea monoculture was introduced in the 1990s. Many farmers in the area had obtained their first tea plants from this station, and so Tian Benping's networks of friends and acquaintances, including within the government hierarchies, were very wide.

But a look at the invitation cards clarified the situation: in fact it is not a husband who invites guests to a birthday, but generally it is the children who celebrate the birthday of their parents. Tian Benping's son, Tian Qiang, is a local businessman in the township of Bashan, and he is exposed to the very constraints that his father Tian Benping had pointed out to me: to maintain a wide network of relationships means that one has to attend many celebrations during the year. And if you do not hold a celebration for a very long time, you will lose a substantial amount of money. For this reason, Tian Qiang felt obliged to hold a great celebration for the sixtieth birthday of his mother – an occasion that other families just marked with their closest relatives. Tian Qiang was therefore the main host at the celebration; even though he was no longer living in the village, all his business partners and friends came up to his parents' house in the village on that day.

For many ordinary villagers, and in particular for those that are relatively poor, the expense in presents (*renqing*) given at such occasions presents a considerable financial burden. I often asked how much people spent each year on money-presents. In peasant households it was said that expenses for presents were usually between 1000 and 4000 Yuan per household per year. Often I felt that there was much exaggeration, sometimes understatement as well, but according to the lists of money-presents I have seen, this sounds realistic. Furthermore, I think it is reasonable to assume that for many households in Zhongba, about a quarter of their annual income is spent in this way.

To someone giving out money-presents year after year, the kind of consideration that Tian Benping was suggesting becomes quite persuasive. In particular, such occasions as birthdays, or when children made it into university or into the army, offer themselves as perfect opportunities to hold a celebration to recoup gift money. Weddings and funerals demand considerable expense for the ceremonies themselves, including the costs of ritual exchanges between affines, and they have to be celebrated with a banquet.[7] The celebrations of birthdays, and of entries into university or the army, do not involve much ritual activity, and incur no additional costs for the host, aside from the standard banquet. They could be celebrated without invitations and without a huge banquet, and in fact in the past, they often were. But now, precisely because they are relatively simple and cheap to organize, they present an opportunity to get some of one's *renqing* expenses back – an opportunity on which fewer and fewer people feel they could miss out.

It is not only villagers who criticize this trend; local government is also concerned about the immense increase in money-gifts and the 'commercialization' of family celebrations. In the commentaries and campaigns of local government and media, there are certain elements of Maoist discourse, as well as of contemporary 'modernist' discourse, in particular related to 'population quality' (*suzhi*). During the Maoist era, a whole new literature emerged that characterized such family celebrations as 'extravagance and waste' (*puzhang langfei*), and contrasted them with older ideals of 'hard work and thrift' (*qinjian jieyue*). Nowadays they are similarly condemned as a 'backward' practice, but not so much as 'capitalist decadence' as they were under Maoism.

Most of the practices identified as 'Confucian propriety' (*li*) had been thoroughly condemned during the Maoist era. The 'Confucian doctrine' (*lijiao*) was an instrument of landlords and capitalists used to oppress the peasants. Hence all of these practices were tightly controlled until the 1980s. Whilst political control is much looser now, there is still a considerable propaganda effort to curb such 'waste' linked to 'backward' practices.

The local TV station of Enshi city frequently broadcast programmes that castigated this 'decadent' and 'backward' custom.[8] What follows are excerpts from reports in the local newspaper, *Enshi Evening News*:

> In the last couple of years, the custom of 'inviting for a wine' (*zheng jiu*) has become more and more popular in the countryside. There are countless causes to invite guests, and many peasants unwillingly have to accept the invitations. What is emerging is a vicious circle of 'I'm afraid to go to a wine – but I have to go there – I myself also host a wine' (*pa chijiu – bu de bu chijiu – ziji ye zheng jiu*). All this does not suit the development and progress of society, and the construction of a socialist new countryside.

The report goes on to describe the hardships of ordinary people that have to spend too much money in presents, and then concludes:

That this bad custom would stop is the hope of many people. So how should the custom of 'holding banquets' be kept in limits? One should keep to the principle of combining attack and rewards, apply various measures, and implement an integrated set of policies.

Build a new and different atmosphere of public opinion. The relevant departments have to run propaganda and education campaigns in the countryside to fight against the excesses (*da cao da ban*) in holding banquets, and establish civilized and new morals (*wenming xin feng*). In newspapers and magazines, broadcasting and TV, and commentary columns and slogans, and many other forms, an intense atmosphere of propaganda shall be built up. Use the people and occasions next to yourself to disseminate the harms of networks of relationships (*renqing wang*) that are always wider knit and bigger, and the advantages of modest celebrations when it is the occasion. At the same time, TV, broadcasting, newspapers, announcement boards etc. should be used to expose those who 'hold banquets for nothing' (*wu shi zheng jiu*), or those who look for an occasion to hold a banquet (*zhao shi zheng jiu*). Do propaganda on the civilized and new customs of holding moderate and simple weddings and funerals.

Put up constraints to customs of holding banquets through the self-government of villages (*cunmin zizhi*). Set up and perfect rules in the villages for the appropriate scope and limits of holding banquets through the assemblies of village representatives.

Increase control, and promote better customs amongst the people by giving exemplars through the attitudes of government and party. An important reason for the spreading of abnormal expressions of human relations (*renqing*) is that there is a minority of party members and officials who are taking a lead in holding banquets (*zheng jiu*). Doing so, they are corrupting the conduct of party and government, and also undermining the morals of the people. To uproot these wrong customs of '*renqing*', the control over party members and officials has to be increased, and cases of party members and officials holding huge celebrations have to be investigated and dealt with in the strictest manner. (Enshi Wanbao 2007d)

Sometimes there are reports on the successful implementation of propaganda campaigns:

To guide the peasants towards a correct consumer behaviour, a committee from the People's Congress of Moudao township has organized broadcasts and TV-programmes, assemblies and smaller groups of representatives and various others campaigns of different forms; in this way propaganda was conducted amongst the masses of the people of the entire township on a grand scale towards changing the customs, according with the principle of simplicity in family celebrations, propagating the correct treatment of the relationships between production and life [expenses], accumulation and consumption, the immediate and the long term. (Enshi Wanbao 2008)

These propaganda efforts meet with a mixed response on the ground. Whilst some older people relate the criticisms of this new custom to Maoist discourses, others are rather sarcastic about it. This is especially so because many of the biggest family celebrations are hosted by businessmen and officials. Officials themselves face the double necessity of representing the party and the state on the one side, and maintaining good relations (mediated by money-gifts) with many people – without which they would be unable to get things done.

The Funeral of the Secretary's Father

Sun Jundong was one of the most successful officials in Bashan township. After three years as the party secretary of the township, he was elevated to a position of vice party secretary in a neighbouring county, the next rank in the hierarchy of party and government. In the spring of 2007 I had the unexpected opportunity of attending the funeral of his father. Liang Xianpei and another man had arrived at the office of Dr Hu. They told Dr Hu and me that they were going to play the *suona* and drums in a funeral band, and asked me if I wanted to join them.

The home of the Sun family is in one of the most remote villages of Bashan township, about two hours' drive by car into the mountains from the market of Bashan. On the dirt road we saw numerous SUVs, black Audis and Volkswagens that are the vehicles used by government officials and businessmen. This was the last night of the funeral, and from the moment we arrived at 5 P.M. until late in the evening, the clanging noise of firecrackers did not cease for a single moment. According to local custom, about three dozen neighbours and relatives help to prepare the food and host the guests at a funeral. At this funeral there were about one hundred helpers, all with their names listed on a beautiful painted poster on the side-wall of the house. On the other side a programme was stuck detailing the performances and rituals for the evening, all written in fine calligraphy. According to local tradition, the coffin is laid out in the central room of the house which is called the 'hall of filial piety' (*xiaotang*) during the funerary period. The hall was richly ornamented with carved bamboo sticks and coloured paper, including various paintings and several huge tablets describing the life of the deceased in poems. All this was done by teacher Lei, a well-known 'man of culture' (*wenren*) and former head of the 'office for culture' in a neighbouring township. He also led the performances and rituals in the evening, which included speeches in classical Chinese, a mourning ceremony where all the twenty-four music bands were marching and playing, songs and couplets sung to all close relatives and important guests, mourning songs for the deceased and his family, mourning dances around the coffin, and lion dances.

This was by far the biggest and most lavish funeral that I saw during my time in Bashan. It was also a huge show of power and money. According to the red books, there were about 70,000 Yuan of money-presents given at this funeral. That is an immense amount, when compared to the conventional sums that ordinary farmers are dealing with: 10,000 Yuan is the annual income for a family that is above average in the region, and it is also the average sum of the money received at a wedding or a funeral.

My attendance at this funeral certainly produced some uncertainties and awkwardness. On the one hand I was a foreign guest, and everyone in the local government and most ordinary people in the surrounding villages knew about my presence, and that I was walking around the villages, observing, talking and asking odd questions to local residents. On the other hand, I was not invited to this celebration, and at some points it was not clear to me whether I was welcome. My neighbours from the village who were playing music had said that I should go, and pay reverence to the former secretary of Bashan. But Sun Jundong himself did not say a single word to me during the night, even after I had given a short funeral oration upon the invitation of the ceremonial coordinator. Some relatives of the Sun family, businessmen in Enshi and Wuhan, were extremely friendly to me, and told me that I should film the event as well. There was even a camera man amongst the helpers, filming the whole event. When I asked him if it would be possible to get a copy of the film, he said that unfortunately this was reserved for the members of the Sun family.

Late in the evening, a professional music group was singing couplets to every important relative and honoured guest. Their rhymes commended or mocked people's characteristics, achievements, and particularities, and at the end the person always had to give some tip to the singers. After many others, they came to me as well, and sang some verses about the 'outsider' (E. *waima*) who had come to pay respect to the Sun family. I got nervous and asked my neighbours how much it would be appropriate to give. An old man next to me said 'not too much, maybe 50 Yuan.' Another disagreed and said it should be just 'symbolic' (*yisi yisi*), a lucky number like 12 Yuan might be fine. So I gave 12 Yuan to the singer when he came to me. His partner had already started to sing rhymes about another person, when Sun Jundong went over to the entertainment group, and told them something. Now the singer came back to me, and rhymed that 'actually he is the guest of us all, we cannot accept his gift' – and gave me the 12 Yuan back.

It is clear that Sun Jundong was in a quandary here. On the one hand he had to present himself as the impeccable leader, a representative of the

高之让
zíǐ

high morals of the party and the government. On the other hand he also had to live up to the demands of filial piety (*xiao*) and what was expected as proper (*li*) and virtuous (*daode*) behaviour from him and his family after the death of his father. He obviously tried to be both, and to represent his family in both respects. In addition to that, the funeral gave him the opportunity of receiving huge amounts of gifts from officials trying to establish a relationship of patronage with him. After all, he was the highest official in the township and is now a powerful cadre at the county level – a very important man to know in the lower government offices. Last but not least, many officials, friends, relatives and business partners will reciprocate the gifts that he has given them in the past.

When the funeral was discussed in Bashan's gossip mills, the accusation that by holding such a massive funeral Sun Jundong was really engaging in 'feudal' and 'corrupt' practices frequently came up. A week after the funeral, the topic was mentioned amongst the officials of Shuanke village, and Fang Bo, the party secretary of the village, asked me in front of some other officials if I had gone to the funeral. Later when we had a cigarette on the side, Fang Bo asked again 'How was it at the funeral? Don't you think that it was really luxurious and decadent (*haochi*)?' Without waiting for my answer, he switched into dialect and said to the village accountant beside him that 'people of Sun's rank should not engage in this kind of activities'. My impression was that Fang Bo could not hide his feelings of *Schadenfreude* about Sun having exposed himself to my prying presence. A couple of days later, I met teacher Song and had a long conversation with him about the funeral. Teacher Song is retired and works now as the janitor of the primary school. For most of the day, he sits in a little lodge next to the gate of the school and reads classical novels or books about the heroes of the revolution. That afternoon, I told him about my impressions of the funeral, and also about my insecurity regarding the reaction of the Sun family. He said that everyone in Bashan knows that this was undoubtedly the biggest funeral that Bashan has ever seen – 'since the beginning of the world' he said, smiling (*pangu kai tian yilai*). He was not referring to the pomp that I had seen, the banquet and the musicians, which I thought was the measurement. He knew of other funerals where there had been about forty bands of musicians, compared to only twenty-four at Sun Jundong's house. The bands are only sent by the daughters and son-in-laws of the family, and hence show how many affines someone has. What people in Bashan were really talking about these days, teacher Song said, was the amount of money given. Most of the secretaries and higher level officials in Bashan had given presents, and it is unlikely that most of them had appeared at the funeral itself, only the closest ones, Teacher Song estimated. Accordingly, much more money must have been given than the 70,000 Yuan recorded in the red book of presents. He said that in the past 'the thunder was big and the rain was little', but now 'the thunder is little, and the rain is big' (*lei xiang xiao, yu lai da*) – meaning that now there is less noise and pomp but more money-presents. Song confirmed that Sun Jundong would be worried about me coming and witnessing all that, as he would fear that I could report it. And then he told me about several cases of officials in similar situations who had been convicted of corruption.

The funeral of Sun Jundong's father illustrates that cultural intimacy is something quite different to the 'cultural resistance' of the 'subaltern'. The one who was embarrassed in this case was one of the most powerful local leaders. Both local villagers and government officials shared a common discourse about propriety, and a common understanding that the outside representation and the local practice of holding family celebrations stand in a tense relationship to one another. What is crucial is how the contradictions are negotiated. In their demeanour and speech at the funeral, Sun Jundong and his guests enacted local ideals of proper behaviour, in this case the ritual of a funeral, which is one of the most important services of children to their parents, expressing as it does their filial piety (*xiao*). Hosts and guests are supposed to behave according to rules and etiquette that can be summarized under the heading of Confucian 'propriety' (*li*). But in the privacy of everyday talk, both villagers and fellow cadres would point out how corrupt this behaviour is.

In the conclusion of her book on *The Art of Social Relationships in China*, Mayfair Yang tells a very similar story of a rural cadre called Zhao (Yang 1994: 317–320). Following the huge funerary celebration for his father, a rival official accuses Zhao of 'corrupt and feudal' activities. Zhao is arrested and subjected to party discipline. But the locals all support him, and plead his case in front of higher government officials. For Yang this is an example of ritual being 'a self-organizing Vehicle of the Minjian' (ibid.: 317). In her interpretation, the *minjian*, or the popular realm of *renqing* ethics and *guanxi* production, is an emerging independent social realm opposed to the anonymous exertion of state power. Let me quote at length her interpretation of the events following the funeral of Zhao's father:

> From the people's point of view, the funeral was not a 'backward' or 'feudal' institution, nor was Zhao using his position to extort money and gifts from them, but it provided an important social occasion for repaying debts owed or initiated a new round of debt relationship with Zhao and his family. The local people sought to transform their relationship with Cadre Zhao from an impersonal, administrative, ruler-to-governed top-down relationship into a personal renqing relationship of giving and repaying. It is noteworthy that, counter to the official policy of de-emphasizing and sometimes banning rituals, the local

people attach much social significance to funerary rituals and feasts. The ritual provides a staging ground for the practice of renqing with an official, so that there is a clear association between ritual or feast and renqing, and between ritual, renqing, and good government.

Zhao himself is a cadre whose attitude toward his job is tinged with a heavy renqing perspective and who allows himself to enter into debt relationships with the people. That is why when he got in trouble with his superiors, so many people organized themselves to support him. In this action the people were not just defending Zhao's personal integrity, but also a certain approach to government and the importance of ritual in their social life. In rural Wenzhou, minjian forces have begun to organize themselves and even to prevail against the state, and these forces include the discourse and practice of renqing and ritual. (Yang 1994: 319–320)

Note how Yang makes use of the category of 'the people': they are a unified body who fight for a 'certain approach to government and the importance of ritual in social life'. This approach is characterized by personalized relationships of *renqing* and *guanxi* and it is diametrically opposed to the impersonal administrative relationships of the state. In my example, the people's judgement of a high official who staged a huge funeral was not as uniform. Both the 'popular' realm (which Yang calls by its Chinese name, *minjian*) and the state discourse are much more fragmented. Both ordinary people and government officials use elements of vernacular and of state discourses. I also subscribe to a binary opposition, but it is not one between 'the local people' and 'the state', but between an official, outside representation, and a vernacular, inside practice. At the funeral of Sun Jundong, local villagers and officials were partaking in both discourses: some locals were admiring the pomp of the funeral, whereas other were criticizing it and denouncing the corruption of local officials. Similarly, officials were divided on how funerals should be interpreted; whereas many had to offer money-presents, some were also quite cynical about Sun, especially when talking in private.

A Banquet for my Departure

During my time in Bashan, I went to 'eat wine' (*chijiu*) on about forty occasions. Whilst many people could not understand why I was asking time and again about very ordinary and very obscure things, my interest in family celebrations seemed more reasonable; celebrations provided obvious occasions for me to learn about 'local culture' (*difang wenhua*) and to carry out my 'investigations' (*diaocha*). Frequently my neighbours would inform me when a celebration was taking place, and said I should go. In the beginning I just turned up if I knew about the ceremony, without understanding much of what was happening there. I was never barred from attending, and even though I was not invited by the host to the first events I went to, the host family almost always welcomed me, sometimes rather formally, sometimes more warmly.

In any family celebration, the utmost emphasis is placed on everything happening smoothly and swiftly. Any accident during the preparation or during the celebration itself is considered a bad portent for the host family. The coming of an unwelcome guest is also taken by many people as an omen. But maybe even more objectionable than bearing the presence of an unwelcome guest would be to have arguments and fights which may result from barring someone from participating.[9] And of course, any extra guests add to the number of visitors at the celebration, thus adding to the prestige of the host. Accordingly, there are sayings demanding that a stranger passing by at a 'wine table' (*jiuxi*) should be invited, although in fact this happens rather rarely. If the appearance of a stranger is considered to be an omen, and his presence related to the prestige of the celebration and of the host family, I often wondered how my presence might be interpreted by locals: being a blond foreigner and a 'doctor' (*boshi*) at one of the most prestigious universities of China marked me as someone of extremely high social status, and my ability to speak English, and my possession of gadgets such as a camera and an MP3-player added symbols of progress and modernity. Yet as a complete outsider, a foreigner is also similar to a bandit, a beggar or a ghost: all beings that come from the outside and do not have homes. In fact, one of the most popular swearwords for foreigners is 'ghosts' or 'devils' (*guizi*). Without doubt, a ghost coming to a celebration would be quite a bad thing to happen. More or less jokingly, I was called a 'German devil' (*deguo guizi*) on various occasions. Sitting at a banquet table at the house inauguration of Yang Minghu, which I described in the introduction and chapter 2, Yang Mingya called me this name teasingly several times. Some people were laughing, but then Hu Xungao and Tian Benping, two well-respected men, scolded him in front of everyone else, and explained to him that this is not polite. Yang Mingya tried to defend himself by saying that it was an 'international joke' (*guoji kai wan xiao*), but then the other two cut him off and told him to shut up.

I soon realized that anyone who went to a family celebration was expected to give a money-present. I started to enquire of people whether they thought it would be necessary or appropriate for me to do so too. People were divided on this issue, and the question became an ongoing topic of debate. Many people said that I was a special guest, in a way a guest of the entire Bashan township. Because of my special status as a foreigner and a researcher, they said that I was really an exceptional case: I could just go there, eat and drink, and observe the customs, and would not need to pay. Others said that 'for us, anyone who comes has to give money', implying that I should do so as well. After some time, I decided to do as the locals did (*ruxiang suisu*), and gave the sum that was then the minimally acceptable one of 20 Yuan.[10] People were often surprised that I should have done so, given my 'exceptional' status not only as a foreigner but also as a 'doctor' from one of the most prestigious universities of the People's Republic of China (I was a research fellow at Tsinghua University in Beijing at the time). People often asked me in surprise how they were meant to 'return the present' (*huanli*) to me. Normally, the rule is that any money-present has to be returned to the giver, ideally adding a little bit more. My standard answer became that I regarded it as a question of 'basic etiquette' (*jiben lijie*), and I would pay just enough to cover the expense of the meals I was eating. If I added that two good meals in a local restaurant would be at least as expensive, people would frequently break out into laughter.

Obviously for local people the reciprocity of 'coming and going' (*laiwang*), of which giving such money-presents is an expression, was quite different to my idea of 'paying for a meal'. In fact, most of the families where I had attended a celebration and paid a money-present invited me later to their house for another meal. Several times when I walked past their houses, they would call me over, offer me tea, cigarettes and fruits, and then insist that I should stay for a meal. Only later did I understand that this was not only because people were just 'friendly' and 'welcoming' with me, but that this was another general requirement of *li*; my presence, and the money I had given, had to be reciprocated somehow.

The climax of my visiting local celebrations came towards the end of my time in Bashan, when several people suggested to me that I should organize a 'departure party' (*jianxing*) for myself, so that people would have the opportunity to 'return the gift' (*huanli*) to me, and I would have the opportunity to recover everything that I had spent at all the celebrations I had attended. On this issue, again, people were divided. Those that had suggested the idea to me insisted in particular on two points: firstly, that I had been living in Bashan for such a long time, as a very particular guest. They saw me as the representative of a foreign country – being a 'research fellow/exchange student' at a prestigious Chinese university, etc. – and because of all that I should not just leave without notice. It would be appropriate to celebrate the occasion, so that people would have an opportunity to send me off. Secondly, people would have the chance to return the money that I had given to them at the numerous celebrations that I had attended.

Others argued against it, referring to the trouble it would mean for me to organize such a celebration. Organizing the event at the village administration would mean some trouble negotiating with the officials, who might not be supportive. If it were not held in the office building of the village administration, I could either ask a family to host the event at their house, or rent the tables in a local restaurant. The latter option would mean that I would even lose out in money terms, given that renting the restaurant tables and the costs of the meals would easily overtake the 'income' of the money-gifts. But more importantly, some friends pointed out that if people came to give money-gifts, others could call this 'departure party' a 'wine for nothing' (*wushijiu*), a banquet that would just serve to get some money back. For many friends, it was a cause for much laughter to imagine that a blond foreigner would stage a 'wine for nothing'. All in all, I would put myself in a really awkward situation, and it would be almost impossible to resolve all this smoothly.[11] Considering all the implications, I eventually decided against organizing such a departure party before I left Bashan in autumn 2007.

Conclusion

We have seen so far the huge social importance that family celebrations, in particular weddings and funerals, have in Bashan. Yet propriety in ritual is far from unambiguous: in the local talk about Daoist priests, 'night songs' and cremation, the vernacular commentary and the official state discourse stand apart. But in Bashan at least, the local state tacitly tolerates all these phenomena. Faced with the 'commercialization' of popular ritual, however, local state and government-oriented media are actively engaging in propaganda work to fight against 'wines for nothing', bad customs of 'extravagance and waste'.

In the embarrassment of *li*, or ritual, are the remnants of a Maoist discourse that had violently denigrated Confucianism. Cultural intimacy is not something which is limited to the little people or the 'subaltern' – it is also felt by officials, like the county secretary Sun Jundong. Just like ordinary villagers, the powerful also engage in 'social poetics', i.e. in the practical and strategic use of essentialisms. My examples have shown how people used essentialisms of *li* and of corruption.

Even if the role of literacy is quite different when compared with imperial China, the relationship between intellectuals and ordinary people is arguably still similar. In all the ongoing discourses about *li*, written and published texts, such as the newspaper articles cited, surely have more influence and authority than most words said in conversation; and it is clear that most people in the countryside are not in the position to deliberate about social propriety on equal terms with the party and state apparatus, which also controls local media to a huge extent. Compared to imperial China, the production of the authoritative commentaries on *li* and access to them is very different in a society where a high percentage of the population is literate. In imperial China they were pronounced in classical Chinese (*wenyan*), and written by Mandarins who had gone through a long Confucian education. In contemporary Chinese society they are in vernacular Chinese (*baihua*), promulgated in party campaigns, newspapers, TV and books, readily understandable to everyone.

The way in which people's family celebrations are written and spoken about nowadays contains many elements of Maoist discourse, and of contemporary modernist discourse, which are linked to a whole new set of texts prescribing ritual propriety. Yet locals integrate elements of different discourses, including those of contemporary propaganda, into their commentaries on what constitutes *li*. In a situation where it is obvious to everyone that a successful official, just as much as a successful businessman, needs to participate actively in 'networks of presents/human relations' (*renqing wang*), and sometimes also hold a banquet himself, the way that locals see this form of 'governing by exemplar' must be ironic to some extent.

In the embarrassment of *li*, we have seen how forms of local sociality enter into an ambiguous relationship with the state. Similar relationships will be discussed in the next two chapters, which will deal with gambling and with rural development projects.

Notes

1. A Chinese shawm, an instrument similar to the oboe.
2. Ritualized bathing of the corpse and preparation of soul tablets for the dead – two features of the funerary processes described by Watson – do not exist in Bashan. At the twelve funerals I attended during fieldwork, I have never seen a ritual bathing of a corpse, nor was it mentioned. However, utmost emphasis is placed on the way the deceased person is dressed with the 'clothes of long life', *shouyi*, also *lianyi*, E. *laoyi* (while Watson deems special clothing for the deceased optional). I have also never seen soul tablets written at funerals. Brown (2004) has argued that the lack of this custom distinguished the local population from orthodox Han Chinese culture from early on. Whilst Watson includes the ceremonial hammering of nails into the coffin into his standardized sequence, in Enshi the use of nails for a coffin is a taboo. It is said here that putting a nail into a coffin, or nailing it, would bring very bad luck, and prevent the deceased from finding peace. Funerary rites in Bashan are in all these respects fairly close to the standardized ritual sequences of central China. In the Enshi region there are also local customs of 'funerary dances' (*tiao sang*), and even love songs at funerals have been documented (see Guo 1992: 218–238), customs

that are unique to this region. Less constrained by ritual orthodoxy, but also dangerously unconventional, such customs are again characteristic of remote areas. That is, areas further remote than Bashan, which is fairly close to the city of Enshi. In Bashan, however, these customs were unheard of.

3. The Spring Sacrifice Festival is a traditional Chinese festival that has become extinct in many other regions (Wu 2003: 293, footnote 22). The date of the festival is not given in today's peasant almanacs, but most older people know how to determine it: 'The method is to find the first wu-day from the day of the beginning of spring; the wu day will return every ten days, and the fifth wu-day will be the Spring Sacrifice Festival (*sheri*). For instance, the *sheri* of 2001 was the 22nd day of the second lunar month' (Wu 2003: 295). The 'wu' is number five of the ten heavenly stems (*shi tiangan*), with which dates are marked in traditional Chinese calendars. Around this festival, it is common to invite relatives and friends for a meal called *shefan*, which is a rice dish made of sticky rice, wormwood, and other herbs. This is particular to the Enshi region, and the ways in which it is prepared serve as a marker of regional identity (Wu 2005).

4. These men were generally in their fifties or older and so most of them smoked tobacco leaves, which they rolled into rough, small cigars (E. *yezi yan*). Men in their twenties or thirties almost never smoke tobacco leaves, but filter cigarettes instead.

5. For instance, when reciting the legendary history of China, ballads would often conclude with the glorious victory of Communism and the establishment of the People's Republic.

6. Most people know them only by their nicknames: Kang was the second son of his father, and Xia has a huge beard. Kang II even has his name written like that in the book of presents, and most people do not know his full name.

7. Weddings and funerals are also those celebrations that contain much more diverse ritual activity, in particular the 'centring' described above, when compared with birthdays, for instance. In the latter, the main elements are really just the banquets and the money-presents.

8. E.g. the programme 'Today at half past nine' with the report 'anfang zhengjiu' (An undercover enquiry into the customs of holding banquets), 5 September 2007, Enshi TV.

9. Whilst a great deal of attention is paid to reciprocity in the money-presents given, similar reciprocal behaviour can be expected if someone starts a fight at a celebration. Stories are told about hosts who took revenge by starting an even more violent fight at the next celebration of the family of the one who started the fight.

10. As many locals do, I listed all the expenses in money-presents during my time in Bashan (see Appendix C). A small number of people who trusted me well showed me the lists of these expenses, which amounted to an average of 3000 Yuan for a relatively well-off family in Zhongba. However, I do not have any systematic data on the exact amounts of money given. I was slightly embarrassed to ask about the exact amounts of money that they gave or received – and I could not hope to ever reach data sets as exact as the one Yan Yunxiang could get hold of (Yan Yunxiang 1996). In my estimates I am reliant on what people told me, on local gossip, and on occasional glimpses into the 'account books' at the celebrations.

11. One of my neighbours, Auntie Tian, told me it would be like 'carrying a three-and-a-half *jin* bass on its tail' (*san jin ban de luyu – daozhe ti*): normally a bass is carried by its head, with a string through its jaw. Taking it by its slippery tail fin would be rather impractical, especially if it is as heavy as three-and-a-half *jin*. It is like approaching something in such an unreasonable way that the undertaking is bound to fail.

Chapter 6

GAMBLING AND THE MOVING BOUNDARIES OF SOCIAL HEAT

Just about two weeks after my arrival in Zhongba village, some young men offered to teach me *zha jinhua*. *Zha jinhua* – 'bash the golden flower' – is a card game similar to poker but with only three cards for each player. The gamblers, usually half a dozen or more, take turns putting money on the table, each betting on the combination of cards in front of him. Everyone must put in at least one Yuan as an ante, a basic amount at the beginning to enter the betting round. As in poker, each player has three options: to increase the highest previous bet, to match the highest previous bet and 'call', or to give up his hand. Each game is worth an average of 50–100 Yuan, and only lasts a couple of minutes.

I vividly remember the first evening I spent with these young men; notes of ten, fifty, and a hundred Yuan were speedily handed over the low table. Most players placed their bills on the table softly, but now and then someone would hit the table with his palm to underscore his defiance of the others' bets. In the beginning I didn't understand why the rustling heap of banknotes constantly shifted from one player to another. The action was taking place so fast that I couldn't keep up with the players or their bets. The ups and downs of the game were constantly accompanied by the jokes and swearwords of the gamblers, and commentary from the bystanders.

'Five.'

'Ten.'

'That's it for me, I fold.'

'I'll take this one.'

'I'll do it. Double raise!'

And so it went on, until the next showdown, when either everyone had drawn level, or all save one had given up their hands. Filled with cigarette smoke, the room resonated with the exclamations, the swearwords, and the comments of the players and the swift clapping of cards and banknotes. It was 'noisy and hot' (E. *naore*), quite literally.

Sitting there, I was surprised, almost shocked, at the amounts that these young men were gambling with – easily more than a week's income from a job in Beijing, Shanghai or Guangzhou, let alone what they could earn in the odd jobs they could find locally. I thought of what I had read before embarking on my fieldwork about the huge inequalities in wealth in China today, about neoliberal regimes and 'casino capitalism' (Strange 1986). Could it be that I had encountered here something akin to what the Comaroffs had called 'the occult economies' of 'millennial capitalism and the culture of neoliberalism' (1999; 2000)?

In the context of rural China, it seems that such an argument holds quite well: in fact, most of the young people migrating to the cities to work in factories and other low-skill manual jobs are participating in a hugely unequal economy. According to official data, urban per capita incomes were on average three times higher than rural incomes, and five to six times higher if the gap of government spending on public services (health and education in particular) was taken into account (UNDP 2008: 33), but this does not fully reveal the realities that are so visible to most people in the countryside. Both on TV and in their everyday lives in the city they are confronted with glaring inequalities on a daily basis. It is in particular the young who are susceptible to dreams of incredible wealth, who want to 'take the plunge' (*xiahai*), leave the countryside and risk a business enterprise, yet who in the majority of cases end up as wage labourers (*da gong*). How would they explain it to themselves that some 'got rich first', that some in this society are buying cars and houses that they will be never able to buy in a lifetime, and that the countryside where they come from seems more and more stagnant, a place of boredom and dullness? Is not the most obvious explanation simply 'luck' or something like 'magic', just what one would need in gambling? Is the gambling of the marginalized then not just a mirror of rising inequalities and dreams of easy money? A reflection of the frustrations and desires of 'millennial capitalism', and maybe even a form of resistance against it?

Several authors have described contemporary Chinese society in general, and internal labour migration in particular, in terms of 'neoliberalism' and 'millennial capitalism' (e.g. Pun 2003; Yan 2003; Lee 2006). And at least one article situates a particularly spectacular form of gambling in rural China – the *liuhecai* underground lotteries – within the same framework (Bosco et al. 2009). But this is not the direction I want to take here. Following Andrew Kipnis's recent critiques of 'tropes of neoliberalism' in China (Kipnis 2007; 2008), I argue that analysing popular gambling in rural China in terms of 'neoliberalism' would mean positing an absolute and totalizing frame which overlooks social action on the micro and medium level and obfuscates the interplay of local sociality, official discourse, and state control.

After a short introduction on gambling in China, I will look at various forms of gambling in the villages of Bashan township in South-western Hubei province, and try to delineate how they are inter-related with discourses of capability and fate in other areas of life. In gambling itself, one can find certain local expressions around desired forms of sociality, which open up a semantic field of vitality, heat and fire. But there are also many occasions where gambling goes beyond the borders of the socially acceptable. Furthermore, the boundaries of the acceptable in expressions of a vital and 'hot' sociality in general, and of gambling in particular, have changed greatly in recent decades. The central section of this chapter then deals with the different ways in which these boundaries are contested in local communities and in official ideology. In the discourses and practices of gambling, people negotiate the moving boundaries of acceptable sociality between young and old, between urban and rural, and between modernism and traditionalism; this also implies a contestation of the boundaries between state control and market, and between local sociality and official representation in contemporary China.

Gambling in China

Gambling in many different forms has a long history in China (cf. Gernet 1962: 226; Wakeman 1985: 96, 625). There is even the probability that playing cards were first introduced to Europe from China (Wilkinson 1895). According to most accounts, gambling has been a part of rural life for a very long time. For example, C.F. Fitzgerald writes of Dali in Yunnan in the 1930s, that the people there 'are rather fond of gambling, card games being the favourite with adults, and dice with children' (Fitzgerald 2005 [1941]: 191).

While all gambling was forbidden during the Maoist era, since the 1980s many different forms of gambling and betting have become increasingly common. There are now various state sanctioned lotteries, of which the national sports and welfare lotteries are the biggest. Lottery sales are growing rapidly, and the revenue from legal lottery sales in China was already ranked eighth or ninth largest in the world in 2006 (Schmittzehe & Partners 2006: 9). The scope of illegal gambling and betting is even larger, with revenues up to ten times that of legal lotteries, according to some estimates (ibid.: 19). In recent years, the *liuhecai* underground lottery, for instance, has spread rapidly over many regions of central China (Bosco et al. 2009). In this chapter, I will not deal with legal or underground lotteries – none of which were common in the villages of Bashan at the time of my fieldwork in 2007.[1] Instead I focus on mahjong and various local card games which will be described below. These forms of gambling have become the most frequent leisure activity in Bashan in recent decades, and they are mostly condoned by local government.

This surge of various forms of gambling – in particular the more spectacular illegal forms, such as the underground lotteries – invites explanation, and the context of a rapidly changing, 'neoliberal' economy seems to suggest itself. In a recent article, Bosco et al. describe in precisely these terms the *liuhecai* underground lottery that has spread rapidly throughout most regions of central China during the last decade (Bosco et al. 2009). They first reject the argument about 'occult economies' made in other parts of the world, where people reacted to the sudden arrival of commercialization and capitalism by viewing 'the growth of money as magical and open to occult manipulation' (ibid.: 51). According to Bosco et al., this argument does not hold for the growth of underground lotteries in contemporary China, which has a long tradition of commerce and markets. In rural China, they suggest, 'it is not the lack of sophistication in the market economy, but the accompanying frustrations and desires of consumer capitalism, and the growing gap in wealth, that underlies the lottery craze' (ibid.: 53). At pains to find an alternative interpretation for the apparent 'irrationality' of the underground lotteries, Bosco et al. conclude that this 'irrationality' makes sense once seen 'in the context' of an economy where luck, speculation, and corruption play a large role (ibid.: 54). The lottery is 'remarkably similar' to speculation, it 'captures the alchemy of neoliberalism: "to yield wealth without production"' (ibid.: 56); in sum, the lottery is yet another example of 'millennial capitalism'.

It is this conclusion of an otherwise very rich ethnography with which I have problems. Bosco et al. yield to what Latour has called 'the temptation to jump to the "context"', providing the absolute scale of the 'Big Picture' or 'panorama' on which everything can be seen (Latour 2005: 185ff.). Various recent attempts at describing contemporary Chinese society in terms of 'neoliberalism' or 'millennial capitalism' (e.g. Pun 2003; Yan 2003; Lee 2006) fall into the same trap: framing their analyses in these big terms obscures broader differences between various forms of (neo-)liberal and anti-liberal governance, their implementation, and the ongoing political negotiations of actors on the ground. By positing a social whole instead, the trope of 'neoliberalism' masks more than it reveals, as Andrew Kipnis has argued forcefully (Kipnis 2007).[2]

Most ethnographies of gambling do map out some 'context', i.e. they provide some correlations and associations between gambling and the socialities in which it takes place. Several recent anthropological interpretations of gambling have done so, while avoiding the leap to a totalizing picture. Evthymios Papataxiarchis for instance has described the idioms of spendthrift behaviour and 'disinterested sociality' in gambling on Lesbos (Papataxiarchis 1999), and Thomas Malaby has explored how people confront uncertainty and contingency in gambling on Crete (Malaby 2003). Both Paptaxiarchis and Malaby argue that gambling reflects something else of the wider social context in which it takes place. Yet they are careful not to leap too many scales and not to give a total panorama of Greek society.

Ellen Oxfeld (1991, 1993) and Paul Festa (2007) have offered analyses of gambling in Chinese communities which similarly privilege social action at the micro and medium level.[3] While both deal with mahjong in places far away from central China (the first in a Chinese community in Calcutta, and the second in Taiwan), several of the features they describe share some resemblance with gambling in Bashan.

Ellen Oxfeld starts from the apparent contradiction between the 'entrepreneurial ethic' of a Chinese community of tanners in Calcutta and the propensity, in particular, of adult males for high-stakes gambling. In her words gambling 'mimics and re-enacts both the risks and possible gains of entrepreneurship, but it does so within an arena contained by both temporal and spatial restrictions' (Oxfeld 1991: 255). Drawing on Goffman's model of 'fateful action' (Goffman 1967), Oxfeld interprets mahjong gambling as an action that is 'problematic', 'consequential' and 'done for its own sake', and hence a great occasion for the display of character; beyond that, it expresses wealth and status, and possibly 'the central contradictions of the community's ethos', in the sense of Geertz's 'deep play' (Oxfeld 1991: 256, quoting Geertz 1973). Even though there are certain similarities, the place and role of both the 'entrepreneurial ethics' and of gambling in rural China in 2007 differ from that of overseas Chinese communities. Nonetheless, like Oxfeld, I want to focus on the internal contradiction between striving and luck/fate that becomes apparent in gambling.

Paul Festa, in his analysis of mahjong gambling in Taiwan, also takes these two elements as distinctive parts of the social imagery of gambling. Using the theoretical framework proposed by Roger Caillois (2001 [1958]) for the study of play, Festa distinguishes four modes of play: *agon* (competition), *alea* (chance), *mimesis* (simulation) and *ilinx* (vertigo). Using Caillois's formal distinctions, Festa then provides the cultural content of mahjong gambling in Taiwan. First, he argues that '*agon* and *alea* animate dominant aspects of sociopolitical culture in Taiwan', as in the 'martial *agon*' which men cultivate in politics and in the military. Festa connects the element of chance in gambling with certain images of the state, where both personal and national aspirations are linked together, as in the official lotteries, or in the astounding ways in which the state is also seen as an element of 'fate' in individuals' lives. The third element of mimesis is a 'martial imaginary' that is invoked at the mahjong table. The militarization of the island of course has a lot to do with the cross-straits conflict and the perceived threat of the PRC. The mainland also shares a history of militarization that is, however, different in many respects: perhaps most importantly, there is no compulsory military service, and so for most men in Bashan, physical movements at the mahjong table were unlikely to remind them of military drill. Festa concludes his article by suggesting that there are elements of vertigo and possession (*ilinx*) in mahjong, which might contain possibilities of a 'sympathetic agonism' that is 'internalized and generalized' by 'mahjong mimesis'. Such a 'sympathetic agonism' might in the end partake 'in the production of a public space marked by democratic plurality, progress, and change' (2007: 117). That mahjong could mimic a 'sympathetic agonism' of democratic plurality in Taiwan seems a bold speculation to me. But be that as it may, the agonies of democratic development are surely very different across the Taiwan Strait.

As Festa argues, gambling animates certain 'imaginaries' intimately linked to the state. Yet these imaginaries are locally specific in Bashan, and they are linked to the state in different ways from those Festa may have observed in Taiwan. Before coming back to what might be 'simulated' or 'mimicked' in ordinary gambling in Bashan, let us have a look at what is concretely produced in gambling, according to local folk theory: social heat.

The Ambiguities of Social Heat

In Bashan any notable social event should be 'noisy and hot' (E. *naore*, P. *renao* or *honghuo*). The liveliness, noise, and heat implied in the word *naore* are the ideal characteristics of a festival, a banquet, a market, and of gambling. Houses that are high up in the mountains and far away from roads are said in the vernacular to be 'lonely' and 'cold'. Contrasted to this is the 'liveliness' and 'hotness' of the street and the market. This is related to the cultural ideal of having a household that is 'lively and hot' of which the most obvious sign would be many children crowded under one roof.[4] Coming together for any eventful gathering – temple fairs, banquets, or gambling for instance – produces social heat and 'red-hot' exuberance according to a kind of 'sociothermic theory of sociality', as Adam Chau has called it. Using examples such as men's drinking games and temple fairs, he has described this field of social heat as 'red-hot sociality' and a Chinese kind of 'folk event production' (Chau 2006: chapter 8; see also Chau 2008). Yet this kind of 'red-hot sociality' is not unequivocally evaluated positively: temple fairs were prohibited for long periods of time as feudal superstition and, for many urbanites, the drinking games which Chau cites as examples of the production of 'red-hot sociality' (Chau 2008: 493–494) are signs of coarse and uncivilized peasantness. The negotiation around the social heat produced in gambling and how it is evaluated differently by different actors is thus precisely the focus of this article.

In the case of gambling, the ambivalence of social heat parallels the general distinction between 'social gambling' and 'problem gambling'. In Chinese, this opposition is matched closely by the two words that are most commonly used for 'gambling': *wan* and *du*. The first is more entertainment and play, whereas the second clearly denotes the involvement of money and betting. As Pina-Cabral and Chan illustrate in their analysis of gambling in Macao, the decision as to whether a certain game is better described as one or the other is certainly a question of perspective – frequently the gamblers themselves will prefer to speak of *wan* (Pina-Cabral 2002: 82ff). This *wan* side of gambling is also extremely important for the celebration of kinship, of friendship, even of relatedness in general. To 'play' (*wan*) together is the best way of cementing a relationship. *Wan* can involve gambling, but also many other social activities, such as playing games of any kind, eating, making an excursion, chatting, joking, etc. The social exchanges in these activities should ideally be lively, hot, and noisy (E. *naore*), in short, they should produce 'social heat'. It is the other side of gambling – *du* – that is purely associated with betting and money. High-stakes card games played by young men, such as the one mentioned at the beginning of this article, are almost unequivocally called 'gambling' (*du*). There are other games, in particular the pastimes of elders, which will be just as unequivocally called *wan*. But perhaps the larger part of these practices lies in between those two extremes, and there is a lot of ironic playing with the positioning of these forms of gambling with respect to what is socially acceptable and what is not.

Zha jinhua, the game mentioned at the beginning of this chapter, is not in fact the most common one in Bashan, and is generally reserved for young men. The games most frequently played in the villages of Bashan are mahjong and two card games: *dou dizhu* ('struggle against the landlord') and *shaofo* (P. *shaohu*, 'pull and win'). These games are played on the most diverse occasions, during weddings, funerals, and other family celebrations, and also often on rainy days at home. During the 'idle' period of the peasant calendar (*nongxian*), and in particular at the time of the Spring Festival, many people will gamble all day with their families, or with relatives and neighbours. The period of the Spring Festival is a time of permissiveness, of amusement in the home amongst relatives and close friends that more often than not takes the form of gambling.[5] Such forms of gambling will be unequivocally called '*wan*' – which is more the 'play' side of gambling.

Photograph 6.1 Just for fun (*hao wan'r*)

Similarly encouraged, if to a somewhat lesser extent, is the gambling at family celebrations like weddings, funerals and house inaugurations.

Setting up a gambling table and providing guests with a set of mahjong tiles or playing cards belong to the proper ways of hosting a guest, together with offering cigarettes and a meal. This is particularly relevant for families of higher social standing, where guests are frequent and hosting is a sign of distinction; gambling equipment is a necessary household asset in such families. Guests can include friends, business partners and officials, and entertaining guests and spending time together in 'amusement' and 'play' (*wan*) is the best – and often necessary – way of establishing and maintaining good relationships. Before exploring the intricacies of gambling further, it is necessary to make explicit the images of fate and luck that are very often associated with such families as they play an important role in the social idiom in which gambling is viewed and evaluated.

Fate and Fire

In chapter 3, I mentioned the opposition between capability (*nengli*) and life/fate (*ming*), according to which achievement and failure are judged (see Wang 1998). People give contradictory statements about the co-relation between capability and fate, and prefer to judge others ('she is capable', 'that's his fate') rather than assess their own success or happiness. If speaking about themselves at all, people might give ex-post explanations or excuses of something deemed inevitable. It is indeed difficult to claim at any time that someone's life has been happy and successful. The criteria for happiness were traditionally sons, wealth, and long life, but sons can become prodigal, wealth can invite jealousy, and old people can fall ill. Moreover, these traditional criteria have become highly ambiguous in recent decades, most obviously the aspiration for many sons. Family planning is strictly enforced in Bashan, and government propaganda continuously repeats that 'girls are just as good as boys'. The pursuit of material wealth was strongly condemned under Maoism, and though it has once more become fully legitimized, in order to become a marker of happiness and success wealth also needs to be continuously exchanged in proper ways. Regarding all these measurements of 'happiness', it is crucially important to demonstrate one's success to others at appropriate times and in appropriate ways. This display of happiness and success invariably includes conspicuous consumption and the production of 'social heat', as for instance in banquets and family celebrations. Hence to be able to produce social heat is constitutive of living in a socially meaningful way, and showing one's life-fate (*ming*) to others – and perhaps constitutive of having a life-fate (*ming*) at all.[6]

In this sense, it is not coincidental that the word for 'luck' that is commonly used in Bashan – *huoqi* – is also related to warmth and fire. In a standard Mandarin dictionary *huoqi* means 'anger, temper; heat in human body; cold-resistant capacity; internal heat', but in the local dialect it is generally used in the sense of luck (P. *yunqi*). Another very similar word can also be used as an attribute signifying luck and good fate: *huose*. This is explained by locals as similar to saying that someone's 'flame' (P. *huoyan*) is 'high'. There are at least two senses to this word. One is spiritual, meaning that one's 'life-force' is strong; thus, one could say that ghosts will not attack someone whose *huose* is good, because they would fear him, whereas they would attack someone whose *huose* is not good. The other sense, which is much more commonly used by young people, means basically that someone is capable, tough, and impressive.[7]

This semantic field of heat, vitality and success stretches from the proper warmth of a social occasion (E. *naore*), to luck (E. *huoqi* and *huose*), and can also be extended to how a business should be: like fire (*huo*). Saying that a business is going like 'fire' (*huo*) means that it is going exceptionally well – 'like a house on fire'. And this relationship is certainly not only semantic: people who are successful in business will have many reciprocal relationships (*laiwang*), which can be seen in the fact that they frequently receive guests and partake in the 'heat' of celebrations, of commensality, and of amusement (*wan*), which in turn often means gambling together.

Commensality in hosting a guest also reveals in particular ways the verticality and horizontality of the relationships between the people at the table: there will be a clear positioning of the seats at the table according to criteria of age, rank, and power. Inferiors, sitting on the 'lower seats' (*xiawei*), will invite those at the 'higher seats' (*shangwei*) to drink. (The 'lower seats' are generally closer to the doors and the 'higher seats' opposite the door, where the ancestral shrines were placed in farm houses.) An important guest will invariably sit at such a higher seat. In these toasts, one can clearly see an expression of homage on the one side (the inferior invites the superior), and of reciprocity on the other (both drink exactly the same amount) (cf. Pharoah 2005: chapter 4). Just as there is a particular emphasis on formality and equal participation when inviting someone to eat and to drink, the same is true with gambling. Gambling means placing one's luck in the hands of that ruthless arbitrator – the mahjong tiles or the cards. Everyone sticks to the rules, and there is an elaborate ethics of proper behaviour and of paying one's gambling debts. But just as with commensality, hierarchical relationships are plainly visible in gambling. During gambling, the powerful and rich generally end up showing that the 'fire' (E. *huose*) of their life is higher, by demonstrating their indifference to the loss of huge sums, or by winning. Often the inferiors will let them win in order to make the superior feel good, a form of indirect 'gift' to them. If the social distance between the superior and the others is too great, the superior can also simply refuse an invitation to gamble, blocking the occasion for reciprocity and mutual indulgence in social heat all together.

This element of 'fire' is parallel to what is called *yun* in the standard Chinese expression for 'luck' (P. *yunqi*). Both categories are more susceptible to human influence than is *ming*, which is 'fate', but also just simply 'life'. Fire-like luck (P. *yunqi*, E. *huoqi*) stands more for the everyday contingency, which can be manipulated by everyday means. It can be seen within gambling, and immediately so, after every round. *Ming* (fate/life), however, has to do with the outside limits of gambling, and its place in the wider social environment. One's *ming* will not be changed in one round of gambling, but it is still visible in the way one participates in gambling rounds – or does not. Through participation in gambling, people show that they are ready to take risks; in particular they take the risk of losing money at high stakes. The higher the stakes, the higher is the prestige of those who dare to participate. The propriety of such behaviour, in particular of the powerful, is much talked about. And so are the boundaries of gambling, of that which goes beyond what is socially expected as 'entertainment' and mutual amusement (*wan*) in social 'heat' and becomes unsocial gambling (*du*).

Boundaries of Gambling I: In Local Sociality

The contrary evaluation of the willingness to take high risks is crucial for the boundaries of socially accepted gambling in local sociality. If participation in gambling shows that one's *ming* is really powerful, this is even more the case if the stakes are high, and the respective games are 'based entirely on luck' (*wanquan shi huoqi*), as people sometimes said about mahjong and the local card games *dou dizhu* and *shaofo*. When asked directly, most gamblers would say that in these games the ratio of luck and capability is about eighty to twenty per cent, respectively.[8] But while some people (especially young men) would interpret this high risk as a display of strength and character, others (especially older people) would condemn it as irrational and immoral.

At least sometimes the risk taking of the young seemed to be excused as youthful folly, or even positively acknowledged as manly bravery.[9] Several middle-aged men told me that they did not gamble much today but that when they were young, they were tremendous gamblers. Such was the case of one man in his thirties; we were leaving the house where some neighbours had been gambling for about ten days in a row during the 'idle months' (*nongxian*) of the peasant calendar, and on the way home he burst out 'mahjong, mahjong, mahjong; all the time mahjong. It is so boring and useless.' I asked him why then he gambled at all, if it was just boring? He answered that there is just nothing else to do. 'Anyway, it's just fun (*hao wan*), there are no big stakes in there.' When he was young, he went on, he gambled much more. And he would not lose tens or hundreds of Yuan, like now, but tens of thousands of Yuan in just one night. In this way, men often played down their gambling now as mere 'entertainment' (*wan*), but still insisted that they had experience with much riskier and more hazardous gambling when they were young.

Contrary to this acknowledgment of risk taking in high-stakes gambling, many others condemned the gambling attitudes of the young and described as erroneous and misguided the belief that one could show daring strength and power through gambling. If gamblers failed to fulfil social expectations, in particular earning enough money to marry, they would face fierce criticism, both from their family and from outsiders. Even worse was the case of a married man who gambled away all of his family's wealth. Such examples were often referred to as people who had a bad 'fate' (*ming*), as had their parents, who might have been hard-working people.

A case in point in Zhongba was Hu Yanglong. His father Hu Xun-gao had been extremely hard-working, to the extent that the neighbours would often call him a 'model worker' (*laodong mofang*). He had never been officially awarded this honorific title, however; to the contrary, during the Maoist era, he had been classed as a 'rich peasant' and hence had suffered a great deal in 'struggle sessions' and everyday humiliation. Against many odds, and with a lot of hard work, he had built a huge tea factory in the 1980s. One of the first major tea factories in Zhongba, at a time when there was less competition on the tea market, it yielded substantial profit for the family. Far from retiring, the model worker started several other enterprises, toiling day and night. He was one of the first to grow his own tea shoots, and he also had a minor construction business. When there was nothing else to do, he made chairs and tables at home, as he was also a skilled carpenter and joiner. At the time of Hu Yanglong's marriage, his father was building a huge new house for his son on the market street of Bashan, on land belonging to Hu Yanglong's father-in-law. This marriage was considered an extremely good match, the father-in-law providing wealth and building lots on the market place and Hu Xungao building two houses, one of which they later sold to build the next tea factory.

Hu Yanglong was the youngest of three sons; his two older brothers inherited the original tea factory and the family home, whereas he got the house on the market street. He was clearly the favoured one, a rather common pattern locally for the youngest son. His father had from the outset demanded too much of the other sons; the oldest son had left the area some fifteen years earlier to work in another province, while the second son had had several major fights with Hu Xungao. Being the most favoured and youngest son, Hu Yanglong had never worked much in his life. He got involved in some small tea business but preferred to spend his time playing mahjong and visiting brothels.

Soon after I had made his acquaintance, the village officials told me not to spend time with him: 'This guy is up to no good', they said. Yet some young men would also speak in awe of his exploits at the gambling table, and tell stories about him and his companions. In 2007, after several fights with his wife related to gambling debts, he divorced her, and the family had to sell the house on the market. In local gossip he was then mostly described as a 'spendthrift' and 'prodigal son' (*baijiazi*), and not even the young men who had respected him before had any good words to say about him. It was clear that he had transgressed the boundaries of what was acceptable. The risks he had taken had been too high, and instead of displaying a mighty *ming*, he had shown not only that he had no 'luck', but also that his *ming* was bad.

This kind of condemnation by talk and gossip in the village community is well documented in the literature on rural China (see for instance Kulp 1925: 325–326). Citing cases like Hu Yanglong's, older people frequently complained about the morals of the day. Like corruption and prostitution, such gambling was a kind of social heat which had became debauched and destructive. In comments such as this, gambling was often linked with exploitation[10] and speculation[11] to form a morality tale of social decline.

Let me now introduce a form of gambling which stands at the opposite of high-stakes mahjong in all aspects: a local card game, played mostly by old men, and unequivocally accepted as pastime and entertainment (*wan*).

The Shaofo *Game*

Mahjong is probably the most common form of gambling in the Chinese world, and is sometimes ironically called a distinctive trait of Chinese civilization. In Bashan, another form of gambling stands in just such an ironic relation to local belonging and tradition: a card game called *shaofo* or *changpai*. In various forms, this game can be found in many areas of central and south-western China, but each locality has its own rules and its own sets of cards. In Bashan the game consists of four sets of twenty-four long cards with one Chinese character painted in calligraphy on each of them.

Photograph 6.2 The *shaofo* game

The calligraphy is rather intricate, and so at first it was impossible for me to decipher it. When I asked for the meaning of the characters on the cards, a twenty-year-old man told me that it is 'Kong Yiji, you know, the Kong Yiji of Lu Xun'. That did not help me either, until an old man pointed out to me that this is the story of 'Kong the second brother (*Kong Lao'er*). You know, in China we have Kong the second.' And then he told me legends about this man Kong. It began to dawn on me that this must be Kongzi, i.e. Confucius.

The twenty-four characters form eight verses of three characters each, and make up a poem:

shang da ren	His Greatness
qiu yi ji	Confucius
hua san qian	has taught three thousand students
qi shi xian	of which seventy became virtuous scholars.
er xiao sheng	A young student like you
ba jiu zi	should study from eight or nine sages
jia zuo ren	should learn how to be benevolent
ke zhi li	and hence understand courtesy and manners.

The rules of the game are similar to mahjong; people pull cards from the stock in turn, and the one who first reaches a full combination of all his cards in families of three, or sets of three or four of the same card, wins.

What is remarkable about *shaofo*, however, is the social confinement within which it takes place: it is exclusively older men who play the game, and it is played mostly on occasions where it clearly does not conflict with other demands. The accusation of wasting time instead of doing productive work almost never appears here; people play *shaofo* only on the right occasions, that is, on rainy days when there is not much to do anyway, when visiting relatives or on holidays.

Furthermore, as if the ideals of Confucian ethics and propriety written on the playing cards demanded it, this game almost never takes place with very high stakes, nor is it played all night. It is primarily a pastime for older men. This stands in stark contrast with high-stakes mahjong, played by the likes of Hu Yanglong. Whilst the latter is generally judged as 'gambling' (*du*), *shaofo* obviously remains within the accepted boundaries of play and amusement (*wan*). Yet *shaofo* carries with it another kind of ambiguity, which is the ambiguity of a traditionalism which is an essential part of local sociality and at the same time a source of lingering embarrassment vis-à-vis outsiders and the modernist state discourse.

Boundaries of Gambling II: Cultural Intimacy and the State

The cards of the *shaofo* game, and the poem about Confucius on them, stand in an ambivalent relationship to dominant and official orthodoxy. On the one hand, they stand for uprightness and conformity, invoking solemn verses and ideals, and the social confinement of gambling. But they also represent a parody of the archaism of the classical language of Confucian ethics – and of sentences that have been repeated countless times, and mostly only half understood.

The verses on the *shaofo* game were commonly used in late imperial China to teach reading and writing to boys, who had to copy the characters written with brushstrokes, and memorize the verse. In doing so, sons were supposed also to learn the ways of 'benevolence' (*ren*) and 'propriety' (*li*). The stories that old men still tell about 'Kong the second' and his deeds fulfil a similar purpose: they generally have a clear moral which is invariably phrased in the Confucian idiom of filial piety (*xiao*), loyalty (*zhong*), benevolence (*ren*), and propriety (*li*).

What the young man first told me when I asked about the meaning of the characters on the cards is nonetheless intriguing: he simply referred to the 'Kong Yiji of Lu Xun', and gave no further explanation. The short story *Confucius* (*Kong Yiji*) by Lu Xun belongs to the canon of required reading that any middle school student in the People's Republic has to study. In the short story a bedraggled Confucian scholar is mockingly called by the nickname 'Confucius' (*Kong Yiji*). Kong Yiji speaks the arcane language (*zhi hu zhe ye*) of the scholar-officials, but he is impoverished and known as a thief and a drunkard. The narrator describes him at the inn, where he usually gets drunk, whilst the other guests are poking fun at him. Written in 1918, the short story is a parody of the anachronism and emptiness of the classical language of Confucian ethics, and with it of traditional China in its totality.[12]

This short story became a core text of the radical critique of the Confucian tradition from the May Fourth Movement in 1919 onwards. Its radical turn against tradition was rather limited to urban intellectuals during the first decades of the twentieth century. Yet over the course of the century, the extraordinarily forceful rejection of tradition would become hegemonic discourse in China. The slogans of the May Fourth Movement – 'Destroy the Shop of Confucius' (*dadao kongjia dian*) and put 'Science and Democracy' (*kexue yu minzhu*) in its place – were taken over by the Chinese Communist Party. During the Maoist era, similar slogans, including the rejection of the Confucian tradition, were taught in school and endlessly repeated in class struggle sessions, over radios, loudspeakers, and on wall newspapers (*dazibao*).

Even though much has changed regarding the public evaluation of Confucianism, the memory of this past still lingers, and means that elements of popular Confucianism are still a source of embarrassment. Let me now quote a description of *shaofo* that reflects a sense of embarrassment about the Confucian ethics of propriety, or *li*. The following is a blog entry on the internet written by a young man from the provincial capital Wuhan, probably an employee or government official, musing on *shaofo*:

> In the evening some old people sat down next to the road in the shadow of the trees and played a card game together. [He went closer, and discovered, to his surprise, that the poem of 'His Greatness Confucius' was written on the cards.] These 24 characters originally had been the 'textbooks' used in feudal society to teach writing and educate children. [...] Confucius had been the patron saint for which every feudal dynasty (*fengjian wangchao*) since the Han was beating the drums; obviously these 24 characters refer to Confucius and the basics of his thought, and they are imbued with feudal ritual and rules (*fengjian lifa*). But the fact that the vast masses of working people made this poem into a card game for entertainment is really quite interesting. Who says that the rules and etiquette of Confucius chagrined the working people? Your emperor treated it as the highest doctrine, and used it as a 'textbook' to tyrannize students, you say? As for me, I play with this form, play with it in the same way I would play mahjong – what do you want to do about that?
>
> [...]
>
> This is just a card game, why think so much?
>
> (Guangming Shibei 2007)

It should be noted that this was written in 2007; the modernist condemnation of the Confucian doctrine still had its grip on the mind of at least this blogger. This provides quite a glaring contrast to the re-appropriation of Confucianism by the government and mainstream media that was taking place at the same time in the cities and via academic circles. In recent years, the Chinese government has established Confucius Institutes all over the world, and the study of the Confucian classics is a declared priority. TV shows in which university professors discuss the works of Confucius, Mencius, and other classics of Chinese philosophy, history, and literature are hugely popular. The most popular of these is *Lecture Room* (*baijia jiangtan*), a programme where intellectuals discuss the classics and relate them to issues of contemporary everyday life. The most successful TV Confucians are Yu Dan and Yi Zhongtian. Their books, in particular Yu Dan's comments on the Confucian Analects (Yu 2006), have become huge bestsellers over the last couple of years. Actually one of my neigh-bours in Zhongba, a farmer and retired village official, also read one of Yi Zhongtian's books in the evenings after working in the fields. This all goes to show that the modernist denial of the Confucian tradition has long ceased to be hegemonic. In fact, for many urban Chinese the kind of Cultural-Revolution style condemnation of Confucianism has itself be-come an embarrassment, a show of uncivilized peasant despotism.

As the Confucian morals represented by the characters on the *shaofo* cards have become highly ambiguous, so have the Confucian morals rep-resented by the rounds in which *shaofo* is actually played. It is in these rounds that the strongest judgements about the lack of morality of the young can be heard. But for many of the young, the rounds and card games of the old men represent village-level gossip and peasant narrow-mindedness, exactly those things that have to be left behind if one is to enter 'the big world' (*da shijie*) of the cities. Recalling the ambiguities of popular Confucianism and potentially representing peasant backward-ness, these games are not strictly encouraged by officialdom. They are tacitly permitted – but definitely not publicly displayed.[13] After all, *shaofo* itself is also a form of gambling.

Shaofo is also barely ever mentioned in the local media. The intricate ambiguities associated with it are more muted, especially when compared with high-stakes card games and mahjong. Every now and then, high-stakes gambling is loudly condemned in the newspapers and on TV, and there are regular reports about businessmen and officials who have been punished for taking part in gambling (e.g. Enshi Wanbao 2007a, 2007e). In a similar vein, high-stakes gambling is often portrayed in the newspapers as the pastime of thugs and shady elements in society (e.g. Enshi Wanbao 2007b, 2007f). In newspaper articles and political announcements, 'gam-bling' (*dubo*) is not presented as the flip side of economic development, but as a residue of 'backward' peasant culture, in the same category as lack of hygiene and 'feudal superstition'.[14]

The irony here is that it is precisely those who try hardest not to be peasants, that is, migrant workers, rural businessmen and officials, who are the focus of such attacks. They themselves always describe their ac-tions as harmless 'entertainment' (*wan*), and yet the 'fire-like' sociality that is created by such entertainment is something that is frowned upon by the authorities. Officials in particular are the targets of regular government campaigns against gambling. However, as everybody knows but no one can quite say publicly, there are good social reasons to explain why local officials are very often heavy gamblers. Besides individual propensities and the boredom of a life in the civil service, there is another reason for the frequency of gambling amongst officials: it serves the function of es-tablishing tight relationships with superiors, peers and business partners, in the celebration of lively, vital and 'hot' sociality. Such relationships, welded by social heat, are often necessary to be an effective official or businessman.

Officials, the businessmen who collaborate with them, and the migrant workers who aspire to become businessmen, all have to engage with the moving boundaries of socially acceptable gambling on an everyday basis. The official discourse of newspapers and TV is not yet very sophisticated here: gambling is either not mentioned at all, or is strongly condemned. But elsewhere in China, gambling – mahjong at least – has already become the object of a normalizing discourse related to the government's aim of creating frameworks of 'civilized' leisure activities.

So argues Paul Festa, for instance: using the example of governmental and academic discourses on mahjong, he describes the emerging normalizing framework and 'moral regulation' of mass consumer culture in the People's Republic (Festa 2006). Dealing primarily with consumption, these discourses also elaborate on notions of civility and national belonging. Festa's examples for these 'mahjong politics' are exclusively textual, mainly focusing on one treatise entitled 'The Study of Mahjong' (*majiangxue*) by Sheng Qi, which proposes an academic investigation on mahjong, and gives recommendations for 'healthy mahjong' (*jiankang majiang*), which would be a proper expression of Chinese culture, as opposed to degraded 'popular mahjong' which is simplified and mostly involves betting.[15] Predictably, Festa concludes that there are countless contestations around this discursive construction. He observes 'that popular mahjong and the gambling that accompanies it are alive and well' (2006: 26), and that there is an 'official ambivalence over whether or not to promote healthy mahjong', which, however, 'merely underscores the party-state's unequivocal antipathy for popular mahjong, ensuring that playing mahjong in contemporary China will remain at once a personal and political act' (Festa 2006: 28).

In the countryside of Enshi, such a sophisticated 'moral regulation' of mahjong does not yet exist; the promotion of 'healthy mahjong' is unheard of here. In the official and government discourses in Bashan, there is simply no positive evaluation of gambling that would point towards the normalizing moral framework described by Festa. This might arrive soon, but so far, gambling is either tacitly condoned (as is *shaofo*, mostly), or publicly denounced as corrupt practice.

As a practice that is both crucially important for local sociality and a potential source of external embarrassment, gambling in these forms is an expression of cultural intimacy, to use Michael Herzfeld's term (2005). This sense of intimacy arises from the tension between a modernist outside representation (where gambling is continuously condemned) and the continuation of local practices, which partly contradict the former. If talking to an outsider (an urbanite, a government official, or an anthropologist), people refer to *shaofo* with characteristic gestures of irony or embarrassment: such a game is presented as a curiosity, an oddity, and potentially a troublesome relict of peasant traditionalism.

The card games played by old men do not represent anything nearly as dangerous and unruly as the games of the young. Yet, the high-stakes games of the young, of officials, businessmen, and migrant workers, also reproduce vital and hot sociality – a sociality that is the more intimate because it is frequently deplored in official discourse. The conflict between this local form of sociality and the ideological representation of gambling as a social pathology has to be confronted continuously. In the everyday practice of 'social poetics' (Herzfeld 2005), people creatively bring together outside representations and inside knowledge, and negotiate the moving boundaries of socially acceptable heat.

Conclusion

I began this chapter with the hunch about 'occult economies' and 'millennial capitalism' which occurred to me when I was watching young men gambling in Bashan. Admittedly, most of the other forms of gambling that I have described here are clearly less spectacular. But even for the high-stakes gambling of young men, an explanation in terms of 'neoliberalism' would overlook the everyday contention of the boundaries of social heat which I have described here.

Over time I had to realize that there were many aspects to the different forms of gambling common in Bashan which a description in such terms would overlook. If the analyst imposes an absolute and objectivist interpretative framework such as 'neoliberalism' or 'millennial capitalism', social action at the micro and medium level (captured here in the concepts of 'social heat' and 'cultural intimacy') either gets completely lost from view or becomes a mere after-product of the posited whole. Instead of locating gambling in contemporary rural China somewhere inside the 'bigger picture' of 'neoliberalism' or 'millennial capitalism', I have suggested here that through the local idiom and practice of 'social heat' it could be better understood as a changing way of socializing and of displaying social success. Additionally, it epitomizes the contradictions between old and young, rural and urban, and local sociality and official/state discourse.

In this chapter I have described how local notions of capability, luck and fate relate to a kind of 'social heat' that is characterized by a certain ambiguity: while expected and necessary sometimes, it can also turn into deplored anti-social indulgence. From there I traced the boundaries of acceptable forms of 'entertainment' (*wan*) against that which should be condemned as 'gambling' (*du*), both in local sociality and vis-à-vis the local state. But the ways in which the boundaries of socially acceptable gambling are drawn in local sociality and in official discourse are partly contradictory. Official discourse largely condemns gambling as backward 'peasant' activity, and extends this blanket condemnation to forms of gambling which are essential to local sociality (for which *shaofo* was a prime example). Yet on the other hand, official discourse misdescribes the high-stakes gambling which is popular precisely among those who try hardest not to be peasants but to be assertively modern (local politicians, businessmen, and migrant workers).

Older people, when asked about the morals of the time, frequently named gambling, prostitution, and the lack of filial piety as the principal signs of the decline of public morality. As regards gambling, it seems to me that this does not refer to gambling *per se* – which has long existed in China – but to the fact that gambling nowadays is increasingly expanding outside the confines within which it was socially acceptable and even expected. The production of 'social heat' – the liveliness and warmth that is good and proper on the one hand, but can spill over into corruption and chaos on the other – is crucial to both the accepted norms of old, and to the new values and expectations of the market economy. The discourses and practices of gambling epitomize the moving boundaries of this social heat, including the boundaries of what is acceptable within local sociality, and the outside boundaries of local sociality itself.

Notes

1. The welfare and sports lotteries are generally limited to urban regions and are more popular with people who have medium or high incomes. In Bashan there existed one lottery station in 2007, which was generally frequented by older men from the township. I have never seen anyone from the surrounding villages buy a lottery ticket there. The *liuhecai* underground lottery was very common in the Yangzi plains of Hubei in 2007, but had not yet arrived in the mountains of this region.
2. A related problem is whether the society and economy of contemporary China is 'neoliberal' at all. Referring to its oligarchic corporatist state and party, the strengthening of personalist ties, and the persistence of highly un-egalitarian hierarchies, Kipnis (2008) and Nonini (2008) argue against using 'neoliberalism' to describe contemporary China.
3. Many ethnographies mention the topic in passing (e.g. Kulp 1925: 325–326; Hsu 1948: 26, 65; Watson 1975: 168), but to my knowledge Oxfeld (1991; 1993: chapter 4), Festa (2007), and Bosco et al. (2009) are the only texts providing focused anthropological analyses of Chinese gambling.

4. Since family planning was enforced in the 1980s, most families have only one or two children.

5. 'Both the New Year season and the Autumn Festival are times of increased licence. Gambling is sanctioned by custom if not by law' (Feuchtwang 2001 [1992]: 112).

6. Adam Chau imagines that in contrast to the Cartesian cogito, 'a Chinese peasant philosopher' might have said 'I make social heat (*honghuo*), therefore I am' (2008: 485).

7. In standard Chinese the equivalent in this sense would be *lihai*. The character "*li*" means originally sharp, fierce, and dangerous; it can also mean 'evil ghost', as in '*ligui*'.

8. Festa's gambling partners in Taiwan gave the same ratio of skill and luck for mahjong (Festa 2007: 109).

9. Some women also gamble for high stakes, but most 'problem gamblers' are male. Women would also claim that their own gambling is 'just for fun', no matter how high the stakes are; but only rarely did I hear women boast about the sums they lost or won at the gambling table, while this was more common with young men. It would be interesting to explore further the importance of risk taking for the performance of masculinity (as Paul Festa has done in his writing on mahjong in Taiwan, see Festa 2007).

10. A teacher from the local primary school explained this to me with a saying: 'the gentleman loves money, and he knows morally appropriate ways to get it' (*junzi ai qian, qude you dao*). The good-for-nothing (*xiaoren*), however, does not have morals; he will use exploitation (*boxue*) and gambling (*dubo*) to accrue wealth.

11. The real estate market in bigger Chinese cities has been exploding, with prices for apartments rocketing in recent years; many people in the countryside, especially those who aspire to an apartment in a city, have been following these development closely, and they also frequently mentioned that this boom is driven by speculation and profiteering (*touji daoba* or *touji maimai*). Just like 'exploitation' (*boxue*), 'speculation' (*touji daoba*) was an activity that the 'bad classes' would engage in and be accused of under Maoism. I was told stories of neighbours who were criticized in class struggle sessions for selling minor goods like chairs or vegetables on the black market; they were said to have gone astray onto the 'capitalist road' and to want to engage in speculation and profiteering (*touji daoba*).

12. In his other classic short story *Diaries of a Madman*, Lu Xun had depicted the consequences of Confucian teachings in even more dramatic terms: whilst studying extensively the four books and the five classics, the narrator sees the words 'Eat People!' (*chi ren*) emerge between the lines of these texts. He falls into paranoia, increasingly convinced that the people in his surroundings, including his doctor and his brother, are prepared to eat him. All these people are heartless and false, and bound to a tradition that is really cannibalistic. Shortly after its first publication, Wu Yu wrote an essay in which the message was further reduced to a simple equation between Confucianism and cannibalism (Wu 1985b [1919]). This argument was frequently cited by radical intellectuals to exemplify the cruelty of Confucianism, the 'doctrine of *li*' (*lijiao*). Lu Xun's short stories are reprinted in Lu Xun (2004).

13. In summer 2007 I visited the neighbouring township Songtaiping, which is known locally as the origin of *shaofo*, and where until now *shaofo* cards have been printed. During this short visit, I was given several introductions to the local situation, mostly about the local economy and culture. Even though local officials are nowadays often 'digging out' (*wajue*) anything that could count as 'local culture', the *shaofo* game was mentioned only once, as an anecdote and with a benign smile on the face of the official who told me about it.

14. A report entitled 'Fascination for Rural Construction and Forgetting Adversities' portrays a stereotype of what the results of successful rural development should look like: 'Now the villagers and neighbours live together in solidarity and harmony, the villagers are actively devoted to rural construction; gambling (*dubo*) and playing cards (*dapai*), disputes over trifles (*che pi la jin*), heterodoxy and superstition (*xiejiao mixin*), do not exist in this village, and instead development, construction and knowledge are quietly on the rise' (Songtaiping Township 2006).

15. 'Ideally, then, to play healthy mahjong would involve the self-cultivation of civilizing norms and, at the same time, the reproduction of Chineseness as a commercial value to be capitalized by the regime of accumulation' (Festa 2006: 26).

Chapter 7

FACE PROJECTS IN RURAL CONSTRUCTION

In the novel *An Ordinary World*, Lu Yao writes about rural life and politics in central China from 1976 to 1983, the years between the end of the Maoist era and the beginning of 'reform and opening'. In 1980, Old Gao, a senior leader in the central government, comes to visit the small town where he was born, and announces that he wants to meet his former classmates from middle school. Many of them are peasants and very poor, and the local cadres of the county are afraid that they will give a very poor picture of the situation in the region. Thus they want to instruct all of Old Gao's schoolfellows to tell him only positive things, and they organize a tour to the most prosperous villages of the county – all so that Old Gao will receive a very good impression. In the decisive meeting of the local cadres, Tian Fujun, one of the heroes of the novel, is the only one who has the courage to stand up and denounce the situation: 'What he wants to know is the real situation. But if we so obviously fake and stage up an image, "hoodwink those above and delude those below" (*man shang qi xia*), we do not only commit a mistake, but a crime!' (Lu 2002 [1989]: 177).

After this intervention the local leaders do not dare to instruct the former classmates, and let them talk with Old Gao. Eventually the poor farmers and the leader from the central government have a 'meeting of telling bitterness' (*suku hui*); the farmers can reveal all their poverty and suffering to Old Gao.

Countless examples can be found in Chinese history of the basic constellation in this story: there is the good official in whom the ordinary people can trust, and who will denounce the misdeeds of corrupt minor officials. If only people can reach him, he will surely condemn the counterfeit and report the real situation.[1] And there are the petty minor officials, who try to improve their own image and that of the region they are governing. That these minor officials would go from pretending to building 'Potemkin villages' and even to barefaced lying seems to have become more common in the last century, when concrete demands, quotas and targets for local officials increased rapidly. In reality, one denunciation – such as Tian Fujun's in the novel – is barely enough to lead to a decisive change. I had plenty of opportunities to observe similar situations, and the negotiations, denunciations, and compliancy amongst villagers and local officials during my fieldwork in Bashan.

Since the 1950s, most rural areas in China have undergone countless administrative reforms. The scope and title of administrative units has changed on average every six years in Bashan, which is probably representative of most regions in central China. In 2003, the last administrative reform in Bashan brought together on average three villages into one new administrative village, with an average population of about 5000 inhabitants. The officials of these new administrative villages are closely connected with the township government, and are mainly responsible to them. At the same time, the abolition of the general agricultural tax meant a dramatic relaxation of the relationship between farmers and local officials. In many cases, one side-effect was that this relationship became one of indifference on both sides. Local officials often have few obligations or reasons to maintain links with the rural population, and at the same time farmers have little bargaining power in relation to local government.[2]

In such an environment, many officials find themselves more reliant than ever on the benevolence and assessment of their superiors within the government hierarchies. They are frequently under pressure to implement development programmes that are mainly assessed by higher officials during brief visits. To satisfy their superiors, and to safeguard their own chances for promotion, local officials frequently settle for building a façade of successful 'development'. These showcases have entered the jargon of local politics in China as 'face projects' (*mianzi gongcheng*) or 'image projects' (*xingxiang gongcheng*). On the most obvious level, these expressions are meant to criticize development programmes that are aimed at 'building face' for local government, constructing a mere 'façade' of local development for the gaze of higher government levels – yet there is more to them than that. In this chapter I will describe some of the rural development programmes that have been implemented in Zhongba, and explore the discourses of 'face' surrounding them. Starting with the façade of the houses of Zhongba, this is also about the 'face' of local families and local officials.

The 'face' of the houses of Zhongba also resonates with the broader theme of the two previous chapters, cultural intimacy. Michael Herzfeld has developed this concept on the basis of an earlier outline of *disemia*. Disemia, in his definition, is 'the formal or coded tension between official self-representation and what goes on in the privacy of collective introspection' (2005: 140; see also Herzfeld 1982). In its linguistic form, this is diglossia: the contrast between a national language and vernaculars. But, 'the phenomenon is by no means confined to language' (Herzfeld 1985: 25, footnote 5): the relationship between façade and interior in architecture, for instance, can become another expression of the same tension. The binary opposites in this coded tension are claimed and attributed both by ordinary people and by the powerful. This interplay, and in particular the use of essentialisms and stereotypes in it, is what Herzfeld calls 'social poetics' (2005: 21ff). In this chapter, I will show how ordinary people and government officials make strategic use of images of development and of stereotypes of the 'good official'. The local discourse on 'face projects' is a case in point, exemplifying as it does the various uses of stereotypes, and how they are employed towards different ends (such as denunciation or excuse for instance). Beyond that, local discourses on face bespeak a common knowledge of appropriate social expression and a shared background knowledge; i.e. something behind the face which is not shown, but known by those who understand.

Rural Construction in Zhongba

In the last decade, the abolition of the general agricultural tax was probably the most momentous policy change for many farmers in China. For the first time in history, farmers did not have to pay the 'emperor's food tributes and the country's taxes' (*huang liang guo shui*) anymore. Instead of levying taxes, the national government has gradually increased public spending in rural areas and introduced subsidies to agricultural producers.[3]

The abolition of the agricultural tax was part of a wider change in the development of rural policies. In 2005 the politburo of the Communist party announced that it would make rural development one of its foremost priorities for the 11th Five-Year Plan (2006–2011) with the 'Construction of a Socialist New Countryside' (*shehui zhuyi xinnongcun jianshe*). The central objectives of this policy are to promote 'modern agriculture and local industry' through 'scientific research and innovation', to 'ensure the steady increase of rural incomes by abolishing rural taxes and optimizing land use rights', and 'to deliver more efficient and adapted public services such as healthcare, education, financial services and environmental protection' (Ye 2006: 12).

Since 2006, the rural development policy of Enshi prefecture has followed these national guidelines. Here as well, countless offices and departments of party and government have issued statements detailing the contents of the new agricultural policies. They are generally prefaced with reminders of the contents of national polices. One document issued by the city government of Enshi in 2006, for example, cites the following aims of 'Rural Construction':

1. Scientific planning, actively constructing a civilized village on the provincial level
2. Adjust structures, and do everything to raise the income of the farmers
3. Advance the construction of a new civilized countryside, and raise the level of culture of the villagers
4. Develop education and hygiene, raise the population quality (*suzhi*) and living quality (*shenghuo zhiliang*)
5. Strengthen the construction of governance, raise villagers' capacity for self-governance. (Enshi City 2006a)

In this outline we find many of the focal points of governmental modernization policies: scientific development (*kexue fazhan*), civilization (*wenming*) and cultural level (*wenhua shuiping*), population quality (*suzhi*), self-governance (*zizhi*) and raising incomes (*zengjia shouru*). Other government documents give more concrete objectives, often again in numbered titles. In Enshi prefecture and Enshi city, the set targets were given in the formula: 'Five changes, three constructions, two improvements and one opening' (*wu gai san jian liang tigao yi gongkai*). This breaks down in the following way:

- Five changes: roads, water system, kitchen, toilet, and pig sty
- Three constructions: hygienic school campus, individual household methane gas tank, more productive and market-oriented agricultural industry
- Two improvements: local government co-ordination and individual cadres' 'quality' (*suzhi*)
- One opening: more transparency in village government affairs.

In what follows, I will describe the implementation of these policies in Zhongba. For most ordinary people, they meant only a continuation of earlier developmental policies that had long been in place. In 2000, for instance, Zhongba was chosen as a 'civilized village' (*wenming cun*) of Hubei province, and at the same time an 'Outline for the construction of a civilized Zhongba village' (*Zhongba cun chuangjian shengji wenmingcun guihua*) was drawn up by the township government, and several developmental programmes implemented. In fact Zhongba had been a showcase for government policies since the Maoist era. In the 1970s it was given the title of a 'red flag brigade' (*hongqi dadui*), in the 1980s it became a 'model village' (*shifan cun*), and numerous other titles abounded later, amongst them 'civilized village' (*wenming cun*) and 'village of comfortable living standards' (*xiaokang cun*). These honorary titles keenly express the changing ideological orientations: from the red flag of a revolutionary brigade, to a civilized and 'well-off' (*xiaokang*) little village. The special attention Zhongba has been receiving for decades from local government is based on at least two factors: its geographical advantages (it covers a relatively flat area and is located just next to the township seat, whereas most other villages in Bashan are either extremely mountainous or far away from the township seat); and the fact that many officials in the township government are from Zhongba, or have close bonds with some villagers.

Yet if the 'New Socialist Countryside' was partly a continuation of earlier policies, it also brought with it new focuses and policies. Not least, it brought particular development programmes and subsidies. The government structure that implemented the development programmes is rather complicated. From the thicket of policy doctrines, working groups, and programmes that have been established and implemented in Zhongba over recent years, I want to elaborate here on the work of the village committee, together with a working group of cadres from the city government, in the summer of 2006.

Following several internal documents and strategic plans from higher party levels at the prefecture and city level, a 'working group' of cadres from the village, township and city level was established, whose task it was to lead and organize these programmes. This working group included four cadres from the city government, of which one was from the Department for Education, one from the Council for Minority and Religious Affairs, and two more from the city government office.

In Zhongba, the 'Rural Construction' carried out by this working group in 2006 included workshops, training sessions and subsidies for agricultural production, but that was only a minor part. Another part of the development programme was a complete renovation of the village administration building. Until 2003 this building had been the Zhongba primary school; the primary school was then closed (primary students now attend school in the market town in Bashan), and the huge building was converted into the village administration. The most important part, however, was the renovation of houses and the improvement of hygienic installations. That meant mainly that many houses that were visible from the principal asphalt road of Zhongba were painted on the outside, and given stylized gable ornaments, scrolls with calligraphy, and lamps. Some of the costs were subsidized directly by the government, some given in materials (such as tiles, concrete, lamps, paint, etc.), and the rest had to be procured by the farmers themselves. In a few households, the government also supported farmers who were improving the hygienic installations of their kitchens, toilets, and pig sties.

It was impossible for me to determine exactly what kind of support and how much money certain households received. But these topics were undoubtedly much discussed, especially when I had just arrived in Zhongba. Even though the development programmes in Zhongba continued for most of my time there in 2006 and 2007, at the time of my arrival (May 2006), the officials were working under tremendous pressure. The reason for the huge efforts towards a 'New Countryside' in these two months was that a visit of a high official from the provincial government of Hubei province had been announced for the beginning of July. When representatives of the provincial government were due to visit, everything had to appear at its best. During this time, officials of the working group, and others from the village and township government, met in the village administration building every day, and went to peasant households to negotiate the details of the work to be done at certain households.

Whilst guidelines for the distribution of money and material were published and put on the announcement board of the village, no one outside the working group and the higher levels of government could really follow the detailed distribution of the money coming from higher government levels. The two single criteria for the availability of funding and material for this programme to the local farmers were clear to most people: first, proximity to (in fact, visibility from) the public road around Zhongba; and second, the closeness of personal relationships to leading cadres in the various levels of government.

Three families, among those most favoured by the local government, received money to renovate their kitchens and toilets, and were even given computers. Xiang Jixiang's household is probably the one that got most out of the government subsidies. In 2005, he started to build a complete new house, with three stories, and two balconies on each side. His house was the only one that was built in the style of Daliangxi, a village closer to the city of Enshi, where a whole new village centre was built with all houses in uniform 'minority culture' style. Outside his house, a little terrace was built with a fence of columns, and three street lamps.

Even though Xiang Jixiang did not have a kinship relationship with any one of the leading cadres, he has very good relationships with several of them, and created those relationships of 'fictive' kinship which are unfailingly efficacious. His five-year-old son has one 'adoptive father' (*gan die*) and one 'adoptive uncle' (*rende jiujiu*) amongst the leading cadres responsible for the development programmes. Other villagers would often point out the relationship that Xiang Jixiang had with the cadres in the township government; whereas he would always emphasize both to me and to other villagers that he was working very hard to build his new house.

Another two families in the same village unit as Xiang Jixiang were also amongst those that appeared to be continuously receiving government subsidies. They are in fact relatives of the former head of the township of Bashan, Yao Kejin, who was a very charismatic leader, and, if some people are to be believed, almost single-handedly introduced the new tea varieties to Zhongba in the 1990s.[4] He Tingqian, who married into the Yao family, and came into the village as a son-in-law, told me proudly about two brothers of his wife (cousins of Yao Kejin) who are working now in the city government.

Other families who had built new houses along the public road also received subsidies. One case was my neighbour Tian Shanwei, who had recently built one of the biggest houses in Zhongba. In 2007 the family completed the brickworks of a three-storey home. According to Tian Shanwei, the new house will have a living space of 330 m², will be equipped with six balconies, and will cost him altogether probably around 150,000 Yuan. Even though the village government had initially opposed this massive building right next to the village administration, he later received some support. This was due not least to his continuous efforts at building good relationships with the officials of the township. Once the Tan family had got permission to build a new house, the township officials consulted with him on the architectural plan and the façade. Because of Tian Shanwei's decision to build a façade in the same 'minority style' that Xiang Jixiang and others had used, he received some support for painting and carved windows.

In stark contrast to the families mentioned so far, the majority of the households only got minor subsidies to paint the front of their houses facing the public road. And most families whose houses were located away from the asphalt road received nothing. For obvious reasons, it is impossible to determine the flows of money, the amounts given to particular households for 'rural construction' and what was given to a particular official. In all cases, the actual support given by government was only a minor part of the money needed to build a house. The officials were supposed to work together with the farmers' households to re-model their houses in a particular fashion.

In Zhongba, many people talked about the development programmes in very disparaging terms, including many of those who had received government subsidies. People complained that others were getting more, that the material that the government was offering was of a bad quality, and that the government officials were siphoning money into their own pockets. One comment I often heard was that 'they are helping the rich, and not the poor' (*tamen fu fu, bu shi fupin*), turning the expression for 'poverty alleviation' (*fupin*) on its head. People whose farms were higher up in the mountains, away from the asphalt road, sometimes invoked the village community, not using the word for village (*cun*), but that for 'brigade' (*dadui*): 'We are all from one brigade (*dadui*), how can it be that only those next to the road are getting money?'

The 'brigade' was the administrative unit of the Maoist era, which was abolished in the 1980s. Whilst even the villagers close to the public road, especially the older generation, often routinely used the notion of their 'brigade', the village cadres never used it. For them the development programmes were focused on individual households, 'village groups' (*xiaozu*), 'model districts' (*shifan qu*), and the administrative village.

In some cases, people chose to refuse government support, if they thought the proposals or the money offered useless. Some particularly confident people refused the government support outright, if it was only enough to paint the outside of their houses. Wang Guohui, whose house is next to the public road but facing away from the road, explained to me: 'Secretary Fang and Director Guan came over, and offered to paint the back side of my pig's barn. The front side of my house, they said, I could do myself. I said "what use that would be?" If they wouldn't help me to do the front side of my house, I don't want their money at all.'

But some months later, just before the marriage of his son Wang Wei (described in chapter 4), Wang Guohui was renovating his house together with his son. They built a new kitchen for the young couple, with a new stove with tiled surfaces, tiled walls, and a storage room. This time his son Wang Wei approached the village secretary for support, and received a proportion of the tiles from the government, to the value of about 600 Yuan. They paid for all the other material, and the wages, themselves.[5]

Over at the Yang family hamlet, Yang Yuanbing told me that several officials from the working group came over to his house (which is about 200 m from the public road, and can be seen from there), and offered to help him if he would plaster and paint the outside walls. He refused, and said, 'how would that help me if the house inside is still the same as before?' Yang Yuanbing went on to say that the 'Construction of a New Countryside' is just a pretext (*kouhao*) for the local cadres to get money from above. They would use only parts of it, to do some superficial work, such as painting the outside walls, and then channel the bigger part into their own pockets: 'What they do here is just a face project (*mianzi gongcheng*), and most of the money they take for themselves. Look at them, what tobacco they are smoking, and what kind of houses they are constructing for their own families! Could they afford that if they would really just use their meagre official salary?'[6]

With such extreme cases of favour and rejection, the general image was clear to most: that the development programmes at that time would only be implemented in the houses next to the public road, and that those who stood on good terms with government officials would have a better chance of receiving support. In particular, those local farmers who had not benefited from the development programmes criticized them and described them as 'face projects' (*mianzi gongcheng*).

Amongst Officials

The government structure that implemented the development programmes is rather complicated. As mentioned, during the year 2006, a working group of officials from several government levels was stationed in Bashan and collaborated with the township and village officials. According to the documents that accompanied their appointment for the working group in Zhongba, they were to stay in Zhongba for one year, but two were earlier assigned to other posts, one of which was clearly a promotion.[7]

The village committee of Zhongba had six members in 2006 and 2007, of which three were local villagers, and three, including the secretary of the party branch, were outsiders that had been assigned by the township government. But the village committee had only a secondary function in the development programmes of 2006; its major functions were tasks such as family planning, maintenance of roads, conflict mediation, etc. Aside from village committee and the party branch, there are plenty of other organizations, including the village militia (*minbing*), women's association (*funü lian*), democratic financial accounting working group (*minzhu licai xiaozu*), democratic control working group (*minzhu jiandu xiaozu*), etc., all of which are subordinated to the village committee and the party branch.

The cadres who were not local farmers in Zhongba either lived in the market town of Bashan, or in the city of Enshi. They had 'reciprocal relations' (*laiwang*), such as regular exchanges of presents at family celebrations, only with very few villagers, mostly with the other cadres, and with households that were successful in the tea trade. All of the cadres of this working group, and of the village committee and party branch of Zhongba, are outsiders to the village. There are only three cadres who are locals: two older men who act as representatives of the village groups that are further away from the centre of Zhongba, and Zhu Yuan, who is the village mayor.

Most of the cadres who are not locals do not have close relationships with the majority of the villagers. They will in all probability serve for only a relatively short time in this one particular village. At the same time, the party secretary and the cadres of the working group were facing relatively high expectations from higher government officials. Their relative success in these programmes would be a criterion for potential promotions within the government hierarchies.

During my time in Zhongba, I spent a great deal of time with these officials. Even though my relationship with them generally remained somewhat tense, I was sometimes invited to participate when outside visitors came to 'inspect' (*kaocha*) the advancements of local development and the general situation in the village.

A Visitors' Tour

The common route on which visitors would be taken by local government officials went around the asphalt road on Bashan Slope to the tea plantations near the Xiang and Yao family homes. The little paths inbetween the tea fields here are conveniently paved with concrete, so that they can be walked upon by people wearing leather shoes or high heels. Then the visitors would inspect a house, where they would see hygienic kitchens, pig barns and toilets, street lamps and brick-laid waste containers (see photograph 7.1). On occasions, they would also be shown the computers and library about production techniques and rural development at the house of the Yao family. From there they might end their visit after a short stop at the village administration. Such visits sometimes occurred as often as once per week, especially during the summer, and I was asked to participate in several of them. Let me give an example of such a tour.

Photograph 7.1 The model household

One morning in March 2007, the village cadres told me that I should join them in taking around some visitors from the Office for Civil Affairs of Hubei province. They were preparing a research report on transparency in local government, and would spend two days in Bashan interviewing cadres and farmers. Half an hour later, two officials and a young researcher from a university in the provincial capital Wuhan arrived in a black Volkswagen, accompanied by officials of the township government. After an introduction to the village, given by the local cadres, everyone was treated to tea and cigarettes, and the three guests interviewed some local farmers.

The farmers were asked what they knew about the government at the township and village levels, how local elections worked, about conflicts in the village and possible conflict solutions, and about petition letters. Without exception, the farmers all delivered a perfect image of the village, without any conflicts. They knew about local elections, and the village announcement board. When questioned about possible methods of conflict solution, including petition letters, they told the researchers that there were extremely few conflicts in the village, and definitely no petition letters.

The three peasants who had been invited were either relatives of cadres in the township government, had worked in the village administration, or belonged to those households that were amongst those that had received considerable support in the development programmes. What they said to the researchers was clearly exaggerated, and I could only wonder about the results of their research.

After the interview I was asked to join them on their trip around Zhongba to see something of the tea plantations and the village. I got into a car with Fang Bo, the village secretary, and two other men from the township government. Fang Bo was swearing a lot, and complaining repeatedly to the others that he was informed only the night before that the visitors would come today and do their investigation; if he had known earlier, he could have prepared it much better. One of the cadres from the township government, obviously Fang Bo's superior, did not answer. The driver asked where he should go to, and Fang Bo suggested driving around the public road to the Memorial Arch. The higher official from the township government ordered us to just go on the old 'visitors' tour' (*canguan de lu*) on the northern loop to Bashan Slope, which the driver then did. No one was at home at the houses of the Xiang and Yao family. We left the car and walked over the concrete paths through the tea plantations, and the guests tried to talk to an old neighbour who crossed the way, but he did not answer much. The cars soon went down to Bashan, where we all had lunch together at the restaurant opposite the township government.

I myself was surprised at several things that day: first of all, that the visitors seemed to accept completely what they were told by local officials and in particular by the three farmers in the village administration. Second, that on this day the cadres seemed completely open and unconcerned about my presence on this visit. After all, there had been lots of signs of mistrust and suspicion linked with my research in the village.

But it seems that to most people on this day it was perfectly clear that this was just a mandatory presentation, in which it was not necessary to emphasize in the slightest anything that could be interpreted negatively for the village cadres and local 'development'. Afterwards I told my neighbour Tian Shanwei about the events and about my astonishment, and he said that I might have finally understood what all the 'Rural Construction' and the visits from above are about.

Admitting the Face Projects

Another aspect of face that is of real interest here is that talking of 'face projects' might not only amount to a critique of the negative aspects of local development programmes. After all, it is also a way for local officials to point out their own limitations in implementing them. This way of talking about it presented itself to me in several discussions I had with local cadres when discussing the programmes.

Several cadres admitted that this is a 'face project', intended to build up 'face' and pride for the locals and for the local government. This was in fact, as I gradually realized, the best way of describing the flaws of the development programmes; for many cadres, when talking in private, it was the only possible way to relate to the problems in the Rural Construction programmes and to draw attention to their own limitations, whereas it would obviously have been unwise to speak openly about injustice or corruption.

One evening in early summer 2007 I accompanied the secretary of Zhongba, Fang Bo, together with two other cadres, to the funeral of one of their colleagues, the secretary of another village. We arrived very late, and then sat around the coffin waiting for the customary meal. Mr Lei, a relative of the family of the deceased, was talking for a long time with Secretary Fang about his post in Zhongba, village politics and the possibilities of economic development. When talking about the 'Construction of a New Countryside' programmes in Zhongba, Lei first complimented Fang Bo on having obtained, as a young cadre, such an outstanding job as secretary of the model village. Fang Bo said that it was rather difficult, because people had high expectations, and there were constantly visitors who came to see how these programmes were progressing. He came to admit that because of all the ongoing visits it is rather difficult to build up any long-term projects there. In particular, capacity training and work-shops in technology were really difficult to organize. For, after all, 'it is still a face project', he concluded.

Over the course of several conversations, Secretary Fang told me more about the pressures that he is facing: officials from the city government come regularly to control and watch what has been done here for 'rural construction'. He and the other local officials can only work piecemeal, and it would definitely be impossible to include all households. They have to first help a selection of the people and let some 'model households' (*shi-fan hu*) develop, and then the others can follow.

On another occasion in the summer of 2007, I was having lunch with Yao Zhishun, an official of the city government's Foreign Affairs Bureau, at the house of a relative of his in Bashan, together with three other distant kinsmen of his. As the official in the city government directly responsible for me and my research, Yao Zhishun was always very careful to empha-size the positive aspects of rural development and government policies in China as a whole, and in Bashan in particular. During lunch, we had a long conversation about the changes in Bashan in recent years. Whilst Yao Zhishun pointed all that had been achieved, two other men at the table were much more sceptical – perhaps they had not even realized that he was an official in the city government. They referred to the inequality in the distribution of government funds, and stressed that we were focusing on just one village, whereas all the other villages in the region were poor. Yao Zhishun responded that development could not happen everywhere at the same speed, and that other places that were left behind now would catch up later. In the end he admitted that Zhongba was a 'face project' and a 'model of development' that could guide others in the future.

These two quotations show, I think, that calling these development pro-grammes 'face projects' is not simply a way of criticizing them, but also a way of excusing their shortcomings. The 'face' of the programmes here is of crucial importance within the government hierarchy. As a local govern-ment showcase, Zhongba is visited regularly by higher officials and gov-ernment offices from Enshi, Hubei province, and even the national gov-ernment. Numerous reports have been written and published in local and provincial media on this village. Because of all this attention, the image that Zhongba can generate is extremely important for local government.

It often seems as if this was the most important task of the local offi-cials: to guard the image, the 'face' of the village vis-à-vis outsiders. The appropriate expression of 'face' is necessary when dealing with borders between 'insiders' and 'outsiders'. In a way, every social expression needs a proper 'face'.[8] A 'face' is not least the outward, visible side of some-thing, and the Chinese word for 'face', *mian*, can also mean 'appearance' or 'outside'.[9] But it can also mean the border to something behind. Here it signifies a border between life in the villages and those outsiders that are shown the development programmes. The officials are not only responsible for the implementation of government policies and projects, but also for the propriety of their appearance.

For such 'face projects', there needs to be a separation between insiders and outsiders. The officials from higher government levels, separated as they are from local reality, can only accept what they are shown. This works particularly well in the context of loosened relationships between local cadres and farmers. In general, neither the local cadres, nor the visitors, will ever venture very far into the slopes behind the public road, nor do they need to. But there have been government officials, remembered and imagined, who have gone there.

The Good Official

It was the villagers who had their houses further away from the public road who talked more frequently and openly with me about the development programmes. In fact, in the beginning, after my arrival in the village, many people thought that I might be close to the officials, and sometimes approached me to ask for support with building or refurbishing their houses, or to report their situation to the cadres.[10] Later on, when people had understood that the influence I had on the decisions of the officials was minimal, some of them lost their interest in me. But others often asked me which officials were around in the village office, and about the progress and plans in the development programmes. There was endless gossip about the personal relations, motivations and plans of particular officials.[11]

Besides the puzzlement caused by a foreigner who apparently had both a high level of education and money available, and yet still was spending so much time amongst 'peasants' (*nongmin*), I may have sometimes prompted another memory: the one of an upright official who might report the 'real' situation to higher levels of government, which are imagined to be just and benevolent.

I spent several nights during the Spring Festival period at the family home of Zhao Mucai in one of the neighbouring villages. Zhao Mucai is one year older than me, and had already been married. The previous year his wife and his baby son had been killed in an accident with a motorbike, and since then he had been living at home, working with his father. He had worked on construction sites in Fujian and Guangzhou, but now his greatest worry was to buy a new house of bricks and concrete and find another bride for himself. His father is not very well received by most neighbours in their hamlet, and he had many arguments and fights, mostly about the borders of their fields and the construction of the public road here, which should have led through one of their fields. His mother wrote many petition letters, and thanks to their fighting they made it twice into the newspaper of Enshi city, which she proudly showed to me. Even though she can read and write, her son Zhao Mucai is illiterate, and so his chances are clearly limited. I had randomly struck up a conversation with Zhao Mucai on the road once, and he had invited me several times to visit their house. His parents treated me extremely politely and invited me warmly to as many meals as I could eat and nights as I could stay at their house.

During the evenings I spent at their home, Zhao Mucai's mother often told me about all the suffering they had to endure at the hands of their neighbours and local officials, and about the overall corruption and malice of the local cadres. She even showed me a story that had been published about their case in the Enshi daily newspaper. I read that she had met the head of Enshi prefecture in person, in a session that he had organized for people coming to petition him. He had received her, and she had told him all the injustice that they had to suffer in the village. The chairman immediately sent a group of officials to her village to investigate the case. But still, the legal issue remained unsolved.

The mother emphasized to me that the officials at the higher levels of government are generally highly educated, civilized and have a 'high population quality' (*suzhi gao*) – all meaning that they are good and benevolent. She backed that up by saying that she had met many officials on all levels, from the village to the prefecture level, and that the best official she had met was the head of the entire prefecture of Enshi.

Although it had become clear to the family that I did not have any obvious influence on local officials, it still seems that my presence at their house gave them some impression of my being an outside official that could shortcut the government hierarchies and report to those much higher up. Several weeks later I visited the home of the Yao family, together with Yao Zhishun, the official from the city government. Yao's brother there asked me about my visits to Zhao Mucai's family, and said that I should not believe his parents, as they were just troublemakers. He happens to be one of the village officials Zhao Mucai's mother is feuding with.

As I alleged above, this hope for an upright official is a trope that comes up in many stories and legends. But there are certain new aspects to it, which have a lot to do with the transformation of local politics under Maoism. One decisive element of Maoist ideology was the direct representation of 'the masses of the people' (*renmin qunzhong*), and in particular 'the peasants' (*nongmin*), by the government and the party. At an unprecedented level, local government penetrated rural life, and in this the good official was no longer the learned scholar or the powerful local boss, but the official who was closest to the 'masses', an official who was himself a peasant or a worker. The highest ideal promulgated was 'to serve the people' (*wei renmin fuwu*). According to the official ideology, the rural cadres, and during the Cultural Revolution also the intellectuals, had to 'eat, live and work together with the peasants' (*yu nongmin tong chi, tong zhu, tong laodong*). This formula was still pronounced for the officials of the working groups implementing the 'New Countryside' programmes in 2006.[12]

In one and a half years, however, I had never heard of any government official spending a night in a farmer's house. Several village officials sometimes stayed overnight in the village administration, but never the officials of the 'Rural Construction' working group from the city government. Older farmers in particular often pointed out the differences between the officials now and the 'good officials' of the Maoist era.

There are also clear differences amongst the officials now, and in particular between the older village cadres and the younger ones who are employed full-time as government officials. Up until 2003, all village cadres were ordinary farmers from the village. They were mostly older men, who were also respected as men of standing in the village. They often acted as coordinators at family celebrations, such as weddings, funerals and house inaugurations. The younger cadres who do not live in the village only participate very rarely in any such family celebration, and obviously do not have such close links to the people in the village.

Clearly, the standards according to which such village cadres are evaluated locally are also extremely different. Whereas the older cadres had to contend with the judgement, gossip and respect of villagers, the younger cadres are mainly responsible to their superiors in the government hierarchies.

As well as these old peasant cadres and the new full-time professional cadres, a new type of official is now becoming very common in rural China: the farmer, who is both a successful businessman, and a local official. The village mayor of Zhongba is a particularly good example of this. Zhu Yuan was the first woman to be elected village mayor of Zhongba in 2006, following a year when there had been no village mayor in office. In the administrative reform which affected the whole of Bashan township, Zhongba village was brought together with two other villages, Bailong'gou and Houmei. I cannot ascertain how village elections had worked beforehand, but there were apparently no village elections in 2003, and in 2004, Zhu Yuan was elected. Most villagers I asked about the elections told me that they are meaningless, and that it is the cadres themselves who chose the village mayor. Zhu Yuan married into the village: her husband Yi

Hongyun is a relatively wealthy man, the boss of two small tea factories, and one of the bigger tea traders in Zhongba.[13]

Zhu Yuan was born in the same village as the former party secretary of Zhongba, Yi Biwen and several people told me that they had had a very close relationship since they went to school together, and that this was the primary reason behind her election as village mayor.

I had the opportunity of attending the birthday of Yi Hongyun's mother in March 2007. This event was one of the biggest celebrations held in a household in Zhongba that I attended; all together there were fifty-five tables of ten people each. The money that was given, as was recorded in the red books commonly used for such celebrations amounted to at least 20,000 Yuan. There were also many officials of the township and city government present, a privilege granted to very few people in the village. Yi Biwen, the former secretary of the party branch of Zhongba, came, accompanied by another man from the township government and brought the money-presents of eight more people from the township government. It is obvious that many people would also use this kind of family celebration as a 'hidden' way of establishing a closer relationship with the couple. Being completely accepted as a form of gift giving, a birthday present might be much simpler than approaching the couple in private, and offering them a 'red envelope' (*hongbao*) to get things done.[14] In this family celebration the collective power and standing of Yi Hongyun and Zhu Yuan are made visible; they are clearly people that are 'in society' (*shehui shang de ren*), that is, they have demonstrated that they have social capability, and maintain a huge network of relationships. As such, both are individuals that have 'face' (*mianzi*).

Yi Hongyun and Zhu Yuan are major recipients of the development programmes in Zhongba. To many official visitors, the couple is presented as an example of successful local peasant-entrepreneurs, rather than as local leaders who are helping in the implementation of developmental policy. They live in the village, and are not the people who take the bigger decisions in the implementation of the development programmes; but they also command a very prestigious position in the village community, and they bring together many networks of kin, friends and colleagues. And here the necessary links between the locals of the village and higher government are formed. Ordinary villagers would much rather approach them than those officials who were outsiders to the village. Hence they are also the necessary intermediaries between villagers and those officials who are often less familiar with the locals.

We have arrived at a point where it seems clear that one would miss out a good part of the complexity of 'face projects', if one simply translated the phrase in terms of its initial meaning, as the 'superficiality' of 'Potemkin villages' built to please higher government officials. In everyday discourse, the notion of 'face' refers to authoritative respect that is based on the capability of establishing and maintaining social relationships. One could say that every proper social expression needs 'face'. Even the go-betweens that help in the implementation of the 'face projects' need it, as it demonstrates the social capability required to maintain meaningful relationships with both officials and villagers. This is probably now the main task of many village officials.

Such a capacity is perhaps best illustrated in the family celebrations of the likes of Zhu Yuan and Yi Hongyun. Most of the people who have meaningful social relationships ('comings and goings', *laiwang*) with the couple participated in their birthday party. On this occasion, one can see the inside and the outside of this household: the people who belong to it, and those who are related to it as relatives, friends, neighbours, colleagues, business partners, etc. The arrival of the guests and their presentation of gifts on the one side, and the reception and hosting on the other, demand the proper treatment of the border between 'insiders' and 'outsiders' – another aspect of the spatial and moral practice of *li*.

The most basic unit of an 'inside' and 'outside' is that of a household. The outside appearance of a household is the façade of the house. It is not only local government officials who are concerned about the façades of farm houses in Zhongba, but also the ordinary people living in these houses.

Ordinary People and Face Projects

One answer that cadres often gave when confronted with the discontent of villagers who lived away from the public road was that the government only had limited means, that one had to start with a 'pilot project' (*shidian*) to provide a 'model' (*shifan*) and then slowly others would follow suit. What has happened in Zhongba seems to justify that to some extent: most peasants who can afford it are trying to build new houses next to the public road. As was described in chapter 2, during the last years there has been a boom in house construction in Zhongba, and hence many house inaugurations. These new houses of bricks and concrete are preferably built at a 'hot' location close to the street and the market town.

Even with the most favoured households, the support given in the government development programmes only constitutes a minor part of the resources needed to build a new house (cf. Appendix D). The efforts of local families to construct new houses precede the development programmes. In the village group of Memorial Arch, for instance, about a dozen new brick houses were being built in 2006 and 2007. In 2006 the working group of the 'Rural Construction' programmes had been busy in Bashan Slope and Fragrant Forest, and when they arrived in Memorial Arch in 2007, several houses had been finished already.

In the choice of a suitable place (next to the asphalt road), the building materials (bricks, cement, tiles) and architectural style, the 'face project' of the government and the aspirations of villagers are far from incompatible.[15] A decisive difference, however, is that for ordinary villagers the main motivation is the desired appearance of their own houses, whereas for the officials it was about the appearance of 'the village' and the 'Rural Construction' programmes. Even though there are perceptible similarities between the objectives of local officials to build face projects and the ambitions of villagers to build new houses, it is in fact only the government projects that are called 'face projects'. Calling them so is in itself something that is marking out a border: such talk never takes place in public, but always in the rather private sphere of insiders.

There are huge barriers to such talk becoming public, most importantly the fact that most rural dwellers do not have the possibilities or the capacity to participate in any public discussion of such projects. The presentation and appearance of these villages to outsiders is orchestrated by local government and the media, and large numbers of officials continuously watch and monitor this outside representation.

An example might illustrate this. The following is the entry by a netizen on a city government Internet bulletin board. It is the only mention of 'face projects' in relation to the implementation of the 'Construction of a Socialist New Countryside' programmes in the region that I found in a somewhat 'public' arena:

Why is the Rural Construction in Enshi only focusing on Zhongba in Bashan, Yanqiao in Songtai, and Dazhu in Fengtan? [these are all villages that are prominent showcases]. The basic conditions of all these places is already all very good, there is no doubt that they are places to experiment (*shidian*), but only doing 'face projects' (*mianzi gongcheng*) and 'image building projects' (*xingxiang gongcheng*) is betraying the original meaning of 'Constructing a New Countryside'.

The answer reads as follows:

Dear netizen!

First of all, thank you so much for your interest in the 'Construction of a Socialist New Countryside' in Enshi City. 'The Construction of a Socialist New Countryside' has already been in process for two years in our city. 'The Construction of a Socialist New Countryside' is a completely new undertaking, and there is no previous model or experience on which it could be based. [...] The enforcement of the construction of model villages is done to provide a model for other villages to study the 'Construction of a New Countryside'. [...] Referring to what you call a 'face project', these are in fact the model villages (*shifan cun*) of our city.

Again, thank you very much for forwarding your opinion and suggestion about the 'Construction of a New Countryside' in our city.

The Office for Agriculture of the Party Branch of Enshi City

The Department for Agriculture in the City Government of Enshi

First of all, it is clear that the majority of the villagers in Zhongba are not able to participate in this kind of 'public' debate on rural development. Very few of those living in the countryside ever go online and participate in discussion groups.

The signature given for the answer makes it clear that this is no intimate chat on the Internet, where many things can be said in a nonchalant way. The question is presented in a rather informal style; however, the answer moves into the diction of bureaucratic and official prose. It is a government body that declares: these are not 'face projects' but 'model villages'. This is but one example of how outside representations are checked and controlled. The flipside of such constraint, however, is a local community of intimate knowledge.

Communities of Complicity

The negotiations around 'face projects' also relate to wider concerns about the corruption of local officials. In fact, the 'Construction of a New Countryside' programme is only one in a host of other subsidies programmes. Another support payment is given to tea farmers via the 'turn farmland into forest' (*tuigeng huanlin*) programme. Tea plantations conveniently count as 'productive forest' and so farmers who have dried out their paddy fields and planted tea shrubs receive a subsidy for a certain period. That is but one minor example of all the support payments that local governments in recognized 'poor districts' (*pinkun diqu*) receive from the provincial and national levels of government. As well as these transfer payments from higher government levels, the township government still has several local sources of revenue: taxes and fees levied from private enterprises, several government enterprises, and recently a new 'development district' (*kaifa qu*) in the Bashan plain. All this is well known amongst local farmers, and they would frequently allege that the responsible officials pocketed part of the transfer payments and the local revenues. A common local commentary about official corruption is that the government hierarchy from the central government downwards works like a funnel with several sieves. At every government level, money is filtered out, officials enrich themselves from the lump sums that the central government is investing, and therefore almost nothing reaches the farmers.

Connected to this way of seeing the governmental hierarchy are the notions of the 'good official' described above, and the theory that the higher up the governmental ladder you go, the better are the officials. Local villagers frequently pointed out to me that the central government, represented by Chairman Hu Jintao and Premier Wen Jiabao, does actually care about the peasants, and promotes good policies. Yet further down the government ladder, officials get increasingly worse. Many people felt that the worst are the cadres at the township level, who are in close everyday contact with ordinary people, yet also further removed from village life when compared with village level officials. Such everyday interactions with township officials are tied to economic and social interests, whereas the relationship of farmers with the central state is more symbolic and moral, and is mediated at various levels. Guo Xiaolin has described this as a 'bifurcated state', in which people keep placing hope and confidence in the central government, even when local government becomes increasingly predatory (2001: 436ff).

But even though people often complain about local officials and have very pointed opinions about them, they still have to approach them for ID cards, marriage certificates, permits to build houses, family planning issues, land conflicts, etc. In particular when it comes to complicated issues, locals prefer a personal relationship and contact with an official. My neighbour Tian Shanwei, for instance, often lectured me on the 'art of relationship-making' (*guanxi xue*). When he was planning to build his new house in the summer of 2007, the village officials initially opposed his plan. He then invited the vice secretary of the township government for several meals at the best restaurant in Bashan, and offered him several boxes of expensive cigarettes. Tian Shanwei also pointed out to me that he had chosen this secretary because he shares the same surname with him, even though he is not a direct relative. After this treatment, the village government eventually granted him the permission to build his new house.

Despite these personal ties with officials, government propaganda continuously emphasizes impartiality and formal equality. Concomitantly, party education programmes focus on raising the 'quality' (*suzhi*) of cadres and their behaviour (cf. Murphy 2006). At the same time, locals like Tian Shanwei, or the neighbours and officials offering cash to Sun Jundong (at the funeral in chapter 5), are clearly aware that it is most important to have a personal bond with officials, in which 'human feeling' (*renqing*) is properly expressed through gifts. Similarly, it is clear to most people that a cadre whose behaviour was too urbanized, and who was friendly with anyone who asked him for something, would not gain respect from his peers and hence become rather ineffective.

From the perspective of some academic observers, such phenomena would be part of what they call 'state involution' in contemporary China (Siu 1989a, 1989b; Wang 1989; Lu Xiaobo 2000). Lu Xiaobo, for instance, points out an 'organizational involution' within the Chinese party state. He defines this involution as

> a process whereby a revolutionary party, while adopting and expanding many 'modern' (i.e. rational, formal, impersonal) structures, [...] fails to adapt itself to, and be transformed by, the routinization and bureaucratization that characterize modern bureaucracy. At the same time, it is unable to maintain its original distinctive competence and identity. Its members make adjustments and adaptations neither through revolutionary ideologies nor modern institutions and practices, but through reinforced and elaborated traditional modes of operation. (Lu 2000: 22)

Lu adds that such 'neotraditionalism' produces 'disillusioned, status-conscious, and undisciplined cadres, who in the manner of pre-revolutionary [...] local officials, put the interests of more intimate secondary and primary groups above those of the regime' (Lu 2000: 23). Rachel Murphy has used Lu's framework to analyse how party education campaigns work to maintain this 'organizational involution': the campaigns deflect systemic critique and instead blame the problems of corruption on the ethical misbehaviour of individuals. She concludes that the 'ritualization' of the education campaigns reproduces the top-down party hierarchy, and the personalistic networks within (Murphy 2007).

It is not only academic observers who conclude that personalistic networks and informal dealings fulfil systemic functions in a supposedly impersonal bureaucracy. Both villagers and cadres are well aware that personal relations with officials are most important and reliable. But they do not pronounce that in public. People share a knowledge of the 'involutionary cancer' of personalistic and informal relations; if cadres do admit them in private, then it is rather a rueful recognition. The embarrassed or ironic ways in which such things are said indicate a shared understanding of local mechanisms of power. Such practices produce a community of complicity – and this is similar to those who engage in *fengshui*, or in wasteful funerary celebrations. All these practices have in common the fact that their outside representation is overwhelmingly negative, whilst they are really essential in everyday life.

In this chapter, I have described 'face projects' as the building up, protection, and surveillance of certain borders between 'inside' and 'outside'.

I have dealt with the images and practice of rural development in this village, and with the position and constraints of local officials in development programmes which are called 'face projects'. We have seen that there are different standards according to which local officials might be judged and respected. People measured the officials entrusted with the implementation of such government programmes against two other role-models: the idealized official who enquires about the local situation; and the contemporary official-cum-businessman. But even though sometimes they denounced local cadres when comparing them with the idealized 'good official', in most situations people dealt with the local government representatives in a pragmatic way.

Some villagers denounced the 'face projects' of the government as superficial, and even some officials admitted that they were 'face projects'. Yet for the officials, this served as an excuse for their actions which was only ever made quietly and in private. In official prose and announcements, they would be called 'models' for emulation, as in the answer the government office gave to the online contribution.

What emerges behind this symbolic struggle is an intimate space of common knowledge, or a 'community of complicity'. This notion is not meant to imply that the object of this intimate knowledge and complicity is a true 'neotraditionalism', more 'true' than the official representation of a rationalized political system and a modern citizenry. This would indeed be the logical consequence of the 'involution' argument: that the modern and rational is only a false mask barely concealing the neotraditionalist 'truth'. In my argument, both the modernist representation and the traditionalist self-knowledge are true. 'Communities of complicity' are formed by those who share an intimate knowledge of the boundaries – the faces – of modernism and traditionalism.

Notes

1. There are many stories and legends about the 'good official', in whom ordinary people can trust to prevent a false report (e.g. Feuchtwang 2001 [1992]: 60–62). Amongst the peasants and the poor a popular figure was Bao Zheng, also called Bao Qingtian (999–1062 C.E.), who was a judge in Kaifeng during the Song Dynasty. In the north China plains people prayed for justice at countless temples built for 'Judge Bao'. There have been numerous stories, operas, theatres, TV series and films dealing with Judge Bao, until the present day. Perhaps the most famous good official in Chinese history, uprightly fighting for moral righteousness, dreaded by his fellow officials, and finally laid off to a non-relevant post, is Hai Rui (1514–1587 C.E.). Notwithstanding the complexity of the historical person (see Huang 1981, chapter 5), the legend of Hai Rui has become a symbol which has been used countless times, most famously in the theatre play *Hai Rui Dismissed from Office*, written in 1961 by the historian and vice-mayor of Beijing, Wu Han. Even though first praised by Mao Zedong, later the

play was fiercely criticized for hinting at Mao's dismissal of Peng Dehuai who had opposed the Great Leap Forward in 1959. The play was then used politically against 'rightists elements' at the beginning of the Cultural Revolution, amongst them its author Wu Han. He was humiliated in public 'class struggle' sessions, tortured, and died in prison in 1969 (cf. Fisher 1982).

2. See Wang and Chen 2004 for an assessment of the general situation of rural officials after the eradication of the agricultural tax, and the other contributions to Li and Dong 2004 for overall evaluations of different aspects of the agricultural reform policies.

3. Cf. Li 2008. The 'peasant burden' that was so much talked about in the 1990s – including heavy taxes and illegal tax collection that in several regions led to violent unrest – has lost certainly a lot of its impact. At the same time there exist huge regional disparities in the pace of tax reductions.

4. See chapter 3 on his role in the introduction of tea monoculture in Bashan.

5. In Appendix D I have included estimates for the subsidies given to the households of Xiang Jixiang, Tian Shanwei, and Wang Guohui.

6. In general, officials would smoke tobacco that cost at least 10 Yuan a pack; and it is true that most of them have relatively big houses in the market town of Bashan, or even apartments in the city.

7. The second one had come to this post as a kind of 'pre-retirement' assignment. He had served as the head of a township, and from there had moved to a post in the Department of Minority and Religious Affairs. The second post is at the same level in the administrative (and salarial) hierarchy in the government, but in fact in this post he has much less responsibility and power. He will probably retire completely within the next five years.

8. For general outlines of the Chinese discourse of face, see Hu 1944 and Ho 1974.

9. One can begin with something very simple: dressing and bodily action. These have to correspond to one's social position and standing. It was always a cause of much surprise to villagers, cadres and businessmen alike that I usually wore cheap clothes, and even the army shoes (E. *gaifang hai*) and the straw shoes (E. *cao hai*) which are usually reserved for older peasants. The cigarettes that one smokes should also be appropriate to one's status. People were astonished to see me smoking the same cigarettes that the peasants smoke, cigarettes that costs two or three Yuan a pack, while they would have expected me to smoke a tobacco costing at least around 10 Yuan a pack.

10. I had been introduced to Zhongba by the city and township government, and was living in the village administration building, next to the village office. For a long time the relationship between me and the local officials was not clear to many villagers. Even though I cannot definitively ascertain this to be true, I believe that towards the end many villagers had understood that the purpose of my stay in the village was quite different to that of the local officials.

11. On the other hand, I almost never heard the local officials talking about the possible motivations or concerns of the ordinary people. This reminds me of the constellation that David Graeber highlighted, namely that people in a subaltern position try hard to understand the situation, motivations and even feelings of those in power, whereas those in the superior position rarely try to empathize with their inferiors (Graeber 2006: 8ff).

12. One of the documents outlining the objectives of the working group in Zhongba reads as follows: '[…] the members of the working group are supposed to eat, live and work together with the peasants' (Enshi City 2006b).

13. Several of the journalist teams that have visited Zhongba have also reported on this household as a model of economic success in Zhongba. According to one report published in a national magazine, Yi Hongyun makes an annual income of 150,000 Yuan from his tea plantations, tea production and business.

14. I also gave 20 Yuan to the family on this occasion. As mentioned in chapter 5, this had become my usual practice when attending family celebrations.

15. And in fact it seems as if the villagers were sometimes proud of their 'face project', of the 'Rural Construction' in Zhongba. On several occasions the local TV station broadcast programmes on the success of government policies in Bashan, and villagers would chat about the television programme, joke about the appearance of their relatives or fellow villagers, and retell stories about this and that government leader or journalist that came to visit. It was even more remarkable to hear old men singing couplets about 'rural construction' at funerals. As described in chapter 6, several elder men sing 'night songs' and entertain the relatives at a vigil around the coffin on the last night of a funeral. On one such night, I heard a man reciting a long ballad in rhyme on the history of China, which ended in a local history of their own place. One of the last couplets dealt with the recent development of the 'tea township' and the 'rural construction' that brought so many visitors – including even 'foreign guests' (*waibing*) – to Bashan.

CONCLUSION

EVERYDAY ETHICS, CULTURAL INTIMACY, AND IRONY

In this book I have explored everyday ethics in contemporary rural China, by giving an ethnographic description of family and work relations, popular ritual, and the local state. Chapter 1 set the stage of this ethnography. In the historical and spatial context in which Bashan is located, we have seen how remote it is in relation to various centres: the civilizational centre of the empire, the central government of the People's Republic, and the capitalist metropolises of contemporary China. Whilst in this first chapter I have emphasized the similarities of such ambiguities in imperial and contemporary times, chapters 6 to 8 dealt with the particularities of the contemporary state. Inbetween I have explored the ways in which people make their own place and their own moral centres. In house construction and work, we have seen how moral frameworks are linked to the family and household. These are spatialized in the house, and reproduced in work. Drawing on the examples of family celebrations, I have elaborated a theoretical perspective on Chinese ritual (*li*) as a moral practice of 'centring'. Yet the categorical moral demands represented in centring practices of ritual always have to be translated and adjusted to contingent realities in different ways. While maintaining some basic principles, the form a house takes can be quite different. Similarly, the kinds of work people engage in are also very diverse. The ways in which success and failure in relation to the family are judged in everyday talk are always manoeuvring between categorical demands and contingent realities. In relationship to wider society and the nation-state, this general ethical dilemma (between what should be and what is) can be found in the opposition between official discourses and vernacular practice, what local sociality should be like and how it really is. This tension produces what Michael Herzfeld calls 'cultural intimacy': the self-recognition of people who are aware that what is dear and important to them is corrupt, backwards, and potentially embarrassing to outsiders. Negotiating such feelings and perceptions reproduces what I call 'communities of complicity', that is, communities of those 'in the know', those who share an experiential horizon and an intimate knowledge. In chapters 5 to 7, I have explored such oppositions between local sociality and the state in the fields of rituals, gambling, and development projects.

In what remains, let me bring together three theoretical fields that have been running through the book: everyday ethics, communities of complicity, and the uses of irony.

Everyday Ethics

In the introduction I referred to a basic distinction between moralities and ethics, defining ethics as the second-level reflection of moralities. Many of the decisions that people take in their everyday lives in Bashan not only include moral evaluations, but are also ethical, in the sense that people need to 'step out' of a status of 'unreflective habitus'. And that is the core argument of this book: much everyday action in Bashan is ethical, because it creatively and reflectively engages different moral frameworks.

Contemporary rural China is thoroughly incorporated into spheres of market exchange and consumerism; the mass media have reached every household; and most of the younger generation have lived for some time at least in the cities. If locals and outsiders still sometimes present Bashan as a remote place of moral innocence, then this presentation itself (for the tourist industry, or in local discourse for instance), has become one moral reference amongst many others that are continuously juxtaposed.

Everyday life in Bashan is characterized by an increased sense of moral challenge and ethical reflexivity. Recognizing the importance of moral frameworks, whilst remaining open to their ironic displacement, I attempt to describe this reflexivity with the notion of 'everyday ethics'. Calling them 'everyday' alludes not only to the ordinariness of these ethics; it is also meant to indicate that the everyday is the realm where ethics are lived out, commented on, and negotiated. In the everyday of now, there is no stable centre in the past and no heroic panorama of a glorious future providing moral frameworks for social action. Instead different moral frameworks – and with them orienting centres, aspirations, and memories – are endlessly placed against many others.

This does not necessarily imply that there is only confusion and arbitrariness (as Liu 2000 might suggest), or a decline of public morality in rural China (as suggested by Yan 2003, for instance). Rather, people are reflectively engaging with moral challenges in everyday life. They are acutely aware of the different meanings and values given to such things as peasant work, ritual, and gambling, and they negotiate these meanings in everyday ethics. Observing the ways in which people in Bashan deal with work, ritual, and the local state, it is abundantly clear that they do not merely re-enact the moral frameworks of 'traditional' rural society. It can be said that people in Bashan have become observers of their own 'tradition' and 'culture', and their everyday talk and action bespeaks an intimate knowledge of the stereotypical representations of rural backwardness (including, for instance, lack of education, superstition, and excessive gift-giving).

Like several other recent descriptions of morality and ethics in China and elsewhere (e.g. Heintz 2009; Oxfeld 2010; Lambek 2010), my outline of everyday ethics emphasizes the importance of the ethical in ordinary life. As various anthropologists have pointed out, much of this new writing implies a departure from the Durkheimian legacy of anthropology, in which morality is collapsed into 'the social', which is thought of as a totality. Like others, I believe there is a risk of 'throwing out the baby with the bathwater' and downplaying the role of the social altogether in favour of individual moral decisions (Yan 2011). Such a removal of the social might take place if we limit the ethical to exceptional moments of 'moral breakdown'. While I adhere to the definition of ethics as the 'reflection of morality', I argue that ethics – defined as reflective engagement with different moral frameworks – cannot be separated from everyday sociality in contemporary rural China. For the rural everyday of now is fraught with ethical challenges. Or, to change 'ordinary' to 'everyday' in Michael Lambek's formulation, the everyday is intrinsically ethical and ethics intrinsically everyday (2010: 3).

The everyday of Bashan now is surely not a rural idyll of primordial time any longer (if it ever was). Anthropologists and sociologists of an earlier generation had separated the progressive and prosaic time of the modern city from the cyclical and poetic time of the countryside. The two were separated by various techniques of representations (the ethnographic present in particular), which achieved a 'denial of coevalness', as Johannes Fabian terms it in his general critique of anthropological representations of the other (1983).

Studies of Chinese modernity, on the other hand, tended to focus on the city, in particular Shanghai (see for instance Yeh 1997, 2007). It was in the everyday life of the city that the rapid social changes of modernity were felt most acutely, both the continuous arousal of the senses and the endless boredom brought about by capitalist rationalization. In this way, the problem of the everyday has often been seen as a distinctive feature of modernity. In recent years, historians of China have suggested a new study of the social history of modernity in China by focusing on everyday life mainly in urban contexts (e.g. Dong and Goldstein 2006).

When anthropologists and sociologists were writing about everyday life in rural China, they were writing about a world where there was no (modern) everyday at all. In his seminal study of *Everyday Life in the Modern World* (1971 [1968]), Henri Lefebvre distinguishes his own concept of the everyday from another 'everyday', which lacked the imprint of the modern:

> The present inquiry should not be confused with those forming part of a popular series: everyday life in different ages and civilizations. Some of the volumes of this series are remarkable, in that they illustrate the *total absence of everyday life* in a given community at a given time. With the Incas, the Aztecs, in Greece or in Rome, every detail (gestures, words, tools, utensils, costumes, etc.) bears the imprint of a *style*; nothing had as yet become prosaic, not even the quotidian; the prose and the poetry of life were still identical. (Lefebvre 1971 [1968]: 29)

Much of Henri Lefebvre's thought on the modern everyday was explicitly contrasted with his image of the rural, as a space and time which lacked the disturbing and exciting feeling of the urban and modern everyday. The epitome of the rural for Lefebvre is the peasant festival: in such celebrations a cyclical time is re-enacted, which contrasts most obviously with the linear and empty time of the prosaic modern everyday (Lefebvre 1971 [1968]: 36ff).

If we follow Levebre's categorical distinction between urban and rural we might say that something similar actually took place in several of the seminal texts of Chinese anthropology. Anthropologists of China wrote about an everyday that was not an 'everyday' in Lefebvre's sense at all. There was no everyday life in the sense that the ordinary routines of work and festival had become problematic. Instead of the urban routine of capitalism and state institutions, instead of the constant arousal of the senses, instead of a fundamental aesthetic and ethical pluralism, in the remoteness of village life there was only re-living and re-enacting a primordial mode of being in the world.

It is one of the main arguments of this book that this kind of disturbing feeling of the everyday has at last arrived in rural China. What distinguishes the remoteness of the villages of Bashan now is that it is both interrupted and amplified by numerous connections with several centres, most importantly the metropolitan centres of capitalist development in contemporary China. If everyday life in the countryside is not quite the same as in the metropolis (of Wuhan, Beijing, or Shanghai, for instance), then the shadows of urban life and its consumerist culture are very much present here as well. Examples of this are the changes in house construction (described in chapter 2), and the arrival of all kinds of consumer goods. Among the younger generation, literacy is close to universal, and the mass media (TV in particular) have reached most farm households. Both work and consumption are increasingly integrated into market economies, not least because of large-scale labour migration. The family and the household continue to be the basic units of production and consumption, and of ritual exchange, yet all these social spheres are now mediated by commodities, and in all these areas, people have to take moral decisions on an everyday basis. In addition, there is an omnipresent official discourse that provides continuous commentary on local practice. People confront all this in everyday life, which is characterized now by contingency and heightened moral ambiguities.

One major factor which encourages moral uncertainty is the ever-lasting presence of a reified (national) culture in everyday life. Together with this comes an increased intensity of the twists and tensions between vernacular practices and official discourse. I have tried to conceptualize the tension between local sociality and official representation here with the notions of 'cultural intimacy' and 'communities of complicity'.

Communities of Complicity

Cultural intimacy is felt as a rueful self-recognition based on the apparent contradictions between official representation and vernacular practices. Stories told about *fengshui* (such as those in chapter 1) illustrate a certain ambiguity between peripheral locality and a centre which is characteristic both of late imperial and contemporary China. But the sense of cultural intimacy linked to *fengshui* and other superstitions was greatly intensified by the state formation processes of the twentieth century, in particular during the Maoist era. In the embarrassment of *li*, or ritual, lie the remnants of a Maoist discourse that had violently denigrated Confucianism. What characterizes contemporary attitudes towards practices such as geomancy, ritual, and corruption more than anything is a discursive uncertainty. And this is perhaps the biggest difference from similar practices in earlier times: I imagine that up to the 1930s it would have been close to impossible in the villages of Bashan to crack a joke about *fengshui* or about the principle of *li*. Now they have to be treated with irony.

The ambiguities between local sociality and the state in rural China are intensified by the omnipresence of the party-state and the memories of violence, in particular the trauma of the Cultural Revolution. Whilst the power and presence of the state is undeniable, the messages it sends out and the decisions that officials take are extremely unpredictable. From the most obvious contradiction (a communist government invoking Marx and Mao, heading a capitalist economy) to the everyday verbal warfare amongst minor officials (such as the discussion around the funeral of Sun Jundong's father, and those about the 'face projects' of Zhongba), it is often far from clear what actually counts as the directive. Ordinary people and officials refer to stereotypical social roles (such as that of the backward peasant and the good official, for instance); sometimes they embarrass themselves by giving interpretations that others take as outdated or too bold; and sometimes they are ironic about them.

Cultural intimacy is not something that is limited to the little people or the 'subaltern'; it is also felt by officials, like the county secretary Sun Jundong. Just like ordinary villagers, the powerful also engage in 'social poetics', i.e. in the practical and strategical use of essentialisms. My examples have shown how people used essentialisms of *fengshui*, of *li*, of corruption, of gambling, and of face. Confronting arguments made about 'state involution', I have pointed out that in fact a knowledge of and familiarity with practices that others might call 'corruption' or 'involution' is common amongst officials and villagers, and this shared knowledge defines communities of complicity.

Regarding the valuation and control of much everyday action, there are now powerful outside representations, promulgated in schools, government offices and by modern media (in particular newspapers, the Internet, but also the 'Maoist modern' of wall papers, scrolls, and loudspeakers)[1] – and an everyday local sociality that more or less contradicts what is written and announced in the outside representations. Because of this tension, such local socialities are felt to be 'intimate' spaces. If the lived contradictions are pointed out, or made visible, the first reaction may be an awkward smile. With a fellow insider, it is just as possible to become ironic: it is actually quite clear to most participants and to the initiated that there exists such a lived contradiction. And embarrassment, irony, and all that is said as an aside are not understood by everyone, and so they re-produce the boundaries of a community of complicity.

The tropes of indirection which reproduce such communities are numerous, and I have highlighted in particular awkwardness and irony. It should be emphasized that when they are put 'into action', they imply a properly ethical stance: a reflective engagement with moral frameworks.

Ironies

Both in the recognition of cultural intimacy, and in the heightened reflexivity of everyday ethics, I have emphasized the role of irony. In the introduction I quoted Richard Rorty who draws attention to the danger of humiliation that ironic re-description entails. In several chapters, I have portrayed the uses of irony made by ordinary people, which are obviously quite different to those created by the liberal ironist based on his reading of novels and ethnographies. It has been argued that although he claims to be indifferent to our drives towards moral (ontological, metaphysical, etc.) consistency, Richard Rorty himself is ultimately prompting a 'final closure' in the commonly shared sense of pain and suffering. Even though he refused a common human essence and an a priori ontology, in the end his proposition to base solidarity on a shared sensitivity to pain and humiliation might amount to something similar: if not a notion of a unified and autonomous self, then at least an acknowledgement of a human drive towards a consistent self, as humiliation denies to others precisely that capacity to build up consistent selves.[2] But whether or not empathy with suffering is universal, it is significant that Rorty privileges one form of learning this empathy, that is, reading texts.

There remains the question of whether people who do not have the leisure to read have the same potential to be 'liberal ironists'. Is the 'liberal ironist' not really a liberal who can afford to be ironic because he is well provided, indeed oversaturated, with cultural stimulation? If so, would he miss the ironies of his own social position, and in particular the ironic potential of 'ordinary people' who could re-describe him, possibly even resulting in a ludicrous caricature?

It is here where the ironies of an anthropologist part company with those of artists, writers, and philosophers. Reading ethnographies might be one way of learning empathy with others, but doing fieldwork is quite a different one. The anthropologist qua fieldworker is forced to recognize the ironies of his own attempts to empathize with others and ultimately, of his trade as a 'professional' observer and writer, and even of his own existence. If ethnography can include ironies of re-description in Rorty's sense, the experience of fieldwork invariably includes ironies of embarrassment in Herzfeld's sense. Irony always cuts both ways, and as such it has an equally unsettling potential for the participant observer. In this ethnography, I have tried to convey some of the ironies of my own position as fieldworker and anthropologist.

As an undergraduate student, I chose to study anthropology in order to learn more about the 'objects' of development and colonialism. Having grown up on a farm in Bavaria, I had a deep interest in the problems of rural development and agricultural politics. After an experience as a volunteer in South America, I wanted to study peasant movements in the 'Third World'. My first research proposal for a PhD was on rural development and peasant identity in China; however, conveying these ideas to local officials and ordinary people alike was a difficult undertaking. My attempts at translation and at participation in everyday life led to count-less situations of embarrassment and irony. Yet I believe that at least in some instances, I became something other than a mere intruder. Through my mistakes, I learned at least some aspects of how to talk and behave properly, of how to do 'face-work', as Goffman termed it (1955). In doing so, I became sensitive to parts of an intimate space of local knowledge, and at least at times I felt that I was close to being a member of a 'community of complicity'.

As described in several chapters, my participation in family celebra-tions played a major role here. The house inauguration with which I 'in-augurated' this book was in fact a crucial turning point in my fieldwork: it was the first time that I somehow felt part of a local community, after having spent more than six months in Bashan. Also essential was my giv-ing presents at the banquets, which made me vulnerable to the ridicule of both local insiders and urban outsiders. The same is true of my par-ticipation in gambling; here it was even more obvious that I was entering something that was quite clearly an embarrassment to the outside world (and so people warned me every so often that I should not gamble too much and not with certain people). But even though I might have taken some minor steps towards the perspective of a cultural insider, I could never escape my basic conditioning as an outsider and a foreigner. Time and again I was reminded during my fieldwork that I was not only repre-senting myself, but also 'Germany' and 'the West'; and vice versa, it often appeared that my experiences in Bashan would represent 'China' to both myself and the wider world outside China.

Community and a sense of belonging is created not so much in the moments when people actually get together, but in the ongoing business of dealing with the necessity of separating and coming together again. It is never possible to stay together forever, and hence any get-together always has to face a 'separation constraint' (Stafford 2000). The dialectical movement between separation and reunion then is really what builds a sociality, and not just the social effervescence of being together. My own separation constraint was always looming in Bashan, and it surely pre-conditioned the nature of the interaction that I had with people there. Just as in the everyday ethics that I have described, my own encounters with people in Bashan were riddled with ironies, not the least in the ways in which they and I managed to frame our encounter at the end of my time in Bashan.

The most felicitous framing, I think, I found with Wen Yunfu. Through our countless conversations, Old Wen and I became good friends. When my departure from Bashan was imminent, he asked me several times to take a photo of us together. And every time he said it, he would add with a smile that I should write on the photo that this is 'a Chinese peasant and a German scholar'. I always refused humbly, and said that I did not count as a scholar, nor was he a real peasant.

Before I left Bashan, we did take the photo, and with the help of a Chinese friend, I found a much better way of expressing our encounter, and the ambiguities of both our personalities. In literary Chinese, festive occasions are always accompanied by written scrolls (*duilian*), which poetically capture the occasion in a parallel structure. The scroll we commissioned for the picture of Old Wen and me was the following: 'A friendship across ages: An 80-year-old peasant-merchant happily meets a young German scholar. A 27-year-old descendant of farmers serendipitously encounters an old Chinese sage' (see photograph 8.1).

Even though some government officials had also become friends, many kept a certain distance from me. My precarious status as a foreigner, a 'guest of the people's government', compelled me to exercise utmost caution with anything that was politically sensitive, including such diverse things as criminality, corruption, superstition, and the workings of the local government. Let me give a last example of the (mis)understandings reached. The following is an excerpt from a newspaper article that appeared in the *Enshi Evening News* in December 2006. By then I had spent six months in Bashan. A friend from the local university in Enshi had told a reporter from the local newspaper about my presence, and together with the township government, a press team came over to interview me

Photograph 8.1 A friendship across ages

and film me for one day. One result was the following newspaper article, entitled 'A German Lad in Bashan':

> In the village of Zhongba, Bashan Township, Enshi City, people can now frequently see a tall, blond young foreigner walking from house to house. This is Hans Steinmuller, a PhD student from the London School of Economics and Political Science in England. His Chinese name is Shi Han, and originally he is a German from the city of Munich. This 1.82 m tall PhD student is only 26 years old, and he speaks German, Chinese, English, and Spanish fluently. When this reporter interviewed him on the 3ʳᵈ December, Shi Han pronounced the following phrase in all four languages: 'The rural reconstruction in Bashan Township and Zhongba village is done very well.'³

As well as the newspaper article, there was also a short film clip about me which was broadcast on local TV. While most peasants do not read newspapers and do not have cable TV (which is necessary to receive Enshi TV), several villagers had seen the news, and talked to me about it afterwards. Some spoke about it in rather high tones, saying that my appearance was 'an honour' for the people of Bashan. But others, in particular people I was very close and familiar with, had different reactions. Two of them stand out.

Tian Dejun mentioned the matter once in a conversation on the slopes, when I was picking tea with him and his son. He asked me: 'Didn't you appear last week on Enshi TV as well? And you said that the rural reconstruction programme is done so well? I tell you, look at the houses here, off the street: the government doesn't do anything. This fucking reconstruction programme sucks. They serve themselves, and don't serve the people.'⁴

Tian Shanwei, the man who was plagued by rheumatism and then also built a new house, also had his opinion on the TV programme and newspaper article. In fact he praised me for having done it. When we came to speak about the TV programme he said to me that 'finally you have understood how propaganda works here and what the rural reconstruction programmes are all about.' They are about building up a 'face' (*mianzi*), a façade that looks nice, he added. We continued the conversation, and I mentioned my anxieties about writing a good PhD thesis and finding a job. He answered that all this should not be a problem for me. Now that I had understood how things work, nothing would be easier: 'Just write long praises of rural development, the good side of the things you saw here. Then get your friends in the university and in the government to publish it. I'm sure you'll do well.'

There are categorical demands and platitudes about what it means to work, to be member of a family, to be a peasant or an intellectual, to be Chinese or German. Yet surely the contingent realities of doing all these things never quite meet all the categorical demands and correspond to the platitudes. One trope through which such displacements can be expressed is irony.

Several ethnographies of rural China published in the last decade conclude with a tone of weariness and concern over the moral uncertainty, and the decline of morals in rural society (e.g. Yan 2003; Liu 2000; Tan 2010). It seems to me that similarly many writings on 'family values', 'work ethics', 'nationalism', 'civil society' and 'democratization' in China assess the messy social realities against the yardstick of absolute and objective concepts of social analysis. What I want to draw the reader's attention to is the 'literal' closure of the ambiguous realities of the social world which such approaches aim to achieve. The goal is a full-scale, 'complete' definition of concepts like 'the individual', 'civil society' or 'democracy', and the lived realities of ordinary people are then measured against this categorical concept. This is not to say that such enquiries do not have intellectual value – in fact many of them are examples of serious scholarship. But what I have proposed here starts from different premises. Against the potential freezing of representations and ossification of lived realities, I have attempted to advocate a way of thinking and representation which remains open to the ambiguities between lived experience and abstract representation. Irony is one way of grasping these, both for peasants and intellectuals.

Notes

1. All these media introduced in the Maoist era are still regularly used in Zhongba. Two enormous loudspeakers hang from the roof of the village administration of Zhongba. In fact, they were installed right next to the window of the room where I was sleeping, and they woke me up more than once. One winter morning in late 2006, for instance, the loudspeakers started to clang at 8 A.M. The pop song 'Three Happy Treasures' (*jixiang sanbao*) and other chart hits rang out at a volume loud enough to reach the surrounding valleys. This was rather common at that time, when the working group was implementing the 'Construction of the New Countryside' programmes. They regularly announced meetings or new regulations using the loudspeakers – always preceded by a pop song, presumably to give a more up-to-date feel to this old-fashioned way of spreading propaganda. I never really got used to having the loudspeakers right next to my window on the balcony of the village administration building, given the ear-battering volume that made it impossible to hear your own words. I had to get up. Two village officials were already in the office, sitting around the little radiator warming their feet. I asked them what 'movement' (*huodong*) there would be today, and they answered 'no movement today': the loudspeaker was just 'good fun' (*hao wan'r*). Instead of venting my anger, I had to join in with their laughter.
2. Joas (2000 [1997]: 159ff), for instance, points out this possibility of a 'final closure' in Rorty's writings on irony and solidarity.
3. See Appendix A for a translation of the entire article.
4. The last sentence echoed Mao Zedong's famous slogan 'to serve the people' (*wei renmin fuwu*).

$\mathcal{C}\!\!\!\sim$

A German Lad in Bashan

Enshi Evening News, 9 December 2006

In the village of Zhongba, Bashan Township, Enshi City, people can now frequently see a tall, blond young foreigner walking from house to house. This is Hans Steinmuller, a PhD student from the London School of Economics and Political Science in England. His Chinese name is Shi Han, and originally he is a German from the city of Munich. This 1.82 m tall PhD student is only 26 years old, and he speaks German, Chinese, English, and Spanish fluently. When this reporter interviewed him on the 3rd December, Shi Han pronounced the following phrase in all four languages: 'The rural reconstruction in Bashan Township and Zhongba village is done very well.'

Shi Han came to China for the first time in July 2005 as an exchange student of the London School of Economics at Tsinghua University in Beijing. His original plan was to stay for one and a half years in China. In December 2005, he came to Enshi for the first time. Already upon the first visit this beautiful and magical land left a strong impression on him, and the kind-heartedness and hospitality of the Enshi people moved him deeply. Even though he then travelled through Hunan, Chongqing, Anhui, and several other provinces, he finally decided to do the empirical research for his PhD thesis in Enshi. Among his reasons for choosing Enshi, Shi Han told the reporter, the friendly reception by the city government of Enshi and the Hubei Institute for Nationalities touched him greatly. But even more important was that when he came to Enshi for the first time, he already felt the strong flavour of local folk culture (*minzu wenhua*).

That he chose Bashan as his final field-site, cannot be separated from the friendly support and the suggestions of Xu Chuanjing, the head of the party association of research students at the Hubei Institute for Nationalities, and several other teachers at this institute. When Shi Han arrived in Enshi for the first time, Xu Chuanjing was charged with the task of receiving him. Shi Han did not book a hotel, but instead stayed in the small and simple dormitory for research students at the university. Sharing the same interests and fields of study, the two research students quickly became good friends.

According to the villagers and officials of Zhongba, when Shi Han first arrived in Zhongba, he was not used to the habits and customs here. The most typical example is that when eating, he always insisted on paying his bills ['*AA zhi'*, i.e. go Dutch]. When smoking tobacco, he only smoked his own cigarettes, and did not offer cigarettes to others. But after some time Shi Han realized that the rule of dividing the bill after a meal does not apply in China. As a student of social anthropology, Shi Han has an excellent ability to adapt to different environments. It is almost unbelievable how much he has learned in the six months since he started living in Zhongba last May: when he goes to farmers' houses now, he knows that he has to offer tobacco to the host first, and has even learned to say modestly 'this is just very bad tobacco' (E. *pie yan*); if he is asked about his father, he can talk about 'my old man' (E. *laohan'r*) so and so; he can say many words in the local dialect; when others offer him cigarettes, he knows that he has to reciprocate...

Talking about tobacco, Shi Han has some other observations. He smokes cigarettes for about 3 to 5 Yuan a pack. In England he has a scholarship paying the equivalent of 76000 Yuan per year, so obviously it is not because he cannot afford better tobacco. So why does he smoke this [very cheap] tobacco? Actually it is because he realized that the local peasants all smoke very cheap cigarettes. When he offered them tobacco for 15 or 20 Yuan, they were embarrassed to take out their own cigarettes. To avoid such an awkward situation for the peasants, Shi Han only smoked cigarettes for 3 to 5 Yuan a pack from then on. Some time ago, a group of research students came to Zhongba to visit him, and Shi Han exchanged his cheap tobacco for the expensive tobacco the research students had brought for the same reason! [so that the other research student in turn could exchange cheap cigarettes with the peasants].

So what does he do on a typical day? During the day, he walks over to the farmers' houses, observes and tries to understand the local conditions; when he meets farmers building new houses or engaged in other activities, he comes over to help, and does the tasks of a simple worker (*xiao gong*); when he meets people in the tea plantations, he helps pick and cut the tea; when there are funerals and weddings, the 'red and white matters' (*hongbai xishi*), he never fails to join in, because these are the best opportunities to understand local customs and habits. His evenings he either spends watching TV in the village administration building, or collects and arranges his research material at the computer, but every night before sleeping, he writes in his diaries.

Actually, his time limit of one and half years in China has just ended. But Shi Han finds now that this time has not been long enough, and he has already made an official request to his university to stay here another couple of months. He wants to wait until the Chinese New Year, and only return to his own country after this holiday. The villagers of Zhongba also said that they would welcome Shi Han enthusiastically to spend the New Year here.

Photograph A.1 Shi Han does research to understand the situation of peasant families

Photograph A.2 Carrying a bamboo basket, he participates in farm work

APPENDIX B

EXPENSES FOR THE CONSTRUCTION OF A HOUSE

Construction Materials

Item	Price	Transport Costs	Quantity	Expenses
Sand lime bricks	0.26/brick	0.07/brick	50,000 bricks	16,500
Concrete	420/ton	20/ton	20 tons	8800
Medium sand	60/m³	20/m³	24 m³	1920
Fine sand	100/m³	20/m³	20 m³	2400
Pebbles	60/m³	20/m³	24 m³	1920
Gravel[1]	60/m³	20/m³	15 m³	1200
Steel bars	5700/ton	10/ton	2.5 tons	14,275
Big doors[2]	500/wing	-	4 wings	2000
Small doors[3]	250/wing	-	10 wings	2500
Carved wooden windows[4]	800/window	-	4	3200
Ordinary windows[5]	300/window	-	5	1500
Varied expenses[6]	6000	-	-	6000
Sub-total				62,215

Wages

Item	Price	Quantity	Expenses
Brick laying	0.15/brick	50,000 bricks	7500
Pouring floor concrete	6.5/m²	240 m²	1560
Installation of formwork for floors	15/m²	240 m²	3600
Varied work, unskilled labour	80/day	30 days	2400
Sub-total			**15,060**
Total			**77,275**

This is a list of the materials and wages needed for the construction of a two-storey house with a ground area of 100 m², and a floor space of 240 m². Material costs and wages are average costs in Bashan township in 2007. The numbers are based on data provided by Song Yong, a young official from Zhongba, and interviews with two companies selling construction material in Bashan. Where the costs of items differed, I determined an arithmetic mean. The quantities are based on Song Yong's estimates, double-checked with my observations at construction sites. Transport costs are calculated for a distance of around one to two kilometres from the township. Transport costs increase proportionally with the distance of the construction site from the township and the quality of the roads. The items listed here are limited to the construction of the main structure of one house, including masonry, concrete floors and ceiling, windows and doors. Further decoration, plastering, and internal installation (water and electricity) are not included. All expenses are given in Yuan RMB.

Notes

1. Gravel is mainly used for the foundations; the amount has to be adjusted to varying circumstances.
2. Transport costs for doors and windows are included in the prices. Prices for big doors vary according to material and style from 400 to 800 Yuan per wing of a door.
3. Prices for small doors vary according to material and style from 200 to 500 Yuan per wing.
4. Prices for carved wooden windows vary according to material and style from 800 to 1400/window or 250/m². Here I assume that wooden carved windows are used only for the front of the house, and ordinary windows for the back- and side-walls.
5. Prices for ordinary windows vary according to material and style from 250 to 500 Yuan per window.
6. This includes meals, liquor, and cigarettes for workers. According to local custom, every worker has to receive one pack of cigarettes per day, and has to be hosted with good meals and liquor.

APPENDIX C

LIST OF MONEY-GIFTS AND TASKS

The following are lists of the money-gifts I offered, and the specific tasks I was invited to take on at family celebrations during fieldwork in Bashan.

List of Money-Gifts

Date (Lunar Calendar)	Date (Gregorian Calendar)	Occasion	Amount given (Yuan RMB)	Estimate of money received by host (Yuan RMB)
2006-6-11	2006-7-6	House inauguration	20	
2006-7-10	2006-8-3	House inauguration	8	
2006-7¹-1	2006-8-24	Funeral	50	8000
2006-10-1	2006-11-21	Funeral	20	
2006-12-6	2006-12-26	Birthday	20	10,000
2006-12-18	2007-2-4	Wedding	20	10,670
2006-12-19	2007-2-5	Wedding	20	15,000
2006-12-24	2007-2-11	Wedding	50	
2007-1-10	2007-2-27	Wedding	50	
2007-1-12	2007-3-1	Wedding	20	
2007-1-14	2007-3-3	Birthday	20	20,000
2007-1-16	2007-3-5	Wedding	20	
2007-1-18	2007-3-6	Wedding	20	
2007-1-18	2007-3-6	Wedding	20	14,000
2007-1-19	2007-3-6	Wedding	20	
2007-1-21	2007-3-10	Birthday	20	9000

2007-1-22	2007-3-11	Wedding	20	
2007-1-29	2007-3-17	Birthday	20	
2007-2-8	2007-3-26	Funeral	20	12,000
2007-2-18	2007-4-6	Birthday	20	10,000
2007-2-27	2007-4-14	Wedding	20	
2007-3-2	2007-4-18	House inauguration	20	7000
2007-3-3	2007-4-19	Funeral	20	
2007-3-10	2007-4-26	Wedding	50	18,000
2007-3-15	2007-5-1	Wedding	20	9000
2007-6-19	2007-8-1	Funeral	30	
2007-7-10	2007-8-24	Birthday	20	11,000
2007-7-1	2007-8-30	Son passed entry exam to university	20	10,000
2007-8-8	2007-9-18	Wedding	20	
2007-8-8	2007-9-18	House inauguration	30	7500

List of Specific Tasks

Family	Date (Lunar Calendar)	Date (Gregorian Calendar)	Occasion	My Task
Yang Minghu	2006-12-2	2007-1-19	House inauguration	Receiving guests (*ying bin*)
Wang Wei	2007-1-19	2007-3-8	Wedding	Packing dowry (*qu qin*)
Yao Kegui	2007-3-15	2007-5-1	Wedding	Offering cigarettes (*feng yan*)

Notes

1. This year had an intercalary seventh month, i.e. a second seventh month (*runyue*).

APPENDIX D:

SUBSIDIES GIVEN TO THREE HOUSEHOLDS

Case 1: The Xiang Family

Item	Cost	Subsidy received
Exterior painting	1500[1]	1500
Carved windows	2240	1120[2]
Four lamps	400	200
Painting of interior walls	1000[3]	1000
Tiles for two bathrooms	800	800
Tiles for cooking surfaces, storage shelves, and stove	500	500

Case 2: The Liu Family

Item	Cost	Subsidy received
Exterior painting	1500[1]	1500
Carved windows	2240	1120[2]

Case 3: The Wang Family

Item	Cost	Subsidy received
Tiles for cooking surfaces, storage shelves, stove, and toilet	600	600

All amounts are given in Yuan RMB. Subsidies were given during the implementation of the 'Construction of a Socialist New Countryside' programmes described in chapter 7. These numbers are estimates based on interviews with the household heads. The Xiang and the Liu family have only recently built their new houses, both directly next to the public road. The Wang family house was built in 1998, and extended in 2004. The houses in case 1 and 2 are very big, with the total costs of house construction amounting to at least 150,000 Yuan (see Appendix B for the costs of house construction).

Notes

1. This was divided into 1000 Yuan for material and 500 Yuan for wages. The household had to cater for two workers eating two meals a day for about three working days.
2. These carved windows were subsidized on the basis of window area: 70 Yuan were paid for 1 m², assuming an entire area of 16 m².
3. Resulting from an estimated wall area of 500 m², and a cost of 2 Yuan per m². Wage labour was not calculated for interior painting.

GLOSSARY

aiyue	哀乐
an guiju	按规矩
an jian	按件
anquan	安全
ansu	安宿
bai gandie	拜干爹
bai ganma	拜干妈
baihua	白话
baijia luntan	百家讲坛
baijiazi	败家子
bang mang	帮忙
bao	报
baogai	宝盖
baogong	包工
baogu fan	包谷饭
baozi	包子
bashan	巴山
ba zi	八字
beifen	辈分
beishi	背时
benhu	本户
boshi	博士
boxue	剥削
bu limao	不礼貌
caichu	菜厨
cai lanzi li kan xingshi	菜篮子里看形势
canguan de lu	参观的路
cao hai	草鞋
cha ma dao	茶马道
changpai	张牌
cha xiang	插香
chaye shang shuitian, hui dao wu jiu nian !	茶叶上水田 回到五九年!

che pi la jin	扯皮拉筋
chi he wan le	吃喝玩乐
chi jiu	吃酒
chi ren	吃人
chuange	橡各
chui niu wang	吹牛王
chunpu	纯朴
chuzhong	初中
cun	村
cunmin zizhi	村民自治
da cao da ban	大操大办
dadao kongjia dian	打倒孔家店
dadui	大队
dagongzai	打工仔
dai xiao	戴孝
da jia	打架
da lian gangtie	大炼钢铁
dao	道
dao ban'r	倒板儿
daode	道德
daoshi	道士
da pai	打牌
da shijie	大世界
da zi bao	大字报
daxue	大学
da yezi	大叶子
da ye luogu	打夜锣鼓
da yue jin	大跃进
da zhaohu	打招呼
dazibao	大字报
deguo guizi	德国鬼子
diangong	点工
diaocha	调查
diaojiao lou	吊脚楼
difang wenhua	地方文化
difang tese	地方特色
difangzhi	地方志
dili	地理
dongliang zhi cai	栋梁之才
dong nei taohua kai ban ye	洞内桃花开半夜
fang zhong guizi jie wu geng	房中贵子结五更
dongzu ting	侗族厅

dongzu xiang	侗族乡
dou dizhu	斗地主
du	赌
du bo	赌博
duilian	对联
en yi fengsu san bian shuo	恩邑风俗三变说
erdao fanzi	二道贩子
e xi	恶习
fanchu	饭厨
fangbian	方便
fangwei tuoshan	方为妥善
fa shi	法事
feichang ganxie	非常感谢
fengchenghua	奉承话
fengjian lifa	封建礼法
fengjian mixin	封建迷信
fengjian shi zhong	丰俭适中
fengjian wangchao	封建王朝
feng jiu	奉酒
fengshui	风水
fengshui xiansheng	风水先生
feng yan	奉烟
fengyu qiao	风雨桥
fu	福
fu lu shou	福禄寿
funü lian	妇女联
gai kou	改口
gai tu gui liu	改土归流
gan bu shang xingshi	赶不上形势
gandie	干爹
gaifang hai	解放鞋
gaoqin	高亲
geren jia	个人家
gonglu	公路
gua ge renqing	挂个人情
guanke	管客
guanxi	关系
guanxi xue	关系学
guoji kai wan xiao	国际开玩笑
guifanhua	规范化
guizi	鬼子
guiju	规矩

gujin tushu jicheng	古今图书集成
guoli	过礼
hai shi yi ge mianzi gongcheng	还是一个面子工程
handai	寒带
hanzu ren	汉族人
haochi	豪侈
haowan	好玩
heidao	黑道
hei shehui	黑社会
hongbai xishi	红白喜事
hongbao	红包
hong cha	红茶
hongdao	红道
honghuo	红火
hongjinlong	红金龙
hong lou meng	红楼梦
hongqi dadui	红旗大队
hongxing dadui	红星大队
hua	华
huagou luocheng	华构落成
huang liang guo shui	皇粮国税
huanli	还礼
huaren	华人
huashi hou xin shu cheng lin	华室后新树成林
yu zhai qian bian shan ru hua	玉宅前边山如画
huitu luban jing	绘图鲁班经
hunli	婚礼
hunhun	混混
hunpai	荤牌
huo	火
huodong	活动
huopan	火盘
huoqi	火气
huose	火色
huoyan	火焰
huozang	火葬
huzhu	户主
ji lu ban	祭鲁班
jia	家
jiachuan	家传
jiagui	家规
jiali	家礼

jianghu	江湖
jiang yiqi	讲义气
jiangxi laoxianghui	江西老乡会
jiankang majiang	健康麻将
jianxing	饯行
jiaotong bu fangbian	交通不方便
jiapu	家谱
jiating lianchan chengbao zerenzhi	家庭联产承包责任制
jia xian	家先
jiazu	家族
jiben lijie	基本礼节
jin	斤
jinian	纪念
jie liangshu	接梁树
jingji sixiang	经济思想
jiujiu	舅舅
jiuxi	酒席
jixiang sanbao	吉祥三宝
juejin	倔劲
junzi ai qian, qude you dao	君子爱钱取得有道
kai caimen	开财门
kai dao	开道
kai lu	开路
kanyu	堪舆
kaocha	考察
kehu	客户
kexue	科学
kexue fazhan	科学发展
kexue yu minzhu	科学与民主
kong lao'er	孔老二
kong yiji	孔乙己
kouhao	口号
ku li	苦力
laiwang	来往
laoban	老板
laodong mofang	劳动模仿
lao gai	老街
laohan'r	老汉儿
lao mu	老墓
laonianren	老年人
laoyi	老衣
lei xiang xiao, yu lai da	雷响小雨来大

li	礼
liangkou kaiqi yi cun ba	梁口开起一寸八
erzi ersun dou fada	儿子儿孙都发达
lianyi	殓衣
libai	礼拜
liben	礼本
lichun	立春
ligui	厉鬼
lihai	厉害
liji	礼记
lijie	礼节
lijiao	礼教
limao	礼貌
li mubei	立墓碑
linse	吝啬
lishang wanglai	礼尚往来
liuchu renkou	流出人口
liu ji kanyu manxing	刘基堪舆漫兴
liulang	流浪
liumang	流氓
lishang wanglai	礼尚往来
lisu	礼俗
liyi	礼仪
lizhuo	礼桌
lu ban shu	鲁班书
lunyu	论语
luogu dui	锣鼓队
luohou	落后
luopan	罗盘
mafan	麻烦
man shang qi xia	瞒上欺下
majiang	麻将
majiang xue	麻将学
mao laohan'r	毛老汉儿
mei you falü de gainian	没有法律的概念
mei you gou fei mei you ji jiao	没有狗吠没有鸡叫
mengzi	孟子
mian	面
mianpi hou	面皮厚
mianzi gongcheng	面子工程
miaotang	庙堂
mijiu	米酒

minbing	民兵
ming	命
mingpao	鸣炮
mingyun	命运
mingzi	名字
minjian	民间
minjian wenhua	民间文化
minzhu jiandu xiaozu	民主监督小组
minzhu licai xiaozu	民主理财小组
minzu tese	民族特色
minzu wenhua	民族文化
minzu xiang	民族乡
modou	墨斗
mu	亩
nanfang	男方
naore	闹热
nei	内
neijing	内景
nengli	能力
nian jing	念经
nongli	农历
nongmin	农民
nongmin fudan	农民负担
nongmin jiaoyu	农民教育
nongxian	农闲
nongye xue dazhai	农业学大寨
nüfang	女方
pa chijiu – bu de bu chijiu – ziji ye zheng jiu	怕吃酒 – 不得不吃酒 – 自己也整酒
pangu kai tian yilai	盘古开天以来
pei shi zimei	陪十姊妹
pian	骗
pie yan	撇烟
pinkun diqu	贫困地区
piqi	脾气
po si jiu li si xin	破四旧立四新
pu	朴
pusu	朴素
putonghua	普通话
puzhang langfei	铺张浪费
qi	气
qi pi lang	七匹狼

qiancheng si jin	前程似锦
qiao bu qi ni	瞧不起你
qing zuxian	请祖先
qinjian chijia	勤俭持家
qinjian jieyue	勤俭节约
qin pa ku zheng	勤扒苦争
qing ke	请客
qingming	清明
qu chi jiu	去吃酒
quekou	缺口
qugongsuo	区公所
qu qin	去亲
rao guancai	绕棺材
rao guan sa hua	绕棺撒花
ren	仁
renao	热闹
rencai	人才
rende jiujiu	认得舅舅
renmin qunzhong	人民群众
renqing	人情
renqing wang	人情网
renshi	认识
rongmei jiyou	容美记游
ruxiang suisu	入乡随俗
san guo yan yi	三国演义
san jin ban de luyu – daozhe ti	三斤半的鲈鱼 – 倒着提
sanji xianren dili	三极仙人地理
san nian man xiao	三年满孝
san nong wenti	三农问题
saomang yundong	扫盲运动
seba	啬巴
shang	上
shang da ren	上大人
qiu yi ji	邱乙己
hua san qian	化三千
qi shi xian	七十贤
er xiao sheng	尔小生
ba jiu zi	八九子
jia zuo ren	佳作仁
ke zhi li	可知礼
shang gai	上街
shang liang	上梁

shang liang jiu	上梁酒
shangmen nüxu	上门女婿
shang ming	上名
shangwei	上位
shangyehua	商业化
shaobing	烧饼
shaocha	烧茶
shaofo	绍和
she	社
shehui bentilun	社会本体论
shehui shang de ren	社会上的人
shehuizhuyi xin nongcun jianshe	社会主义新农村建设
shengchan fazhan	生产发展
shenghuo	生火
shenghuo zhiliang	生活质量
shenkan	神龛
sheri	社日
shidian	试点
shifan	示范
shifan cun	示范村
shifan hu	示范户
shifan qu	示范区
shifu	师傅
shinanfu	施南府
shi tiangan	十天干
shiwai taoyuan	世外桃源
shouyi	寿衣
shuang xi	双喜
shui hu zhuan	水浒传
shushu	叔叔
shou	寿
si nonghuo	死农活
si shu	四书
siji facai caiyuan guang	四季发财财源光
tiaotiao cailu dou tongchang	条条财路都通畅
sixiang gongzuo	思想工作
songshi	讼师
songgun	讼棍
su ku	诉苦
suku hui	诉苦会
supai	素牌
suzhi	素质

suzhi di	素质低
suzhi gao	素质高
tang	堂
tangwu	堂屋
tai shou	太守
tai tou jia nü	抬头嫁女
di tou jie xifu	低头接媳妇
tamen fu fu, bu shi fupin	他们扶富不是扶贫
tan pengyou	谈朋友
taohua shan	桃花扇
taowu	套屋
taohuayuan ji	桃花源记
tian chang di jiu, di jiu tian zhang	天长地久地久天长
tiandi	天地
tian di jun qin shi wei	天地君亲师位
tiao sang	跳丧
tiaoxi	调席
touji daoba	投机倒把
touji maimai	投机买卖
tu	土
tuannianfan	团年饭
tudi	徒弟
tu fangzi	土房子
tuigeng huanlin	退耕还林
tujiazu miaozu zizhizhou	土家族苗族自治州
tuli tuqi	土里土气
tusi	土司
tuzang	土葬
wai	外
waibin	外宾
waidiren	外地人
waima	外马
waijing	外景
wajue	挖掘
wan	玩
wanquan shi huoqi	完全是火气
wei geren fuwu, bu shi wei	为个人服务不是为老百姓服务
laobaixing fuwu	
wei renmin fuwu	为人民服务
wen	文
wenhua	文化
wenhua shuiping	文化水平

wenming	文明
wenming cun	文明村
wenming xin feng	文明新风
wenren	文人
wenyan	文言
wu gai san jian liang tigao yi gongkai	五改三建两提高一公开
wu jiu bu zheng liyi	无酒不正礼仪
wu shi jiu	无事酒
wu shi zheng jiu	无事整酒
wu xing	五行
xia	下
xia gai	下街
xiahai	下海
xia kuli	下苦力
xiang shangji huibao	向上级汇报
xiang zhengfu	乡政府
xian'r bing	馅儿饼
xiao	孝
xiao cai ban bian liang	小菜半边粮
xiaodao	孝道
xiao gong	小工
xiaokang	小康
xiaokang lou	小康楼
xiaokang cun	小康村
xiaonian	小年
xiaoqi	小气
xiaoren	小人
xiaotang	孝堂
xiaozu	小组
xiawei	下位
xicai	洗菜
xie baogao	写报告
xie	邪
xiejiao mixin	邪教迷信
xike	稀客
xingshi	姓氏
xin mu	新墓
xingxiang gongcheng	形象工程
xiong	凶
xi you ji	西游记
xuesheng wa'r	学生娃儿
xun	旬

xunzi	荀子
yacha	芽茶
yanerke	燕儿客
yanzi	燕子
yang fangzi	洋房子
yang lou	洋楼
yangyu fan	洋芋饭
yege	夜歌
yeshi	夜市
yezi yan	叶子烟
yijing	易经
yili	仪礼
yi muguang wei xian	以目光为限
ying bin	迎宾
yingxiong	英雄
yinsi	阴祀
yinyang xiansheng	阴阳先生
yisi yisi	意思意思
you chan san zhuan sheng guizi,	右缠三转生贵子
zuo chan san zhuan dian zhuangyuan	左缠三转点状元
sheng guizi,	生贵子
dian zhuangyuan,	点状元
zhujia fada wanwan nian	主家发达万万年
you pu er hua	由朴而华
youtiao	油条
you wenhua	有文化
yuanzi	院子
yule	娱乐
yu nongmin tong chi, tong zhu, tong laodong	与农民同吃同住同劳动
yunqi	运气
zangli	葬礼
zengjia shouru	增加收入
zha jinhua	炸金花
zhang moshi	掌墨师
zhao shi zheng jiu	找事整酒
zheng jiu	整酒
zhengwu	正屋
zhi hu zhe ye	之乎者也
zhi ke	支客
zhipan	执盘
zhiza	支杂

zhong	忠
zhong	中
zhongba	中坝
zhongba cun chuangjian shengji wenmingcun guihua	中坝村创建省级文明村规划
zhongtang	中堂
zhongyong	中庸
zhouli	周礼
zhu yang ji	猪羊祭
ziwei gaozhao	紫薇高照
zizhi	自治
zongguan	总管
zuo shengyi	做生意
zupu	族谱
zuzhang	族长

BIBLIOGRAPHY

Abrams, P. 1988. 'Notes on the Difficulty of Studying the State', *Journal of Historical Sociology* 1(1): 58–89.

Ahern, E.M. 1974. 'Affines and the Rituals of Kinship', in A.P. Wolf (ed.), *Religion and Ritual in Chinese Society*. Stanford: Stanford University Press, pp. 279–307.

———. 1979. 'Domestic Architecture in Taiwan: Continuity and Change', in R.W. Wilson, A. Auerbacher Wilson and S.L. Greenblatt (eds), *Value Change in Chinese Society*. New York: Praeger, pp. 155–70.

Anagnost, A. 2004. 'The Corporeal Politics of Quality (*suzhi*)', *Public Culture* 16: 189–208.

Ardener, E. 1989 [1987]. '"Remote Areas" – Some Theoretical Considerations', in M. Chapman (ed.), *Edwin Ardener: The Voice of Prophecy and Other Essays*. Oxford: Blackwell, pp. 211–23.

Bailey, F.G. 1969. *Stratagems and Spoils*. Oxford: Blackwell.

———. 1991. *The Prevalence of Deceit*. Ithaca: Cornell University Press.

Bakken, B. 2000. *The Exemplary Society. Human Improvement, Social Control, and the Dangers of Modernity in China*. Oxford: Oxford University Press.

Bashan Township. 2006. *Bashan Lishi Tai Zhang Zhuyao Biaozhi* (Major Indexes of the Historical Accounts of Bashan), collected and reported by Chen Xiaochun.

Bell, C. 1992. *Ritual Theory, Ritual Practice*. New York: Oxford University Press.

Benjamin, W. 1982. *Das Passagen-Werk*, ed. by R. Tiedemann. Frankfurt am Main: Suhrkamp.

Berman, M. 1983. *All that is Solid Melts into Air: The Experience of Modernity*. London: Verso.

Billeter, F. 1984. 'Pensée Occidentale et Pensée Chinoise: le Regard et l'Acte', in J.-C. Galey (ed.), *Différences, Valeurs, Hiérarchie. Textes offerts à Louis Dumont*. Paris: EHESS, pp. 25–51.

Bosco, J., L.H.-M. Liu and M. West. 2009. 'Underground Lotteries in China: The Occult Economy and Capitalist Culture', *Research in Economic Anthropology* 29: 31–62.

Bourdieu, P. 1991. *The Political Ontology of Martin Heidegger*, transl. P. Collier. Stanford: Stanford University Press.

Bray, F. 1994. *The Rice Economies: Technology and Development in Asian Societies*. Berkeley: University of California Press.

———. 1997. *Technology and Gender. Fabrics of Power in Late Imperial China*. Berkeley: University of California Press.

Brown, M. 2002. 'Local Government Agency. Manipulating Tujia Identity', *Modern China* 28(3): 362–95.

———. 2004. *Is Taiwan Chinese? The Impact of Culture, Power, and Migration on Changing Identities*. Berkeley: University of California Press.

Bruun, O. 2003. *Fengshui in China: Geomantic Divination between State Orthodoxy and Popular Religion*. Honolulu: University of Hawai'i Press.

———. 2008. *An Introduction to Feng Shui*. Cambridge: Cambridge University Press.

Burns, J. 1987. 'Political Participation of Peasants in China', in V.C. Falkenheim (ed.), *Citizens and Groups in Contemporary China*. Ann Arbor: Center for Chinese Studies, pp. 91–122.

Caillois, R. 2001 [1958]. *Man, Play and Games*, transl. M. Barash. Urbana: University of Illinois Press.

Cao Jinging. 2000. *Huanghe bian de Zhongguo. Yi ge Xuezhe dui Xiangcun shehui de Guancha yu Sikao* (China along the Yellow River. A Scholar's Observations and Reflections on Rural Society). Shanghai: Shanghai Wenyi Chubanshe.

Capdeville-Zeng, C. 2008. *La Conception Chinoise du 'Ritual' (li) en Chinois*, unpublished presentation at the Groupe de travail d'anthropologie sociale comparative, 22 and 29 January 2008, EHESS, Paris.

Chau, A.Y. 2006. *Miraculous Response. Doing Popular Religion in Contemporary China*. Stanford: Stanford University Press.

———. 2008. 'The Sensorial Production of the Social', *Ethnos* 73: 485–504.

Ch'en, J. 1992. *The Highlanders of Central China. A History 1895-1937*. London: M.E. Sharpe.

Chen Duxiu. 1917. 'Jiu Sixiang yu Guoti Wenti' (The Old Thinking and the Problems of the National Polity), *Xin Qingnian* 3(3): 3, online at http://www.southcn.com/NEWS/COMMUNITY/shzt/youth/forerunner/200404281032.htm [accessed on 15 March 2009].

Chen Guidi and Wu Chuntao. 2004. *Zhongguo Nongmin Diaocha* (Report on the Chinese Peasantry). Beijing: Renmin Wenxian Chubanshe.

Chen Zhongshi. 2008 [1993]. *Bailu Yuan* (White Deer Ground). Beijing: Wenhua Yishu Chubanshe.

Cohen, A.P. 1998. 'Review of Cultural Intimacy: Social Poetics in the Nation-State by Michael Herzfeld', *American Ethnologist* 25(1, Special Book Review Issue): 7–8.

Comaroff, J. and J.L. Comaroff. 1999. 'Occult Economies and the Violence of Abstraction: Notes from the South African Postcolony', *American Ethnologist* 26(2): 279–303.

———. 2000. 'Millennial Capitalism: First Thoughts on a Second Coming', *Public Culture* 12(2): 291–343.

Coppet, D. de. 1992. 'Comparison, a Universal for Anthropology: From Re-presentation to the Comparison of Hierarchies of Values', in A. Kuper (ed.), *Conceptualizing Society*. London: Routledge, pp. 59–74.

Corsín Jiménez, A. 2003. 'On Space as a Capacity', *Journal of the Royal Anthropological Institute* 9(1): 137–53.

Croll, E. 1994. *From Heaven to Earth: Images and Experiences of Development in China*. London: Routledge.

Day, A. 2008. 'The End of the Peasant? New Rural Reconstruction in China', *boundary* 2: 49–73.

Derrida, J. 1987. *De l'Esprit. Heidegger et la Question*. Paris: Galilée.

Dillingham, R. and C. Dillingham. 1971. *A Survey of Traditional Architecture in Taiwan*. Taizhong: Donghai University.

Dong, M.Y. and J. Goldstein (eds). 2006. *Everyday Modernity in China*. Seattle: University of Washington Press.

Duara, P. 1987. 'State Involution: A Study of Local Finances in North China, 1911-1935', *Comparative Studies in Society and History* 29(1): 132–61.

Dutton, M. 1998. *Streetlife China*. Cambridge: Cambridge University Press.

Eberhard, W. 1966. *Erzählungsgut aus Südost-China*. Berlin: Walter de Gruyter.

———. 1970. 'Chinese Building Magic', in W. Eberhard (ed.), *Studies in Chinese Folklore and Related Essays*. Bloomington: Indiana University Folklore Institute, pp. 49–65.

Ebrey, P.B. 1991. *Chu Hsi's Family Rituals: A Twelfth-Century Chinese Manual for the Performance of Cappings, Weddings, Funerals, and Ancestral Rites*. Princeton: Princeton University Press.

Elvin, M. 1972. *The Pattern of the Chinese Past*. Stanford: Stanford University Press.
———. 1984. 'Female Virtue and the State in China', *Past and Present* 104: 111–52.
Enshi City. 1996. *Enshi Shizhi* (Gazetteer of Enshi City). Wuhan: Wuhan Gongye Daxue Chubanshe.
———. 2006a. *Zhongba Cun: Qiangzhua Xin Nongcun Jianshe Yu. Quanmian Tigao Wenming Xin Cun Jianshe Shuiping. Enshi Shi 2006 Nian Sanji Ganbu Huiyi Dianxing Cailiao* (Zhongba Village: Seize the Opportunities of the New Countryside. Increase Comprehensively the Levels of Rural Construction), government announcement.
———. 2006b. *Wu Gai San Jian. Rang Tumiao Shanzhai Piankai Wenming Hua* (Five Changes and Three Constructions. Let the Flowers of Civilization bloom in the Mountain Villages of the Tujia and Miao Minorities), government announcement.
Enshi City Propaganda Department, Office of the People's Government of Enshi City, Council of Minority Affairs of Enshi City (eds). 1994. *Xidu Enshi* (Enshi, the Capital of Selenium), Enshi City Government.
Enshi County. 1982 [1868]. *Enshi Xianzhi* (Gazetteer of Enshi County), Tongzhi Period (1862–1875).
Enshi Prefecture, Bureau of Statistics. 2007. *Enshi Zhou Tongjia Nianjian* 2006 (Statistical Yearbook of Enshi Prefecture 2006).
Enshi Wanbao (*Enshi Evening News*). 2007a. 'wo zhou sanqi dangyuan ganbu canyu dubo anli bei quanshen tongbao' (The Case of Gambling of Three Cadres from Different Levels of Enshi Prefecture has been Publicized in the Whole Province), 2 January 2007.
———. 2007b. 'dubo shule qian toudao luo fawang' (Lost Money in Gambling – Thief Caught in the Nets of the Law), 28 March 2007.
———. 2007c. 'enshi lao cheng de "'yanerke"' (The Yanerke of the Old Town of Enshi), 25 May 2007.
———. 2007d. 'renqing ru zhai: guanyu hefeng nongcun zhengjiu zhi feng de diaocha' (When renqing become a Debt: A Report about the Customs of Hosting Banquets in Hefeng County), 15 August 2007.
———. 2007e. 'guanyu Li Zeyu dengren canyu dubo wenti de tongbao' (Report about the Problem of Li Zeyu and Several Others who Engaged in Gambling), 29 September 2007.
———. 2007f. 'dubo shule qian xing qie bei zhuahuo' (Lost Money in Gambling – Delinquent was Caught), 29 October 2007.
———. 2008. 'moudao renda yindao nongmin jianqing renqing fudan' (The People's Congress of Moudao Township Guides the Peasants towards Reducing the 'Burden of Presents'), 2 February 2008.
Enshi TV. 5 September 2007. 'anfang zhengjiu' (An Undercover Enquiry into the Customs of Holding Banquets), in the programme 'jinwan jiudian ban' (Today at half past Nine), online at http://www.enshi.cn/20070525/ca81357.htm [accessed on 1 November 2008].
Entwisle, B. and G.E. Henderson (eds). 2000. *Re-Drawing Boundaries. Work, Households, and Gender in China*. Berkeley: University of California Press.
Fabian, J. 1983. *Time and the Other: How Anthropology Makes Its Object*. New York: Columbia University Press.
Farias, V. 1987. *Heidegger et le Nazisme*. Paris: Verdier.
Fan Wei. 1992. 'Village Fengshui Principles', in R.E. Knapp (ed.), *Chinese Landscapes. The Village as Place*. Honolulu: University of Hawaii Press, pp. 35–46.
Faubion, J.D. 2001. 'Toward an Anthropology of Ethics: Foucault and the Pedagogies of Autopoiesis', *Representations* 74: 83–104.
Faure, D. 1999. 'The Emperor in the Village: Representing the State in South China', in J.P. McDermott (ed.), *State and Court Ritual in China*. Cambridge: Cambridge University Press, pp. 267–98.

Fei Xiaotong. 1999 [1991]. 'Wuling Xing' (Journey in the Wuling Mountains), *Fei Xiaotong Wenji* (Collected Works of Fei Xiaotong) 12, Beijing: Qunyan Chubanshe, pp. 238–55.

Fernandez, J. and M. Taylor Huber (eds). 2001. *Irony in Action. Anthropology, Practice and the Moral Imagination*. Chicago: University of Chicago Press.

Festa, P. 2006. 'Mahjong Politics in Contemporary China: Civility, Chineseness, and Mass Culture', *positions: east asia cultures critique* 14(1): 7–35.

———. 2007. 'Mahjong Agonistics and the Political Public in Taiwan: Fate, Mimesis, and the Martial Imaginary', *Anthropological Quarterly* 80(1): 93–125.

Feuchtwang, S. 2001 [1992]. *Popular Religion in China: The Imperial Metaphor*. London: Routledge.

———. 2002 [1974]. *An Anthropological Analysis of Chinese Geomancy*. Bangkok: White Lotus.

———. 2004. 'Curves and the Urbanisation of Meifa Village', in S. Feuchtwang (ed.), *Making Place: State Projects, Globalization, and Local Responses in China*. London: UCL Press, pp. 163–79.

———. 2005. 'Three Gestures in a Poetics of Place: Chinese Settlement and Disruption', in T. Atkin and J. Rykwert (eds), *Structure and Meaning in Human Settlements*. Philadelphia: University of Pennsylvania Museum of Archaeology and Anthropology, pp. 107–21.

Fisher, T. 1982. '"The Play's the Thing": Wu Han and Hai Rui Revisited', *The Australian Journal of Chinese Affairs* 7: 1–35.

Fitzgerald, C.P. 2005 [1941]. *The Tower of Five Glories. A Study of the Min Chia (Bai Ethnic Minority) of Ta Li, Yunnan*. Hong Kong: Caravan Press.

Foucault, M. 1984. 'Polemics, Politics, and Problematizations: An Interview with Michael Foucault', in P. Rabinow (ed.), *The Foucault Reader*. New York: Pantheon Books, pp. 383–85.

Freedman, M. 1970. 'Ritual Aspects of Chinese Kinship and Marriage', in M. Freedman (ed.), *Family and Kinship in Chinese Society*. Stanford: Stanford University Press, pp. 163–87.

———. 1979 [1967]. 'Rites and Duties, or Chinese Marriage', in G.W. Skinner (ed.), *The Study of Chinese Society. Essays by Maurice Freedman*, Stanford: Stanford University Press, pp. 255–72.

Fried, M.H. 1953. *The Fabric of Chinese Society: A Study of Social Life of a Chinese County Seat*. New York: Praeger.

Fuller, C.J. and V. Benei (eds). 2001. *The Everyday State and Society in Modern India*. London: C. Hurst.

Gardiner, M.E. 2000. *Critiques of Everyday Life*. London: Routledge.

Geertz, C. 1963. *Agricultural Involution*. Berkeley: University of California Press.

———. 1973. 'Deep Play: Notes on the Balinese Cockfight', in C. Geertz (ed.), *The Interpretation of Cultures*. New York: Basic Books, pp. 412–53.

———. 1980. *Negara, the Theatre State in Nineteenth Century Bali*. Princeton: Princeton University Press.

Gernet, J. 1962. *Daily Life in China on the Eve of the Mongol Invasion, 1250-1276*. Stanford: Stanford University Press.

Gibeault, D. (forthcoming). 'L'Autorité comme Echange : la Chine', in D. Gibeault and S. Vibert (eds), *Autorité et Pouvoir en Perspective Comparative, Textes en Hommage à Daniel de Coppet*.

Gibson, T.P. 1986. *Sacrifice and Sharing in the Philippine Highlands: Religion and Society among the Buid of Mindoro*. London: Athlone Press.

Goffman, E. 1955. 'On Face-work: An Analysis of Ritual Elements of Social Interaction', *Psychiatry: Journal for the Study of Interpersonal Processes* 18(3): 213–31.

———. 1959. *The Presentation of Self in Everyday Life*. New York: Anchor.

———. 1967. *Interaction Ritual: Essays in Face to Face Behavior*. New York: Anchor.

Graeber, D. 2004. *Fragments of an Anarchist Anthropology*. Chicago: Prickly Paradigm Press.

———. 2006. 'Beyond Power/Knowledge. An Exploration of the Relation of Power, Igno-rance and Stupidity', Malinowski Memorial Lecture, 25 May 2006, London School of Economics, online at http://www.lse.ac.uk/collections/LSEPublicLecturesAndEvents/pdf/20060525-Graeber.pdf [accessed on 19 February 2009].

Gu Cai. 1991 [1704]. *Rongmei Jiyou* (Travel Notes from Rongmei), ed. and annotated by Gao Runsheng. Tianjing: Tianjing Guji Chubanshe.

Guang Lei. 2003. 'Rural Taste, Urban Fashions: The Cultural Politics of Rural/Urban Differ-ence in Contemporary China', *Positions* 11(3): 613–46.

Guang Ming Shi Bei. 2007. 'Shang Da Ren Jiu Yi Ji…' (His Greatness, Confucius, …), blog entry 13 August 2007, online at http://iron-connon.blogbus.com/logs/7645107.html [ac-cessed on 1 February 2008].

Gumbrecht, H.U. 1997. *1926. Living at the Edge of Time*. Cambridge MA: Harvard University Press.

Guo Xiaolin. 2001. 'Land Expropriation and Rural Conflicts in China', *The China Quarterly* 166: 422–39.

Guo Yuhua. 1992. *Si de Kunrao yu Sheng de Zhizhuo. Zhongguo Minjian Sangzang Yili yu Chuan-tong Shengsi Guan* (The Affliction of Death and the Persistence of Life. Popular Rituals of Burial and Funeral and The Traditional View of Life and Death in China). Beijing: Zhongguo Renmin Daxue Chubanshe.

Gupta, A. 1995. 'Blurred Boundaries: The Discourse of Corruption, the Culture of Politics and the Imagined State', *American Ethnologist* 22: 375–402.

Hamilton, G.G. 1989. 'Heaven is High and the Emperor is Far Away', *Revue europeenne des sciences sociales* 27: 141–67.

Han Min. 2001. *Social Change and Continuity in a Village in Northern Anhui, China: A Response to Revolution and Reform*. Osaka: National Museum of Ethnology.

Harootunian, H.D. 2000a. 'In the Tiger's Lair: Socialist Everydayness Enters Post-Mao Chi-na', *Postcolonial Studies: Culture, Politics, Economy* 3(3): 339–47.

———. 2000b. *History's Disquiet: Modernity, Cultural Practice, and the Question of Everyday Life*. New York: Columbia University Press.

Harrell, S. 1987. 'The Concept of Fate in Chinese Folk Ideology', *Modern China* 13(1).

———. 1995. 'Introduction: Civilizing Projects and the Reaction to them', in S. Harrell (ed.), *Cultural Encounters on China's Ethnic Frontiers*. Seattle: University of Washington Press, pp. 3–36.

Harrison, H. 2001. *China: Inventing the Nation*. London: Arnold.

Hay, J. 1983a. 'The Human Body as a Microcosmic source of Macrocosmic Values in Callig-raphy', in S. Bush and C. Murck (eds), *Theories of the Arts in China*. Princeton: Princeton University Press, pp. 74–102.

———. 1983b. 'Values and History in Chinese Painting I: Hsieh Ho Revisited', *Res* 6: 73–111.

Hayes, J. 1985. 'Specialists and Written Materials in the Village World,' in D. Johnson, A.J. Nathan and E.S. Rawski (eds), *Popular Culture in Late Imperial China*. Berkeley: University of California Press, pp. 75–111.

He Xiaogui. 2008. 'Enshi Shejie' (The *She* Holiday of Enshi), *Minzu Dajiating* 1: 50–51.

Heidegger, M. 2006 [1927]. *Sein und Zeit*. Tübingen: Niemeyer.

Heintz, M. 2009. *The Anthropology of Moralities*. New York: Berghahn Books.

Herzfeld, M. 1982. 'Disemia', in M. Herzfeld and M.D. Lenhart (eds), *Semiotics 1980*. New York: Plenum, pp. 205–15.

———. 1985. *The Poetics of Manhood. Contest and Identity in a Cretan Mountain Village*. Prince-ton: Princeton University Press.

———. 2005. *Cultural Intimacy: Social Poetics in the Nation-State*. New York: Routledge.

Hevia, J. 1995. *Cherishing Men from Afar: Qing Guest Ritual and the McCartney Embassy of 1793.* Durham NC: Duke University Press.

Highmore, B. 2002. *Everyday Life and Cultural Theory. An Introduction.* London: Routledge.

Hirschkind, C. 2001. 'Religious Reason and Civic Virtue: An Islamic Counter-Public', *Cultural Anthropology* 16(1): 3–34.

Ho, D.Y.F. 1974. 'On the Concept of Face', *American Journal of Sociology* 81: 867–84.

Holm, D. 1991. *Art and Ideology in Revolutionary China.* Oxford: Clarendon University Press.

Hostetler, L. 2001. *Qing Colonial Enterprise: Ethnography and Cartography in Early Modern China.* Chicago: University of Chicago Press.

Howell, S. 1997. 'Introduction', in S. Howell (ed.), *The Ethnography of Moralities.* London: Routledge, pp. 1–24.

Hsu, F.L.K. 1948. *Under the Ancestors' Shadow. Chinese Culture and Personality.* New York: Columbia University Press.

Hu Hsien-chin. 1944. 'The Chinese Concept of "Face"', *American Anthropologist* 46(1): 45–64.

Huang, P. 1985. *The Peasant Economy and Social Change in North China.* Stanford: Stanford University Press.

———. 1990. *The Peasant Family and Rural Development in the Yangzi Delta 1350-1988.* Stanford: Stanford University Press.

Huang, R. 1981. *1587. A Year of No Significance: The Ming Dynasty in Decline.* New Haven: Yale University Press.

Huang Shu-min. 1998. *The Spiral Road. Change in a Chinese Village Through the Eyes of a Communist Party Leader.* Colorado: Westview Press.

Jing Jun (ed.). 2000. *Feeding China's Little Emperors: Food, Children, and Social Change.* Stanford: Stanford University Press.

Joas, H. 2000 [1997]. *The Genesis of Values,* transl. G. Moore. Cambridge: Polity.

Joseph, G. and D. Nugent (eds). 1994. *Everyday Forms of State Formation: Revolution and the Negotiation of Rule in Mexico.* Durham NC: Duke University Press.

Joyce, J. 1968 [1922]. *Ulysses.* London: Penguin.

Kipnis, A.B. 1997. *Producing Guanxi. Sentiment, Self, and Subculture in a North China Village.* Durham NC: Duke University Press.

———. 2006. 'Suzhi: A Keyword Approach', *The China Quarterly* 186: 295–313.

———. 2007. 'Neoliberalism Reified: *suzhi* Discourse and Tropes of Neoliberalism in the People's Republic of China', *Journal of the Royal Anthropological Institute* 13(2): 383–400.

———. 2008. 'Audit Cultures: Neoliberal Governmentality, Socialist Legacy, or Technologies of Governing?', *American Ethnologist* 35: 275–89.

Kleinmann, A. 1998. 'Experience and its Moral Modes: Culture, Human Conditions, and Disorder', *The Tanner Lectures on Human Values,* Stanford University, 13–16 April.

Knapp, R.G. 1986. *China's Traditional Rural Architecture: A Cultural Geography of the Common House.* Honolulu: University of Hawai'i Press.

———. 1989. *China's Vernacular Architecture: House Form and Culture.* Honolulu: University of Hawai'i Press.

———. 1999. *China's Living Houses. Folk Beliefs, Symbols and Household Ornamentation.* Honolulu: University of Hawai'i Press.

Kong Shangren. 1993 [1702]. *Taohua Shan* (The Peach Blossom Fan), ed. and annotated by Wang Jisi, Su Huanzhong, Yang Deping. Beijing: Renmin Wenxue Chubanshe.

Krohn-Hansen, C. and K.G. Nustad (eds). 2005. *State Formation: Anthropological Perspectives.* London: Pluto Press.

Ku Hok Bun. 2004. *Moral Politics in a South China Village: Responsibility, Reciprocity, and Resistance.* Oxford: Rowman & Littlefield.

Kulp, D.H. 1925. *Country Life in South China: The Sociology of Familism. Vol.1, Phoenix Village, Kwantung.* China, New York: Columbia University.

Laidlaw, J. 1999. 'On Theatre and Theory: Reflections on Ritual in Imperial Chinese Politics', in J.P. McDermott (ed.), *State and Court Ritual in China.* Cambridge: Cambridge University Press, pp. 399–416.

———. 2002. 'For an Anthropology of Ethics and Freedom', *Journal of the Royal Anthropological Institute* 8(2): 311–32.

Lambek, M. 2000. 'The Anthropology of Religion and the Quarrel between Poetry and Philosophy', *Current Anthropology* 41: 309–20.

———. 2004a. 'Introduction: Irony and Illness – Recognition and Refusal', in M. Lambek and P. Antze (eds), *Illness and Irony: On the Ambiguity of Suffering in Culture.* New York: Berghahn, pp. 1–20.

———. 2004b. 'Rheumatic Irony: Questions of Agency and Self-Deception as Refracted through the Art of Living with Spirits', in M. Lambek and P. Antze (eds), *Illness and Irony: On the Ambiguity of Suffering in Culture.* New York: Berghahn, pp. 40–59.

———. 2008a. 'Value and Virtue', *Anthropological Theory* 8(2): 133–57.

———. (ed). 2010. *Ordinary Ethics. Anthropology, Language, and Action.* New York: Fordham University.

Lambek, M. and P. Antze (eds). 2004. *Illness and Irony: On the Ambiguity of Suffering in Culture.* New York: Berghahn.

Latour, B. 2005. *Reassembling the Social: An Introduction to Actor-Network-Theory.* Oxford: Oxford University Press.

Leach, E.R. 1960. The Frontiers of 'Burma', *Comparative Studies in Society and History* 3: 49–68.

Lee Haiyan. 2006. 'Nannies for Foreigners: The Enchantment of Chinese Womanhood in the Age of Millennial Capitalism', *Public Culture* 18(3): 507–29.

Lefebvre, H. 1968. *La Vie Quotidienne dans le Monde Moderne.* Paris: Gallimard.

———. 1971 [1968]. *Everyday Life in the Modern World,* transl. S. Rabinovitch. London: Harper and Row.

Li Changping. 2001. *Wo xiang Zongli shuo Shihua* (Telling the Prime Minister the Truth). Beijing: Guangming Ribao Chubanshe.

Li Changping and Dong Leiming (eds). 2004. *Shuifei Gaige Beijing xia de Xiangzhen Tizhi Yanjiu* (Research on Rural Governance against the Background of the Tax Reforms). Wuhan: Hubei Renmin Chubanshe.

Li, L.C. 2008. 'State and Market in Public Service Provision: Opportunities and Traps for Institutional Change in Rural China', *The Pacific Review* 21(3): 257–78.

Liu, L.H. 1995. *Translingual Practice. Literature, National Culture, and Translated Modernity – China, 1900-1937.* Stanford: Stanford University Press.

Liu Xin. 2000. *In One's Own Shadow: An Ethnographic Account of the Condition of Post-reform Rural China.* Berkeley: University of California Press.

———. 2002. 'Remember to Forget: Critique of a Critical Case Study', *Tsinghua Shehuixue Pinglun* December 2002: 343–95.

Lu Hanchao. 1999. *Beyond the Neon Lights: Everyday Shanghai in the Early Twentieth Century.* Berkeley: University of California Press.

———. 2006. 'Out of the Ordinary: Implications of Material Culture and Daily Life in China', in M.Y. Dong and J. Goldstein (eds), *Everyday Modernity in China.* Seattle: University of Washington Press, pp. 22–51.

Lu Hanlong. 2000. 'To be Relatively Comfortable in an Egalitarian Society', in D. Davis (ed.), *The Consumer Revolution in Urban China.* Berkeley: University of California Press, pp. 124–44.

Lu Xiaobo. 1997. 'The Politics of Peasant Burden in Reform China', *The Journal of Peasant Studies* 25(1): 805–31.

———. 2000. *Cadres and Corruption. The Organizational Involution of the Chinese Communist Party*. Stanford: Stanford University Press.

Lu Xun. 2004 [1922]. *Na Han* (Cry). Beijing: Yanshan Chubanshe.

Lu Yao. 2002 [1989]. *Pingfan de Shijie* (An Ordinary World). Guiyang: Guizhou Renmin Chubanshe.

Luhmann, N. 1991. 'Paradigm Lost: On the Ethical Reflection of Morality: Speech on the Occasion of the Award of the Hegel Prize 1988', transl. D. Roberts, *Thesis Eleven* 29(1): 82–94.

Macauley, M. 1998. *Social Power and Legal Culture: Litigation Masters in Late Imperial China*. Stanford: Stanford University Press.

MacIntyre, A. 1981. *After Virtue*. London: Duckworth.

———. 1988. *Whose Justice? Which Rationality?* London: Duckworth.

———. 1990. *Three Rival Versions of Moral Enquiry*. London: Duckworth.

Mahmood, S. 2005. *Politics of Piety. The Islamic Revival and the Feminist Subject*. Princeton: Princeton University Press.

Malaby, T.M. 2003. *Gambling Life. Dealing in Contingency in a Greek City*. Urbana: University of Illinois Press.

Malinowski, B. 1922. *Argonauts of the Western Pacific. An Account of Native Enterprise and Adventure in the Archipelagoes of Melanesian New Guinea*. London: Routledge & Sons.

Mann, S. 1987. 'Widows in the Kinship, Class, and Community Structures of Qing Dynasty China', *Journal of Asian Studies* 46(1): 37–56.

Marx, K. 1962 [1867]. 'Das Kapital. Band I. Kritik der politischen Ökonomie', in *Karl Marx/ Friedrich Engels – Werke*, Band 23. Berlin: Dietz Verlag.

Masini, F. 1993. *The Formation of Modern Chinese Lexicon and its Evolution towards a National Language: The Period from 1840 to 1898*. Berkeley: University of California Press.

McDermott, J.P. 1999. 'Emperor, Elites, and Commoners: The Community Pact Ritual of the Late Ming', in J.P. McDermott (ed.), *State and Court Ritual in China*. Cambridge: Cambridge University Press, pp. 299–351.

Mitchell, T. 1991. 'The Limits of the *State*: Beyond Statist Approaches and Their Critics', *American Political Science Review* 85(1): 77–94.

Mueggler, E. 2001. *The Age of Wild Ghosts. Memory, Violence, and Place in Southwest China*. Berkeley: University of California Press.

Murphy, R. 2002. *How Migrant Labor is Changing Rural China*. Cambridge: Cambridge University Press.

———. 2006. 'Citizenship Education in Rural China: The Dispositional and Technical Training of Cadres and Farmers', in V.L. Fong and R. Murphy (eds), *Chinese Citizenship: Views from the Margins*. London: Routledge, pp. 9–26.

———. 2007. 'The Paradox of China's Official State Media Reinforcing Poor Governance: Case Studies of a Party Newspaper and an Anti-Corruption Film', *Critical Asian Studies* 39(1): 63–88.

Musil, R. 1994 [1930–1942]. *Der Mann ohne Eigenschaften*. Berlin: Rowohlt.

Naquin, S. 1988. 'Funerals in North China: Uniformity and Variation', in J.L. Watson and E.S. Rawski (eds), *Death Ritual in Late Imperial and Modern China*. Berkeley: University of California Press, pp. 37–70.

Ni Fangliu. 2008. *Dao Mu Shi Ji* (The Recorded History of Grave Robbery). Beijing: Gongren Chubanshe, online at http://book.qq.com/s/book/0/12/12335/index.shtml [accessed on 1 March 2009].

Nonini, D.M. 2008. 'Is China Becoming Neoliberal?', *Critique of Anthropology* 28: 145–76.

Oxfeld, E. 1991. 'Profit, Loss, and Fate: The Entrepreneurial Ethic and the Practice of Gambling in an Overseas Chinese Community', *Modern China* 17(2): 227–59.
———. 1993. *Blood, Sweat, and Mahjong: Family and Enterprise in an Overseas Chinese Community*. Ithaca: Cornell University Press.
———. 2010. *Drink Water, But Remember the Source: Moral Discourse in a Chinese Village*. Berkeley, CA: University of California Press.
Papataxiarchis, E. 1999. 'A Contest with Money: Gambling and the Politics of Disinterested Sociality in Aegean Greece', in S. Day, M. Stewart and E. Papataxiarchis (eds), *Lilies of the Field: Marginal People who Live for the Moment*. Boulder CO: Westview Press, pp. 158–75.
Peng Linxu. 2000. 'Tujiazu Minzhu ji Yinshi Wenhua Bianqian' (The Transformation of the House and Food Culture of the Tujia Minority), *Hubei Minzu Xueyuan Xuebao* 18(1): 6–13.
Perdue, P.C. 2005. *China Marches West: The Qing Conquest of Central Eurasia*. Cambridge MA: Harvard University Press.
Perry, E.J. 1999. 'Crime, Corruption and Contention', in M. Goldman and R. MacFarquhar (eds), *The Paradox of China's Post-Mao Reforms*. Cambridge MA: Harvard University Press, pp. 308–29.
Peterson, G. 1994. 'State Literacy Ideologies and the Transformation of Rural China', *The Australian Journal of Chinese Affairs* 32: 95–120.
Pharoah, R. 2005. *Visions of Authority: Hierarchy, Leadership and Power in Central China*, unpublished PhD dissertation. University of London.
Pina-Cabral, J. de 2002. *Between China and Europe. Person, Culture and Emotion in Macao*. London: Berg.
Proust, M. 2002 [1913–1927]. *A la recherche du temps perdu*. Paris: Gallimard.
Pun Ngai. 2003. 'Subsumption or Consumption? The Phantom of Consumer Revolution in "Globalizing" China', *Cultural Anthropology* 18(4): 469–92.
Radcliffe-Brown, A.R. 1952. *Structure and Function in Primitive Society*. London: Cohen and West.
Rawski, E.S. 1988. 'A Historian's Approach to Chinese Death Ritual', in J.L. Watson and E.S. Rawski (eds), *Death Ritual in Late Imperial and Modern China*. Berkeley: University of California Press, pp. 20–36.
Ribeiro, G.L. 2006. *El capital de la esperanza. La experiencia de los trabajadores en la construcción de Brasilia*. Buenos Aires: Antropofagia.
Robbins, J. 2004. *Becoming Sinners: Christianity and Moral Torment in a Papua New Guinea Society*. Berkeley: University of California Press.
Roberts, J. 2006. *Philosophizing the Everyday. Revolutionary Praxis and the Fate of Cultural Theory*. London: Pluto.
Rorty, R. 1980. *Philosophy and the Mirror of Nature*. Oxford: Blackwell.
———. 1989. *Contingency, Irony, and Solidarity*. Cambridge: Cambridge University Press.
Ruf, G.A. 1998. *Cadres and Kin: Making a Socialist Village in West China, 1921-1991*. Stanford: Stanford University Press.
Ruitenbeek, K. 1986. 'Craft and Ritual in Traditional Chinese Carpentry', *Chinese Science* 7: 1–24.
———. 1993. *Carpentry and Building in Late Imperial China: A Study of the Fifteenth-Century Carpenter's Manual Lu Ban jing*. Leiden: E.J. Brill.
Schmittzehe & Partners. 2006. *Review of China's Gambling Sector: Focus on Mainland China's Lottery with Brief Coverage of Macau and Hongkong*, online at http://www.sand-pconsulting.com/admin/upload/s%20Gambling%20Sector%20September%202006.pdf [accessed on 20 January 2010].
Schurmann, F. 1968. *Ideology and Organization in Communist China*. Berkeley: University of California Press.

Scott, J.C. 2001. 'La montagne et la liberté, ou Pourquoi les civilisations ne savent pas grimper', *Critique International* 11: 85–104.

———. 2009. *The Art of Not Being Governed: An Anarchist History of Upland Southeast Asia.* New Haven: Yale University Press.

Seeberg, V. 1990. *Literacy in China: The Effects of the National Development Context and Policy on Literacy Levels, 1949-1979.* Bochum: Brockmeyer.

Selden, M. 1993. 'Family Strategies and Structures in Rural North China', in D. Davis and S. Harrell (eds), *Chinese Families in the Post-Mao Era.* Berkeley: University of California Press, pp. 139–64.

Shahar, M. and R. Weller (eds). 1996. *Unruly Gods. Divinity and Society in China.* Honolulu: University of Hawai'i Press.

Shirk, S.L. 1992. *The Political Logic of Economic Reform in China.* Berkeley: University of California Press.

Shue, V. 1988. *The Reach of the State.* Stanford: Stanford University Press.

Siu, H.F. 1989a. *Agents and Victims in South China. Accomplices in Rural Revolution.* New Haven: Yale University Press.

———. 1989b. 'Socialist Peddlers and Princes in a Chinese Market Town', *American Ethnologist* 16(2): 195–212.

Skinner, G.W. 1964. 'Marketing and Social Structure in Rural China, Part I', *Journal of Asian Studies* 24(1): 3–43.

———. 1965a. 'Marketing and Social Structure in Rural China, Part II', *Journal of Asian Studies* 24(2): 195–228.

———. 1965b. 'Marketing and Social Structure in Rural China, Part III', *Journal of Asian Studies* 24(3): 363–99.

———. 1985. 'Rural Marketing in China: Repression and Revival', *The China Quarterly* 103: 393–413.

Skinner, G.W. and E. Winckler. 1969. 'Compliance Succession in Rural Communist China: A Cyclical Theory', in A. Etzioni (ed.), *A Sociological Reader on Complex Organization.* New York: Holt, Rinehart and Winston, 2nd ed., pp. 410–38.

Sommer, M.H. 2000. *Sex, Law, and Society in Late Imperial China.* Stanford: Stanford University Press.

Songtaiping Township. 2006. *Mizui Wangfan Xin Nongcun* (Fascination for Rural Construction and Forgetting Adversities), unpublished announcement.

Stafford, C. 2000. *Separation and Reunion in Modern China.* Cambridge: Cambridge University Press.

State Administration of Radio, Film, and Television. 2009. *Guang Dian Zong Ju Guanyu Jiaqiang Hulianwang Shiting Jiemu Neirong Guanli de Tongzhi* (Notice of the State Administration of Radio, Film, and Television about Strengthening the Administration of the Visual and Audio Programmes on the Internet), online at http://www.chinasarft.gov.cn/articles/2009/03/30/20090330171107690049.html [accessed on 31 March 2009].

Stein, R. 1979. 'Religious Taoism and Popular Religion', in H. Welch and A. Seidel (eds), *Facets of Taoism.* New Haven: Yale University Press, pp. 53–81.

Steinmüller, H. 2010. 'How Popular Confucianism became Embarrassing: On the Spatial and Moral Center of the House in Rural China', *Focaal* 58: 81–96.

Strange, S. 1986. *Casino Capitalism.* Oxford: Basil Blackwell.

Strassberg, R.E. 1983. *The World of K'ung Shang-jen: A Man of Letters in Early Ch'ing China.* New York: Columbia University Press.

Tan Tongxue. 2007. 'Paths and Social Foundations of Rural Graying: The Case of Two Townships in Southern Hunan', *Chinese Sociology & Anthropology* 39(4): 39–49.

———. 2010. *Qiaocun you dao. Zhuanxing xiangcun de daode quanli yu shehui jiegou* (The Way of Bridge Village. Moral Power and Social Structure in a Rural Society Under Transformation). Beijing: Sanlian Shudian.

Tang Xiaobing. 2000. *Chinese Modern: The Heroic and the Quotidian*. Durham NC: Duke University Press.

Taylor, C. 1976. 'Responsibility for Self', in A. Rorty (ed.), *The Identities of Persons*. Berkeley: University of California, pp. 281–99.

———. 1985. *Philosophical Papers*, 2 volumes. Cambridge: Cambridge University Press.

———. 1989. *Sources of the Self: The Making of Modern Identity*. Cambridge: Cambridge University Press.

———. 1997. *Philosophical Arguments*. Cambridge MA: Harvard University Press.

Thompson, S. 1988. 'Death, Food, and Fertility', in J. Watson and E.S. Rawski (eds), *Death Ritual in Late Imperial and Modern China*. Berkeley: University of California Press, pp. 71–108.

Tian Qingwang. 2007. 'Tujiazu Shenkan Wenhua Yanjiu' (Research on the Culture of the Ancestral Shrines of the Tujia), in *Youshui Liuyu Lishi yu Wenhua Kaocha. Chengguo Huibian* (Research on the History and Culture of the Youshui River Basin. Report on Results), (ed.) Jishou Daxue Minzuxue Renleixue Yanjiusuo, Jishou Daxue Youshui Liuyu Lishi yu Wenhua Zhongxin. Jishou: Jishou Daxue Youshui Liuyu Lishu yu Wenhua Zhongxin, pp. 161–72.

Trotsky, L. 1973 [1924]. *Problems of Everyday Life and Other Writings on Culture and Science*. New York: Monad.

UNDP. 2008. *China Human Development Report 2007/2008. Access for All: Basic Public Services for 1.3 Billion People*. Beijing: China Translation and Publishing Corporation.

Wakeman, F. 1985. *The Great Enterprise: The Manchu Reconstruction of the Imperial Order in Seventeenth-century China*. Berkeley: University of California Press.

Wang Aihe. 2000. *Cosmology and Political Culture in Early China*. Cambridge: Cambridge University Press.

Wang Jian. 2003. 'Sidian, Sisi yu Yinsi: Mingqing Yilai Suzhou Diqu Minjian Xinyang Kaocha' (Official Ceremony, Private Cults and Licentious Cults: Research on Popular Beliefs in the Suzhou Region during the Ming and Qing Dynasties), *Shilin* 2003(1): 1–7, online at http://www.sass.org.cn/eWebEditor/UploadFile/20060321141240589.pdf [accessed on 5 March 2009].

A———. 2003. 'Du "Liwu de Liudong"' (Reading 'The Flow of Gifts'), in Wang Mingming (ed.) *Piaobo de Dongcha* (Wandering Observations). Shanghai: Sanlian Chubanshe.

———. 2006. 'Cha ji qi "tazhe"' (Tea and its 'Other'), in Wang Mingming (ed.), *Xin yu Wu You* (Travels between Heart and Objects). Guilin: Guangxi Shifan Daxue Chubanshe.

Wang Shaoguang. 1989. *From Revolution to Involution: State Capacity, Local Power, and [Un]governability in China*, unpublished manuscript.

Wang Ximing and Chen Tao. 2004. 'Nongcun Shuifei Gaige yu Jiceng Zhengfu Nengli Jianshe' (Rural Tax Reform and the Construction of the Capacity of Local Government), in Li Changping and Dong Leiming (eds), *Shuifei Gaige Beijing xia de Xiangzhen Tizhi Yanjiu* (Research on Rural Governance under the Background of the Tax Reforms). Wuhan: Hubei Renmin Chubanshe, pp. 310–25.

Ward, B. 1985. 'Regional Operas and their Audiences: Evidence from Hong Kong', in D. Johnson, A.J. Nathan and E.S. Rawski (eds), *Popular Culture in Late Imperial China*. Berkeley: University of California Press, pp. 161–87.

Watson, J.L. 1975. *Emigration and the Chinese Lineage*. Berkeley: University of California Press.

———. 1982. 'Of Flesh and Bones: The Management of Death Pollution in Cantonese Society', in M. Bloch and J. Parry (eds), *Death and the Regeneration of Life*. Cambridge: Cambridge University Press, pp. 155–86.

Watson, J.L. 1975. *Emigration and the Chinese Lineage*. Berkeley: University of California Press.
———. 1982. 'Of Flesh and Bones: The Management of Death Pollution in Cantonese Society', in M. Bloch and J. Parry (eds), *Death and the Regeneration of Life*. Cambridge: Cambridge University Press, pp. 155–86.
———. 1985. 'Standardizing the Gods: The Promotion of T'ien Hou ("Empress of Heaven") Along the South China Coast, 960-1960', in D. Johnson, A. Nathan and E. Rawski (eds), *Popular Culture in Late Imperial China*. Berkeley: University of California Press.
———. 1988. 'Introduction: The Structure of Chinese Funerary Rites', in J. Watson and E.S. Rawski (eds), *Death Ritual in Late Imperial and Modern China*. Berkeley: University of California Press, pp. 3–19.
Weber, M. 1932 [1920]. *Die protestantische Ethik und der Geist des Kapitalismus*. Tübingen: J.C.B. Mohr.
Weller, R.P. 1987. *Unities and Diversities in Chinese Religion*. Basingstoke: Macmillan.
Wen Tiejun. 2000. *Zhongguo Nongcun Jiben Jingji Zhidu Yanjiu. 'Sannong' Wenti de Shiji Mo Fansi* (Research on the Basic Economic System of the Chinese Countryside. Reflections on the 'Three Problems of the Countryside' at the End of the Century). Beijing: Zhongguo Jingji Chubanshe.
———. 2001 [1999]. 'Centenary Reflections on the "Three Dimensional Problem" of Rural China', transl. P. Liu, *Inter-Asia Cultural Studies* 2(2): 287–95.
Wheatley, P. 1971. *The Pivot of the Four Quarters: A Preliminary Enquiry into the Origins and Character of the Ancient Chinese City*. Edinburgh: Edinburgh University Press.
Wiens, H.J. 1954. *China's March toward the Tropics*. Connecticut: Shoe String Press.
Wilkinson, W.H. 1895. 'Chinese Origin of Playing Cards', *American Anthropologist* 8(1): 61–78.
Wolfram, S. 1982. 'Anthropology and Morality', *Journal of the Anthropological Society of Oxford* 13: 262–74.
Wright, A.F. 1977. 'The Cosmology of the Chinese City', in G.W. Skinner (ed.), *The City in Late Imperial China*. Stanford: Stanford University Press, pp. 33–74.
Wu Xu. 2003. *Food, Ethnoecology and Identity in Enshi Prefecture, West Hubei, China*, unpublished doctoral dissertation, University of Alberta, Edmonton.
———. 2005. 'The New Year's Eve Dinner and Wormwood Meal. Festival Foodways as Ethnic Markers in Enshi Prefecture', *Modern China* 31(3): 353–80.
Wu Yu. 1985a [1917]. 'Du 'Xunzi' Shu Hou' (After reading Xunzi), in *Wu Yu Ji* (Collected Works of Wu Yu). Chengdu: Sichuan Renmin Chubanshe, p. 110.
———. 1985b [1919]. 'Chiren yu Lijiao' (Cannibalism and Confucianism), in *Wu Yu Ji* (Collected Works of Wu Yu). Chengdu: Sichuan Renmin Chubanshe, pp. 167–71.
Xiao Ping. 2005. *Huguang Tian Sichuan* (Huguang Fills Sichuan). Chengdu: Shidai Chubanshe.
Xin Jing Bao (New Beijing Newspaper). 'fengshui shi che tou che wei de mixin, hai shi kexue?' (Is Fengshui out-and-out Superstition or Science?), 19 March 2009, online at http://www.chinanews.com.cn/cul/news/2009/03-19/1608315.shtml [accessed on 31 March 2009].
Xu Chuanjing. 2006. 'Wuling Tujiazu Cunluo Yinshi Juzhu Wenhua Bianqian – Yi Baishun Cun Wei Li' (On The Transformation of Food and Residential Culture of Tujia Nationality Villages in the Wuling Area – Shown with the Example of Baishun Village), *Changjiang Shifan Xueyuan Xuebao* 22(5): 65–68.
Yan Hairong. 2003. 'Neoliberal Governmentality and Neohumanism: Organizing Suzhi/Value Flow through Labor Recruitment Networks', *Cultural Anthropology* 18(4): 493–523.
Yan Yunxiang. 1996. *The Flow of Gifts: Reciprocity and Social Networks in a Chinese Village*. Stanford: Stanford University Press.

————. 2000 [1996]. *Liwu de Liudong. Yi ge Zhongguo Nongzhuang Zhong de Huhui Yuanze yu Shehui Wangluo* (The Flow of Gifts: Reciprocity and Social Networks in a Chinese Village), transl. Li Fangchun and Liu Yuze. Shanghai: Shanghai Renmin Chubanshe.

————. 2003. *Private Life under Socialism. Love, Intimacy, and Family Change in a Chinese Village 1949-1999*. Stanford: Stanford University Press.

————. 2005. 'The Individual and the Transformation of Bridewealth in Rural North China', *Journal of the Royal Anthropological Institute* 11(4): 637–58.

————. 2011. 'How Far Can We Move From Durkheim? Reflections on the New Anthropology of Morality', *Anthropology of this Century* 2, online at http://aotcpress.com/articles/move-durkheim-reflections-anthropology-morality/ [accessed on 2 February 2012].

Yang, M.-M.H. 1988. 'The Modernity of Power in the Chinese Socialist Order', *Cultural Anthropology* 3(4): 408–27.

————. 1994. *Gifts, Favors, and Banquets: The Art of Social Relationships in China*. Ithaca: Cornell University Press.

Ye Jingzhong. 2006. *Nongmin Shijue de Xin Nongcun Jianshe* (Construction of a New Countryside: Farmer's Perspectives). Beijing: Shehui Kexue Wenxian Chubanshe.

Ye Jingzhong, J. Murray and Wang Yihuan. 2005. *Left-behind Children in Rural China: Impact Study of Rural Labor Migration on Left-behind Children in Mid-west China*, transl. Song Yuehua. Beijing: Shehui Kexue Wenxian Chubanshe.

Yeh, W. 1997. 'Shanghai Modernity: Commerce and Culture in a Republican City', *The China Quarterly* 150: 375–94.

————. 2007. *Shanghai Splendor*. Berkeley: University of California Press.

Yu Dan. 2006. *Yu Dan lun yu xin de* (Yu Dan's Insights into the Analects). Beijing: Zhonghua Shuju.

Yu Hua. 2005. *Xiongdi. Shangbu* (Brothers, 1st part). Shanghai: Wenyi Chubanshe.

————. 2006. *Xiongdi. Xiabu* (Brothers, 2nd part). Shanghai: Wenyi Chubanshe.

Yu Yingshi. 2004. 'Fu: Tan 'Tian Di Jun Qin Shi' de Qiyuan' (Appendix: About the Origins of [the scroll of] 'Heaven, Earth, Emperor, Ancestors, and Teachers'), in *Zhongguo Sixiang Chuantong ji qi Xiandai Bianqian. Yu Yingshi Wenji Di Er Juan* (The Chinese Tradition of Thinking and its Modern Transformation. Collected Works of Yu Yingshi, vol. 2). Guilin: Guangxi Shifan Daxue Chubanshe, pp. 71–77.

Zhang Qian F. and J.A. Donaldson. 2008. 'The Rise of Agrarian Capitalism with Chinese Characteristics: Agricultural Modernization, Agribusiness and Collective Land Rights', *The China Journal* 60: 25–47.

Zhang Yinjing (ed.). 1999. *Cinema and Urban Culture in Shanghai, 1922-1943*. Stanford: Stanford University Press.

Zigon, J. 2007. 'Moral Breakdown and the Ethical Demand. A Theoretical Framework for an Anthropology of Moralities', *Anthropological Theory* 7(2): 131–50.

————. 2008. *Morality. An Anthropological Perspective*. Oxford: Berg.

Zito, A. 1984. 'Re-presenting Sacrifice: Cosmology and the Editing of Texts', *Ch'ing-shih wen-t'i* 5(2): 47–78.

————. 1993. 'Ritualizing Li: Implications for Studying Power and Gender,' *positions* 1(2): 321–48.

————. 1997. *Of Body and Brush: Grand Sacrifice as Text/Performance in 18th Century China*. Chicago: University of Chicago Press.

Zweig, D. 1989. *Agrarian Radicalism in China, 1968–1981*. Cambridge MA: Harvard University Press.

INDEX

A

Ahern, Emily, 95n8, 97n33, 145–46
ancestor, 149, 153n16, 156
  worship, 43, 54, 55, 65n25, 72, 117,
    135, 147
Ardener, Edwin, 19, 44–45, 62, 64n15

B

backward/backwardness, 19–20, 37, 48,
    61–62, 73–74, 100, 123, 164, 169,
    192, 195, 223, 225, 228
Bailey, Frederick, 34n20
Bakken, Borge, 64n10
banquet, 4, 26, 74, 88–91, 93, 130–132,
    136, 139, 141, 144, 154, 155, 161,
    163–174, 175n7–8, 181, 184, 230
Bao, Qingtian, 220n1
Beijing, 2, 24, 25, 26, 29, 49, 75, 104,
    115–16, 130, 172, 177, 220n1, 226
  dialect, 17
Benjamin, Walter, 14, 15, 19, 33n7, 34n16
Bosco, Joseph, 179, 195n3
Bourdieu, Pierre, 33n6
Bray, Francesca, 24
breakfast, 3, 85, 89, 99, 148
Brown, Melissa, 174n2,
bureaucracy, 18
  bureaucracy and mobilization,
    'reds' and 'experts', 15
  bureaucratic discourse, 217
  bureaucratization, 15, 219
  imperial bureaucracy, 41, 44
  modern bureaucracy, 23, 219

C

cadre. *See* official
Caillois, Roger, 180

calligraphy, 139, 166, 188–189, 202
Cao, Jinqing, 127n12
carpentry, 1–2, 69, 76–86, 91–92
centring, 20, 31, 73, 76, 84, 93, 130–153,
    175n7, 223
Chau, Adam, 21, 95n13, 181–182, 196n6
Chen, Zhongshi, 33n12
Chiang Kai-shek, 60
Chinese
  classical Chinese, 66n32, 87, 133,
    166, 174
  vernacular Chinese (*baihua*), 174
cigarettes, 3, 80, 82, 97n34, 128n16, 132,
    139–142, 148, 152n12, 152n15,
    168, 172, 175n4, 176, 183, 208, 218,
    221n9
civilization
  Chinese civilization, 188
  and remoteness, 43–45
  civilizational centre, 37, 44, 223
  wenming, 19, 49, 51, 54, 61, 138, 201
class
  in Maoist discourse, 49
  labels, 68, 187, 196n11
  struggle, 50
  struggle session, 18, 191, 196n11,
    221n1
Comaroff, Jean and John, 177
commercialization, 179
  agricultural commercialization,
    101, 124
  of family celebrations, 31, 138, 157,
    164, 173
commodification, 100, 120, 124
communities of complicity, 24, 32,
    34n20, 94, 217–220, 224, 227–228

Confucianism, 19–20, 153n16, 157, 173, 191–192, 196n12, 227
    Neo-Confucianism, 151n3
Confucius, 158, 189–191
corruption, 22, 24, 128n22, 169, 170, 173, 179, 188, 195, 209, 212, 217, 219, 227, 228, 231
Cultural Intimacy, 22–24, 32, 157, 169, 173, 190–194, 199, 223, 227–228
Cultural Revolution, 15, 18, 102, 157, 160, 213, 220n1, 227
cynicism, 22–23, 34

D

Daoist priest, 89, 137, 139, 140, 144, 157–161, 173
Deng, Xiaoping, 95n9, 122
diaojiaolou, 69–70, 89
disemia, 199
divination, 55–56, 59, 61, 66n35, 126n2, 129n25, 158
Dong minority. *See under* minority nationality
dou dizhu, 182, 186
dowry, 142, 146–148, 153n18
Duara, Prasenjit, 23

E

Eberhard, Wolfram, 94n5, 96n24, 96n26
Ebrey, Patricia, 151n3
eight characters (*ba zi*), 56–57, 65n23, 131, 146, 149, 151, 153n17
embarrassment, 4, 22–23, 34, 152–175, 189, 191–194, 227–230
emperor, 19, 60, 36, 64n19, 66n34, 72, 84, 95n10, 96n21, 132, 135–137, 142–143, 154, 191, 200
    See also Kangxi, Qianlong, Yongzheng
ethics
    as second-level reflection of morality, 7–8, 13, 224
    Confucian relational ethics, 20
    entrepreneurial ethics, 180
    everyday ethics, 5–24, 31–32, 63, 224–227

everyday, 13–19
    everyday ethics. *See under* ethics
    (Post-)socialist Everyday, 15–19

F

Fabian, Johannes, 225
face
    face-to-face community, 22, 23, 119, 139, 157
    face-work, 22, 228
    mianzi, 32, 67, 94n1, 122, 214–215, 221n8, 228, 232
    project, 199–200, 205–206, 209–211, 214–217, 219–220, 222n15, 228
family
    celebrations, 4, 22, 73, 109, 125, 130–131, 136, 138–144, 150, 154, 157–158, 162, 164–166, 169–171, 173–174, 182–184, 206, 213–215, 222n14, 223, 230
    conjugal family, 5
    division (*fenjia*), 57
    family planning, 75, 95n12, 128n23, 184, 196n4, 206, 218
    history/legends, 40, 50, 52–63,
Faure, David, 137
fate/life (*ming*), 32, 59, 120–122, 129n25, 178, 180, 183–187, 194
Fei, Xiaotong, 63
fengshui, 57–62, 65–66, 69, 73, 89, 91–93, 97n33, 129n25, 142, 158, 219, 227–228
Festa, Paul, 180–181, 193, 195n3, 196n8–9
Feuchtwang, Stephan, 20, 60
filial piety (*xiao*), 86, 137, 144, 156, 158, 166, 168, 169, 190, 195
Fitzgerald, C.F., 178
Fried, Morton, 127n14
funerals, 21, 28, 31, 119, 126n2, 131, 132, 136, 139–142, 144, 154–175, 209, 222n15, 228, 235

G

gai tu gui liu, 39, 63n4, 69
gambling, 22, 24, 32, 61, 62, 80, 85, 147, 159, 176–197, 225, 227, 230

Geertz, Clifford, 24, 33–34, 180
genealogy (*jiapu*), 55
geomancy. *See* fengshui
Gibeault, David, 94n1
Goffman, Erving, 22, 180, 230
gossip, 119, 122, 139, 168, 175n10,
    187–188, 192, 211, 213
Graeber, David, 152n5, 221n11
Great Leap Forward, 15, 18, 102, 106,
    221n1,
great tradition. *See* little tradition
Gu, Cai, 36–37, 39, 49, 56
Gumbrecht, Hans Ulrich, 33n6

H
Hai, Rui, 220n1
Han Chinese, 30, 37, 39, 41, 43, 45, 50,
    69, 128n16, 176n2
Harootunian, Harry, 14–15, 33n7
Heidegger, Martin, 10, 13, 15, 33n6,
    33n8
Herzfeld, Michael, 23, 157–158, 193–194,
    199–200, 222, 229
house altar, 54, 97n33, 142–145, 147,
    149–151
household, 93, 215
    head, 73, 125, 146
    Household Responsibility System,
        102, 125, 127n8
    industry, 126n4
    model household (*shifan hu*), 107,
        207, 210
    as unit of production and
        consumption, 125, 227
Hsu, Francis L.K., 93n14
Huang, Philip, 126n4
Huang, Shu-min, 96n26
Huguang, 39, 63n5–6

I
immorality, 42
    decline of public morality, 5–6, 195,
        224
    lack of morality of the young,
        117–118, 192
involution, 22–24, 126n4, 219–220, 228

irony, 6–12, 22, 34n20, 61, 194, 228–233

J
jianghu (rivers and lakes), 119–120, 125,
    128n22
Joyce, James, 13, 19

K
Kangxi emperor, 36
Kipnis, Andrew, 177, 179
Kleinmann, Arthur, 32n4
Kong, Shangren, 36, 63n1
Krakauer, Siegfried, 14, 33n7

L
Laidlaw, James, 6–8, 32n2, 133–134
Lambek, Michael, 6–8, 11–12, 225
land reform, 16, 18, 34n14, 68, 95n7
Latour, Bruno, 179
Leach, Edmund, 44
Lefebvre, Henri, 33n9, 226
legalism, 19–20
Li, Changping, 127n12
lineage, 38, 43, 54–58, 61–62, 64n20,
    65n25, 67–68, 75, 91, 117, 136, 141,
    145
    branch name (*tang*), 79, 141
    elder (*zuzhang*), 132, 137
    ritual, 137
    rules of a lineage (*jiagui*), 54, 61
literacy, 17–19, 34n15, 138, 173, 227
little tradition, 56
Liu, Xin, 5–6, 12, 34n14
liumang (hooligan), 118, 128n20
local sociality, 22–23, 31–32, 61, 94,
    126, 157, 174, 177–178, 186–189,
    193–195, 223–224, 227–228
lottery
    liuhecai underground lottery,
        177–179
    welfare lotteries, 178, 180, 195n1
Lu, Ban, 2, 4, 69, 79, 81, 84, 94n5, 96n24
Lu, Hanchao, 123
Lu, Xun, 189–190, 196n12
Lu, Yao, 129n24, 199
Luhmann, Niklas, 32n4

M

Macartney, George, 134–135

Mahjong, 88, 153n18, 178, 180–189, 190, 192–193, 196n8–9, 197n15

Malaby, Thomas, 180

Malinowski, Bronislaw, 19, 45, 64n16

Mao, Zedong, 15, 60–61, 64n21, 65n30, 72–73, 84, 96n21, 160, 220n1, 233n4

    poster of Chairman Mao, 72–73, 97n33, 142, 144, 147–149

Maoism

    discourse/language, 47, 113, 160, 164, 166, 173–174

    era, 18, 47–48, 50, 53, 55, 59–61, 72, 85, 102, 122, 126n6, 156–157, 160, 164, 178, 187, 190, 196n11, 199, 201, 205, 213, 227

    government and state, 16–17, 32

    ideology, 212

    morals/ethics, 126, 138

    propaganda, 228, 233n1

    revolution, 17

market, 5, 45, 91, 123, 126n3–4, 179

    black market, 113, 196n11

    commodity market, 99, 100, 118, 124

    economy, 19, 179, 195, 227

    exchange, 224

    'hot' market, 74, 181

    marketing system, 101

    periodical peasant market, 48, 101–104, 126n5, 127n8–9, 128n17

    price, 41, 113

    real estate market, 196

    state control and markets, 178

    street, 20, 118–119, 187

    supermarket, 47–48

    tea market, 48, 103, 107–108, 111–114, 124, 187

    town, 4, 40, 48, 52, 53, 58, 67, 69, 73, 74–76, 88, 106, 107, 116, 117, 131, 152n12, 154, 158, 202, 206, 215, 221n6

        marriage market, 75

Marx, Karl, 109, 227

McDermott, Joseph, 137

migrant labour, 108, 114–116, 124

ming. See fate/life

minority nationality (*shaoshu minzu*), 30, 43, 45, 50–51, 56

    culture, 52, 62, 156, 203

    classification, 43, 50, 56–57, 64n20

    district, 30, 39, 47, 50, 56, 156

    Dong minority, 46

    politics, 50–51

    style (*minzu tese*), 97n31, 204

    Tujia minority, 30, 39, 47, 50–51, 56, 64n12,

model

    household. See *under* household

    village, 26, 30, 97n31, 201, 209, 216–217

    worker, 187

modernity, 12, 14–16, 123, 138, 171,

    Capitalist modernity, 17

    Chinese modernity, 225

    and the city, 90–91, 225

    Everyday modernity, 15–16, 33n7

    Western modernity, 12, 16, 33n7, 134

    See also tradition

morality, 5–8, 11–13, 19–22, 32n1–4, 34n19

    local moral world, 62–63

    Maoist morals/ethics, 126, 138

    moral frameworks, 4–5, 8–9, 12–13, 19–22, 31, 93–94, 100–101, 118, 120, 123, 126, 193, 223–225, 228

    of brotherhood, 120

    of ritual, 132, 224–225

    space, 8, 20, 93

    See also immorality, ethics

motorbike passenger service, 116, 128n18

Mueggler, Erik, 24, 35n23

Murphy, Rachel, 128n18, 219

Musil, Robert, 13–14, 19

N

names and naming, 55–56, 62, 62n21, 65n24

    generational name, 55–56, 64n21

list of names in celebrations, 3, 131,
162, 166
nicknames, 95n18, 175n6, 190
See also surname
neoliberalism, 64n18, 177, 179, 194,
195n2

O

official/cadre, 206–211
'the good official', 198–199, 211–215
official discourse, 22, 93, 128n22, 157,
177, 193–195, 223, 227
opium, 46, 101, 126n4
orthopraxy, 137
Oxfeld, Ellen, 180, 195n3

P

Papataxiarchis, Evthymios, 179–180
Party, 61, 165, 166, 168, 174, 195n2, 200
communist party, 16, 97n30, 190
discipline, 169
education, 219
hierarchy, 219
nationalist party (KMT), 60
secretary, 27, 29, 166, 168
state, 193, 219, 227
Pina-Cabral, João de, 182
place names, 53–54
population quality (*renkou suzhi*), 19,
49, 51, 61, 138, 164, 201, 212, 218
propaganda, 16–17, 29, 33n12, 157,
164–166, 173–174, 184, 218, 232,
233n1
prostitution, 188, 195
Proust, Marcel, 13, 19
putonghua, 29, 115

Q

Qianlong emperor, 42, 59, 134–135

R

Radcliffe-Brown, Alfred Reginald,
133–134
Rawski, Evelyn, 137
red-hot (*renao*), 21, 74, 181–184
See also social heat

Reds and experts. *See under*
bureaucracy
remote/remoteness, 19–20, 37–38,
43–45, 62, 64n15, 74–76, 112, 121,
152n12, 175n2, 223–224, 226
renqing, 34n19, 131, 133, 162–165,
169–170, 174, 218
Ribeiro, Gustavo Lins, 109
ritual, 1–2, 4, 19, 21, 22, 24, 31–32, 54,
62, 69, 77, 79–93, 131–139, 142,
144–145, 151
imperial ritual, 134–137, 142, 151
Li, 21, 31, 131–139, 152n6, 153n16
See also funerals, weddings
Rorty, Richard, 9–12, 152n7, 228–229
Ruitenbeek, Klaas, 94n5, 96n19

S

Schurmann, Franz, 15
science/scientific (*kexue*), 61, 66n35,
190, 201
See also social science
Scott, James, 43–44
Seeberg, Vilma, 34n15
Shanghai, 3, 15, 49, 99, 104, 114, 116, 121,
130, 177, 225, 226
shangmen nüxu. See uxorilocal
marriage
shaofo (P. *shaohu*), 182, 186, 188–195,
196n13,
Shinan (Enshi), 39, 59
Simmel, Georg, 14, 33n7
Skinner, G.W., 101–103, 126n6, 127n9
social heat, 21, 76, 95n13, 176–197
See also red-hot (*renao*)
Socialism
Chinese Socialism, 15, 18, 85, 127n7
National Socialism, 33n8
social poetics, 23, 173, 194, 200, 228
social science, 120, 133, 152n5
spring festival, 3, 54, 96n19, 99–100,
110, 114, 126n2, 130, 145–146, 161,
182, 211
spring sacrifice festival (*sheri*), 155–156,
175n3
suona, 154, 161, 166, 174n1

superstition, 18, 24, 41, 57, 60, 66n35, 72, 92, 93, 157–161, 182, 192, 197n14, 225, 227, 231
surname 50, 72, 106, 218
single-surname hamlets and villages, 67–68
suzhi. See population quality

T
Taiwan, 65n29, 95n8, 97n33, 145, 180–181, 196n8–9
Tang, Xiaobing, 18
tao hua yuan (land of peach blossoms), 36–37, 63n2, 63n3
Taylor, Charles, 8–9, 12
tea
industry, 103, 114, 124
introduction of tea monoculture, 105–108
labour, 108–111
market/marketing, 48, 103, 111–114, 124, 187
tobacco, 48, 100, 101, 105, 152n12, 152n15, 158, 175n4, 205, 221n6, 221n9
toponym. *See* place name
tourism, 38, 46–52, 51, 62, 224
Township and Village Enterprise (TVE), 103, 108
tradition, 188, 190, 225
Confucian tradition, 190, 192
and the countryside, 90–91
local tradition, 166
neo-traditionalism, 219–220
traditionalism, 24, 178, 189, 194, 220
Trotsky, Leon, 15
Tujia minority. *See under* minority nationality

U
uxorilocal marriage, 75, 146, 150

V
vernacular discourse, 22, 157, 170, 173

village
village elections, 208, 213–214
village secretary, 108, 208

W
wage
labour, 31, 85, 91, 124–125, 126n4, 177
piece-wage, 109–110
time-wage, 109–110
Wang, Mingming, 120, 133
WASP, 45
Watson, James L., 137–138, 155, 174n2
weddings, 21, 28, 31, 86, 109, 119, 121–122, 126n2, 130–153, 161–165, 173, 175n7, 182, 183, 213, 235
Weller, Robert, 97n33
Wen, Tiejun, 127n12
Wright, Arthur F., 66n33
Wu, Han, 220n1
Wu, Yu, 196n12

X
Xiang, Shunnian, 36, 39
xiao. See filial piety
xiaokang, 95n9, 122
xiaokang cun, 201–202
xiaokang lou, 70–71, 89

Y
Yan, Yunxiang, 5–6, 12, 132–133, 152n4, 175n10, 224, 225, 233
Yang, Mayfair M.H., 20, 169–170
Yi, Zhongtian, 191–192
yiqi, 119
Yongzheng emperor, 39, 69
Yu, Dan, 196
Yu, Hua, 128n19, 151n1
Yu, Yingshi, 95n10

Z
Zigon, Jarrett, 7–8, 13, 32
Zito, Angela, 134–138, 142, 151

CPSIA information can be obtained
at www.ICGtesting.com
Printed in the USA
JSHW051450151221
21288JS00007B/173